"Doing business internationally is a country-by-country challenge, and *Macro Talent Management gives* us a world tour, not available elsewhere, of the government policies, demographics, and the other attributes that affect how employers hire, develop, and manage a workforce across the major countries of the world. An important resource for doing business and learning about business around the world."

—**Peter Cappelli,** *George W. Taylor Professor of Management, Director—Center for Human Resources, The Wharton School, University of Pennsylvania, USA*

"This book is truly unique due to its cross-country, multidisciplinary nature. The authors are explaining very complicated things in a clear, easy-to-understand language. This is a very useful book for both academics and practitioners, including policy makers."

—**Nikolai Rogovsky,** *Head, Knowledge Management Coordination Team, International Labour Office, Geneva, Switzerland*

"This remarkable text, edited by the leading names in the field and including a stellar list of contributors, examines talent management in North America, Australia, and five European countries. If you want to understand talent management, read this book!"

—**Chris Brewster,** *Henley Business School, University of Reading, UK*

Macro Talent Management

Macro Talent Management: A Global Perspective on Managing Talent in Developed Markets is the first book to focus specifically on country-level activities aimed at attracting, developing, mobilizing, and retaining top talent for economic success in developed markets. The book serves as a guide that orients the reader toward activities that increase their country's global competitiveness, attractiveness, and economic development through strategic talent management.

This book brings together leading experts from around the world to address such issues as cross-border flows of talent, diaspora mobility, knowledge flows, global labour markets, and policies.

Bringing together research from the fields of human resource management, international business, economic geography, comparative international development, and political economy, this is a definitive, comprehensive treatment of the topic aimed at advanced students and practitioners.

Vlad Vaiman, Professor, School of Management, California Lutheran University, USA.

Paul Sparrow, Emeritus Professor of International Human Resource Management, Lancaster University, UK.

Randall Schuler, Professor, Rutgers University, USA, Visiting Scholar, University of Lucerne, Switzerland.

David G. Collings, Professor of Human Resource Management, Dublin City University, Ireland.

Routledge Global Human Resource Management Series
Edited by Randall S. Schuler, Susan E. Jackson, and Paul Sparrow

Routledge Global Human Resource Management is an important series that examines human resources in its global context. The series is organized into three strands: Content and issues in global human resource management (HRM); specific HR functions in a global context; and comparative HRM. Authored by some of the world's leading authorities on HRM, each book in the series aims to give readers comprehensive, in-depth and accessible texts that combine essential theory and best practice. Topics covered include cross-border alliances, global leadership, global legal systems, HRM in Asia, Africa and the Americas, industrial relations, and global staffing.

Dedication: The late Professor Michael Poole was one of the founding series editors, and Professors Schuler, Jackson, and Sparrow wish to dedicate the series to his memory.

For a full list of titles in this series, please visit www.routledge.com

Managing Human Resources in Asia-Pacific (second edition)
Edited by Arup Varma and Pawan S. Budhwar

Human Resource Management and the Institutional Perspective
Edited by Geoffrey Wood, Chris Brewster, and Michael Brookes

International Human Resource Management (fifth edition)
Policies and Practices for Multinational Enterprises
Ibraiz Tarique, Dennis Briscoe, and Randall S. Schuler

Contemporary HR Issues in Europe (third edition)
Michael Dickmann, Chris Brewster, & Paul Sparrow

Globalizing Human Resource Management (second edition)
Paul Sparrow, Chris Brewster & Chul Chung

The Global Human Resource Management Casebook (second edition)
Edited by Liza Castro Christiansen, Michal Biron, Elaine Farndale, Bård Kuvaas

Global Leadership (third edition)
Research, Practice, and Development
Mark E. Mendenhall, Joyce S. Osland, Allan Bird, Gary R. Oddou, Michael J. Stevens, Martha L. Maznevski, and Günter K. Stahl

Macro Talent Management
A Global Perspective on Managing Talent in Developed Markets
Edited by Vlad Vaiman, Paul Sparrow, Randall Schuler and David G. Collings

Macro Talent Management in Emerging and Emergent Markets
A Global Perspective
Vlad Vaiman, Paul Sparrow, Randall Schuler and David G. Collings

Macro Talent Management

A Global Perspective on Managing Talent in Developed Markets

Edited by Vlad Vaiman, Paul Sparrow,
Randall Schuler and David G. Collings

NEW YORK AND LONDON

First published 2019
by Routledge
711 Third Avenue, New York, NY 10017

and by Routledge
2 Park Square, Milton Park, Abingdon, Oxon, OX14 4RN

Routledge is an imprint of the Taylor & Francis Group, an informa business

© 2019 Taylor & Francis

The right of Vlad Vaiman, Paul Sparrow, Randall Schuler and David G. Collings to be identified as the authors of the editorial material, and of the authors for their individual chapters, has been asserted in accordance with sections 77 and 78 of the Copyright, Designs and Patents Act 1988.

All rights reserved. No part of this book may be reprinted or reproduced or utilised in any form or by any electronic, mechanical, or other means, now known or hereafter invented, including photocopying and recording, or in any information storage or retrieval system, without permission in writing from the publishers.

Trademark notice: Product or corporate names may be trademarks or registered trademarks, and are used only for identification and explanation without intent to infringe.

Library of Congress Cataloging-in-Publication Data
Names: Vaiman, Vlad, 1971– editor. | Sparrow, Paul, editor. | Schuler, Randall S., editor.
Title: Macro talent management : a global perspective on managing talent in developed markets / edited by Vlad Vaiman, Paul Sparrow, Randall Schuler and David Collings.
Description: 1 Edition. | New York : Routledge, 2018. | Series: Routledge global human resource management series | Includes bibliographical references and index.
Identifiers: LCCN 2018006465 (print) | LCCN 2018013481 (ebook) |
 ISBN 9781315200200 | ISBN 9781138712386 (alk. paper) |
 ISBN 9781138712409 (alk. paper) | ISBN 9781315200200 (ebk)
Subjects: LCSH: Employee motivation. | Job enrichment. | Employees—Attitudes. | Corporate culture.
Classification: LCC HF5549.5.M63 (ebook) | LCC HF5549.5.M63 M328 2018 (print) | DDC 658.3/14—dc23
LC record available at https://lccn.loc.gov/2018006465

ISBN: 978-1-138-71238-6 (hbk)
ISBN: 978-1-138-71240-9 (pbk)
ISBN: 978-1-315-20020-0 (ebk)

Typeset in Times New Roman
by Apex CoVantage, LLC

Contents

List of Figures ix
List of Tables x
List of Contributors xi
Foreword by Randall Schuler, Susan E. Jackson and Paul Sparrow xviii

Introduction: Macro Talent Management in Developed Markets: Foundations for a Developing Field 1
PAUL SPARROW, VLAD VAIMAN, RANDALL SCHULER AND DAVID G. COLLINGS

1. Macro Talent Management in the United States: Framework, Context, Processes and Outcomes 17
RANDALL SCHULER, IBRAIZ TARIQUE AND SHAISTA KHILJI

2. Macro Talent Management in Canada: A Review of the National Context, Competitive Strengths and Future Opportunities to Attract, Develop and Retain Talent 40
KARIN KING

3. Macro Talent Management in the UK: Patterns of Agency in a Period of Changing Regimes 70
PAUL SPARROW

4. Macro Talent Management in Germany: A Strong Economy Facing the Challenges of a Shrinking Labor Force 101
MARION FESTING AND KATHARINA HARSCH

viii • Contents

5. Macro Talent Management in Spain: Is the Sun Rising Again?   123
   ADORACIÓN ÁLVARO-MOYA, EVA GALLARDO-GALLARDO
   AND JORDI PANIAGUA

6. Macro Talent Management in Denmark: The Origins of Danish
   Talent Paradox   154
   DANA MINBAEVA, TORBEN ANDERSEN, NIKOLAJ LUBANSKI,
   STEEN ERIK NAVRBJERG AND RONJA MARIE TORFING

7. Macro Talent Management in Finland: Contributing to a
   Rapidly Evolving Knowledge Economy   170
   PAUL EVANS, ADAM SMALE AND INGMAR BJÖRKMAN

8. Macro Talent Management in the Netherlands: A Critical Analysis
   of Growing and Retaining Talent in the Netherlands   190
   MARIAN THUNNISSEN, JOOP SCHIPPERS AND PAUL BOSELIE

9. Macro Talent Management in Australia: Balancing Industrial
   Relations, Isolation and Global Competitiveness   206
   SHARNA WIBLEN AND ANTHONY McDONNELL

Appendix: Useful Research Sources, Talent Rankings
and Cross-Country Indices   223
Index   227

Figures

0.1	The General Framework for Macro Talent Management	5
1.1	Talent Management in Global Context: A Conceptual Framework of Macro Talent Management (MTM)	19
2.1	Macro Talent Management in Canada	42
2.2	Mini-Case: Canadian MTM Context and Environment: Example of Government Policy and Immigration	50
2.3	Mini-Case: Canadian MTM Core Functions and Processes: Example of Corporate Strategy and Leadership	55
2.4	Mini-Case: Canadian MTM Outcomes: Example of Economic Development and Competitiveness	61
3.1	Alternative Futures for the Skills and Productivity Challenge	81
3.2	The Processes Through Which the Economic, Technological and Cultural Context Shapes and Conditions Talent Management Acquisition in the UK	93
3.3	The Processes Through Which the Macro Context Shapes and Conditions Talent Management Growth and Development in the UK	94
3.4	The Processes Through Which the Macro Context Shapes and Conditions Talent Management Attraction and Retention in the UK	96
4.1	Population Pyramid Age Structure	105
4.2	Global Talent Competitive Index—Germany	115
4.3	Well-being Index in Germany	116
5.1	GDP per capita, (PPP constant 2011 international $) in Spain, United States (US), Italy, Germany and Portugal (1990-2016)	124
5.2	Population Growth (annual %) in Spain, US, Germany, Italy and Portugal (1980–2012)	129
5.3	Net Migration in Spain, US, Germany, Italy and Portugal (1972–2012)	129
5.4	Population by Age in Spain	131
5.5	Unemployment, Total (% of total labor force) (modeled ILO estimate) in Spain, US, Germany, Italy and Portugal (1991–2017)	143
6.1	Skills, Talent Attraction and Image of the Selected Countries	155
6.2	Macro Talent Management	157
7.1	Finland's GTCI 2017 Country Profile by Pillar	176

Tables

1.1	Global Competitiveness Index Pillars Related to Education and Talent Management	22
1.2	IMD World Talent Ranking	22
1.3	World Bank's Doing Business Index	23
1.4	Labor Market Regulations	23
1.5	Global Talent Index	24
1.6	Global Competitiveness Index Pillars	29
1.7	Human Capital Indicies Using Four Pillars and Five Age Categories	29
1.8	The Global Talent Competitiveness Index (GTCI): Two Pillars More Applicable for Education	32
1.9	The Global Talent Competitiveness Index (GTCI): Four Pillars More Applicable for MTM	33
1.10	Programme for International Student Assessment (PISA)	33
2.1	Macro Talent Management in Canada: Context and Environment	43
2.2	Macro Talent Management in Canada: Core Processes and Functions	49
2.3	Macro Talent Management in Canada: Outcomes at the National Level	57
2.4	Macro Talent Management: Opportunities for Canada	63
5.1	Spain, Italy, France, Germany and US Rank (out of 190) According to the DB 2018 Rank World Bank's Doing Business Index*	135
5.2	Spain, Italy, France, Germany and US Rank (out of 138) According to the Global Competitiveness Index 2016–2017	138
5.3	Spain, Italy, France, Germany and US Rank (out of 63) According to the IMD World Talent Ranking 2017	139
5.4	Spain, Italy, France, Germany and US Rank (out of 118) According to the Global Talent Competitiveness Index (GTCI) 2017	140
5.5	Spain, Italy, France, Germany and US Rank According the *Programme for International Student Assessment* (PISA) 2015	141
5.6	Spain, Italy, France, Germany and US Rank (out of 130) According to the Global Human Capital Index 2017	142
7.1	GTCI Rankings of Top Ten Countries (out of 118): Overall and by Pillar	171

Contributors

Adoración Álvaro-Moya is Associate Professor of Economic History at CUNEF (Madrid). PhD in Economic History by Universidad Complutense of Madrid, she has been visiting fellow at Universities of Reading and York. Her research, focused on the long-term effects of foreign direct investment in late developing economies, has been awarded twice by the Spanish Association of Economic Historians. Having published near twenty articles and book chapters, including at *Business History* and *Business History Review*, she serves on the boards of indexed *Revista de Historia Industrial* and open-accessed *Journal of Evolutionary Studies in Business*.

Torben Andersen is Associate Professor at Aarhus University (Ph.D. from Copenhagen Business School), and has in his research focused on international and structural aspects of human resource management. He was Editor of the Danish HRM handbook for more than 10 years and is Senior Editor of *European Journal of International Management*. Torben has occupied management positions in academia for 2 decades and he has worked at University of Warwick (UK), Auckland University of Technology (New Zealand), and University of Bamberg (Bavaria, Germany).

Ingmar Björkman is Professor of International Business and Dean of Aalto University School of Business in Finland. His research interests focus on people management issues in an international context in particular. His work has been published in a range of leading journals within the areas of international business and management. He received the *Journal of International Business Studies* Decade Award in 2014 together with Dana Minbaeva, Torben Pedersen, Carl Fey, and H.-J. Park. His latest book is *Global Challenge: International Human Resource Management* (2017, third edition, Chicago Business Press), co-authored with Vladimir Pucik, Paul Evans and Shad Morris.

Paul Boselie, PhD, MSc, is Professor and Research Director in the Utrecht School of Governance at Utrecht University, The Netherlands. His research traverses human resource management, institutionalism, strategic management, and industrial relations. He currently focuses on public-value creation, employer engagement, health care management, professional performance, and talent management. Paul's teaching involves bachelor, master, PhD, and executive education. He is a member of the editorial board of the *Journal of Management Studies* and *Human Resource Management Journal*, and he is an associate editor of the *International Journal of Human Resource Management*. His 2010 and 2014 textbook, Strategic HRM—A Balanced Approach, is popular in bachelor and master programs.

David Collings is Professor of HRM at Dublin City University Business School where he is co-Director of the Leadership and Talent Institute. He previously held academic appointments at the University of Sheffield and National University of Ireland Galway and visiting appointments at King's College London, Nanyang Business School, Singapore and Cornell University as a Fulbright Scholar. His research and consulting interests focus on talent management and global mobility. A key focus of his recent work is on understanding how employees add value in organisations and how organisations can support key employee groups, including international assignees, in generating sustainable performance. From 2014 to 2017 he has been named as one of the most influential thinkers in the field of HR by *HR Magazine* and in 2015 he was awarded the President's award for research by Dublin City University. He has published numerous papers in leading international outlets and nine books. He sits on a number of editorial boards including *Academy of Management Review, Journal of Management* and *Journal of Management Studies*. He is incoming joint Editor-in-Chief at *Journal of World Business and* former Editor in Chief of *Human Resource Management Journal* and the *Irish Journal of Management*.

Paul Evans is the Shell Chaired Professor of Human Resources and Organizational Development, Emeritus, and Emeritus Professor of Organizational Behavior at INSEAD. His research focuses on people management in an international context, and particularly on global talent management. He is Academic Director of INSEAD's Global Talent Competitiveness Index, assessing 120 countries and undertaking focused studies for its annual report. His most recent book is *The Global Challenge: International Human Resource Management* (third edition, 2017, Chicago Business). Paul has been described in the press as one of the most influential people in international human resource management, joining in 2013–2016 the European list of the Most Influential Thinkers in HR. He has been advisor to more than 200 multinational corporations, and he has taught courses as visiting professor at universities in North America, Europe, Russia, Brazil and China, winning awards for his teaching and research. He has a PhD in Management and Organizational Psychology from MIT, an MBA from INSEAD, and he is a graduate in law from Cambridge University.

Marion Festing is Professor of Human Resource Management and Intercultural Leadership and the Academic Director of the ESCP Europe Talent Management Institute. Former responsibilities at ESCP Europe include her work as the European Research Dean and the Dean of the Berlin Campus. She is the incoming editor-in-chief of the *German Journal of HRM* and was an associate editor of the *International Journal of Human Resource Management*. Marion is also the German Ambassador to the HR Division of the Academy of Management. Her current research interests are concerned with International Human Resource Management with a special emphasis on strategies, talent management, (female) careers, rewards, performance management as well as diversity and inclusion in various institutional and cultural contexts. She has written or co-authored over one hundred book chapters and journal articles and published in international journals such as *Human Resource Management, International Journal of Human Resource Management, Human Resource Management Review, Academy of Management Perspectives, Journal of*

World Business, Management International Review, Economic and Industrial Demography, and *European Management Journal.* In a three-continental team together with Peter J. Dowling (Australia) and Allen D. Engle (USA) she has published the seventh edition of their textbook on International Human Resource Management.

Eva Gallardo-Gallardo is Assistant Professor of Management at the Universitat Politècnica de Catalunya-BarcelonaTech. She holds a PhD in Business by the Universitat de Barcelona, and has been visiting fellow at University of Minho, Universitat de València, and HU Applied Sciences Utrecht. Her research has focused on talent management, with a particular interest in understanding the formation and evolution of the field, its dynamics, and its conceptual boundaries. Having published papers in leading academic journals in the field of Management and Human Resource Management, she serves on the boards of the *International Journal of Human Resource Management* and the *Journal of Organizational Effectiveness: People and Performance.*

Katharina Harsch is research assistant and PhD student at the Chair of Human Resource Management and Intercultural Leadership and an affiliated researcher for the Talent Management Institute at ESCP Europe, Berlin Campus. Her main research focus centers on talent management from different angles, concentrating on various working environments. For instance, former research projects have focused on talent management in family businesses in German-speaking countries or talent management in small- and medium-sized companies. She gained practical experience at the Bosch Training Center of Robert Bosch GmbH and designed a globally standardized career development program for experts. Moreover, Katharina Harsch worked in the area of talent management/career development at MHP, a Porsche Company.

Shaista Khilji is Professor of Human and Organizational Learning & International Affairs at the George Washington University, and founding editor-in-chief of the *South Asian Journal of Business Studies* (Emerald Publications). Shaista has a well-established expertise in talent development, cross-cultural management, change and leadership. Her most recent work focuses upon exploring organizational inequalities, advancing understanding of macro-level global talent development, and humanizing leadership education. She has recently served as the Co-PI of a US Dept. of State funded project that focused upon women's empowerment in Pakistan. In addition, she has led efforts within GW to develop the next generation of USNA and US Coast Guards leaders. Shaista has authored more than 100 papers, publishing many scholarly articles in tier-1 academic journals. She has won many awards including the Best Reviewer, Outstanding Service, Service Excellence, Best Paper, and VALOR Award for cross-disciplinary work. Shaista has taught and trained a diverse audience in Asia, Europe, North Africa and North America. She has served as a consultant to many public and private sector organizations.

Karin King is a guest lecturer, instructor and doctoral researcher in the Department of Management of the London School of Economics and Political Science in London, UK. Karin's teaching focuses on leadership, organizational behavior, international management and strategic human resource management. Her academic work in talent management has been presented in the Academy of Management annual meetings and appears in peer-reviewed journals including *Employee Relations, Journal of Global Mobility,* and *Journal* *of Organizational Effectiveness People and Performance.* Karin's work has been recognized with *Journal of Global Mobility* Best Paper Award (titled "Talent Management in the Business: HR's central role"); Emerald Literati Award for Highly Commended Manuscript (titled "Global Talent Management: Introducing a Strategic Framework and Multi-Actor Model) and Teaching Excellence Award (Department of Management) at the London School of Economics. Karin is also an experienced practitioner having held leadership roles in global human resources and in professional services, responsible for the design and delivery of consulting projects for clients. In her ongoing consulting work with leaders and organizations, Karin draws on practical insight from both her professional and academic work to support leaders in their design, implementation and evaluation of talent management in alignment with business-specific priorities.

Nikolaj Lubanski is Director for Talent Attraction at Copenhagen Capacity, the official investment promotion agency of Greater Copenhagen. At Copenhagen Capacity, he assists Danish companies in attracting the right highly skilled international candidates—and has innovated the way in which we reach the attention of international candidates through digital channels and direct marketing. Nikolaj is passionate about research and knowledge-sharing, and is the author of several books and publications within the area of innovation, labour-market issues and management. Most recently he has co-authored a book on *Talent Attraction Management* introducing some best practice guidelines to Talent Attraction for Cities, Regions and Countries. Born to a Polish-Danish family and having worked in several countries, international mobility lies at the heart of everything he does.

Anthony McDonnell is Head of the Department of Management & Marketing and Professor of Management at the Cork University Business School, University College Cork, Ireland. Prior to joining UCC, Anthony was a Reader in Management at Queen's University Belfast. Anthony is currently the (Co)Editor-in-Chief of *Human Resource Management Journal* and Adjunct Senior Research Fellow at the University of South Australia. He is a previous recipient of the Australian and New Zealand Academy of Management Early Career Researcher Award. Anthony sits on the editorial boards of the *Journal of World Business*, *Employee Relations* and *International Journal of Human Resource Management* amongst others. His primary research interest and area of expertise is in the areas of talent management and international management, and more specifically, the HRM approaches of MNCs across countries. His work has been published in the leading journals including *Human Resource Management, Journal of World Business, Industrial and Labor Relations Review* and *Human Relations*.

Dana Minbaeva is a Professor of Strategic and Global Human Resource Management at Copenhagen Business School. Her research on strategic and international HRM, knowledge sharing and transfer in MNCs has appeared in such journals as *Journal of International Business Studies*, *Journal of Management Studies, Human Resource Management*, and many others. She received several national and international awards to research achievements, including the prestigious JIBS Decade Award 2013. Dana is the founder of the Human Capital Analytics Group: www.cbs.dk/hc-analytics.

Steen Eric Navrbjerg is an Associate Professor at FAOS—the Employment Relations Research Centre, Department of Sociology, University of Copenhagen, Denmark. His research focuses on shop steward-management corporation at company level, employers' organization, multinational companies' effect on Industrial Relations and collective bargaining. Steen has published several research reports on a variety of subjects within the area of Industrial Relations and HRM, and he has published in outlets such as *Human Resource Management Journal, International Journal of Human Resource Management, Journal of Industrial Relations and Economic* and *Industrial Democracy*. As part of FAOS he is in close contact with central actors in the Danish labor market model, both practitioners and politicians. Steen is also a member of the international ETUI WorkPlaceEurope network.

Jordi Paniagua is Assistant Professor of Economics at the University of Valencia, Department of Applied Economics II. Jordi has an academic and applied specialization in Foreign Direct Investment (FDI) and online networking. In his academic career, he has published papers in leading academic journals in the field of international economics and business. Jordi has worked as telecommunications engineer in multinational enterprises and served in public administration in the area of FDI promotion. He has consulted to multinational companies and to public bodies, like NATO, the World Bank and UNCITRAL. His research interests include gravity models of trade and FDI, and its interplay with migration, trade law, energy and social media networks.

Joop Schippers is a full professor of Labour Economics at the Faculty of Law, Economics and Governance at Universiteit Utrecht (the Netherlands). He is one of the coordinators of the research program "The Future of Work" and has for almost forty years studied the relation between the labour market and social inequality. More in particular his focus has been on gender and age differentials in the labour market. His multidisciplinary oriented research combines a theoretical perspective with quantitative and qualitative empirical research and is often policy related. He obtained grants from both the Dutch government and the European Union for large projects in FP 4–7. For his continuous contribution to the dissemination of scientific knowledge to a broader audience he received in 2012 the first PubliPrice. He has served on several royal committees and is currently a member of the Monitor Committee that sees to the implementation of the law on equal representation of men and women in boards of governance and supervisory boards in the Netherlands.

Randall Schuler is Distinguished Professor of Strategic International Human Resource Management and Strategic Human Resource Management in the Department of Human Resource Management at Rutgers University. He is also on the faculty of University of Lucerne (Switzerland), Center for HRM as a Visiting Scholar and a Visiting Scholar at Lancaster University Management School (UK). He is a Fellow of the American Psychological Association, a Fellow of the British Academy of Management, a Fellow of the Society for Industrial and Organizational Psychology, and a Fellow of the Academy of Management. Currently he is co-editing a GLOBAL HRM Series for Routledge Publishing, London England, with P. Sparrow and S. E. Jackson. It is comprised of more than twenty-five books and involves more than 400 authors from around the world.

Adam Smale is a Professor of Management at the University of Vaasa, Finland. His research interests focus on talent management, HRM, careers, and knowledge transfer in multinational corporations. He has written a popular teaching case on global talent management in the Case

Centre (case no. 415–111–1) and has published a number of articles in journals such as the *Journal of International Business Studies*, *Human Resource Management*, *Journal of World Business*, *International Business Review*, and *The International Journal of Human Resource Management*. Professor Smale sits on the editorial boards of *Human Resource Management Journal* and the *Journal of Organizational Effectiveness: People and Performance*. He is the HR Ambassador for Finland in the Academy of Management HR Division and the Finnish representative in both CRANET (www.cranet.org) and the Cross-Cultural Collaboration on Contemporary Careers (www.5C.careers).

Paul Sparrow is Emeritus Professor of International HRM at Lancaster University Management School and was Director of the Centre for Performance-led HR from 2006–2016. In 2016, he was awarded the USA's Society for HRM Michael R. Losey Award for lifetime achievement in human resource research and research contributions that impact the HR management field. He is regularly voted amongst the Most Influential HR Thinkers by *Human Resources* magazine, listed from 2008–2012 and 2014–16. His research interests include cross-cultural and international HRM, HR strategy and the employment relationship. He has several writing collaborations from which his latest books are: *Globalizing HRM, Strategic Talent Management*; *Do We Need HR?*; *International HRM*; *Contemporary HR Issues in Europe*; and *Human Resource Management, Innovation and Performance*. He is senior editor of the *Journal of Organizational Effectiveness: People and Performance* and editorial board member for *Human Resource Management, International Journal of Human Resource Management, British Journal of Management, Human Resource Management Review, Cross-Cultural Management: An International Journal, International Journal of Cross-Cultural Management, European Management Review* and *Career Development International*.

Ibraiz Tarique is Professor of HRM and the Director of Global HRM Programs at the Lubin School of Business, Pace University, New York City campus. His academic research interest is in IHRM with a focus on issues related to global talent management and investments in human capital. His publications include articles in the International Journal of Human Resource Management, Journal of World Business, Human Resource Management Review, and International Journal of Training and Development and several book chapters. He is the co-author of International Human Resource Management: Policies and Practices for Multinational Enterprises, a comprehensive textbook, which provides a foundation for understanding the theory and practice of IHRM.

Marian Thunnissen is Professor at the School of HRM and Applied Psychology at Fontys University of Applied Sciences in Eindhoven (The Netherlands). She has over 20 years of experience in research, teaching and consulting. Her current research is focused on the identification, attraction and development of talent, in particular in the public sector. Her recent interests concern a "team-based" TM approach, the impact of contextual factors on developing and implementing TM, and the dilemmas and tensions organizations experience in implementing TM. Marian finds it very important to share her knowledge with organizations and HR practitioners, in order to support them in an evidence based TM approach. Her work is published in *Human Resource Management Review, International Journal of HRM, Personnel Review* and *Employee Relations*. Marian has (co-)authored several book chapters on TM, e.g. on TM in practice, TM in the public sector and TM in academia. Marian is the editor-in-chief of the *Dutch Journal of HRM*, which aims to build a bridge between theory and practice.

Ronja Marie Torfing is Talent Attraction Manager at Copenhagen Capacity, the official investment promotion agency of Greater Copenhagen. In Copenhagen Capacity, she assists Danish companies in attracting highly skilled international candidates within IT/Tech, Life Science and Engineering through digital channels and matchmaking with candidates from Copenhagen Capacity's talent pool. Ronja is also responsible of measuring how many international candidates Copenhagen Capacity help find a way to a company in Greater Copenhagen. She holds a Master within Political Science and are passionate about how to strengthen the talent attraction initiatives in the region. Hereunder creating the best framework for not only attracting but also receiving and retaining the international specialists in Denmark through various initiatives together with municipalities, educational institutions and other relevant partners.

Vlad Vaiman is Professor and the Associate Dean at the School of Management of California Lutheran University and a visiting professor at several premier universities around the globe. Vlad has published three very successful books on managing talent in organizations as well as a number of academic and practitioner-oriented articles and book chapters in the fields of talent management and international HRM. His work appeared in *Academy of Management Learning and Education, Human Resource Management, International Journal of Human Resource Management, Human Resource Management Review, Journal of Business Ethics*, and many others. He is also a founder and Chief Editorial Consultant of European Journal of International Management (EJIM), an SSCI/ISI indexed publication, and an editorial board member of several prestigious academic journals. Vlad is a highly sought-after consultant and speaker—he is frequently invited to speak on both professional and academic matters to a number of global corporations and highly acclaimed universities around the world.

Sharna Wiblen is a Lecturer (Assistant Professor) in the Sydney Business School at the University of Wollongong. Before earning a PhD at the University of Sydney, Sharna played a pivotal role in two competitively awarded government funded projects with colleagues at the University of Sydney Business School and amassed over 15 years of industry experience having worked as a management consultant, human resource, recruitment and selection coordinator. Sharna works at the boundaries of talent management and information technologies. More specifically, her research critically analyses how "talent" is conceptualized within organizational boundaries, how these meanings are enacted, and the structure, composition, alignment and desired outcomes of talent management policies and practices, including talent acquisition, talent identification and talent development. Her research also examines the role that various information technologies (such as Enterprise Resource Planning Systems, Human Resource Information Systems, Social Media etc.) play, or do not play, in strategic talent management.

Foreword

Global HRM is a series of books edited and authored by some of the best and most well-known researchers in the field of human resource management. This Series is aimed at offering students and practitioners accessible, coordinated and comprehensive books in global HRM. To be used individually or together, these books cover the main areas in international and comparative HRM. Taking an expert look at an increasingly important and complex area of global business, this is a groundbreaking new Series that answers a real need for useful and affordable textbooks on global HRM.

Several books in the Series, **Global HRM**, are devoted to human resource management policies and practices in multinational enterprises. Some books focus on specific areas of global HRM policies and practices, such as global leadership, global compensation, global talent management and global labour relations. Other books address special topics that arise in multinational enterprises, such as managing HR in cross-border alliances, managing global legal systems, and the structure of the global HR function. There is also a book of global human resource management cases. Several other books in the Series adopt a comparative approach to understanding human resource management. These books on comparative human resource management describe HRM topics found at the country level in selected countries. The comparative books utilize a common framework that makes it easier for the reader to systematically understand the rationale for the similarities and differences in findings across countries.

Because the topic of macro talent management is just emerging, we thought it would useful to be as thorough as possible and cover as many countries as possible. The responsiveness of authors far exceeded our expectations, and consequently created the need to convey the chapters into two books that can be used either separately or together. This book, *Macro Talent Management: A Global Perspective on Managing Talent in Developed Markets*, is a book that focuses on the talent management systems in the USA, Canada, the UK, Germany, Denmark, Spain, Finland, The Netherlands and Australia. As we define macro talent management, the chapters cover the quality of a country's political system, educational system, labor systems, social and cultural systems, and its economic and many other systems that help determine country-level conditions that help determine and shape the types and levels of a country's talent. Using this information MNEs can inform their decisions about where to locate operations around the world, and how they might best prepare to address shortfalls in needed talent, e.g., through human resource management interventions such as training and development, if they must enter a country for reasons other than the levels and types of talent. Country leaders can also use this information to help craft national and regional level policies and practices to help elevate the types and levels of talent in their citizens. Each country is described in a chapter written by scholars knowledgeable about their particular country. Extensive use is made of existing and available databases so that readers can access much more information than is contained in the chapters. An appendix is included to provide further references that will enable the user to keep up to date with contemporary statistics and events.

This Routledge series, **Global HRM,** is intended to serve the growing market of global scholars and practitioners who are seeking a deeper and broader understanding of the role and importance of human resource management in companies that operate throughout the world. With this in mind, all books in the Series provide a thorough review of existing research and numerous examples of companies around the world where applicable. Mini-company stories and examples are found throughout the chapters where applicable. In addition, many of the books in the Series include at least one detailed case description that serves as convenient practical illustrations of topics discussed in the book.

Because a significant number of scholars and practitioners throughout the world are involved in researching and practicing the topics examined in this Series of books, the authorship of the books and the experiences of the companies cited in the books reflect a vast global representation. The authors in the Series bring with them exceptional knowledge of the human resource management topics they address, and in many cases the authors have been the pioneers for their topics. So we feel fortunate to have the involvement of such a distinguished group of academics in this Series.

The publisher and editor have played a very major role in making this Series possible. Routledge has provided its global production, marketing and reputation to make this Series feasible and affordable to academics and practitioners throughout the world. In addition, Routledge has provided its own highly qualified professionals to make this Series a reality. In particular, we want to indicate our deep appreciation for the work of our Series editor, Sharon Golan. She has been very supportive of the **Global HRM** Series and has been invaluable in providing the needed support and encouragement to us and the many authors and editors in the Series. She has moved on and Lucy McClune has taken over her role. So together, Sharon and Lucy, along with the entire staff especially Judith Lorton, have helped make the process of advancing this Series an enjoyable one. For everything they have done, we thank them all. Together we are all very excited about the **Global HRM** series and hope you find an opportunity to use *Macro Talent Management: A Global Perspective on Managing Talent in Developed Markets*, and all the other books in the Series!

Randall Schuler
Rutgers University, University of Lucerne Center for HRM,
and the Lancaster University School of Management

Susan E. Jackson
Rutgers University, University of Lucerne Center for HRM,
and the Lancaster University Management School

Paul Sparrow
Lancaster University Management School

July 2018

Introduction
Macro Talent Management in Developed Markets: Foundations for a Developing Field

Paul Sparrow, Vlad Vaiman, Randall Schuler and David G. Collings

Pespectives on Managing Talent

This book—*Macro Talent Management: A Global Perspective on Managing Talent in Developed Markets*—is the first of two volumes that we have edited on the topic of Macro Talent Management (the other being *Macro Talent Management in Emerging and Emergent Markets: A Global Perspective*). These two books represent the first comprehensive discussion of the rapidly evolving field of Macro Talent Management (MTM) on the market. Together they serve as an orientation to researchers and as a guide to practitioners aiming to understand and increase their country's global competitiveness, attractiveness, and economic development in order to ensure high-quality talent management within their countries. Macro talent management (MTM) incorporates activities aimed at attracting, mobilizing, developing, and retaining top talent within an organization. As such, it has also major implications for organizations, including multinational enterprises and nongovernmental organizations (NGOs), and individuals, as well as countries.

But the essence of MTM is conceptualized at the country-level, and as such guides country-level processes and their outcomes. These books, therefore, will be concentrating on country-level talent management systems, providing an invaluable insight into their environments, processes, and outcomes. Common to both of the books is the view that a macro perspective is best analyzed at the level of country. At this level of analysis it becomes easier to see what relationships exist between factors such as government policies, institutions, or approaches taken to mobility, and the processes that firms use in their talent management. It is possible to assess whether such relationships may be more, or less integrated. It is easier to link such MTM to important outcomes such as productivity, economic development and competitiveness. We are at an important juncture in globalization, with many debates taking center stage in both international and national arenas.

Across the two books we have pulled together a team of 45 academics from around the world to analyze the MTM arrangements in an array of 16 different countries, and to provide insight into two pan-national developments in this area. Except for the introductory chapters written by the volume editors, and the two final chapters of the second book that pull out some important pan-national developments, each chapter by the contributors to the two books is structured in a similar manner. The editors have provided authors with specific guidelines on how the chapters should be structured, and each chapter was subjected to editorial review to ensure a consistent look and feel across the contributions. Thus in each chapter, contributors illustrate the external environment of MTM in their country of interest and expertise, then explain the processes through which a country facilitates (or hinders) its economic development and competitiveness of their citizens and corporations, as well as increases (or decreases) its attractiveness to global talent, and finally, describe the outcomes in terms of the country's competitiveness, attractiveness, and economic development that materialized as a result of the MTM processes. Each chapter ends with both the implications of MTM activities and recommendations for individuals, organizations, policy makers, and the country's economy as a whole, as well as opportunities for further research on MTM in the country of interest. All chapters contain numerous exhibits and up-to-date references. In addition, each book has an appendix that the reader can use to find even more complete information than can be included in just a single chapter. Furthermore, the numerous websites in the appendix are useful for staying up-to-date with the current statistics and events as they unfold. We believe that the comparative analysis in our two books will help develop the topic of talent management in important new directions.

The importance of managing talent in the business context increased significantly in the 1990s when a group of McKinsey consultants coined the phrase 'war for talent' to emphasize the vital importance of employees to the success of top performing companies (Michaels, Hanfield-Jones, & Axelford, 2001; Scullion & Collings, 2018). While certainly that thrust into managing talent was and is important, it tended to focus mainly on the more individual and organizational levels (whether under the term "talent management" (TM) or "global talent management"), and thereby minimized several macro or country factors of the global environment that were also proving to have important implications—be they positive or negative—for managing talent at individual and organizational levels (Khilji & Schuler, 2017; Collings, Mellahi, & Cascio, 2017; Lanvin & Evans, 2017; Evans & Rodriguez-Montemayor, forthcoming; Hays, 2017; Khilji, Tarique, & Schuler, 2015; *Oxford Economics*, 2014; Al Ariss, Cascio, & Paauwe, 2014). This seems to be the case, despite the long-standing interest in talent management in the macro (country) level that pre-dated the 1990s. In particular, nongovernmental organizations such as the World Economic Forum (WEF), IMD's World Competitiveness Center, and the Organization for Economic Cooperation and Development (OECD) began publishing reports about the importance of talent, education and quality of a country's workforce in the 1980s.

Since these earlier studies in the 1980s, several studies have highlighted the macro, country, view of talent management (Khilji & Schuler, 2017; Sparrow, Brewster, & Chung, 2017; Cooke, Saini, & Wang, 2014; Khilji et al., 2015; *Oxford Economics*, 2014; *World Economic Forum*, 2016; Lanvin & Evans, 2014, 2015, 2017). These studies and reports showed that many governments have joined the hunt for global talent by actions such as developing immigrant friendly policies. Some governments have also focused on luring back skilled diaspora, and many others have made serious investments in education and human development of their own citizens with the purpose of spurring economic growth by upgrading local capabilities and building innovative capacities for the firms in their countries (Lanvin & Evans, 2014, 2015, 2017; Evans & Lanvin, 2015; Khilji et al., 2015).

Active involvement of governmental and nongovernmental organizations (NGOs), and several consulting firms, in attracting and developing talent makes managing talent truly a global issue, which reaches beyond a single organization and its talent management activities. It also draws attention to complexity of the macro environment within which organizations develop their talent management systems, and individuals make career choices (Khilji & Schuler, 2017; Khilji et al., 2015). Managing talent in the macro context also incorporates cross border flow of talent, diaspora mobility, and government policies to attract, grow, develop and retain the talent nationally for innovation, productivity and competitiveness, which facilitates talent management activities within organizations.

It is, therefore, important that the scope of TM extend beyond an individual and organizational analysis to incorporate the macro level in order to fully comprehend the complexities of managing talent in today's globalized world, where organizations are not only competing with each other but where governments, organizations and their societies have also joined the race to improve how they grow, nurture, and develop talent in their countries (Sparrow et al., 2017; Lanvin & Evans, 2014, 2015, 2017; Ragazzi, 2014). As such, we adopt the definition of macro TM (MTM) as:

Factors such as the demographics, the economic, educational, social and political conditions of countries and the policies, programs and activities that are systematically developed by governmental and non-governmental organizations expressly for the purpose of enhancing the quality and quantity of talent within and across countries and regions to facilitate productivity, innovation and competitiveness of their domestic and multinational enterprises for the benefit of their citizens, organizations, and societies for long term advantage.

(Khilji & Schuler, 2017, p. 400)

By promoting the macro perspective of talent management, we want to broaden the scope of talent management beyond its current primarily micro (individual level) and meso (organizational level) foci. What we are describing, therefore, is not "talent management" or "global talent management" (GTM) (which are both more focused on the individual and organizational levels), but MTM in the global context, which is focused on the macro level, or country level (it can be a single country, regions and cities within a country, or even several countries). At this macro level, talent issues—whilst potentially still focused on dominant sectors or skill groups—will impact the working lives of a large majority of a country's population.

This book *Macro Talent Management: A Global Perspective on Managing Talent in Developed Markets* offers the first comprehensive discussion of Macro-level Talent Management (MTM) in this newly emerging field. It serves as an orientation to scholars and as a guide to professionals, policy makers and societal leaders aiming to increase their country's global competitiveness, attractiveness, and economic development by ensuring high-quality talent management at individual, organizational, and country levels. Unlike the micro and meso perspectives on talent management and global talent management, the macro view that concerns the country-level activities aimed at attracting, developing, mobilizing and retaining top talent has received little attention from scholars, professionals and societal leaders alike until recently (*cf.* Tarique & Schuler, 2010; Farndale, Pai, Sparrow, & Scullion, 2014; Khilji et al., 2015).

The book and its focus on MTM also broadens the scope of global talent management to involve cross border flows of talent, diaspora mobility, and policies to attract, grow, develop and retain national talent in ways that facilitate their own MTM strategies and activities to one of global labor mobility and knowledge flows.

Thinking about talent management in this macro context calls for an understanding of the way in which these macro-level issues—for example, shifts taking place in global labor markets, the diaspora effect and brain circulation—create new questions and challenges for organizations, especially multinational enterprises (MNEs) around global mobility, the need for an integrated human development agenda, and links between talent flows and learning. It shifts the focus of activity within MNEs in response to these developments, as they see new opportunities to work around the long term structural trends in global labor markets, such as skills shortages, over education and skills under-utilization, changes in demography and wage pressure thresholds. It also creates questions around the balance between global integration and local responsiveness, as it is evident that country-level labor market strategies, strategies for growth, and the competitiveness of various national and local labor markets might mean that MNEs will develop unique and different strategies across their operations depending on the importance of various labor markets. Hence, there is a clear need to adopt a country-level perspective on MTM in the first instance. MNEs must now look at external collaborations in global cities, business clusters and industrial districts, national governments and institutions and across regional economies.

Just as nation states, regions and globally connected cities—and their many institutions and actors—are learning how best to survive and compete in a more globalized world and create new activities, MNEs are no different. Some people and functions inside MNEs will increasingly start to make the necessary connections between their own internal activities, and progressively collaborative activities that support the development of global talent and its management both at the individual level and at the broader institutional level. Global talent professionals and HR professionals might equally pursue these more macro-agendas.

The concept of MTM, then, is increasingly shaping the requisite GTM strategies of MNEs (Vaiman & Collings, 2014). It means that the core functions of GTM when seen from a micro or meso perspective—such as talent planning, talent acquisition, talent development, talent retention, the importance of talent flow, and knowledge spillovers and learning—need to be seen in a broader context. The emerging field of MTM brings together research from the fields of HRM, international business, economic geography, comparative international development and political economy, amongst others.

This book also enables the Routledge Global HRM Series to capture this new development. It aims to outline the interconnected nature of MTM environment, processes, and outcomes that in their entirety encompass an intricate world of a country's GTM system. The contributors—focusing on countries of their expertise—will help us both illustrate the importance of the topic and fill the gap in our knowledge about GTM systems and outcomes in different nations.

MTM Framework

To help facilitate our discussion in this chapter, we utilize a general framework of MTM that encapsulates macro environmental factors, processes and outcomes that flow from our definition of MTM. This general framework is illustrated in Figure 0.1. Because this framework is relatively new, chapter country authors have been free to adapt it as they see appropriate for their countries.

While Figure 0.1 is our framework of MTM for the purposes of organizing our thoughts on MTM, it also reflects the underlying frameworks that are being used by several NGOs

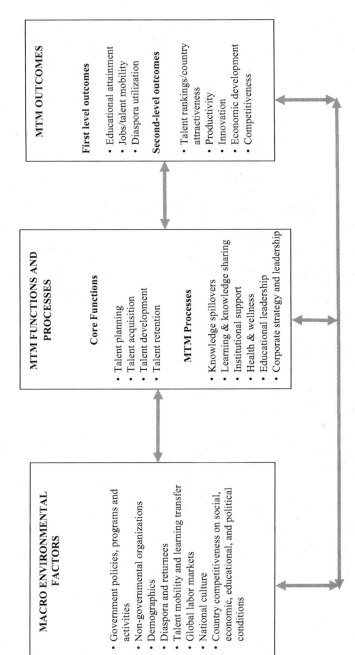

Figure 0.1 The General Framework for Macro Talent Management

Adapted from S.E. Kliiji, I. Tarique and R. S. Schuler, Incorporating the Macro View in Global Talent Management. *Human Resource Management Review*, 25 (3): 236–248, 2015.

(such as the WEF, the ILO, INSEAD, IMD and the World Bank) and consulting firms (such as McKinsey, Hays, and Boston Consulting Group (BCG)) to similarly describe a country's level of talent management capability (infrastructure) as it endeavors to be more competitive and productive vis-à-vis other countries of the world. The headlines of reports from these organizations and firms typically rank the overall success of talent management and/or country level competitiveness and productivity based upon its talent management infrastructure. But these overall rankings can be thought of as the outcomes of a country's macro environmental factors and the MTM processes as shown in Figure 0.1. Fortunately, these reports also provide the extensive details behind these overall rankings.

Thus, using similar frameworks to Figure 0.1, the reports essentially obtain the detailed country information from a wide variety of sources that measure the macro environmental factors and the MTM processes shown in Figure 0.1. Then the reports combine that information and construct rankings of the countries around the world on the MTM outcomes/consequences, also shown in Figure 0.1. While some of these reports, notably from the World Economic Forum, gather and report on more information than related to solely talent management, our focus in this chapter is on that information related to talent management at the country level (including local levels such as cities and states). More specifically, the information used here to illustrate our framework and reflected in many of the chapters in this book is largely based on the reports from:

- The World Economic Forum and its Global Competitiveness Index
- The World Economic Forum and LinkedIn and their Human Capital Report
- The Global Talent Index from the Economist Intelligence Unit and Heidrick & Struggles
- INSEAD and its Global Talent Competitiveness Index
- IMD and its World Talent Ranking Factors
- OECD and its Programme for International Student Assessment (PISA)
- The World Bank and its indicators of Doing Business; and Employing Workers
- Hays Global Skills Index

While the talent management contributions of consulting firms are often more focused on the company and individual levels, some also relate to the country level. Notable examples of consulting firms include McKinsey, the BCG and its Global Leadership and Talent Index (GLTI), Hays Plc and its Global Skills Index, the BCG and its Perspectives Reports, Deloitte, PWC, the Economist Intelligence Unit, Heidrick & Struggles and Adecco. Professional associations, such as the World Federation of People Management (WFPMA), Society for Human Resource Management (US), CIPD (UK), and SHRI (Singapore), also contribute significantly to our understanding of MTM. The various authors of our country chapters utilize information from the sources of information that they have found most useful for describing their countries.

There are of course different frameworks that could be used to guide our choices as to which countries to analyze. It is already evident from the comparative HRM literature that there are different varieties of capitalism around the world, and that the political economy of a country can serve to shape many aspects of HRM. In both books we have therefore included countries from different political economies, but in so doing, have arrived at an underlying position about this literature. For example, a distinction is often drawn between the liberal market economies (LME) and coordinated market economies (CME) (Soskice & Hall,

2001). Liberal market economies (LMEs) are defined by dispersed shareholder systems, arms-length competitive relations, formal contracting, supply-and-demand price signalling, reliance on mobile assets whose value can be realised, and deregulated or looser hire and fire labor market arrangements. The USA is an archetype LME. In contrast, coordinated market economies (CMEs) are characterised as having more strategic forms of co-ordination, with long-term employment strategies, close ties between firms and banks, and systems shaped by "institutional complementarities" such as frameworks between labor relations and corporate governance, labor relations and the national training system, and corporate governance and inter-firm relations. Germany is an archetype CME.

However, despite this categorization into two dominant varieties of capitalism, distinct and often subtly deep differences remain (Hancké, Rhodes, & Thatcher, 2007; Vaiman & Brewster, 2014). The variety of capitalism literature does not capture differences, for example, across Europe, which includes countries such as France, Italy and Spain, with their large state-owned sectors and Mediterranean Mixed Market Economies, or the recent arrivals to the capitalist scene of countries in Central Europe, nor Scandinavian economies, which whilst being seen as CMEs can be characterised as being a specific variant that has a social democracy form of political economy, which begins with its attitudes that favour the integration of trade unions into the business system and a universal welfare state.

In line with those who extended the varieties of capitalism literature to incorporate greater variation of national business models, we also believe a simple LME-CME distinction is too broad to capture and understand the complexities of talent management at a country level. At country level, we often need to understand complex domestic changes, especially in the areas of welfare states and labor markets.

What becomes evident, as we dig into the subtleties of national and industrial cultures at country level, and how these impact each country's MTM agenda, is that it is very hard to simply "export" talent philosophies from one location to another, even though policy setting elites are often tempted to do so. This is not our intention. Rather, as was made clear by the earliest cross-national research, we suspect that the whole (MTM) system only works if it is embedded into the appropriate institutional *and cultural* set. This became clear from research into phenomena such as the Japanization of manufacturing and the export of their production systems globally (Turnbull, 1986; Ackroyd, Burrell, Hughes, & Whitaker, 1988; Turnbull, Oliver, & Wilkinson, 1992), but also research into communication and decision making practices (Pascale, 1978), high commitment work systems (Wood, 1995) and industrial relations arrangements such as co-determination (Ichniowski, Kochan, Levine, Olson, & Strauss, 1996). Where any one function does not really exist, then you have to find its "functional equivalence", i.e., something which creates equivalence at the macro level. This notion of needing to find a functional equivalent has also been understood by looking at differences in culture, or in specific value. Where you are trying to recreate an HRM practice or function that worked well in one culture, how can you substitute or make up for the missing cultural values that in reality made the original HRM practice effective? You can only do this by understanding the function that such differences in culture or values served, and by understanding how you can achieve similar objectives through what may be different (often called parallel) practices or institutions (Pascale, 1978; Bensaou, Coyne, & Venkatraman, 1999; Gudykunst, 2000).

We now provide a summary of the country level chapters which provide an overview of MTM in developed markets.

8 • Paul Sparrow et al.

This Book on Macro Talent Management in Developed Markets

We have had to make some choices in terms of which countries it would be best to cover, which of the two books to place each country into, and how to sequence or group the different country chapters. The book is organized into country chapters that will enable the reader to understand how well countries are doing on many factors associated with the MTM, namely, the macro environmental factors of MTM as depicted in Figure 0.1. Because authors had the freedom to approach the general topic of MTM from their own country perspective, the reader will experience a rich variety of materials and discussions and even expansions and modification of the general framework of MTM.

An important distinction that might be made across countries in terms of their approach to MTM is to consider the ways in which countries that represent either developed or emerging markets (and those countries deemed emergent—having made a recent transition to developed status) approach the topic. Coming from an investment perspective based on the performance and reliability of securities, countries have been categorized as developed or emerging based on financial listings such as FTSE, MSCI, S&P, and Dow Jones. The International Monetary Fund also has a listing.

In this first of the two books we have brought together analyses of countries that are seen as developed markets. Countries that are classed as having developed markets are typically the most advanced in economic terms, with high levels of per capita income. As such, they have highly developed capital markets, and regulatory systems. Developed markets are found mostly in North America, Western Europe, and Australasia, including nations like the United States of America (USA), Canada, Germany, the U.K., Australia, New Zealand and Japan.

We hope that the many country chapters in this book will help both researchers and policy makers understand the comparability of MTM systems across countries—our adoption of a common analytical framework for each country is intended to facilitate this. We hope that the various chapters will signal the necessary adjustments that might be needed from one country to another as they try to both respond to the challenges of, and mutually compete in, the area of talent management.

United States of America

We begin with the North American perspective. In the original *Routledge Global Human Resource Management Series* Werner (2007) grouped the USA and Canada together under a common North American cluster. Both countries faced a common set of factors in terms of the economic, political, legal, technological and socio-cultural environment. Both have common HRM functions and structures, somewhat similar national and corporate cultures, and there are deep economic ties between the countries and numerous bilateral institutions. That said, there are also key differences between the USA and Canada, such as for example, their approach towards immigration and migrant labor (Horak, Farndale, Brannen, & Collings, 2017). We have therefore included separate chapters on the United States of America and Canada to capture the commonalities and uniqueness of the two MTM systems.

Chapter 1 on the USA by Randall Schuler, Ibraiz Tarique and Shaista Khilji develops their original MTM framework (Khilji et al., 2015; Khilji & Schuler, 2017) and "populates" this new framework with examples from the USA. The chapter makes four major contributions to the book:

1. It reviews the current underpinnings of the macro, or country, view of talent management, noting the belief across governmental and nongovernmental organizations,

consulting firms and policy bodies that there needs to be an upgrading of local capabilities and building of innovative capacities for the firms within, and across, countries in order to spur economic growth.
2. It identifies a range of metrics and indices that provide valuable comparative data (see also the Appendices in this book) and lays out some of the assumptions on which these recent metrics are based.
3. It introduces two developments important for the US but also of increasing global relevance: the role of being a leading market for international graduate education and the linked importance of immigration; and having a growing population.
4. It provides us as researchers with a language and set of ideas that enable us to share and compare our analysis across a range of countries. It introduces the notion of core MTM *functions* and *processes*. It uses a range of essential action verbs that explain how the impact of the macro environmental factors influences important outcomes or has important consequences. They may *transfer*, or *mediate*, or *shape*, or *modify* the core processes of talent planning, acquisition, development and retention. Finally, the chapter makes clear that we need to think about how these processes occur over time, or in sequence, and how they create primary and secondary effects on talent management.

Canada

In Chapter 2 Karin King analyses MTM in Canada. Although its position in North America and links to the USA through the North American Free Trade Agreement (NAFTA) have created strong cultural and institutional links to the USA, the Canadian economy is becoming increasingly internationalized, through connections via the Comprehensive Economic and Trade Agreement (CETA) with the EU and historical arrangements with the Commonwealth. It has a highly educated workforce, with strong adult literacy rates and very high levels of investment in tertiary education. The chapter makes the following contributions to the book:

1. As a nation, Canada was founded on international migration and strongly-held values of international collaboration, and this need continues (two in five Canadians are either immigrants or the child of immigrants). It has a long-standing structurally set of institutions designed to import and then distribute talent across its geography through within-country migration systems for skilled workers, long-standing reliance on analytical and labor market forecasting practices, and a national culture designed to welcome talent from both local, national and far reaching places.
2. As a consequence of remaining a high net importer of talent, it has developed a highly structured skills-based program aligned to targeted skillsets, based on transparent rules that assist in creating a sense of fairness and inclusiveness.
3. It is also the first of the countries analyzed in the book for whom the management of its own diaspora of globally-dispersed highly-educated and internationally-experienced talent, and the need to avoid the risk of periodic "brain drains" to the larger US economy, is important.
4. Canada has made investments in international educational collaborations and initiatives aimed at establishing standards of education abroad which transparently align to Canadian standards.
5. Canada is also one of the countries that can claim to be able to compete on 'soft power' and a national employer brand based on the attractiveness of its culture, national policies and political ideologies—it fairs well in its ability to attract highly-skilled foreign talent to its business environment.

United Kingdom

The book then has eight chapters that analyze a selection of European countries: the UK, Germany, Spain, Denmark, Finland, and the Netherlands. It is particularly useful to examine country-level differences across Europe, for as the varieties of capitalism and comparative HRM literatures remind us, there is still remarkable diversity found in national business systems across Europe as a region (Larsen & Mayrhofer, 2006; Collings, Scullion, & Vaiman, 2011; Vaiman & Holden, 2011; Dickmann, Brewster, & Sparrow, 2016).

Chapter 3 by Paul Sparrow analyses the MTM context in the UK. The chapter makes the following contributions:

1. It develops the notion of *patterns of agency* and *webs of action* at country level that serve to *condition* the conduct of talent management. There are few generalizable or preferable recipes for MTM—the patterns that emerge in the UK need not, or would not, necessarily work in a different national context. National strategies are embedded in, and managed through, complex webs of action. The dominant patterns in the UK concern: the HRM culture; specific qualities of being an advanced economy; the industrial structure; the link between skills and productivity; the comparative advantage of vocational and education training strategies, the impact on education strategies; the impact of globalized sector labor markets on large national employers; and the growing impact of London as a global city.
2. It draws upon institutional theory to argue there is a need not just for new talent management practices in the UK, changes in the structures in which these practices will need to become embedded, and changes in the regimes (the overriding expectations and planned way of doing things for a given issue-area around which actors tend to converge) currently in place.
3. It draws attention to the importance of the HRM culture and the assumptions made about what makes a manager effective. It also argues that a number of *qualities of the UK as an advanced economy* have had a bearing. Important roles are played by historical accumulations of human capital, a highly globalized economy (around a tenth of the UK's assets and liabilities and more than five times the value of its GDP come from foreign direct investment).
4. It draws attention to the importance of industrial structure, the gross value added (GVA) that comes from dominant sectors, and the networks that foster skills clusters, support innovation activity, links between education providers and industry to strengthen market signals on industry skill demand, and access to finance. More problematic for the UK is the link between its skills base and productivity, the weakness of its vocational and education training strategies, the impact of its education strategies, and the need to rebalance its immigration strategies.
5. Finally, the chapter introduces work on future skills scenarios to the book, the impact of digitalization and artificial intelligence upon these, the role played by globalized sector labor markets, and the growing impact of London as a global city.

Germany

In Chapter 4 on Germany, Marion Festing and Katharina Harsch review the MTM context in the first of the coordinated market economies (Soskice & Hall, 2001) covered in the book. Its approach to talent management stands in contrast to those seen in the opening chapters

Introduction • 11

in the book, which cover liberal market economies. Unemployment is relatively low, but as the world's industrial structure continues to evolve, Germany has to continue to innovate and find markets suited to its relatively high labor costs, an ageing population and shrinking working age population. The chapter makes the following contributions:

1. It helps us understand how many of the generic talent management challenges seen across the globe are tackled in a country in which the state takes a strong role in providing an educational context in the social market economy, and there is a tight relationship between the national business system and human resource management on the corporate level. As the largest European economy, Germany engages actively in talent management. It faces an interesting mix of positive short term context but a significant set of medium to longer term challenges. It has a well-performing export-led economy, a resilient and adaptive industrial structure based around SMEs, a strong vocational education and training institutions and a tight system of state regulations for industrial relations.
2. It shows how a tightly integrated approach to regulation can be targeted on specific outcomes. Attention in Germany is now being directed at various talent management challenges through various laws, regulations, ordinances and regional and federal initiatives aimed at improving the efficiency of the labor market, through the integration of the recent influx of refugees, further improvements in the economic participation of equality of women, and the encouragement of returnees from the overseas diaspora. A similar approach is being adopted to address the challenges of digitization.

Spain

A defining characteristic of the political economy of Europe is variation in the socio-economic arrangements. On the one hand, we see significant moves towards mutual trade, monetary union and single market regulation within the EU, and common government initiatives aimed at developing institutional solutions to the problems of economic governance through many small changes in the operation of the underlying institutional framework (many of these changes are noted in the various country chapters). On the other hand, analyses of the HRM context across Europe in the *Routledge Global HRM Series* continue to show that whilst it can still be linked to country clusters linked by Mediterranean, Western European, Central and Eastern European, and Nordic geography—different sets of social and economic forces continue to shape contemporary IHRM in Europe, and these issues must be layered into any analysis of HRM practices (Dickmann et al., 2016).

In Chapter 5 Adoración Álvaro-Moya, Eva Gallardo-Gallardo, and Jordi Paniagua analyze MTM in Spain. In the varieties of capitalism literature, Spain is characterized as a "mixed market economy" or "state-influenced mixed market economy" and is often seen as part of a Mediterranean periphery to Europe, alongside countries such as Italy and Portugal. Industrialization, institutional reform, economic stabilization and liberalization gathered pace relatively recently, from the 1960s and 1970s onwards, and the country has experienced more volatile patterns of economic growth, contraction and unemployment than seen in the EU as a whole. It has experienced noticeable increases in inwards migration, with 10% of residents now being foreigners, but the majority of working age migrants have a low or middle educational attainment. Weaknesses persist around educational investment and outcomes, productivity, and labor market security, but the country has advanced on its position on most talent management indices. The chapter makes the following contributions to the book:

1. Spain is one of those countries that has experienced variation in migration inflows and outflows, recently experiencing a negative migratory balance between 2009 and 2016, raising fears about a brain drain, and only recently returning to being a net importer of talent. The chapter draws attention to initiatives that can be used to reverse migration flows, and to market the country as a brand to attract labor.
2. It shows that immigration is not always perceived in the same way across cultures or political economies. The authors argue that given Spain's recent history and experience of both emigration and immigration, it is perceived as a vehicle to enhance democratic values and, compared to other countries, is not perceived as a threat to national identity.
3. It reminds us that regional variations can be important. There is internal variation in policies that might affect talent management at a macro level, as regional governments have jurisdiction to intervene in education, infrastructures and taxation issues, and internal migration across regions needs to be managed.
4. Finally, it draws attention to the challenges faced in economies in which microenterprises are important (they account for 40% of employment compared to 20% in Germany), family ownership is a factor, and sole self-employment is a growing trend.

Denmark

The first Nordic/Scandinavian country examined in the book is Denmark. In Chapter 6 Dana Minbaeva, Torben Andersen, Nikolaj Lubanski, Steen Erik Navrbjerg and Ronja Marie Torfing analyse MTM of Denmark. Denmark is another economy that is highly dependent on foreign trade and investment, and that has an economy influenced strongly by a small number of dominant sectors (rather like the UK discussed in Chapter 3). Unlike the UK, however, it is a coordinated market economy, with high levels of regulation through collective-agreement and a centralized bargaining system. The chapter makes the following contributions to the book:

1. It shows how talent systems can be overlain on distinctive labor relations models—in the case of Denmark this is its *flexicurity* model—helping us understand how talent management systems can be developed as a cooperation between the state and the social partners.
2. It provides insight into how labor markets can be attractive to many MNCs through competition around the quality of human capital—many Nordic and non-EU MNCs maintain a high local presence because of the availability and quality of human capital. However, Denmark faces potential and significant skills shortages around the high-education skills demographic, raising the threat of some economic activity being outsourced.
3. Such talent debates surface some of the national paradoxes that have to be confronted. On the one hand Denmark has an enviable record of being able to grow talent internally, making it attractive to many firms, but at the same time it struggles to attract external talent. As a consequence, there is as yet not a well-established and -integrated talent management system in Denmark, and institutions are not as coordinated

as might be assumed, notwithstanding new initiatives around pan-national issues such as Industry 4.0.
4. Its analysis of talent paradoxes signals important areas for future research—for example, in Denmark the very macroeconomic factors that allow the country to grow its home talent base (such as education and training philosophies), reinforced by a cultural imperative to make the most of internal labor markets and home talent, might potentially either limit the ability to respond to external talent issues, or confound the country's ability to keep pace with the demands of global talent management.

Finland

In Chapter 7 Paul Evans, Adam Smale and Ingmar Björkman analyze MTM in a second Nordic/Scandinavian country, Finland. They argue that the similarities between Finland and the Scandinavian countries of Sweden, Denmark and Norway outnumber the differences, and so their chapter also serves as an example of the approaches being taken in the Nordic region of Europe. The Finnish economy is undergoing much change, and a rapid transition towards a knowledge economy is taking place. There are important learning points to draw from this disruptive societal transformation, and the chapter explores some of the talent aspects of this transformation. It argues that despite relatively high levels of unemployment, Finland should be seen as a model nation in matching talent to work needs, with relatively high levels of employability and a sense amongst employers that skills shortages are not stark. The chapter presents the distinctive features of talent management in Finland, and makes the following important contributions to the book:

1. It highlights the role played by a country's educational philosophy, which in the case of Finland emphasizes a learning-how-to-learn orientation even from pre-school years, an emphasis on egalitarianism and an early bifurcation of students into academic and vocational tracks, and a pattern of close collaboration between key stakeholders involved in talent management.
2. It is also evident that in an economy the size of Finland, national champion organizations (such as Nokia) can play a significant role in revitalizing the economy. A combination of competition policies, deregulation, and innovation underpinned by education and government-supported research helped create industry-leading firm-level capabilities. The subsequent demise of Nokia was met by a similar centrally-coordinated investment process, this time in the SME sector, and it remains to be seen what long-term impact a talent cohort of R&D experts who have been made redundant and released into a job market will have on a planned-for entrepreneurial eco-system.
3. It also brings the Global Talent Competitiveness Index (GTCI) frame of analysis into the book (Lanvin & Evans, 2017; Evans & Rodriguez-Montemayor, forthcoming).

The Netherlands

In Chapter 8 Marian Thunnissen, Joop Schippers, and Paul Boselie analyze MTM in the Netherlands. The Netherlands has a high level of GDP per capita, and an economy tightly integrated into the global trade system, and developed around a well-functioning infrastructure and trade hubs such as Amsterdam, Rotterdam and Eindhoven. Of the workforce, 40% work for a small number of MNCs. It is also in the top 10% of countries in terms of the opportunities for firms to attract, identify, develop and deploy talent, has a strong and broadly publically-funded education system, high levels of productivity, and relatively low levels of income inequality. As with many of the other countries analyzed in the book, it has a unique national business system variant (the "polder-model") with 80% of the workforce being covered by collective agreements. However, weaknesses in its system remain, with the authors drawing attention in particular to parallel problems of under-utilization (both in terms of lifelong learning, and also the utilization of specific groups such as women, ethnic minorities and older employees), over-utilization (excessive workloads) of talent, and some systemic biases in the education system. The chapter makes the following contributions to the book:

1. Given the economic geography of the country, the case is made that we should not just focus on conditions that make it easier for firms to attract talent, but also draw upon the literature on smart cities and add offering and protecting a good quality of life for all as an enabler of effective macro talent systems. A country or a region must also be attractive for the talents or employees themselves.
2. It reminds us that the GTCI (Lanvin & Evans, 2017) is of course derived from a strong neo-liberal perspective and set of assumptions (for example around competition, models of education and assumptions about labor flexibility) and that there are other narratives around cooperation to counter-balance competition.
3. Whilst standardized and comparative metrics around MTM are useful, we need qualitative and critical analysis of country systems in order to qualify, contradict or contextualize the messages that should be taken from such metrics.

Australia

Finally, in Chapter 9 Sharna Wiblen and Anthony McDonnell analyze MTM in Australia. As a relatively recent nation state, and one forged from foundation as a penal colony, migration has been pivotal in shaping both early and modern-day Australia. Although clearly a developed market, Australia has a number of distinct characteristics—it was one of the few countries to avoid the Global Financial Crisis (GFC), so the "war for talent" narrative has continued unabated and skills shortages continue at all organizational levels. It has a narrower distribution of income than many Anglo-Saxon cultures, higher real wages growth, a generous minimum wage, labor productivity growth has exceeded increases in real wages for a while, yet there are relatively powerful unions, a small population pool and a distributed array of medium-sized cities (i.e., without a mega-city). Population growth has been driven significantly by net overseas migration, and it is a multicultural nation, with some 30% of the Australian labor force being born outside of Australia. There are domestic Chinese and Indian diaspora, seen as enhancing market links with Asia, and a recognisable Australian diaspora overseas, but immigration is no longer being framed politically as being in Australia's national interest. The more constrained approach to immigration has been taken despite international education being Australia's third-largest export after coal and iron ore, and largest service export. The chapter makes the following contributions to the book:

1. It shows that there are many—and subtly nuanced—paths to effective talent management at a macro level, and a country can have natural production factors that position it outside standard MTM "recipes". Despite scoring only moderately on some of the key talent enablers (though well on many too), Australia still manages to adequately

utilize the skills and capabilities of 71 per cent of its total in the pursuit of national productivity and competitiveness.
2. However, the Australian business structure seems potentially vulnerable to future technological shifts—up to 40% of current jobs are at risk of being lost over the next 15 years. The need to address future technological challenges of course may bring another shift in national strategies, policies and processes.

Conclusion

In this chapter, we have both introduced the topic of MTM and have explained the rationale and structure this particular book on *Macro Talent Management: A Global Perspective on Managing Talent in Developed Markets*. In so doing we have drawn upon the expertise of academics from around the world. We have presented comparable data and analysis of the MTM environment across nine countries. This represents an invaluable source of information for academics and policy makers alike. However, we felt it was important to provide the contributing researchers with a standard MTM framework to help structure their reviews, but also importantly to task the teams with reflecting on their analysis and to identify what they saw as the most important lessons and implications for the developing field of MTM— keeping them to a structure but letting them interpret their country. This has allowed us to analyze each of the chapters in order to surface, in the form of various numbered conclusions, what we in turn see as the generic messages for this new field. We hope that the many insights in this summary chapter provide guidance on the challenges ahead, help establish agreed principles but also debunk a few myths, and do indeed help to lay the foundations for what we and all the contributors see as an important field of study.

References

Ackroyd, S., Burrell, G., Hughes, M., & Whitaker, A. (1988). The Japanisation of British industry. *Industrial Relations Journal*, *19*(1), 11–23.
Al Ariss, A. A., Cascio, W. F., & Paauwe, J. (2014). Talent management: Current theories and future research directions. *Journal of World Business*, *49*, 173–179.
Bensaou, M., Coyne, M., & Venkatraman, N. (1999). Testing metric equivalence in cross-national strategy research: An empirical test across the United States and Japan. *Strategic Management Journal*, *20*, 671–689.
Collings, D.G., Mellahi, K. & Cascio, W.F. (2017). (Eds.) *The Oxford Handbook of talent Management*. Oxford: Oxford University Press.
Collings, D., Scullion, H., & Vaiman, V. (2011). European perspectives on talent management. *European Journal of International Management*, *5*(5), 453–462.
Cooke, F. L., Saini, D. S., & Wang, J. (2014). Talent management in China and India: A comparison of management perceptions and human resource practices. *Journal of World Business*, *49*, 225–235.
Dickmann, M., Brewster, C., & Sparrow, P. R. (Eds.). (2016). *International HRM: Contemporary human resource issues in Europe*. London: Routledge.
Evans, P., & Lanvin, B. (2015). *The world's most talent ready countries*. Retrieved from www.knowledge.insead.edu/talent-management.
Evans, P., & Rodriguez-Montemayor, E. (forthcoming). Talent management in a global context: The global talent competitiveness index. In I. Tarique (Ed.), *The Routledge companion to talent management*. New York: Routledge.
Farndale, E., Pai, A., Sparrow, P., & Scullion, H. (2014). Balancing individual andorganizational goals in global talent management: A mutual-benefits perspective. *Journal of World Business*, *49*(2), 204–214.
Gudykunst, W. B. (2000). Methodological issues in conducting theory-based cross-cultural research. In H. Spencer-Oatey (Ed.), *Culturally speaking: Managing rapport through talk across cultures* (pp. 293–315). London: Continuum.

Hancké, R., Rhodes, M., & Thatcher, M. (Eds.). (2007). *Beyond varieties of capitalism: Conflict, contradictions, and complementarities in the European economy.* Oxford: Oxford University Press.

Hays Plc. (2017). *Hays global skills index 2016.* Retrieved from www.hays-index.com/the-index/introduction/.

Horak, S., Farndale, E., Brannen, M. Y., & Collings, D. G. (2017). International Human Resource Management in an Era of Political Nationalism. *Thunderbird International Business Review*, in press.

Ichniowski, C., Kochan, T., Levine, D., Olson, C., & Strauss, G. (1996). What works at work: Overview and assessment. *Industrial Relations, 35*, 299–334.

Khilji, S. E., & Schuler, R. S. (2017). Talent management in the global context. In D. Collings, K. Mellahi, & W. Cascio (Eds.), *Oxford handbook of talent management.* Oxford, UK: Oxford Press.

Khilji, S. E., Tarique, I., & Schuler, R. S. (2015). Incorporating the macro view in global talent management. *Human Resource Management Review, 25*(3), 236–248.

Lanvin, B., & Evans, P. (2014). *The global talent competitiveness index 2014.* Human Capital Leadership Institute. INSEAD and Adecco Group, Switzerland.

Lanvin, B., & Evans, P. (2015). *The global talent competitiveness index 2015–16.* Human Capital Leadership Institute, INSEAD and Adecco Group, Switzerland.

Lanvin, B., & Evans, P. (2017). *The global talent competitiveness index 2016–17.* Human Capital Leadership Institute. INSEAD and Adecco Group, Switzerland.

Larsen, H. H., & Mayrhofer, W. (Eds.). (2006). *Managing human resources in Asia pacific.* London: Routledge.

Michaels, E., Hanfield-Jones, H., & Axelford, B. (2001). *War for talent.* Boston, MA: Harvard Business School Press.

Oxford Economics. (2014). *Global talent 2021: How the new geography of talent will transform human resource strategies.* Retrieved from www.oxfordeconomics.com/Media/Default/Thought%20Leadership/global-talent-2021.pdf.

Pascale, R. (1978). Communication and decision making across cultures: Japanese and American comparisons. *Administrative Science Quarterly, 23*(1), 91–110.

Ragazzi, F. (2014). A comparative analysis of diaspora policies. *Political Geography, 41*, 74–89.

Scullion, H., & Collings, D. (2018). *Global talent management* (2nd ed.). London: Routledge.

Sparrow, P. R., Brewster, C., & Chung, C. (2017). *Globalizing human resource management* (2nd ed.). London and New York: Routledge.

Soskice, D. W., & Hall, P. A. (2001). *Varieties of capitalism: The institutional foundations of comparative advantage.* Oxford: Oxford University Press.

Tarique, I., & Schuler, R. (2010). Global talent management: Literature review, integrative framework, and suggestions for future research. *Journal of World Business, 45*, 122–133.

Turnbull, P. (1986). The 'Japanisation' of production and industrial relations at Lucas Electrical. *Industrial Relations Journal, 17*(3), 193–206.

Turnbull, P., Oliver, N., & Wilkinson, B. (1992). Buyer-supplier relations in the UK-automotive industry: Strategic implications of the Japanese manufacturing model. *Strategic Management Journal, 13*(2), 159–168.

Vaiman, V., & Brewster, C. (2014). How far do cultural differences explain the differences between nations? Implications for HRM. *International Journal of Human Resource Management, 26*(2), 151–164.

Vaiman, V., & Collings, D. (2014). *Global talent management, Routledge companion to human resource management.* London: Routledge.

Vaiman, V., & Holden, N. (2011). Talent management in central and Eastern Europe: Challenges and trends. In D. Collings & H. Scullion (Eds.), *Global talent management.* London: Routledge.

Werner, S. (Eds.). (2007). *Managing human resources in North America.* London: Routledge.

Wood, S. (1995). Can we speak of high commitment management on the shop floor? *Journal of Management Studies, 32*, 215–247.

World Economic Forum. (2016). *The human capital report.* Retrieved from www.weforum.org/reports/the-human-capital-report-2016.

1
Macro Talent Management in the United States
Framework, Context, Processes and Outcomes

Randall Schuler, Ibraiz Tarique and Shaista Khilji

Interest in the United States in talent management (TM) increased significantly in the 1990s when a group of McKinsey consultants coined the phrase 'war for talent' in late 1990s to emphasize the vital importance of employees to the success of top performing companies (Michaels, Hanfield-Jones, & Axelford, 2001; Scullion & Collings, 2016). While certainly important, TM tended to focus mainly on the individual and organizational levels, and minimize several macro or country factors of the global environment that have since become more recognized as invaluable for TM at the individual and organizational levels (Khilji & Schuler, 2018; Khilji, Tarique, & Schuler, 2015; *Oxford Economics*, 2014; Strack, Von Der Linden, Booker, & Strohamyr, 2011). This growth in TM at the individual and organizational levels in the United States occurred despite the long-standing interest in talent management in the global context, or the macro (country) level, especially outside the United States. In particular, non-governmental organizations such as the World Economic Forum (WEF), IMD's World Competitiveness Center, and the Organization for Economic Cooperation and Development began publishing reports about the importance of talent, education and quality of a country's workforce in the 1980s.

Since the early 1980s several other studies, many outside the United States, have continued to highlighted the macro, country, view of talent management (Khilji and Schuler, 2018; Sparrow, Brewster, & Chung, 2017; Cooke, Saini, & Wang, 2014; *The Economist*, 2013; Heidrick & Struggles, 2007, 2011; Khilji et al., 2015; *Oxford Economics*, 2014; WEF, *Human Capital Reports*, 2013, 2015, 2016; Lanvin & Evans, 2014, 2015, 2017). These studies and reports showed that many governments have joined the hunt for global talent by developing immigrant friendly policies. Some governments have also been luring back skilled diaspora, and many others have been making serious investments in education and human development of their own citizens with the purpose of spurring economic growth by upgrading local capabilities and building innovative capacities for the firms in their countries (Lanvin & Evans, 2014, 2015, 2017; Evans & Lanvin, 2015; Khilji et al., 2015; Ragazzi, 2014). This has certainly impacted thinking about the macro context of TM in the United States (Khilji & Schuler, 2018).

Thus today, active involvement of various governmental and nongovernmental organizations (NGOs), and several consulting firms, in attracting and developing talent makes TM truly a global issue, which reaches beyond a single organization, and even a single country and their talent management activities. It draws attention to complexity of the macro environment within which organizations in the United States develop their talent management systems, and individuals make career choices (Khilji & Schuler, 2018; Khilji et al., 2015; Khilji & Keilson, 2014). It incorporates cross border flow of talent, diaspora mobility and government policies to attract, grow, develop and retain the talent nationally for innovation, productivity and competitiveness, which facilitates talent management activities within organizations.

It is, therefore, important in the United States that the scope of talent management (TM) extend beyond an individual and organizational analysis to incorporate the macro level in order to fully comprehend the complexities of managing talent in today's globalized world, where organizations are not only competing with each other but where governments, organizations and their societies have also joined the race (Sparrow et al., 2017; Lanvin & Evans, 2014, 2015, 2017; Ragazzi, 2014; *Economist*, 2011). As such, we adopt the definition of macro talent management (MTM) for the United States offered in the Introductory chapter of this book as:

> Factors such as the demographics, the economic, educational, social and political conditions of countries and the policies, programs and activities that are systematically developed by governmental and non-governmental organizations expressly for the purpose of enhancing the quality and quantity of talent within and across countries and regions to facilitate productivity, innovation and competitiveness of their domestic and multinational enterprises for the benefit of their citizens, organizations, and societies for long term advantage.

By promoting the macro perspective, we want to further broaden the scope of TM in the United States beyond its current main focus (on the individual and organizational levels). What we are describing, therefore, is not "global talent management" (which is focused on the individual and organizational levels), but talent management in the global context, which is focused on the macro level, or country level (it is both within a single country and/or across countries). At this macro level, talent is defined to include a large majority of a country's population, similar to companies that pursue an inclusive approach in their talent management activities. However, research has also shown that many countries also pursue an exclusive approach to target a small portion of the workforce (Khilji & Keilson, 2014).

To help facilitate our discussion of MTM in the United States, we build on a framework of MTM that encapsulates macro environmental factors, processes and activities that are broadly presented in Figure 0.1 in this book's Introductory chapter. Because this framework is relatively new (Khilji & Schuler, 2018), we describe its components in more detail and use it to describe the MTM context of the United States. In doing so, we also provide the reader with an extensive set of references and data sources that can used for further elaboration on what is presented in this chapter. These references and sources can also be used for other countries.

While Figure 1.1 is our framework for describing MTM in the United States, it reflects the underlying frameworks that are being used by several NGOs (such as the WEF, the

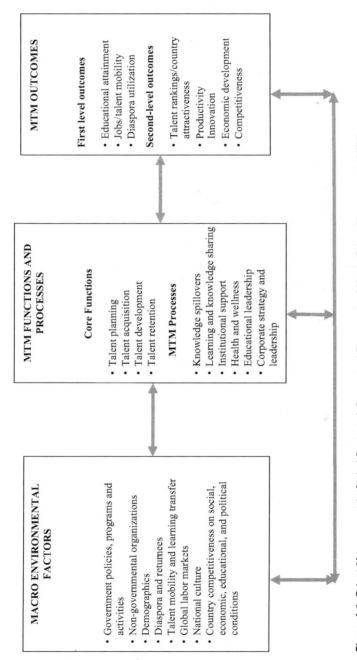

Figure 1.1 Talent Management in Global Context: A Conceptual Framework of Macro Talent Management (MTM)

Adapted from S.E. Khilji and R. S. Schuler, "Talent Management in the Global Context," a chapter in D. Collings, K. Mellahi, and W. Cascio (eds.) *Oxford Handbook of Talent Management*, Oxford Press (Oxford, England, 2018).

ILO, INSEAD, IMD and the World Bank) and consulting firms (such as McKinsey, Hays, and BCG) to similarly describe a country's level of talent management capability (infrastructure) as it endeavors to be more competitive and productive vis-à-vis other countries of the world. The headlines of reports from these organizations and firms typically report the overall rankings of talent management success and/or country level competitiveness and productivity based upon its talent management infrastructure. But these overall rankings can be thought of as the outcomes of a country's macro environmental factors and the MTM processes as shown in Figure 1.1. Fortunately, the reports from these organizations and firms also provide the extensive details behind these overall rankings. Thus, using Figure 1.1, the reports essentially obtain the detailed country information from a wide variety of sources that measure the macro environmental factors and the MTM processes shown in Figure 1.1. Then the reports combine that information and construct rankings of the countries around the world on the MTM outcomes/consequences, also shown in Figure 1.1. While some of these reports, notably from the World Economic Forum, gather and report on more information than related to solely talent management, our focus in this chapter is on that information related to talent management at the country level (which can also include macro levels, i.e., those above the individual and organizational levels, such as cities and states). More specifically, the information used here to describe our framework for MTM in the United States in Figure 1.1 is largely based on the reports from:

- The World Economic Forum and its Global Competitiveness Index
- The World Economic Forum and LinkedIn and their Human Capital Report
- The Global Talent Index from the Economist Intelligence Unit and Heidrick & Struggles
- INSEAD and its Global Talent Competitiveness Index
- IMD and its World Talent Ranking Factors
- OECD and its Performance Indicators of Student Assessment (PISA)
- The World Bank and its indicators of Doing Business; and Employing Workers
- Hays Global Skills Index

While the talent management contributions of consulting firms are often more focused on the company and individual levels, some do relate to the country level as well. Notable examples of consulting firms including McKinsey, the Boston Consulting Group (BCG) and its Global Leadership and Talent Index (GLTI), Hays Plc and its Global Skills Index, the BCG Perspectives Reports, Deloitte, PWC, the Economist Intelligence Unit, Heidrick & Struggles and Adecco. Professional associations also contribute significantly to our understanding of macro talent management such as the World Federation of People Management (WFPMA), and the Society of Human Resource Management (SHRM).

This chapter is organized to enable the reader to begin to understand how well the United States is doing on many factors associated with the macro talent management, namely the macro environmental factors, the MTM processes and the MTM outcomes/consequences as depicted in Figure 1.1. Through the references and the links provided in the references, hopefully this chapter can enable the reader to find many more relevant and specific details associated with Figure 1.1 than can be reported in this short chapter. In addition, these references are used in many of the other chapters in the book to describe countries in addition to the United States being described here. Thus what is described here should be regarded as only the "tip of the iceberg."

The Macro Talent Management (MTM) Environment Factors in the United States

We begin with a general description of the macro environmental factors, which are captured in Figure 1.1 and offer MTM data from the United States and occasional references to other countries for context and comparison.

Governmental Policies, Programs and Activities and Non-Governmental Organizations

We have mentioned previously that many national governments have been pursuing policies that focus upon upgrading and/or maintaining local capabilities and developing innovative capacities through their human talent. Perhaps those most directly associated with country level talent management are associated with educating and developing their populations and making it attractive for individuals from other countries to migrate to them (Martin, 2015). There are, however, more broadly focused characteristics of countries that are also important in making a country an attractive and welcoming place for talent and for MNEs seeking to locate their operations in a particular country. The same can be said for similar activities at the state and local governmental levels. Indeed, the INSEAD report on the Global Talent Competitiveness Index (2017) provides numerous examples of what state and local governments are doing.

Education Focused

Many organizations and consulting firms have been tracking and measuring just how well countries do in this regard, making it easy for countries to see how well they are doing and compare themselves to others. Their work can be found in yearly and bi-yearly reports from the World Economic Forum, INSEAD, the IMD, the OECD, the ILO, the World Bank and the Economist Intelligence Unit.

The data in the following six tables shows that the US, as a large developed economy, scores very well in comparative terms for innovation, the sophistication of business practices and ease of doing business, the institutional environment and level of market development, labor market efficiency, the appeal of its labor market to overseas talent, the country's capacity for developing, attracting and retaining talent, and the quality of its higher education and training sectors. It fares less well (but in the top third) in terms of the investments it makes for health and primary education, and investments in home-grown talent. It faces some particular talent issues, such as the need for more flexibility at all levels of education, wage pressures in high-skilled industries, levels of talent shortages and mismatch, and an uncertain political environment associated with immigration and the image to international students.

For example, the World Economic Forum (WEF) publishes the Global Competitiveness Index that compares and ranks 138 countries on 14 separate country-level pillars. Not all pillars relate directly to education and talent management, but four do: the 4th Pillar (Health and Primary Education); the 5th Pillar (High Education and Training); the 7th Pillar (Labor Market Efficiency); and the 12th Pillar (R&D Innovation). The details of these four are shown in Table 1.1. Details about the entire set of 14 country-level pillars are provided under our discussion of country competitiveness on social, economic, educational and political conditions. The more broadly focused country characteristics mentioned previously are described in detail elsewhere (WEF: *The World Competitiveness Report 2016–2017*: 1–50).

Table 1.1 Global Competitiveness Index Pillars Related to Education and Talent Management

This index looks at the effect of several macro level factors which create the conditions for competitiveness. The overall US Ranking is 3/140 (economies).

Pillar	Description	US Rank
Health and Primary Education	This pillar examines investments in the provision of health services, and the quantity and quality of basic education	46/140
High Education and Training	This pillar measures secondary and tertiary enrollment rates, and the quality of education	6/140
Labor Market Efficiency	This pillar looks at the efficiency and flexibility of the labor market	4/140
Innovation	This pillar focuses on technological innovation	4/140

Source: Schwab, Klaus, et al., 2016–2017. *The Global Competitiveness Report 2016–2017.* World Economic Forum: Davos, Switzerland. www.weforum.org/reports/the-global-competitiveness-report-2016-2017-1/

Table 1.2 IMD World Talent Ranking

This ranking compares and ranks countries on three factors: investment, development, and appeal and readiness. Overall US Ranking is 14/61 economies

Factor	Description	US Ranking
Investment and Development	This factor examines the investment in and development of home-grown talent	23/61
Appeal	This factor focuses on the ability of a country to tap into the overseas talent pool	2/61
Readiness	This factor inspects the context of the talent pool (e.g., the growth of the labor force and the quality of the skills available)	55/61

Source: IMD World Talent Report by the IMD World Competitiveness Center (2015). Institute of Management Development. www.imd.org/wcc/news-talent-report/

The IMD publishes a World Talent Ranking report that compares and ranks countries on three education-focused factors, namely: 1) investment and development, 2) appeal and 3) readiness shown in Table 1.2. Each of these factors is comprised of several more specific sub-factors. For example and most relevant here, the investment and development factor reflects: total public expenditure on education; total public expenditure per pupil; pupil-teacher ratio (primary and secondary); apprenticeship; employee training; and female labor force (see pages 7–8 for a complete description of these three factors and sub-factors in the *IMD World Talent Report 2015*). A country is able to increase its overall country ranking by doing better on these sub-factors while doing the same or better on the other two factors.

The World Bank has its Doing Business Index that ranks countries on several broadly focused characteristics of a country for doing business, from ease of starting a company and tax rates to employability of the workforce, including its skill levels (*Doing Business,* 2016). The broadly focused characteristics are shown in Table 1.3 and describe in detail elsewhere (*Doing Business,* 2016: 264–265).

A more detailed ranking specifically relevant to talent management are the labor market regulations associated with hiring, working hours, redundancy rules, redundancy costs, and job quality as shown in Table 1.4 and described in detail elsewhere (*Doing Business,* 2016: 266–67).

Table 1.3 World Bank's Doing Business Index

This index looks at 10 areas and examines the extent for local entrepreneurs to start and run a small to medium-size business when complying with relevant regulations. Countries are ranked on their ease of doing business. A high score suggests that the regulatory environment is supportive of establishing a new business. Overall US Ranking is 6/189 Economies

Area	US Ranking
• Starting a Business	17/189
• Dealing With Construction Permits	23/189
• Getting Electricity	15/189
• Registering Property	45/189
• Getting Credit	19/189
• Protecting Minority Investors	4/189
• Paying Taxes	15/189
• Trading Across Borders	38/189
• Enforcing Contracts	33/189
• Resolving Insolvency	13/189

Source: Doing Business, Measuring Business Regulations (2016), World Bank Group. (www.doingbusiness.org/rankings)

Table 1.4 Labor Market Regulations

Items from the Doing Business ranking index specifically relevant to "labor market regulations" are grouped into five categories as shown in the table. Within each category are many specific dimensions. There are 37 dimensions in total in these five categories.

www.doingbusiness.org/data/exploretopics/labor-market-regulation

www.doingbusiness.org/reports/global-reports/~/media/GIAWB/Doing%20Business/Documents/Annual-Reports/English/DB16-Chapters/DB16-Labor-Market-Regulation.pdf

See this website to see all the details for the five categories of labor regulations listed in Table 1.4.

Hiring: Five dimensions of hiring, including existence of fixed term contracts; length of those contracts; minimum wage; value added per worker; and incentives

Working hours: Nine dimensions of hours, including maximum working days/week; premium for night work; premium for weekly rest; premium for overtime; restrictions on night work; etc.

Redundancy rules: Nine dimensions of rules, including legal dismissal; third party notification of dismissal; priority rules for redundancy; rules for re-employment, etc.

Redundancy costs: Two dimensions of costs, including weeks of pay for dismissal; notice period for dismissal

Job quality: 12 dimensions of quality, including equal pay for equal work, on-the-job training, paid/unpaid maternity leave, sick leave days, gender nondiscrimination in hiring, etc.

The Economist Intelligence Unit and the consulting firm of Heidrick and Struggles (2007, 2011) compile an index they call the Global Talent Index. And as the title suggests, all seven of its dimensions capture some aspect of talent and talent management, to include: 1) demographics, 2) compulsory education, 3) university education, 4) quality of the labor force, 5) talent environment, 6) openness; and 7) proclivity to attracting talent (Heidrick & Struggles, 2007, 2011). The education-focused dimensions are described and their scores for the US are shown in Table 1.5 and are described in detail elsewhere (*The Global Talent Index Report: The Outlook to 2015*: 19).

Table 1.5 Global Talent Index

This index benchmarks countries on their capacity for developing, attracting and retaining talent. This is based on data indicators from various thematic categories: Demographics, Compulsory education, University education, Quality of the labor force, Talent environment, Openness, and Proclivity to attracting talent. The US is ranked # 1 in both time periods

Global Talent Index 2011 **Top 5 Countries with overall rank**	**Global Talent Index 2015** **Top 5 Countries with overall rank**
United States	United States
Denmark	Denmark
Finland	Finland
Norway	Sweden
Singapore	Norway

Source: The Global Talent Index Report: The Outlook to 2015. Heidrick & Struggles and The Economist Intelligence Unit.
www.economistinsights.com/sites/default/files/downloads/GTI%20FINAL%20REPORT%205.4.11.pdf
www.globaltalentindex.com/pdf/Heidrick_Struggles_Global_Talent_Report.pdf

The consulting firm Hays Plc evaluates 33 countries on seven indicators of global skills including: 1) education flexibility; 2) labor market participation; 3) labor market flexibility; 4) talent mismatch; 5) overall wage pressure; 6) wage pressure in high-skill industries; and 7) wage pressure in high-skill occupations. On a scale from 1 to 10 with a lower score indicating a favorable environment for skills, the US is rated: 1) education flexibility 6.6; 2) labor market participation; 3.7; 3) labor market flexibility 4.8; 4) talent mismatch 10; 5) overall wage pressure 6.5; 6) wage pressure in high-skilled industries 9.9; and 7) wage pressure in high-skilled occupations 4.9.

Schools and Universities

Overlapping with the previous section, this section focuses on a slightly different aspect of macro talent management. Within the current global environment of more knowledge-based economies and job opportunities, educational institutions have also emerged as important players in MTM. They play a rather significant role in developing the human capital base throughout the early life of youth and young adults. This can be measured in the quantity and quality of primary, secondary and tertiary education that countries offer. This is described in more detail in the section of MTM processes.

For this discussion the focus is on providing educational opportunities to individuals of other countries to become attractive destinations for attaining further education. This is an important feature of the US labor market (a similar situation is seen in chapter describing MTM in the UK). So for example, developed countries are forging global partnerships with other universities and exchange programs worldwide to train talent and obtain greater access to the global talent pool (Wildavsky, 2010). Currently, in the United States there are approximately 1 million foreign students enrolled in a variety of higher educational institutions in 2013–2014 (*Institute of International Education*, 2015). These international students gain valuable global experience and often fill important positions upon returning to their home countries, or they may remain in the country of higher education such as the United States (Gareis, 2012). The number of international students, however, who will continue to attend universities in the US is not assured. It depends on the number of student visas that are provided, and the perception of the US as a welcoming country for international students.

In the current political environment there is concern at many universities across the US on the continued application and enrollment levels of international students. These levels can also depend in part on the immigration policies in place.

Immigration Policies

It is clear from the previous examples that talent development has been adopted as a national agenda by many countries (Guo & Al Ariss, 2015; Khilji et al., 2015). Several countries have also been competing for the world's most skilled and qualified workers in an increasingly global labor market via their immigration policies. Kapur and McHale (2005) state, "official pronouncement on immigration policy has been couched in the language of 'national competitiveness', especially in knowledge-intensive sectors" (p. 37). This is clearly apparent in the immigration strategies adopted by countries such as Germany and Canada as well as the United States (Martin, 2013).

The United States has been a popular destination attracting about 20 percent of the world's international migrants. Immigrants account for almost 15 percent of the total 324 million US residents. Adding the US-born children (of all ages) of immigrants means that approximately 80 million people, or one-quarter of the overall US population, is either of the first or second generation (Zong & Batalova, 2015; Jordan, 2017).

Overall, immigration is widely considered to be in the national interest, especially when done legally, since it permits individuals to better themselves as it strengthens the United States (Martin, 2013). The US specifically regulates talent-related immigration with various types of "visas", including the H1-B, H-2B, the L-1 and T-1 visa categories as well as the use of "green cards". The quota limits in these visas may vary subject to Congressional action and Presidential Executive Orders. Companies in the US are often trying to get Congress to expand these visa categories in order to have the opportunity to hire highly educated students graduating from some of the best universities in the country. While visas are given for specific reasons and limited periods of time (with the individual still remaining a citizen of another country), "green cards" represent a more permanent form of admission to the United States and can lead to full status of citizenship. As with visas, the number of individuals able to obtain green cards for employment-based preferences is relatively small, about 15% (Patel, 2016). Future actions by the federal government could include making it easier for MNEs to bring in talented immigrants for longer assignments, although it requires Congressional action that is not always assured. The current political environment in the United States, for example, appears to suggest a pause in the immigration, legal and illegal, that will be permitted. This in turn may induce more programmatic efforts by the US Congress to enhance the talent base of the current population within the United States (*Economist*, 2017; Jordan, 2017).

Demographics and Mobility

In addition to the quality of the talent pool of countries that the country rankings introduced earlier provide, sheer quantity of the talent/population pool is also important for talent management in the global context (Chand & Tung, 2014; Khilji, 2012).

A majority of the future growth in the world population is expected to occur in developing or emerging economies (*Population Reference Bureau*, 2015). As a matter of fact, nearly half of the increment to the world population is estimated to come from only six countries; India (22%), China (11%), Pakistan, Nigeria, Bangladesh and the US (17% at approx. 4%

each). This presents an interesting paradox because on one hand some countries in Asia Pacific and Europe (including France, Spain, Japan and Germany) are aging fast and the proportion of the working-age people in the population is shrinking (McDonnell, Collings, & Burgess, 2012). On other hand, in countries like India, Bangladesh and Pakistan, 31–36% of the workforce is 14 years of age or below (Khilji, 2012; Khilji & Keilson, 2014). These countries are faced with the crisis of making them employable for an increasingly complex and global environment. By 2050, developed countries will not have enough workers to support the higher cost of their aging populations. Developing countries with younger population will not have enough jobs. Khilji and Keilson (2014) argue that a global generational divide is likely to emerge as a workforce issue, where a majority of the young will be based or come from developing countries, and the aging from the developed countries. As a developed country, Japan is already providing lessons in managing an aging talented workforce for other developed countries, such as those in Western Europe (Adachi, Ishida, & Oka, 2015). As a developed country the United States appears to be an exception to population slowdown or actual decline. More specifically,

- Over the next four decades, as fertility rates are projected to continue to fall and modest increases are projected for the overall level of net legal international migration, the US population is projected to grow, albeit more slowly than in previous decades.
- Overall, the percentage of the total population that is under the age of 18 is projected to decrease from 23 percent to 20 percent between 2014 and 2060. Similarly, the working-age population is projected to decrease from 62 percent to 57 percent of the total population over the same interval. In contrast, the percentage of the population that is aged 65 and over is expected to grow from 15 percent to 24 percent, an increase of 9 percentage points. Overall the population is projected to continue aging, reflected in the growth of the percentage of the population that is in the older ages. Because MNEs are not required to retire employees at a certain age, e.g., 65 years, they can continue to employ older workers who are some of their most talented employees.
- Growth of the foreign-born population is projected to exceed that of locals, resulting in an increasing share of the future US population that is foreign born. Specifically, the foreign-born population in the US is currently at about 14% and is expected to increase to 18% by 2065. It had been as low as 4% in 1965 before the passage of the Immigration Act of 1965 (Patel, 2016). According to some, immigrants and their children are likely to be the major source for the growth in the US labor market: "The growth that comes from (first-generation) immigrants and the second generation are going to be the only source of growth in working-age people," said Audrey Singer, an immigration and labor force expert at the Urban Institute. "We don't have a choice right now. We're depending on these two groups to be part of the next generation of workers" (Patel, 2016). Nevertheless, the political conditions within the US at this time may reduce the number of immigrants, legal and illegal, who are permitted to enter the United States.
- Consequently, the US population is projected to become more diverse, as seen in the projected increases in the percentage of the population that is a minority—groups other than non-Hispanic White alone. By 2044, the United States is projected to become a plurality nation (US Census.gov). Again, this projection is now stated more cautiously than before because of the current political environment. More specific information about the US labor market is described next.

Diaspora and Returnees

Two other important factors in the global context of talent management are brain circulation and the efforts to maximize the diaspora effect (Saxenian, 2005; Tung & Lazarova, 2006). Both of these phenomena can have a big impact on governmental programs. For example, those countries with a large population that emigrated elsewhere (mostly to the United States and other developed countries) for better opportunities decades earlier are luring back talented diaspora in order to benefit from their expertise and connections and develop younger talent effectively (such as China, Pakistan and India with their policies to bring back their diaspora for shorter to longer durations (Ragazzi, 2014; Khilji & Keilson, 2014). Because significant numbers of companies in the Silicon Valley depend upon immigrants to the US, continued success by other countries in repatriating their diaspora could diminish the labor supply in the US. This combined with immigration unfriendly policies in the United States, might reduce the supply of high talent individuals for high tech companies such as those in Silicon Valley (*Economist*, 2017). Thus while this discussion of diaspora and returnees (repatriates) could be placed under governmental activities, it is placed here because of its singular importance.

Global and US Labor Markets

A central factor in the global context of TM is the development of global labor markets over the past thirty years. Global labor markets have been created in part due to government-led initiatives that prioritize talent acquisition, retention, and development. These have been facilitated by technological advancements and ease of global communication. In turn, greater workforce mobility, extensive developments of diaspora and international migration (along with the brain circulation and knowledge flows) have exposed the macro implications and country effects of MTM. It is to be expected that both of these macro aspects of MTM will continue to evolve and transform over the next decade based on the characteristics and desires of the large generation of millennials (Generation Y, born 1981–1994) who are now in the position of having and wanting international assignments (PWC, 2015). As we continue to adopt a macro perspective in global talent management, it is important to review how global markets are evolving, particularly in view of a likely "global generational divide" (Khilji & Keilson, 2014). That said, we also need to know the numbers of individuals who are entering the global labor market. Right now, it is estimated that approximately 25,000 new workers will enter the labor market in the developing world every day until 2020, and more than 200 million people globally will be out of jobs; yet, simultaneously, there is expected to be a shortage of around 50 million high-talented job applicants over the coming decade (*The Human Capital Report 2016*: 1).

It is also important to understand the unique labor market of each country. In the United States, while the labor market is growing, the labor force participation rate of 25–54 olds has declined slightly in recent decades, particularly for American men. This has been due in part to an increasing number of men who have dropped out (reduced their participation rate) of the labor force (Applebaum, 2014; Bomey, 2017). More than 20% of American men, about 20 million people between the ages of 20 and 65, had no paid work in 2015 (Chira, 2016). In addition, it has become harder and harder for men to find high-paying jobs, in part to increased technology and automation, globalization and more jobs requiring higher levels of training and education (Applebaum, 2014; Chira, 2016; Bomey, 2017; Miller, 2017; Graham, 2017). One major result of this is the tremendous job-person mismatch, perhaps greater in the US than any other developed economy (Hays, 2017; Graham, 2017). This job loss and job-mismatch now appear to be resulting in declining health which is now becoming a major reason prime-age men are working less and less (Krueger, 2016), thus creating a vicious circle that cries out for massive intervention and remediation.

In addition to knowing labor force participation rates and causes, it is important to be aware of the generational differences in the US labor force. Yes, the US has its share of millennials, but it also has a large number of traditionalists (born before 1946), baby boomers (born 1946–1964), baby busters (Generation X, born 1965–1980), and digital natives (Generation Z, born after 1994). Each of these generational groups is different in many ways and brings substantially different talent to the workplace (PWC, 2015). Thus programs to help return individuals back to work and/or back to school need to consider these generational differences and design activities to reflect such things as learning style differences and preferences (PWC, 2015; Graham, 2017; *Economist*, 2017).

National Culture

While these previously described data indicate where talent pools are likely to be found, additional information about the national culture of a country can be important in establishing a country's reputation as a good place for doing business. For example, culture characteristics such as work orientation, work ethics, comfort with uncertainty and the need for structure at work have been shown to be important characteristics of a country's labor force, that is, its talent (Hofstede, 1980). There is also a plethora of evidence to suggest that national culture can help determine the appropriateness of the many possible talent management policies and practices a company can use in a particular country. For example, talent management policies and practices by companies in the United States tend to reflect country culture characteristics of individualism, tolerance for uncertainty, achievement and relative egalitarianism for all to reach higher levels of success (Cooke et al., 2014; Lanvin & Evans, 2014, 2015, 2017).

While the degree to which a strong relationship between country culture and a company's TM practices is linked to the effectiveness of specific TM practices remains to be explored, companies may still choose to tailor their programs for managing talent with sensitivity to local country culture conditions, especially those that would be supportive of learning, knowledge, innovation, education and achievement (Cooke et al., 2014).

Country Competitiveness on Social, Economic, Educational, and Political Conditions

Country competitiveness is the set of institutions, policies and factors that determine the level of productivity of a country and its level of talent management as indicated by our earlier discussion of the four pillars of the Global Competitiveness Index (WEF, 2016). The level of productivity in turn sets the level of prosperity that can be reached by the society. The WEF ranks these institutions (i.e., pillars) in 138 countries. And while four pillars directly measure *indicators* of talent management, eight of the twelve pillars measure broader aspects of a country's institutional environment including social, economic and political ones. Hence the premise is that the country that scores the best on all 12 pillars is the most competitive and thus the most likely to be productive and provide prosperity for its citizens (thus these are also used in our discussion of Outcomes in Figure 1.1). Efforts to boost the talent management pillars are in vain if not also accompanied by similar efforts to boost all the other pillars. Thus companies that depend upon being able to develop the quality of the labor force in a country, such as the US, may hesitate to enter the country if it does

Table 1.6 Global Competitiveness Index Pillars

This index looks at the effect of several macro level factors which create the conditions for competitiveness. The overall US Ranking is 3/140 (economies).

Pillar	Description	US Rank
Institutions	This pillar examines the institutional environment which includes the legal and administrative framework	30/140
Infrastructure	This pillar looks at the infrastructure of an economy	12/140
Macroeconomic Environment	This pillar examines the stability of the macroeconomic environment of a country	113/140
Goods Market Efficiency	This pillar analyzes efficiency of the goods markets	16/140
Financial Market Development	This pillar examines the well-being of the financial and economic activities	9/140
Technological Readiness	This pillar looks at the agility with which an economy adopts existing technologies	16/140
Market Size	This pillar inspects the size of the markets	1/140
Business Sophistication	This pillar looks at the sophistication of business practices	4/140

Source: Schwab, Klaus, et al., 2016–2017. *The Global Competitiveness Report 2016–2017.* World Economic Forum: Davos, Switzerland. www.weforum.org/reports/the-global-competitiveness-report-2016-2017-1/

Table 1.7 Human Capital Indicies Using Four Pillars and Five Age Categories

This index looks at the effect of several macro level factors which create the conditions for human capital development and utilization. The overall US Ranking is 17th out of 130 countries.

Pillar	Description	US Rank
Education	This pillar has indicators relating to qualitative/quantitative aspects of primary, secondary, tertiary levels for present and future workforce	11/130
Health and Wellness	This pillar contains indicators of a population's physical/mental health	43/130
Workforce and Employment	This pillar is designed to quantify the experience, talent, knowledge and training of the country's people	4/130
Enabling Environment	This pillar captures the legal framework and infrastructure	16/130
0–14 year olds	This pillar captures the enrolment rates, educational attainment, quality of education, rate of child labor	40/130
15–24 year olds	This pillar looks at educational attainment rate and quality, unemployment rate and skills	7/140
25–64 year olds	This pillar captures educational attainment rates, workplace learning, skills and ease of finding skilled jobs	15/140
65 years old and over	This pillar looks at educational attainment rates, unemployment rates and healthy life years beyond 65	16/140

Source: A combination of *The Human Capital Reports* from 2013, 2015 and 2016 (see website references listed in the Appendix to this book). First four pillars from the 2013 report.

not score well on the eight pillars of the WEF that describe the country's social, political, and economic conditions, in addition to the four additional pillars more related to talent management. These eight pillars and their relative competitiveness scores for the United States are shown in Table 1.6.

A more specific analysis of country-level talent conditions is a study conducted by the WEF in conjunction with the LinkedIn Corporation (now a part of the Microsoft Corporation). It originally began in 2013 in a joint effort between the WEF and Mercer Consulting. The latest result of this collaboration is called *The Human Capital Report 2016*. The results of these reports for the United States are shown in Table 1.7. Together these reports highlight several aspects of country-level talent management (referred to also as "human capital"). First they indicate short term and longer term aspects of a country's policies and practices that exist to develop its human capital such as primary, secondary and tertiary education, and training programs in place at the workplace level. In capturing these, the reports reflect how well a country is developing and training its population for current jobs and for future and relatively unknown jobs. So the reports help to measure how well a country has prepared and is preparing its population to in turn help its workforce and economy to be productive. Please note that the four pillars (also referred to in Table 1.7 as Human Capital Index) of education, learning and development are similar (both have the involvement of the WEF), but somewhat different from the four pillars described previously that are part of the twelve pillars of the Global Competitiveness Index. The Human Capital Index (HCIndex) ranks 130 countries on how well they are developing and deploying their human capital potential. The HCIndex assesses Learning and Employment outcomes across five distinct age groups to capture the full demographic profile of a country's human capital and talent (*The Human Capital Report 2016*: 2). The Global Competitiveness Index (GCI) ranks almost 150 countries on workforce health and primary education, high education and training, labor market efficiency and innovation for the country's workforce and economy. So while the GCI focuses on the country's economy, the HCIndex focuses more on the country's human capital development and potential for further development. As a consequence, the rankings can be different: the US ranked #3 on the overall GCI and #39 on health and primary education, #8 on higher education, #7 on labor market efficiency and #4 on innovation, but ranked #24 on the overall HCI.

MTM Functions and Processes

Now we move through our Conceptual Framework of MTM shown in Figure 1.1 to look more closely at what is important at the macro level of MNEs for TM. Broadly speaking, there are two broad categories of activities: Core functions and MTM Processes.

Core Functions

Here we include the essential functions of MTM at the country (also at the state and local) level as:

- talent planning,
- talent acquisition,
- talent development, and
- talent retention

Not surprisingly, these four functions flow rather easily from the macro environmental factors described in the preceding paragraphs. A plethora of research indicates that these core functions transfer/mediate/shape/modify the impact of the macro environmental factors on the MTM outcomes/consequences (Sparrow et al., 2017; Tarique & Schuler, 2010; Scullion, Collings, & Caligiuri, 2010; Khilji et al., 2015). For example, the diaspora effect (mentioned previously) at the country level is associated with a country's ability to plan, attract and retain talent; and education-led initiatives are focused upon developing the human talent. And of course, the quality and quantity of a country's primary, secondary and tertiary educational institutions provide a good indication of the readiness and capability of its current and future workforce.

In addition, a country can add to its talent pool by making itself an attractive place for talent from other countries to come and stay through such activities as its visa and immigration policies, and the quality of its governmental system and infrastructure, all characteristics of its institutions as described by the twelve pillars of the WEF shown in Table 1.6.

Based on these results of the ranking of the WEF, the United States has an overall ranking of #3 in the world, although the specific four pillars for human capital are less favorably ranked as stated previously. This overall ranking alone helps explain the ability of the United States to develop, attract and retain talented employees from around the world. Of course, there are other activities that assist in making countries attractive places for talent. These are described under the next section of Core MTM processes.

Core MTM Processes

Core MTM processes are the activities that influence how, when, why and if the environmental factors transfer/mediate/shape/modify the impact of the macro environmental factors on the MTM outcomes/consequences. These events might include:

- Knowledge spillovers
- Learning and knowledge sharing
- Institutional support
- Health and wellness
- Educational leadership
- Corporate strategy and leadership

Scholars have argued that talent produces knowledge flows, causes spillovers, and can be used for knowledge sharing as well as learning (organizational and national). As discussed previously, it is clear that macro institutional (both governmental and nongovernmental) support, educational leadership, and corporate strategy and leadership can facilitate and/or hinder MTM in an environment. We present these aspects as MTM processes because they describe how talent relates to organizational and country level changes over time, identify patterns of activities and explain an observed relationship between talent and the desired outcomes of (for example) national competitiveness, innovation and economic development (Cooke et al., 2014; Liu, Lu, Filatotchev, Buck, & Wright, 2011; Oettl & Agrawal, 2008).

It is worth repeating that both governmental/ NGO programs and organizational-level activities influence MTM processes. For example, greater global talent mobility stimulates international transmission of ideas (Agarwal, Kapur, McHale, & Oettl, 2011; Kapur & McHale, 2005; Liu et al., 2011), produces knowledge flows (Di Maria & Lazarova, 2009; Carr, Inkson, & Thorn, 2005), enhances learning (Furuya, Stevens, Bird, Oddou, & Mendenhall, 2009) and improves efficiency of the innovation process (Oettl & Agrawal, 2008). As people move and interact across organizations and societies, they provide greater access to knowledge and reduce the need to recreate knowledge that already exists elsewhere. They also gain diverse experiences and hence serve as a prime source of learning for organizations and societies (Di Maria & Lazarova, 2009). The US seems to do well in facilitating the flow of individuals across the world, especially through the facilitation of expatriates around the world.

Helping to quantify some of these characteristics of the Core MTM Processes are the Human Capital Reports. As described earlier, the WEF publishes the Human Capital Reports which focus exclusively on country-level talent management. In these reports, introduced in the discussion on "Country Competitiveness on Social, Economic, Educational and Political Conditions," the WEF ranks countries on four pillars including: education, health and wellness, workforce and employment, and enabling environment. These reports also describe the talent management capabilities in four separate age categories. These four pillars and four age categories are shown in Table 1.7. They help measure the Core MTM Processes and suggest how countries, including the United States, can improve on its talent management rankings.

MTM Outcomes: Evaluations and Rankings

The outcomes/consequences of MTM, as shown in Figure 1.1, are many. Sparrow, Scullion, and Tarique (2014) suggest that it is possible to think of them of occurring over time, or in sequence. For example, the outcomes of educational attainment, jobs, talent mobility, immigration flows and diaspora utilization can be considered first level outcomes that result from the macro environmental factors and the MTM processes. These outcomes are directly related to talent within the country (in terms of its development, retention and utilization). In addition, there are several second level outcomes including talent rankings, country attractiveness, productivity, innovation, economic development and competitiveness. These second level outcomes are more cumulative in nature, are associated with the strengthened economies, and are the direct result of effective first level outcomes. In other words, if a country has managed to enhance educational attainment of its people, create jobs and capitalize on human capital global mobility, these can have a positive impact on enhancing its national innovative capacities, productivity and country competitiveness, indicators of a country's level of talent management as described in the exhaustive work of INSEAD in the Global Talent Competitiveness Index (GTCI) (Lanvin & Evans, 2014, 2015, 2017).

The GTCI ranks countries on six pillars including: enabling, attracting, growing, retaining, vocational and global knowledge. The items from the GTCI most specifically related to education are contained in the pillars for vocational education and global knowledge. As shown in Figure 1.1, we use these two pillars as outcomes as shown in Table 1.8, specifically educational attainment. For each of these two pillars there are almost ten sub-pillars. It is worth taking a look at both GTCI reports in full to appreciate the educational information in these two pillars (Lanvin & Evans, 2014, 2015)

Table 1.8 The Global Talent Competitiveness Index (GTCI): Two Pillars More Applicable for Education

This annual index benchmarks over 100 countries to examine each country's ability to compete for talent. More specifically, these two pillars seem to reflect outcomes of a country's macro-environment, function and processes.

Pillar	US Rank
Labor and Vocational Skills	22/109
Global Knowledge skills	3/109
Grow	We have included this in Table 1.8, the input side because of the *opportunities* a country provides learning rather than an outcome.

Source: Lanvin, Bruno and Evans Paul (2015). *The Global Talent Competitiveness Index. Talent Attraction and International Mobility 2015–16.* INSEAD, Adecco Group, and the human Capital Leadership Institute.
global-indices.insead.edu/gtci/documents/INSEAD_2015-16_Full_Book_Ebook.pdf

Macro Talent Management in the United States • 33

Table 1.9 The Global Talent Competitiveness Index (GTCI): Four Pillars More Applicable for MTM

This annual index benchmarks over 100 countries to examine each country's ability to compete for talent. More specifically, the index looks at each country's ability to grow, attract and retain talent. The overall US Ranking is 4/109 (economies). Please note that these four pillars refer to the input side of the GTCI. There are two pillars (vocational education; and global knowledge) that seem more applicable in our description of outcomes and are presented in Table 1.9.

Pillar	Description	US Ranking
Enable	This pillar examines the regulatory landscape, market landscape and the business-labor landscape	9/109
Attract	This pillar focuses on external openness and internal openness	14/109
Grow	This pillar describes *opportunities* for formal education, lifelong learning and access to growth	3/109
Retain	This pillar evaluates sustainability and lifestyle	2/109

Source: Lanvin, Bruno and Evans Paul (2015). *The Global Talent Competitiveness Index. Talent Attraction and International Mobility 2015–16*. INSEAD, Adecco Group, and the Human Capital Leadership Institute of Singapore. global-indices.insead.edu/gtci/documents/INSEAD_2015-16_Full_Book_Ebook.pdf

Table 1.10 Programme for International Student Assessment (PISA)

This metric examines the extent to which 15-year-old students have acquired important knowledge and skills that are essential for full participation in modern societies.

Pillar	Mean Score in PISA 2012 (Mathematics)	Mean Score in PISA 2012 (Reading)	Mean Score in PISA 2012 (Science)
OECD Average	494	496	501
USA	481	498	497
Shanghai—China *Highest Ranked Country*	613	570	501
Peru *Lowest Ranked Country*	368	384	373

Source: PISA 2012 Results in Focus: What 15-year-olds know and what they can do with what they know. OECD www.oecd.org/pisa/keyfindings/pisa-2012-results-overview.pdf

The remaining four of these pillars have been discussed as characteristics of the macro environment under the heading of "Country competitiveness on social, economic, educational and political conditions", but we have also included them here under the "second-level outcomes," specifically as "talent rankings" and "competitiveness" (shown in Table 1.9).

In another measure of first-level outcomes, the OECD ranks countries on their levels of educational attainment for many age categories of their citizens. One of its most famous rankings is the Program for International Student Assessment (PISA), which ranks 15-year-old students on the basis of the achievement in math, sciences and reading. The United States does relatively poorly on the PISA scores as shown in Table 1.10. This corroborates the relatively low ranking that the United States receives on its primary and secondary education. Many attempts are being made to improve these two levels of education. Presidents Bush and Obama had national campaigns with their "No Child Left Behind" and "Race to the Top", but thus far the achievements are slow in coming. Attempts are also being made closer to where this education is delivered, namely at the state and local levels (www.ed.gov; *New York Times*, 2016: 10).

As referenced earlier in this chapter (Tables 1.3 and 1.4), The World Bank has its Doing Business Index that ranks countries on several aspects of doing business, from ease of starting a company and tax rates to employability of the workforce, including its skill levels (*Doing Business*, 2016). Thus the Index can be regarded as a good measure of the second-level outcomes shown in Figure 1.1.

The Economist Intelligence Unit and the consulting firm of Heidrick & Struggles (2007, 2011) compile an index they call the Global Talent Index. And as the title suggests, all seven of its dimensions capture some aspect of talent and talent management, to include: 1) demographics, 2) compulsory education, 3) university education, 4) quality of the labor force, 5) talent environment, 6) openness; and 7) proclivity to attracting talent as illustrated in Table 1.5 (Heidrick & Struggles, 2015). As described, these dimensions can also be placed earlier in our Framework, specifically under the "macro environmental factors". These dimensions also appear to overlap with some of the early measures of a country's talent/human capital, such as the Human Capital Report pillars (Table 1.7). Thus, the authors of the following chapters in this book might choose to interpret and utilize these dimensions and reports slightly differently.

**Implications/Applications of the Framework:
What Can the Country Do?**

While potentially interesting, we may ask, What is the evidence that any of the aspects of Figure 1.1 actually have practical implications/applications? Fortunately, the summer 2015 issue of the *New European Economy* contains many examples of how countries, states, cities and regions in the United States and elsewhere have become magnets for foreign companies and international organizations to set up base. An example of one consequence of the rankings such as the GTGI Index and the GCI Index having an innovative and flexible workforce is that the United States is the top destination for foreign investment (*Organization for International Investment*, 2016). Of course, this result does not occur in isolation of other macro factors such as a strong institutional framework, a high level of business sophistication, a political environment that welcomes international businesses and individuals, and an investment-friendly legal system and financial market.

And as a consequence of many of these factors within the United States, individual states and localities can further enhance their specific situations to entice foreign investors to locate in their areas. For example, Ohio is one of the top ten most competitive states. More than 3,400 organizations from 42 countries have set up global headquarters in Ohio. And Licking County, which surrounds the capital area of Columbus, is widely recognized as a leading center for manufacturing and technology-enabled expansion (Cullen, 2015). More than 50 of the *Fortune* 500 companies have a presence in Licking County, in the process gaining access to a highly educated workforce. Licking County is focused on STEM-related employers and a willing workforce with developed technical skills developed in part through cutting-edge training and development programs offered through the Career and Technology Center of the county, the Central Ohio Technical College, the Ohio State University and Denison University (Cullen, 2015). Other examples of what specific regions, countries, cities, provinces and towns are doing can be accessed through Lanvin and Evans (2014, 2015, 2017), Evans & Lanvin (2015) and Dua, Lund, Singh, and Ward (2017). Further and more extensive discussion and description of what states are doing for talent improvement and workforce preparation can be found in much more detail in the awarding of the Prosperity

Cup (Arend, 2017). While there are many factors within states that help make it an attractive site for companies to locate, certainly workforce talent preparation and training are essential factors. And virtually all states today have offices of Workforce Development and Training to support the efforts of companies and individuals to enhance their talent readiness. To further validate what states and individuals are doing to enhance their talent and skill development, ACT provides testing for individuals to obtain their NCRC (National Career Readiness Certificate), a certificate that employers nationwide use as a reliable way to verify individuals' work skills and talents (www.act.org).

While these descriptions of what states are doing are brief, they are offered here to illustrate the implications of the MTM Framework shown in Figure 1.1 They also support and complement the broader implications of the various ranking results for the US regarding education, particularly primary and secondary education and technical education. Whether measured by the PISA scores (rankings) the HCIndex scores, the GTCI scores, the Hays Global Skills scores, or the GCI scores, the US needs to improve its quality of primary and secondary education (Miller, 2017). The US Department of Education has just recently released its "Final Teacher Preparation Regulations" that outline a variety of initiatives to encourage state and local governments to improve secondary and primary education which varies a great deal across states, thus supporting the need for broader country-level initiatives, at least at considering the ability of states to fund educational initiatives (*24/7 Wall St.*, 2015; Dua et al., 2017).

Of course even more specific initiatives can be very helpful as well. The automobile companies BMW and FiatChrysler conduct extensive training programs to help ensure a supply of well-trained auto mechanics (Mayersohn, 2017). Work by the consulting firm Accenture and the non-profit group Girls Who Code, is aimed at identifying and improving the factors that make it more attractive for young girls to go into computer programs in primary and secondary schools and then to higher education (Guynn, 2016). And as these various initiatives expand, it is more likely that success in higher education, technical education and continuous education will also improve (Chira, 2016; Bryant & Sarakatsannis, 2016). While perhaps not likely to improve to the level of Finland, Switzerland or Singapore in the near term because of the complexity, it signals a start (*New York Times*, 2016, p. 10). Without these educational changes, the US will continue to fall short of rightfully developing and utilizing its talent. And over the longer term the US may lose its level of competitiveness. In this spirit Congress passed the Workforce Innovation and Opportunity Act in 2014 to help reduce the complexity of the various training programs available to unemployed workers. In addition, there is a clear need to more closely link needed job qualifications with training programs that are being federally and state funded. The US Labor Department's Trade Adjustment Assistance program is one important program that can be made more efficient by closely linking training funds and opportunities with job availability with greater employer involvement (Rotella, 2017; *Economist*, 2017). Congress also passed the 2014 Revitalize American Manufacturing and Innovation Act which has resulted in more than $3 billion to establish a network for manufacturing innovation that includes government research labs, universities and companies (Michaels, 2017). Whether this financial support will continue in the current political environment is uncertain. Current discussions about the continuation of trade agreements the US has with its nearest neighbors, Mexico and Canada, has implications for the financial support that the federal government may be willing to provide to states and local governments.

In addition to major improvements in education, it is argued by many that prime working-age men's health now needs to get more attention (Krueger, 2016). Surveys indicate that

40% of these men not in the labor force have pain that prevents them from returning to work, in contrast to only 19% of the men who are in the workforce (Krueger, 2016).

But making significant improvements in primary and secondary education and individual health is a complex undertaking requiring the contributions and engagement of many. This quote from Klaus Schwab, founder and executive chairman of the World Economic Forum perhaps captures the essence of the situation facing the US:

> Talent, not capital, will be the key factor linking innovation, competitiveness and growth in the 21st century. To make any of the changes necessary to unlock the world's talent—and hence its growth potential—we must look beyond campaign cycles and quarterly reports. Dialogue, collaboration and partnerships between all sectors are crucial for the adaptation of educational institutions, governments, and businesses.
>
> (*Human Capital Report 2016*: 2)

In addition to the type of example from Licking County in Ohio that depends upon actually having private sector jobs, another idea being proposed is for governments to subsidize private employment or even volunteer jobs.

> If the private market isn't creating the jobs people need, then the public sector should engage in direct job creation (programs). A recent study by the Georgetown Center on Poverty and Inequality examined 40 programs over 40 years, and found they were successful at things like improving workers' skills and reducing their dependence on public benefits.
>
> (Miller, 2017)

The 2016 Hays Global Skills report further recommends three activities on the part of governments and businesses working together: 1) address skilled migration to tackle the every-growing skills gap; 2) implement smarter training programs to ensure businesses are future-proofed; and 3) tackle low productivity through better technology (with workers and automation working together) and employee engagement (Tingley, 2017; Hays, 2017; *Economist*, 2017). But as is often said, "easier said than done." Seemingly today more than ever, it is the political environment that may help to determine the extent to which the three activities are implemented effectively and soon enough to make a difference.

Future Research Directions

We would like to offer a word of caution here. The conceptual framework for looking at MTM in the United States and other countries presented in Figure 1.1 should not be viewed as being linear or simple relationships. Scholars argue that societies and organizations are complex social systems (Anderson, 1999). A rapid pace of globalization has also added new elements of complexity to the human dynamics (Lane, Mazenvski, Mendenhall, & McNett, 2004). Accordingly, the MTM model should be viewed as being made up of a large number of parts that interact in a non-simple and linear manner (Phene & Tallman, 2012; Simon, 1962). Applying this understanding to MTM presents it as a system that requires interactions between different partners on a number of issues and levels, representing varying levels of complexity. We would also like to mention that the proposed framework doesn't capture an exhaustive list of trends, outcomes and processes, nor the dynamics of the current political environment in the US (Sparrow et al., 2017). As scholars continue to explore the multiple aspects of macro MTM as a phenomenon, they are likely to unravel and add other issues to this framework, for example, country levels of engagement (e.g., Blessing & White, 2013).

What we have tried to do here is offer a framework that represents a large number of aspects of what many authors consider the macro MTM and illustrate as many of these aspects as possible from the growing body of country level research, using the United States as an example of how this could be done (Khilji & Schuler, 2018; Evans & Lanvin, 2015). We admit that this is an early attempt to do this and as such suggest to other authors to take countries and try to fill in as much relevant country specific information related to Figure 1.1 from the many established secondary sources used here, as well as others that the authors may uncover that might be unique to their countries and also general to all. A large set of websites, several used in this chapter, and several not but that could be useful, are found at the end of this book in the Appendix.

References

24/7 Wall St. (2015). *America's most and least educated states: A survey of all 50*. Retrieved from 247wallst.com/special-report/2015/09/23/the-most-and-least-educated-states.

Adachi, M., Ishida, R., & Oka, G. (2015, March). Japan: Lessons from a hyperaging society, *McKinsey Quarterly*.

Agarwal, A., Kapur, D., McHale, J., & Oettl, A. (2011). Brain drain or brain bank? The impact of skilled emigration on poor country innovation. *Journal of Urban Economics, 69*, 43–55.

Anderson, P. (1999). Complexity theory and organization science. *Organization Science, 10*, 216–232.

Applebaum, B. (2014, December 11). The vanishing male worker: How America fell behind. *The New York Times*, p. 14.

Arend, M. (2017, May). 2017 prosperity cup. *Site Selection Magazine*.

Blessing & White. (2013). *Employee engagement research report*. New York: GP Strategies.

Bomey, N. (2017, January 17). Special report: Automation puts jobs in peril. *USA Today*. Special Report. Also see: Nathan Bomey, *USA Today*. /staff/40767/Nathan-bomey.

Bryant, J., & Sarakatsannis, J. (2016, November). Three more reasons why US education is ready for investment. *Mckinsey*, pp. 1–4.

Carr, S. C., Inkson, K., & Thorn, K. (2005). From global careers to talent flow: Reinterpreting 'brain drain'. *Journal of World Business, 40*, 386–398.

Chand, M. S., & Tung, R. L. (2014). The aging of the world's population and its effects on global business. *Academy of Management Perspectives, 26*(4), 409–429.

Chira, S. (2016, October 16). Men need help: Is Hillary Clinton the answer? *The New York Times*, SR 6–7.

Cooke, F. L., Saini, D. S., & Wang, J. (2014). Talent management in China and India: A comparison of management perceptions and human resource practices. *Journal of World Business, 49*, 225–235.

Cullen, P. (2015, Summer). Finger Lick'in good. *New European Economy*, pp. 78–80.

Di Maria, C., & Lazarova, E. A. (2009). *Migration, human capital formation and growth: An empirical investigation*. SSRN. Retrieved from ssrn.com/abstract=1517647.

Dua, A., Lund, S. Singh, N., & Ward, T. (2017, February). Measuring the state of US states. *McKinsey*, pp. 1–7.

Economist. (2011, November 19). *The magic of diasporas*.

Economist. (2013, January 19). *406, 3-S.5*. Retrieved from www.economist.com/news/special-report/21569572-after-decades-.

Economist. (2017, October 21). *In the lurch*.

Evans, P., & Lanvin, B. (2015). *The world's most talent ready countries*. Retrieved from www.knowledge.insead.edu/talent-management.

Furuya, N., Stevens, M. J., Bird, A., Oddou, G., & Mendenhall, M. (2009). Managing the learning and transfer of global management competence: Antecedents and outcomes of Japanese repatriation effectiveness. *Journal of International Business Studies, 40*, 200–215.

Gareis, E. (2012). Intercultural friendship: Effects of home and host region. *Journal of International and Intercultural Communication*, 1–20.

Graham, R. (2017, February 23). The retraining paradox. *The New York Times Magazine*.

Guo, C., & Al Ariss, A. (2015). Human resource management of international migrants: Current theories and future research. *International Journal of Human Resource Management, 26*(9–10), 1287–1297.

Guynn, J. (2016, October 21). Women in computing to decline even more. *USA Today*, p. 4B.

Hays Plc. (2017). *Hays global skills index 2016*. Retrieved from www.hays-index.com/the-index/introduction/.

Heidrick & Struggles. (2007). *The global talent index 2007–2012*. New York.

Heidrick & Struggles. (2011). *The global talent index report: The outlook to 2015*. New York. Retrieved from www.weknowglobaltalent.com/gti/print/gti/all/1/2012/; www.globaltalentindex.com/pdf/Heidrick_Struggles_Global_Talent_Report.pdf.

Heidrick & Struggles ((2015). *Board monitor survey 2015*. New York.

Hofstede, G. (1980). *Culture's consequences: International differences in work-related values*. Beverly Hills, CA: Sage.

Institute of International Education (IIE). (2015). Retrieved from www.iie.org/.

Jordan, M. (2017, October 27). Citizenship applications in the U.S. surge as immigration talk toughens. *The New York Times*. Retrieved from www.nytimes.com/2017/10/27/us/citizenship-applications-immigration.html.

Kapur, D., & McHale, J. (2005). *Give us your best and brightest: The global hunt for talent and its impact on the developing world*. Washington, DC: Center for Global Development.

Khilji, S. E. (2012). Does South Asia matter? Rethinking South Asia as relevant in international business research. *South Asian Journal of Global Business Research, 1*(1), 8–21.

Khilji, S. E., & Keilson, B. (2014). In search of global talent: Is South Asia ready? *South Asian Journal of Global Business Research, 3*(2), 114–134.

Khilji, S. E., & Schuler, R. S. (2018). Talent management in the global context. In D. Collings, K. Mellahi, & W. Cascio (Eds.), *Oxford handbook of talent management*. Oxford, UK: Oxford Press.

Khilji, S. E., Tarique, I., & Schuler, R. S. (2015). Incorporating the macro view in global talent management. *Human Resource Management Review, 25*(3), 236–248.

Krueger, A. (2016). *Where have all the workers gone?* Boston: Federal Reserve of Boston.

Lane, H. W., Mazenvski, M. L., Mendenhall, M. E., & McNett, J. (2004). *Blackwell handbook of global management: A guide to managing complexity*. Oxford: Blackwell.

Lanvin, B., & Evans, P. (2014). *The global talent competitiveness index 2014*. Human Capital Leadership Institute. INSEAD and Adecco Group, Switzerland.

Lanvin, B., & Evans, P. (2015). *The global talent competitiveness index 2015–16*. Human Capital Leadership Institute. INSEAD and Adecco Group, Switzerland.

Lanvin, B., & Evans, P. (2017). *The global talent competitiveness index 2016–17*. Human Capital Leadership Institute. INSEAD and Adecco Group, Switzerland.

Liu, X., Lu, J., Filatotchev, I., Buck, T., & Wright, M. (2011). Returnee entrepreneurs, knowledge spillovers and innovation in high-tech firms in emerging economies. *Journal of International Business Studies, 41*, 183–197.

Martin, H. (2015, Summer). Top 10 investment locations. *New European Economy*, pp. 90–94.

Martin, P. (2013). The global challenge of managing migration. *Population Reference Bureau, 68*(2). Retrieved from www.prb.org/pdf13/global-migration.pdf.

Mayersohn, N. (2017, April 27). Shortage of auto mechanics has dealerships taking action. *The New York Times*, p. B5.

McDonnell, A., Collings, D., & Burgess, J. (2012). Guest editors' note: Talent management in the Asia Pacific. *Asia Pacific Journal of Human Resources, 50*, 391–398.

Michaels, D. (2017, March 27). Foreign robots invade American factory floors. *The Wall Street Journal*.

Michaels, E., Hanfield-Jones, H., & Axelford, B. (2001). *War for talent*. Boston, MA: Harvard Business School Press.

Miller, C. C. (2017, March 8). How to help humans when the robots come to take our jobs. *The New York Times*, p. B6. For a description of the 40 programs reviewed by the Georgetown Center on Poverty and Inequality. Retrieved from www.law.georgetown.edu/news/press-releases/report-by-georgetown-center-on-poverty-and-inequality-lessons-learned-from-40-years-of-subsidized-employment-programs.cfm.

Oettl, A., & Agrawal, A. (2008). International labor mobility and knowledge flow externalities. *Journal of International Business Studies, 39*, 1242–1260.

Organization for International Investment. (2016). *Foreign direct investment in the United States 2016 report*. Washington, DC.

Oxford Economics. (2014). *Global talent 2021: How the new geography of talent will transform human resource strategies*. Retrieved from www.oxfordeconomics.com/Media/Default/Thought%20Leadership/global-talent-2021.pdf.

Patel, J. K. (2016, October 19). Trump also wants big changes to legal immigration. But how big? *The New York Times*, p. A14.

Phene, A., & Tallman, S. (2012). Complexity, context and governance in biotechnology alliances. *Journal of International Business Studies, 43*, 61–83.

Population References Bureau (2015). *2015 World Population Data Sheet*. www.prb.org.

PWC Millennials Survey. (2015). *Millennials at work: Reshaping the workplace*. Retrieved from www.pwc.com/gx/en/managing-tomorrows-people/future-of-work/millennialssurvey.jhtml.

Ragazzi, F. (2014). A comparative analysis of diaspora policies. *Political Geography, 41*, 74–89.

Rotella, C. (2017, February 26). The pipe fitter. *The New York Times Magazine*, pp. 47–49.

Saxenian, A. L. (2005). From brain drain to brain circulation: Transnational communities and upgrading in China and India. *Studies in Comparative International Development, 40*, 35–61.

Scullion, H., & Collings, D. (2016). *Global talent management* (2nd ed.). London: Routledge.

Scullion, H., Collings, D., & Caligiuri, P. (2010). Global talent management: Introduction. *Journal of World Business, 45*, 105–108.

Simon, R. (1962). The architecture of complexity. *Proceedings of the American Philosophical Society, 106*(6), 467–482.

Sparrow, P. R., Brewster, C., & Chung, C. (2017). *Globalizing human resource management* (2nd ed.). London and New York: Routledge.

Sparrow, P. R., Scullion, H., & Tarique, I. (2014). Strategic talent management: Future directions. In P. R. Sparrow, H. Scullion, & I. Tarique (Eds.), *Strategic talent management: Contemporary issues in international context* (pp. 278–302). Cambridge: Cambridge University Press.

Strack, R., Von Der Linden, C., Booker, M., & Strohmayr, A. (2014). *Decoding global talent*. Boston: Boston Consulting Group.

Tarique, I., & Schuler, R. (2010). Global talent management: Literature review, integrative framework, and suggestions for future research. *Journal of World Business, 45*, 122–133.

Tingley, K. (2017, February 26). The future of work. *New York Times Magazine*, 30–33, 58, 63.

Tung, R. L., & Lazarova, M. B. (2006). Brain drain versus brain gain: An exploratory study of ex-host country nationals in Central and East Europe. *International Journal of Human Resource Management, 17*(11), 1853–1872.

WEF. (2013, 2015, 2016). *The human capital reports*. Retrieved from www.weforum.org/reports/the-human-capital-report-2016.

WEF. (2016). *Global competitiveness report 2016–2017: Country profile highlights*. Retrieved from www.weforum.org/reports/the-global-competitiveness-report-2016–2017–1/.

Wildavsky, B. (2010). *The great brain race: How global universities are shaping the world*. Princeton, CT: Princeton University Press.

World Bank. (2016). *Doing business*. Retrieved from www.doingbusiness.org/rankings; www.doingbusiness.org/~/media/WBG/DoingBusiness/Documents/Annual-Reports/English/DB16-Full-Report.pdf.

Zong, J., & Batalova, J. (2015, February 26). *Frequently requested statistics on immigrants and immigration in the United States*. Spotlight. Retrieved from www.migrationpolicy.org.

2

Macro Talent Management in Canada

A Review of the National Context, Competitive Strengths and Future Opportunities to Attract, Develop and Retain Talent

Karin King

Introduction

As a nation, Canada is a "net importer of talent and skills" and adopts a highly structured, skills-based immigration program. That is, while Canada invests actively in the development of its citizens nationally, Canada additionally requires an influx of educated and skilled individuals to meet the requirements for skilled workforce positions and within that, aims to attract top talent for key positions to support innovation-driven economic growth. Champions of Canada's focus on talent and skills exist at all levels in the nation including the Canadian government, industry stakeholders, and talented individuals who chose Canada for their career and future life. By 2000, the influx of skilled talent with graduate degrees was four times larger than the outgoing flow of Canadian talent with degrees at any level (Statistics Canada 2002) and two in five Canadians (15 years or older) were either immigrants or the child of immigrants (Statistics Canada 2014). Since Canada's founding in 1867, Canada has a long history of national, economic and social development through both immigration into Canada and migration within and across the geographically vast nation. Canada today has established institutions which underpin a long-standing national culture structurally designed to welcome talent from both local national and far reaching places, enriching communities and businesses with an immensely diverse range of talent, skills and international experience.

Canada is strongly positioned to participate in a world of increasing intensity of capital, people and information flows (DHL, 2016), ranked 12th of 31 countries in 2016 for world talent (IMD, 2016), 15th of 138 countries in 2017 for global competitiveness (Schwab & Sala-i-Martín, 2016b), and 30th of 140 countries for global connectedness in 2015 (DHL, 2016). One example of global connectedness which underlies the macro talent management context, is Canada's long-standing membership in the Group of 7 countries, the "G7", comprised of the world's seven largest industrialised democratic nations (along with France, Germany, Italy, Japan, United Kingdom and United States) and which represents the world's most advanced economies with the highest gross domestic product (GDP) (Government Canada, 2017d). Canada is also a founding member of the Organisation for Economic Co-operation and Development (OECD), founded in 1960 dedicated to economic development which today includes 35 member nations (OECD, 2017c). Through this macro connectedness, Canada accesses and develops talent and participates in global and national economic advancement.

Founded on a firm belief in democracy and international relations, Canada is now an established nation and mature economy, which continues to develop through its foundations of international collaboration and a strong investment in the well-being of its citizens and is seen as one of the countries in the world most competitively positioned for future growth (Schwab & Sala-i-Martín, 2016b). Canada is a country which continues to develop through innovation-driven development, the most advanced stage of economic development as defined by the WEF (Schwab & Sala-i-Martín, 2016b). To compete for further economic development and the positive societal outcomes such growth affords its citizens, Canada must attract, develop and retain the talent it requires through effective macro and micro talent management systems.

The focus of this chapter is talent management at the national level in Canada and is presented in five core sections. This first section briefly introduced the topic of macro talent management (MTM) in Canada specifically. The second section introduces the reader to a framework and definition of macro talent management (Khilji, Tarique, & Schuler, 2015) to guide the reader. The subsequent sections present the three components of macro talent management in Canada: the environment and context of MTM; functions and processes which influence MTM and the outcomes of MTM, respectively. A "mini-case" Canadian example is provided to illustrate each of the components. The final section, presents recommendations for key stakeholders of MTM in Canada and priorities for further research, followed by the conclusion.

Macro Talent Management—A Theoretical Framework to Guide the Reader

Talent management has emerged in the past 15 years as a topic of strategic importance influencing an organisation's ability to effectively attract, manage and retain employees who possess the skills, knowledge and abilities required to compete effectively in today's fast-paced global economy (Tarique & Schuler, 2010). Talent management has become a topic of substantial visibility and interest (Cappelli, 2008) to many stakeholders including management, the employee, and the shareholder; however a wider view of stakeholders is required (Collings, 2014). At the highest level, the nation itself and its communities are stakeholders of talent management as a suitable national talent system is required to achieve a nation's aspiration for economic growth and as a fundamental foundation for full employment which enables the quality of life it aspires to for its citizens.

Macro talent management, that is, at the national or country level, is the wider national system in which all organisations within a given nation operate and subsequently design and implement their organisational-specific talent management practices. This wider context and its influence on organisational talent management therefore cannot be ignored. As with any system, there are inter-related component parts which may be influenced to adapt the system (Boulding, 1956). Understanding the Canadian macro talent management system may afford opportunities to Canadian organisations to influence the macro system within which they operate or to adapt organisational-level talent management for greater effectiveness within the national macro context.

This chapter adopts the definition of macro talent management (MTM) by Khilji et al. (Khilji et al., 2015), comprised of three elements: macro environmental context and factors; macro-level processes and functions; and resulting macro outcomes. Using the framework by Khilji et al. (2015) to guide the reader, this chapter reviews MTM specifically in Canada. Figure 2.1 presents the adapted framework for the reader's reference.

The Macro Talent Context and Environment in Canada

This section reviews the macro talent context and environment in Canada, the first of three components of the MTM framework. The Canadian macro talent context and environment is a positive contributor to the overall MTM system in Canada. Key factors comprising the macro context are Canada's governmental and non-governmental policies, financial and institutional environment, educational system, national labour market, population demographics and culture which are described in detail in the following pages. A range of external measures of the macro context exist in the form of national rankings, including national institutions, infrastructure, macroeconomic environment, the financial market development and business sophistication. Table 2.1 presents a summary of available rankings for the Canadian MTM context and environmental factors.

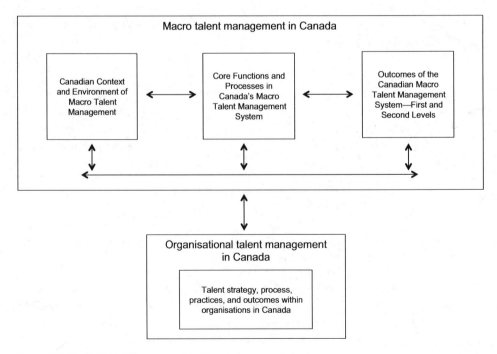

Figure 2.1 Macro Talent Management in Canada

Adapted from Khilji et al. (2015)

Table 2.1 Macro Talent Management in Canada: Context and Environment

Macro talent management component			Ranking	Source
Context and Environment	**Overall Context**	Attractiveness to talent	7th of 188	INSEAD et al. (2017)
		Global talent	8th of 60	(Economist Intelligence Unit 2015)
		Country competitiveness	15th of 138	WEF (2017)
		Top 10 best countries for business	10th of 139	Forbes (2016)
	Economic and Financial	Financial market development	7th of 138	WEF (2017)
		Market size	15th of 138	
		Macro-economic environment	41st of 138	
	Institutional and Regulatory	Regulatory Quality	5th of 118	INSEAD et al. (2017)
		Regulatory landscape	9th of 118	
		Institutions	18th of 138	WEF (2017)
	Infrastructure and Technological	Infrastructure	15th of 138	
		Technological readiness	21st of 138	
	Business Environment	Business and labour landscape	10th of 118	INSEAD et al. (2017)
		Business sophistication	24th of 138	WEF (2017)
	Talent-Specific Context	Proclivity to attract talent	8th of 60	(Economist Intelligence Unit 2015)
		Internal openness for talent	6th of 188	INSEAD et al. (2017)
		External openness for talent	10th of 188	
	Political	Political stability	9th of 118	
	Societal	Personal Safety	9th of 118	
		Openness	21st of 60	(Economist Intelligence Unit 2015)

Canadian Governmental Policies, Programs and Activities

Canada is globally-minded, and hence its national policies and governmental activities reflect this focus. For example, Canada is a founding member and active champion of the United Nations, founded in 1945 (Government Canada, 2017i), "to maintain international peace and security and to achieve international co-operation in solving international problems" (United Nations, 2017) and is the UN's 5th largest donor (Canada, 2017). Canada is an active member nation in the G7 (Government Canada, 2017e) and as host of the annual G7 Summit in 2018, Canada leads the Youth Summit, a dedicated investment in young future leaders designed to provide opportunities for future leaders to participate in global decision making (Government Canada, 2017d). Canada's MTM context is geared towards visible investment in emerging national and global talent.

Canada's intention to actively engage internationally is also visible in its global trading relationships which enable access to global talent and economic development. The North American Free Trade Agreement (NAFTA), for example, established in 1994, facilitates trade between and across North American countries including Canada, the United States and Mexico. Economic analysis of the impact of NAFTA on Canada has been largely positive with significant expansion of exports to the US and more than tripling of agricultural trade in the 20 years since NAFTA entered into force (McBride & Aly Sergie, 2017) and talent flows across borders have contributed positively to economic development.

With a population of only 36.6 million (Statistics Canada 2017), Canada's relationships with the international community are highly relevant to continued national growth and to macro talent management. The Comprehensive Economic and Trade Agreement (CETA), a landmark trade agreement between Canada and the European Union, is a clear statement of Canada's intention to further develop its active involvement in global trade and is a tangible reduction of trade barriers (BBC, 2016). CETA is particularly important to Canada given Europe's continued status as the "world's most globally connected region" (DHL, 2016) and Canada's aging population which mirrors that of other Western countries (Economist, 2017). Through such global participation, Canada invites international collaboration which supports the mobility of talent and the accelerated transfer of knowledge and experience. Canada looks beyond North America and the EU to collaborate with other countries and regions. For example, through Canada's participation in the Commonwealth, a world-wide community of 2.4 billion people and 52 nations, with a shared Charter declaring commitment to inclusiveness (Commonwealth, 2017), the Canadian Government offers scholarships to selected Commonwealth countries as an investment in the development of foreign Commonwealth talent.

Non-Governmental Organisations in Canada

Non-governmental agencies directly contribute to Canada's macro talent management context and environment. For example, MITACS, a national not-for-profit organisation, supports industrial and social innovation in Canada through applied and industrial research in mathematics and sciences. This organisation's activities support the MTM environment in Canada through its attraction of both domestic and foreign direct investment for research in industry and through investment in scholarships programs for research and the training and development of world-class researchers in Canada (MITACS, 2017). Industry-education partnerships in Canada are examples of macro talent interventions through which Canadian industry invests in Canadian talent through education, research and training.

Canadian Financial, Regulatory and Institutional Environment

Canada's financial and regulatory institutions are enabled to facilitate international foreign direct investment and expansion of Canadian firms internationally and a number of fundamental macro conditions are in place which make Canada highly competitive for economic development (WEF, 2017). Seen as one of the top 10 countries in which to do business globally (Forbes, 2016), these fundamentals include the advanced development of financial markets and the degree of business sophistication suitable for advanced economic development (ranked 7th and 24th of 138 countries, respectively) and the presence of institutions and infrastructure which are supportive of economic development (ranked 18th and 15th respectively of 138 countries) (WEF, 2017). Further, Canada's regulatory landscape and quality of regulation are amongst the best in the world (ranked 9th and 5th of 118 countries ranked globally) (INSEAD et al., 2017). Underpinned by political stability and a competitive market size (WEF, 2017), Canada is seen as open for global business. Supported by Canada's institutional foundations, businesses in Canada leverage the talent networks and knowledge which exist within their subsidiaries (Bartlett & Ghoshal, 1986), a recognised channel for competitive advantage through global growth.

Canada's Education System

Canada's commitment to education is evidenced by its exceptionally strong adult literacy rates, ranked as 2nd internationally in 2011 (Economist Intelligence Unit, 2011) and investment in compulsory education for its national population (Economist Intelliengence Unit,

2011). Canada has the largest proportion of tertiary-educated adults of all OECD member countries and invests more on tertiary education, as measured by spend per student, than nearly all other OECD countries (OECD, 2016a). Canada's investment in primary through tertiary education is comparably high as a percentage of public spending amongst OECD countries globally, at 8%, and Canada's public spending is higher than OECD average (OECD, 2014c). As a percentage of GDP, Canada's private spending on education achieves the OECD average (OECD, 2014b).

The University of Toronto, which leads Canada's universities in the annual Times Higher Education (THE) World University Rankings, was ranked 22nd of 1102 institutions globally, and ranked top amongst the six Canadian universities in the top 120 overall. Recent analysis indicates that further governance and investment in the future of research and graduate education in Canada is warranted to further assure that currently strong macro talent foundations remain such for the future (Naylor, 2017).

Canada's National Labour Market and Its Regulation

The health and regulation of its national labour market is a further factor in the MTM context. Canada's labour market is regulated by the Canadian federal government and its 13 provinces and territories. Historically, Canadian provinces began implementation of minimum wage legislation in 1914 (Derry & Douglas, 1922) following which a federal minimum wage was introduced. More recently in 1996, the federal wage was re-configured to become the legislated general adult minimum wage rate, regulated by the province or territory where the work is conducted. Minimum wage legislation today is authorised by the Canadian Constitution and varies by the province or territory that sets the actual minimum wage. Generally, labour laws are seen as less restrictive in Canada than in many other countries, including the European Union, which enables the nation's attraction of talent and business (Heidrick & Struggles, 2015). Wage regulation however, ranked as 47th in 60 countries, may limit some business flexibility in performance (Traxler, Blaschke, & Kittel, 2001).

Canada is seen as a place to do business, ranked favourably at 22nd of 190 countries, indicating an overall ease of doing business (WorldBankGroup, 2017), reflecting the extent to which Canada's existing labour market regulations are supportive of business activities. Canada's flexibility in employment practices such as the use of fixed-term contracts balanced with the protection of workers including restrictions on overtime work, and competitive minimum wage legislation (WorldBankGroup, 2017) supports both business access to talent and the talent themselves.

Canadian Immigration Policies

Canada is a country which, together with the Indigenous Peoples of Canada, has grown historically through successive waves of immigration from all over the world. Indeed, commitment to immigration and multiculturalism are globally-recognised elements of Canada's national culture and societal composition (Javidan, Dorfman, De Luque, & House, 2006). An important component of macro talent strategy for Canada's future, Canada actively manages immigration through a structured skills-based program aligned to targeted skillsets. The Federal Skilled Worker Program and The Federal Trades Program are two examples of programs designed to specify the type of skills and experience required by Canadian industry and then to fast-track qualified and eligible candidates through the immigration process to meet that requirement (Government Canada, 2017a). The high degree of transparency of national immigration programs is likely a strong contributor to the perception that Canada's immigration system is fair and inclusive.

Canadian Population Demographics and Mobility

Canada's population of 36 million has significant ethno-diversity, representing more than 200 ethnic origins and with the highest proportion of foreign-born citizens in the G8 countries (Statistics Canada 2011b,2012). Within Canada, there are 1.4 million Indigenous Canadians, representing 4.3% of the population (Statistics Canada 2011a). Indigenous Canadians or Aboriginal Canadians are terms which refer to the First Nations, Inuit and Métis peoples, whose ancestors originally resided in the part of North America which later became the nation of Canada (Government of Canada, 2011). Canada's Indigenous Peoples have distinct identities, cultures, languages, traditions and communities which are widely dispersed geographically, established in each of Canada's 13 provinces and territories (Government Canada, 2011; Statistics Canada 2002). The First Nations peoples are the largest of the three Indigenous populations in Canada, within which there are 634 distinct First Nations peoples, representing a total population of nearly 900,000 (Government Canada, 2011; Statistics Canada 2011a). The Assembly of First Nations is a national advocacy organisation, representing the First Nations communities and their people in Canada in many dimensions of national policy including education, languages, health, housing, and environment (First Nations, 2017).

Overall, Canada's population is mature, similar to advanced economies, and in contrast to emerging economies, Canada's higher average population age is less favourable for competitive economic development (Economist, 2011). National population demographics underscore Canada's macro talent system requirements for incoming skilled workers and high potential talent flows to meet national and organisational needs for skilled labour and talent. However, Canada's demonstrated ability to attract and recruit foreign talent at a competitive rate is a documented strength, contributing to Canada's ranking of 13th overall for global talent (Heidrick & Struggles, 2015).

Diaspora and Returnees to Canada

"Diaspora networks have always been a potent economic force" and are expected to be even more so today as global migration "allows ideas to circulate in millions of mobile minds" (Economist, 2011). While a strong importer of talent and skilled workers, Canada also has historically contributed senior Canadian talent internationally to contribute in key leadership positions. Of note recently, the former Governor of the Bank of Canada, Mark Carney, was appointed to the position of Governor of the Bank of England in 2013; the first foreigner to lead the Bank (Bank of England, 2013) with valued expertise from Canada's national banking system which was recognised for its strength and stability, particularly in the wake of the global financial crisis. Historically, there have been concerns about the outflow of educated and experienced talent leaving Canada for career advancement or reward in the United States, Europe and beyond (Statistics Canada 2000).

More recently, an emerging trend of educated expatriate Canadians considering attractive career positions at home has been observed, however, empirical analysis of Canada's diaspora is highly limited to date (Statistics Canada 2014; Welsh, 2011). The increasing attractiveness of Canada relative to other countries globally (Lanvin, Evans, & Rodriguez-Montemayor, 2016), such as ranking 3rd country overall for expatriates in a 2016 survey (HSBC, 2016) and the political instabilities of other countries globally may influence Canada's attraction of national and foreign talent. In 2016, the HSBC Group Expat Explorer Survey cited 74% of Canadians as stating they were confident in their country's political stability compared with only 51% of expatriates globally who reported confidence in their country's political stability (HSBC, 2016). However, analysis indicates the opportunity for improved use of pay systems, which are seen to be meritocratic (Heidrick & Struggles, 2015).

Canadian National Culture

As with any national identity and culture, Canada's culture is a representation of Canada's national heritage interwoven historically with generations of economic and social development. Significant studies of culture, such as the GLOBE studies, identify Canada's culture as having several dimensions of note. Specifically, Canada's culture is identified as future-oriented, humane-oriented, values high gender egalitarianism and has a very high performance orientation (GlobeProject, 2004). Leadership in Canada is deemed more team-oriented, participation-oriented and humane-oriented than the average of countries measured in the world-wide study and the degree to which leaders are individualistic is seen to occur less frequently in Canada than in the average of global countries ranked (Globe Project, 2004). This is consistent with Canada's team-oriented leadership style and value of inclusion in workplaces. Canada is also recognised for its openness, ranked 13th of 61 countries in 2015 (Heidrick & Struggles, 2015), all of which are positive elements of talent attractiveness.

The opportunity to communicate with one another is an important element of Canada's cultural foundations, particularly given the diversity of Canada's people as a nation which historically grew largely through immigration. Canada has two official national languages: French and English, originating from the early settlement of Canada and its establishment as a dual language country in 1967. Today Canada enjoys significant linguistic diversity with more than 200 languages spoken as a mother tongue or native language (Statistics Canada 2011c). While millions of Canadian citizens speak two or more languages within their homes, English and French remain strongly positioned as the common foundation in life and work in Canada, such that 98% of Canada's population report the ability to conduct a conversation in either English or French (Statistics Canada 2011c). Use of the English language in Canada is a cultural anchor through which individuals of many diverse cultural and national origins communicate, engage, work and share life in Canada.

Educational experiences can also be seen as one example of how Canadians experience the national culture. The OECD Gender Equality in Education report (OECD, 2012) indicates that Canada's education system performs better than the OECD average in supporting equity in the educational system in three dimensions of equity: gender, social background and immigrant students (OECD, 2012). Importantly, this finding of Canadians' early life experiences in their primary school settings is consistent with overall national cultural measures indicating equality and inclusion in Canada and its workplaces, as reflected in workplace measures of inclusion (Strauss, 2017), which are associated with lower levels of conflicts and higher levels of satisfaction (Nishii, 2013).

Diversity, Inclusion and Openness in Canadian Society and Workplaces

"Diversity is Canada's Strength", an address by the Right Honourable Justin Trudeau, Prime Minister of Canada, delivered in London, U.K. in 2015 reflects diversity as a core value in Canada, culturally and socially (Trudeau, 2015). Consistent with Canada's priorities as a G7 member to "promote respect for diversity and inclusion" (Government of Canada, 2017e), Canada and Canadians value diversity and seek to maintain what are recognised as inclusive national and local cultures. For example, Canada's approach to regulation and management of its labour market has processes which are favourable to diversity and inclusion, such as the availability of lengthy maternity leave policies, legislation which ensures equal remuneration for work of equal value, and protection for periods of unemployment (WorldBankGroup, 2017).

Business communities in Canada also share the value of inclusion and diversity in their workforces and seek to reinforce these through measurement and action. Of Canadian organisations, 87% report employing dedicated Diversity & Inclusion staff to facilitate effective diversity and inclusion practices (Deloitte, 2014). Top Diversity Employers in Canada are identified based empirically on confidential employee feedback, a management effort to further endorse the imperative of diversity and inclusion focused workplaces. This recognition as a Best Diversity Employer is also a visibly positive factor in the national or global talent markets (Mediacorp 2017a). A further example of Canada's commitment to inclusion culturally is a current national initiative in education to improve the effectiveness in the teaching of Canadian history to more effectively include the perspectives of Canada's Indigenous peoples (Globe 2017) through increased teacher capability and effectiveness (Milne, 2017). The presence and history of Indigenous Peoples in Canada long pre-dates the development of Canada as a nation, mainly by European settlers (Government of Canada, 2011). More recently, Canada as a nation and its government have openly recognised historical failures to respect the rights of Indigenous Peoples and have committed to actively address these failures as identified in a review, the Truth and Reconciliation Report (Trudeau, 2017). At its core this endeavour strives for inclusion and values the abundant diversity of Canada's many peoples.

The Center for Competitiveness of IMD Business School conducts an annual analysis of relevance to this chapter's review of macro talent management. The IMD World Talent Ranking is an assessment of each country's ability to develop, attract and retain talent for companies operating within their economy (IMD, 2016) and assesses Canada as very strongly positioned. Specifically, Canada is ranked as 7th in appeal, 9th in readiness and 22nd in investment and development, each of which contribute to the overall ranking of Canada as 12th of 61 countries, (IMD, 2016). Such indicators can be seen as both an outcome of the macro talent management system and also a sub-factor of the context in which macro talent management is subsequently conducted.

Social, Economic, and Political Conditions in Canada

As presented earlier, the World Economic Forum reports annually on cross-country comparison of a nation's institutions, policies and factors which together determine a country's level of competitiveness which facilitates its industrial and social outcomes (Schwab & Sala-i-Martín, 2016b). In addition to the education-related factors presented as one component of the MTM context, other factors of competitiveness measured help to explain the country's institutional environment. They include measures of a country's social, economic and political competitiveness and are relevant to the model of MTM in Canada, presented in Table 2.2.

Societally, life in Canada is seen as a positive lifestyle and offers a high degree of personal safety, ranked respectively at 22nd and 8th of 118 nations globally (INSEAD et al. 2017). Legislation is in place in Canada to protect individual intellectual and private property, consistent with global rankings of personal security and property protection in Canada as 6th of 61 countries (IMD, 2016) and 3rd of 60 countries ranked (Heidrick & Struggles, 2015) in the IMD world Talent Report and Global Talent Index respectively.

Table 2.2 Macro Talent Management in Canada: Core Processes and Functions

Macro talent management component			Ranking	Source
Processes and Functions (including national HR processes)	**Health and Educational**	Health and Primary Education	9th of 138	WEF (2017)
		Higher Education and Training	19th of 138	
		Compulsory Education Quality	17th of 60	(Economist Intelligence Unit 2015)
		University Education	16th of 60	
		Public Spending on Education	8th of OECD	OECD (2014c)
		Private Spending on Education	18th of OECD	
	Labour Force and Market	Labour Market Efficiency	8th of 138	WEF (2017)
		Demographics	23rd of 60	(Economist Intelligence Unit 2015)
		Quality of the Labour Force	7th of 60	
		Preparedness of Students	4th highest	PISA (2015)
	Core Human Capital Processes	Enable Talent	7th of 188	INSEAD et al. (2017)
		Attract Talent	7th of 118	
		Grow Talent	12th of 118	
		Retain Talent	21st of 118	
	Capability and Skills	Global Knowledge Skills	16th of 118	INSEAD et al. (2017)
		Vocational and Technical skills	26th of 118	
		Information Skills (students with at least one home computer)	98.9%	OECD (2014b)

A nation with political stability, Canada is seen to project itself to the world by way of "soft power," that is, the ability of a country to attract support and followers through the attractiveness of its culture, national policies and its political ideologies (Nye, 2009). Canada achieves influence through attraction by use of various instruments of public diplomacy including cultural programs, international education, international broadcasting, trade, and investment promotion (Potter, 2009). Economically, Canada's national performance and GDP output are evidence of a stable advanced nation (Schwab & Sala-i-Martín, 2016b) with high levels of employment (OECD, 2017a). To protect and assure the health of the economy, Canada has instituted strong anti-corruption legislation which is seen as effective in Canada. This is comprised of two key legal instruments of anti-corruption regulation in Canada: the Corruption of Foreign Public Officials Act, and the Criminal Code. As the consequences of corruption are widely viewed as detrimental to Canada's economic growth, businesses and citizens, the consequences and penalties for corrupt activities are significant (MLT Aikins, 2017) as reported by the OECD in 2015 (OECD, 2015a). Canada's has been ranked highly, as 9th of 176 (where top rankings indicate low perceptions of corruption) in a report conducted by Transparency International which ranks countries globally for perceptions of corruption in the public sector (International, 2016), which is important to protecting Canadian culture from the negative risk and consequences of inequality given that inequality contributes to unequal distribution of power in society and unequal distribution of wealth (International, 2016).

To further illustrate the MTM context and environment in Canada for the reader, Figure 2.2 presents a mini-case example of one its sub-components: Government Policy and Immigration.

Overall, the Canadian macro talent context is one of stability, which reflects mature institutions, stable political leadership, and facilitates international trade and talent flows while investing in people through education, technology and the nation's inclusive culture. The next section considers the core functions and processes which interact with the Canadian macro talent context and creates national MTM outcomes.

> **Express Entry – The fast track to skills for Canada**
>
> **Context**
>
> Canada seeks to attract skilled migrants as future permanent residents and citizens for the specific purpose of settling in Canada and participating in and contributing to the Canadian economy and quality of life.
>
> **Core Process**
>
> To accelerate the entry process for migrants with the specific skills Canada requires at any given time, Canada implements the "Express Entry" program. Candidate qualifications are ranked for priority access through an expedited path to residency and employability in alignment with prioritized national talent and skills requirements. The skillset requirements are updated regularly to reflect national and sector-specific priorities.
>
> **Outcomes**
>
> This program is a mutually expedited process for both individuals and the organisations who seek to employ them, achieving the goal of bringing talented and skilled individuals into Canada who are motivated to settle in Canada and contribute to the Canadian economy and quality of life. This active approach to talent pool management and ranking ensures selected candidates deliver the specific skills required to support Canada's national business and economic requirements.
>
> *Source:* Government of Canada (2017a).

Figure 2.2 Mini-Case: Canadian MTM Context and Environment: Example of Government Policy and Immigration

MTM Core Functions and Processes in Canada

This section reviews the second of three components of macro talent management in Canada. They are the core functions and core processes through which Canada facilitates (or hinders) its talent attraction, development and retention, which interact with the national context to achieve macro talent outcomes. Table 2.2 presents an overview of Canada's MTM process and functions.

Core Functions

The core functions of MTM at the country level are defined as: talent planning, acquisition, development and retention (Khilji et al., 2015).

Talent Planning

The national Government of Canada engages regularly in the forecasting of Canadian provincial and national requirements for a diverse and highly skilled workforce to support Canada's established and continually growing advanced economy (Conference Board Canada, 2002). The insight emerging from such analytical practices are reflected in the ongoing policy decisions made by both the Canadian national and regional (provincial or territorial) governments. These may include immigration policies (as presented in the previous section) or investments in education, such as the national apprenticeships programs (Government Canada, 2017c) and sector-targeted university funding. Engagement with industry (Conference Board Canada, 2017) as stakeholders in national workforce and talent planning supports a more informed view for government policy making and an opportunity to proactively intervene on problematic skills challenges, such as a maturing population (Statistics Canada 2017) or specific industrial skills shortages (Conference Board Canada, 2002) for sector-specific expertise

(Ontario Investment, 2016). Recently, industry-government collaboration was implemented in the cybersecurity sector (Deloitte, 2016; OntarioInvestment, 2016) to attract international investment, supported by Canada's post-secondary educational system.

Talent Development in Canada

Within Canada, national and provincial development initiatives support individuals to complete education and enter careers. One example, Canada's Red Seal Program, offers a suite of nationally-managed apprenticeships, registered within a specific province or territory, for individuals to learn and qualify as a skilled apprentice in one of a range of trades and technologies, such as power engineering or master electrician (Government Canada, 2017c). Apprenticeships programs are designed to provide structured on the job training while facilitating employment such that individuals build their skills and experience while earning employment income and formal credentials. The skilled trades and technologies are a long-standing core segment of Canada's industrial workforce and have contributed to Canada's historic performance strengths and innovative competitive advantage in sectors such as oil and gas and natural resources and as such the trades and technology professions are valued highly by Canadians themselves (Skills Canada, 2002).

Canada also contributes to the development of talent internationally. The International Experience Canada Program (Goverment Canada, 2017f), for example, provides eligible youth applicants with a structured employment program to live and work in Canada for a fixed period of time in order to gain international work experience in Canada. The three routes to participation include a specific employer-sponsored visa, a holiday working visa or an international co-op internship. Individuals are selected into talent pools as international candidates and managed through a structured selection process (Goverment Canada, 2017f) through which Canada attracts international talent into Canadian businesses and, reciprocally, foreign candidates gain valuable and sought-after Canadian work experience and career development.

The quality and presence of local managers in Canadian workplaces is also recognised as a functional strength in Canada's MTM, ranked as 3rd of 61 countries (IMD, 2016). The commitment to management capability is an important factor in both management of domestically-educated talent and in the integration of incoming foreign talent into Canadian workplaces and Canadian work standards. Literature indicates that the line manager is an important influencer of employee workplace outcomes such as performance (Alfes, Truss, Soane, Rees, & Gatenby, 2013; Sikora, Ferris, & Van Iddekinge, 2015), use of voice (Townsend & Loudoun, 2015), effective psychological contracts (McDermott, Conway, Rousseau, & Flood, 2013), and the implementation of effective HR practices (Cappelli, 2013; Guest & Conway, 2011; King, 2015; Purcell & Hutchinson, 2007). The line manager has a direct role in effective organisational talent management including identification and retention of employees in high potential and leadership talent pools (Dries & Pepermans, 2012; King, 2016).

Talent Attraction and Retention

Nationally, Canada is a strong attractor of talent, as evidenced by rankings of 7th globally of 188 countries for overall talent attractiveness (INSEAD et al., 2017) and 8th of 60 countries for ability to attract talent (Heidrick & Struggles, 2015), supported by high levels of external and internal openness to talent (ranked 10th and 6th respectively of 188 countries) (INSEAD et al., 2017). Within Canada, companies actively seek to retain talent through a number of strategies. At the national level, one example is through "best employer" strategies. While "best employer" awards are achieved by individual companies in recognition of their organisationally specific talent and workforce practices, Canadian businesses overall aspire to meet those standards and this is reflected in the overall MTM environment in Canada. "Best employer" awards include: Canada's Top 100 Employers, Canada's Best Diversity Employers and Alberta's Top 70 Employers (Mediacorp 2017a); Canada's Top Employers for Young People (Mediacorp 2017b); and Canada's Best Employers 2017 supported by Forbes Inc. (Strauss, 2017). While "best employer" status is often used by companies to compete within Canada for talent at the organisational level, the increasing visibility of these independent measures of workplace quality are also visible in international recruitment. Importantly, many award recipients in Canada are global companies with either headquarters or subsidiaries outside of Canada, and therefore the recognition of "best employer" awards may also contribute to recruitment internationally and global mobility of talent, such as Zurich's ABB in Canada, which placed 3rd in 2016 (Strauss, 2017).

Historically, at the national level, there have been economic periods during which Canada has been challenged to retain its organically grown domestic talent (Service, 2000). For example, in the early 2000s, demand from the United States for medical-technical and postgraduate talent, coupled with a U.S. dollar comparatively stronger than the Canadian dollar, resulted in a "brain drain" to the South. Other coincident factors which influenced this macro talent mobility trend were recent enactment of the North American Free Trade Agreement (NAFTA) in 1994, which made it possible for Canadian citizens to readily obtain U.S. work permits and the U.S. economy's relative strength which had the dual effect of facilitating the expansion of Canadian companies to the South, but also required the relocation of senior company talent to the U.S. to oversee the expansion (Service, 2000). Over time, Canada has sought to attract Canadian citizens to return home with their U.S.-gained experience, most recently through growth in technical sector jobs (Lee, 2017).

Core MTM Processes

The core processes by which macro talent management takes place include a range of processes which vary by country and may include learning and knowledge sharing, institutional support, educational leadership and corporate strategy and leadership (Khilji et al., 2015). A review of these is presented next.

Learning and Knowledge Sharing

Canada participates actively in the global sharing of knowledge. For example, Canada is recognised for its quality of universities as 7th of 60 countries (Heidrick & Struggles, 2015), as measured by the number of those ranked in the world's top 500 universities and also for Canada's quality of university education delivered, where Canada is ranked as 11th of 61 globally (IMD, 2016). When specific knowledge and expertise are required, Canada's macro talent context and environment as discussed earlier, is positioned reasonably well to support both access to that knowledge globally through partnerships and trade, through attraction of foreign talent and through the targeted investment in domestic development of knowledge and skills, such as is the case currently in regards to the development of the Artificial Intelligence (AI) sector, to which Canada has historically been a lead contributor (Alberta, 2017; Deep-Mind, 2017). Given that technological risk is a key risk in global economies currently (WEF, 2016), the Canadian MTM system's ability to flexibly direct increased focus to investments to learning and knowledge where identified (in this case, in Canada's technology capability), may prove to be an important differentiator for Canada's macro talent system and national economy in future.

Further examples are Canada's participation in the OECD, founded by Canada along with other original members, with the specific purpose to support information sharing for cooperative global economic development (OECD, 2017c) and participation of Canadian talent in the UN Council Committees and the G-20. It is through such channels that Canadian talent regularly engage with other top talent and contribute to learning and knowledge sharing.

Institutional Processes That Support Talent in Canada

A number of supportive institutions are in place to facilitate Canadians' employability and participation in the job market and to contribute to Canada's productivity, which facilitates overall quality of the macro talent supply in Canada and also thereby supports the quality of careers for Canadians and residents. In addition to a nationwide employment service and unemployment insurance benefits programme which provides financial benefits during periods of unemployment, specific employment programmes are designed and implemented to support the employment of specific segments of the population. These specific population segments vary over time as needs are identified through government macro national, provincial and sector analysis of workforce trends. Currently, three specific programmes are of visible priority: for Indigenous Peoples; for Canadian Armed Forces veterans or the Royal Canadian Mounted Police; and for youth (Government Canada, 2017g). Highlights of these programmes include educational scholarships for Aboriginal students, career transition services for Canadians leaving military service, apprenticeships and financial assistance programmes for students (Government Canada, 2017g). Underpinning the focus on employment skills and Canada's job market is the national Government's national department of Employment and Social Development Canada (ESDC) whose declared objective is stated as: "To improve the standard of living and quality of life for all Canadians. We do this by promoting a labour force that is highly skilled. We also promote an efficient and inclusive labour market" (Government of . Canada, 2017g). This vision is a clear example of Canada's approach to welcoming and inviting talent into the Canadian job market, whether domestic or foreign, to actively contribute to national economic performance and importantly, also illustrates Canada's cultural focus on enabling positive social outcomes for all.

The Health and Wellbeing of Canadians

Canada has a national health care system which is publically funded and is supported by the health insurance plans established by each of Canada's 13 provinces and territories. This national healthcare provides universal health care coverage to all Canadian citizens and permanent residents (Government Canada, 2017b). Canada's national healthcare system today is largely determined by the Canadian Constitution and was founded in the late 1940s, over a period of years following the end of World War II (Government Canada, 2017b). Prior to that, health services were largely privately funded for hospitals and medical services mandated by the Canadian Constitution. The Canada Health Act ensures that the plans provided by the provinces and territories meet the principles of service and care to the standard expected (Government of Canada, 2017b). The Canadian health care system design is largely based on the model of the National Health Service (NHS) in the United Kingdom. In addition to underlying Canada's commitment to its citizens for social well-being, this national healthcare system reflects the "basic values of fairness and equity that are demonstrated by the willingness of Canadians to share resources and responsibility" for the health and well-being of all Canadians through Canada's health care system (Government of Canada, 2017b). Canada enjoys above-OECD health outcomes indicators such as increased availability of medical services and a trained medical workforce and increased health diagnostic and prevention services (OECD, 2015b). However Canada's current expenditure on health as a percentage of gross domestic product is higher than OCED average and is the 12th highest of OECD countries at 10.3% (OECD, 2017b) and therefore the efficiency of Canada's national healthcare system has been in question in recent years.

Educational Leadership

As described earlier in this chapter, Canada has been recently recognised for its efforts to invest in education and educational quality outcomes as based on analysis of its education from basic through to tertiary and management education (Heidrick & Struggles, 2015; OECD, 2014b, 2014c; Schwab & Sala-i-Martín, 2016b). Canada continues to strive to maintain and extend its educational standards and leadership, both domestically and internationally. Domestically, for example, to actively support the education of Indigenous Canadians, a number of educational initiatives have been established and implemented over many years. One such initiative is the Summer Literacy Camp Program which is now in place nationally and delivered in more than 140 communities across Canada supporting early-childhood aged youth from Canada's Indigenous communities to build their literacy and numeracy skills as a critical foundation necessary for future success in school and work (Alberta 2017).

Canadian governments, nationally, provincially and territorially, also invest further afield in the education of foreign non-Canadian citizens, resident outside of Canada. At first glance this may seem to be an investment beyond the required scope of Canada's macro talent management system, however, with closer examination, such investment can be seen to align well to Canada's long term macro talent planning through educational leadership. For example, in 2017, Alberta Education, the ministry of education for the Alberta Provincial Government, established a partnership with Cambridge International School for Girls in Jalandhar, India, to offer an authorised Alberta Education Curriculum Programme in their schools in Jalandhar. Through this partnership, Cambridge Schools Jalandhar has become the first educational organisation in India to offer the Canadian Alberta Government approved curriculum to Indian national students with quality assured through delivery by Canadian-educated and qualified teachers. Although early in its delivery, this initiative is already being recognised in India as a "doorway to Canadian Universities and Schools" facilitating "easier immigration to Canada" (CityAir News, 2017). This international collaboration aims to benefit both the receiving country, India, as well as the sponsoring country, Canada, through establishing standards of education abroad which transparently align to Canadian standards and thereby future opportunities for careers in Canada or bilateral trade.

Corporate Strategy and Leadership in Canada

Corporate strategy and leadership in Canada's industries often act in complement to and cooperatively with the Canadian government's programs and policies, to lead the way for Canada nationally or regionally with regard to development of the macro talent context to facilitate the attraction of talent for a region or sector or sometimes to help solve challenges in macro talent supply requirements for industry. Historically, one example has been the Canadian oil, gas and energy sector, whose efforts to forecast the skills and workforce requirements at a macro level involved collaboration at the national level with government and across the sector, with peers and competitors, to proactively attract international talent and grow domestic talent to supply a then rapidly growing industry (Conference Board Canada, 2002). Partnering with the Conference Board of Canada (CBoC), an independent not-for-profit organisation which influences Canadian industry and government policy through evidence-based applied research

(Conference Board Canada, 2017), key stakeholders representing the oil, gas and energy industries were influential in drawing attention and action to the forecasted shortage of industry skilled labour from the late 1990s through the early 2000s such that a number of industry-education partnerships and targeted recruitment campaigns were enacted to address the foreseen macro talent supply shortage. Historically and continuing today, the natural resources sectors have attracted and employed some of Canada's most highly skilled and scarce technical talent, a mix of both domestically and internationally qualified and experienced talent.

Currently, the specific case of "deep learning" has come into strategic focus in Canada, or perhaps more precisely, back into focus, in both industry and education. Deep learning essentially refers to learning that is done by machines or computers such as the interpretation of algorithms, patterns and artificial intelligence (AI) and is "expected to have a massive impact on fields like healthcare, banking, manufacturing and transportation" (Murphy, 2017). Canadian Universities are recognised to have contributed strongly to the early development of the field of deep learning (Lee, 2017) and in 2017, the Vector Institute for Artificial Intelligence to conduct research in deep learning was launched by the Royal Bank of Canada (RBC). This is one recent example of corporate strategy contributing directly to attracting and developing talent in Canada which is funded by a collaborative group of 30 Canadian and international businesses including Google, Google's DeepMind and RBC (Murphy, 2017) which aims to attract and develop specialised research talent and expand the applications of AI significantly.

To further illustrate the MTM core functions and processes in Canada, Figure 2.3, presents a mini-case example of one its sub-components: Corporate Strategy and Leadership.

Building Canada's capability in Artificial Intelligence & Deep Learning

Context

Canada invests in competitive talent-based capabilities to attract and develop talent and build innovation-driven economic growth. Through ongoing attraction and development of individual talent, research investment and company partnerships, Canadian research and corporate organisations establish a defined focus and committed investment in the emerging sector of artificial intelligence (AI) and deep learning.

Core Process

DeepMind (founded in London, UK in 2010; acquired by Google's Alphabet Group in 2014) opened its first international AI research office in the Western province of Alberta, Canada, in collaboration with the University of Alberta (UAlberta) (DeepMind, 2017). The CEO of DeepMind explained the decision to open DeepMind Alberta saying "It was a big decision for us to open our first non-UK research lab, (and) is a sign of the deep admiration and respect we have for the Canadian research community." (DeepMind, 2017) in large part due to the talented researchers which attracted the investment (Alberta, 2017).

Outcomes

This focused investment in the Canadian AI sector has generated international visibility for Canada as a continuing leader in AI and Deep Learning, nationally committed to enabling long term investment and to attracting and engaging world-class talent. This is an example of a coordinated effort by key Canadian industry and educational institutions to make sector-specific investments in infrastructure, research and the talent to lead the sector's global development.

Figure 2.3 Mini-Case: Canadian MTM Core Functions and Processes: Example of Corporate Strategy and Leadership

In summary, this section has reviewed the second of three components of the national talent system in Canada. They are the core processes and functions which interact with the national talent environment to leverage the competitiveness and stability of the national context by ongoing investment in the attraction, development and engagement of talent, both domestic and foreign, to contribute to economic and social development. The following section reviews the third component of MTM in Canada and finds that macro talent outcomes are largely supportive of Canada's social, economic and political aspirations.

Outcomes and Consequences of MTM in Canada

This section reviews the third and final component of MTM in Canada: outcomes of the macro talent system. Systems theory (Boulding, 1956) would explain that the macro talent management system produces outcomes which, when measured, generally consider the extent to which a system has been productive and effective (Von Bertalanffy, 1972). The MTM system specifies outcomes as first-level and second-level outcomes (Khilji et al., 2015). In the case of talent systems specifically, the literature tends to consider the effectiveness of the talent system (King, 2015) as its effective attraction, development, deployment and retention of talent. Talent systems are expected to be effective in the ongoing development of human capital (King, 2015) which is argued to be a predictor of firm performance through differentiated firm resources (Boudreau & Cascio, 2017). In the case of macro talent systems, effectiveness is expected at the national level. At the national level then, a country's establishment of a brand for the development of human capital for business advantage would be expected to be a distinct national competitive advantage. This advantage has in part been illustrated by the various competitive outcome rankings of counties described earlier. This section reviews the first- and second-level outcomes of the Canadian macro talent management system, resulting from the interaction of the Canadian macro talent context and environment together with core processes and functions. Table 2.3, presents a summary of the key macro talent outcomes in Canada.

First Level Outcomes

Educational Attainment in Canada

Canada has a highly educated population, as evidenced by OECD ranking of countries based on educational attainment levels (defined as the highest level of education which is achieved by an individual) (OECD, 2014a). Of note, Canada's youth rank above OECD average for foundation skills development, which is a prerequisite for higher education success (OECD, 2014a) and score significantly above the OECD average in mathematics (OECD, 2014a). Overall, Canada's educational system generates outcomes above OECD average as measured by each of three performance dimensions: science, mathematics and reading (OECD, 2012). The language and technical skills of the Canadian workforce are recognised to be exceptionally strong, each ranked at 2nd, along with the quality of local managers which is ranked 3rd amongst the ranked list of countries in the Global Talent Index 2015 (Economist Intelligence Unit, 2011). Overall, the Canadian educational system is assessed as of competitively high quality, ranked 5th of 61 countries for the quality of its educational system (IMD, 2016). Additionally, management recruitment and education practices in Canada result in having competent senior managers readily available (ranked 9th and 15th respectively, of 61 countries ranked) (IMD, 2016) to support emerging and developing talent in Canadian workplaces.

Table 2.3 Macro Talent Management in Canada: Outcomes at the National Level

Macro talent management component			Ranking	Source
Outcomes and Consequences	Business and Investment	Canada—Top 10 Best Countries for Business	10th of 139	Forbes (2016)
		Toronto—Top 20 Cities in the World	17th of 128	A.T. Kearney 2017
		Ease of Doing Business With Canada	22nd of 190	World Bank (2017)
	Talent Attraction and People	Canada's Attractiveness for Talent	12th of 61	IMD (2016)
		Global Talent Competitive Index	13th of 118	INSEAD, et al. (2017).
		Canada—Top 10 for Talent	8th of 60	(Economist Intelligence Unit 2015)
		Canada—Top 3 for Expats	3rd of 45	HSBC (2016)
		People-Specific Pillar of Ranking	16th of 102	WEF (2017)
	Financial and Political	Participation in International Capital Flows	13th of 85	
		GDP per Capita	16th of 140	
		Press Freedom (high)	8th of 137	
		Financial Freedom (high)	3rd of 136	
		Perception of Corruption (low)	9th of 176	Corruption (2016)
	Capability, Knowledge, and Workforce Readiness	Global Knowledge Skills	16th of 118	INSEAD, et al. (2017).
		Preparedness of Students	4th Highest	PISA (2015)
		Labour Market Efficiency	8th of 138	WEF (2017)
		Linguistic Commonality	6th of 140	WEF (2017)
		Labour Freedom	31st of 140	
	Technology, Innovation and Security	Technological Readiness	21st of 138	WEF (2017)
		Innovation	24th of 138	
		Cybersecurity Capability and Competitive Positioning	4th Globally	Deloitte (2016)
		Canada's Connectedness for Global Business	30th of 140	WEF (2017)

Jobs and Employment in Canada

Employment in Canada in 2017 indicates strong employment with an unemployment rate of 5.7%, its lowest rate in over 40 years (Statistics Canada 2018), a rate which is lower than the OECD average. (OECD, 2017a). The work environment is seen to demonstrate high levels of worker motivation and one which demonstrates that attracting and retaining talent is a priority in Canadian companies (IMD, 2016). Foreign talent contribute strongly to Canada's economy through employment and Canada's ability to attract foreign talent is high, ranked at 11 of 61 countries globally (IMD, 2016). Remuneration in the service professions ranks relatively highly in Canada at 11th position of 61 countries assessed (IMD, 2016). Unfortunately, as with other advanced economies, there still exists a gender pay gap such that the gap between the earnings of men and women in Canada is larger than the OECD average (OECD, 2016a). While relatively very highly ranked, at 15th of 188 countries with regard to gender pay gap (INSEAD et al., 2017), this gap persists and is viewed as a constraint to growth by Canadian business leadership. If unresolved, such gaps can become associated with long-term economic limitations as it diminishes the ability of women to save financially (Grant, 2017). Positively however, this earnings gap narrows as educational attainment increases and Canada has been steadily closing the gap over the past 2 decades (OECD, 2016a). Personal disposable income per capita in Canada is rather competitive, ranked as 6th of 61 countries in the Global Talent Index (Heidrick & Struggles, 2015) and is a fundamental factor in the quality of life enjoyed by Canadians in direct recognition of their contribution of skills and motivation as part of Canada's national workforce. However, personal income tax rates in Canada are relatively higher than those of peer countries in the G7, with Canada ranked only as 31st of 61 countries (IMD, 2016). This relatively high rate of personal income tax may be a limitation to Canada in future as global talent competitiveness increases. Overall, Canada's labour market is seen as strongly efficient, ranked as 8th of 138 countries assessed (Schwab & Sala-i-Martín, 2016b) which contributes to the higher than OECD average satisfaction levels which Canadians report when asked to rate their general satisfaction with life (OECD, 2016b).

Talent Mobility

Canada's macro talent system works effectively to attract and hire foreign nationals into the national workforce and is internationally competitive in doing so, as indicated by its ranking of 13th among nations assessed (Heidrick & Struggles, 2015). Canada's intake of talent from abroad includes a high proportion of master's and doctoral graduates (Statistics Canada 2000). This is consistent with the 2016 IMD World Talent Report findings that highly-skilled foreign talent are attracted to Canada's business environment such that Canada ranked 11th of 61 countries globally in its ability to attract foreign highly-skilled talent (IMD, 2016).

Canada supports the within-country migration of skilled workers between provinces and territories in order to support the macro talent system functioning within Canada nationally. Interprovincial mobility processes are used to allow migration of individuals who hold trades, technology and professional qualifications to allow both individual talent and businesses to utilise registered credentials in any province or territory. This has supported both the timely access of Canadian industry to the qualified talent they require and Canadian citizens in their career mobility within Canada.

Canada's talent is mobile internationally and demand for this mobility is generated both within Canada and externally. Valuing the international experience of Canadian talent (Government of Canada, 2017j), the Canadian government offers support to Canadian citizens who wish to travel and work abroad. The International Experience Canada (IEC) program facilitates access to international work experience for Canadians through expedited flexible visa access agreements with the national governments of more than 30 other countries globally (Government of Canada, 2017j). Canadian talent is also in demand globally, driven in part by the recognition of educational quality, educational attainment of Canadians and the globally-oriented mind-set and values of Canadians. There are many examples of Canadian top talent invited into international roles, whether in the public, private or not-for-profit sectors.

Diaspora Utilisation

The Canadian diaspora presents a significant and largely untapped opportunity to Canada. The Canadian diaspora is Canada's expatriate population and includes all Canadian citizens living abroad and all dual passport holders, as defined by Global Affairs Canada, the department which oversees foreign affairs, trade and development, By 2007, Canadians living abroad numbered approximately 8.3% of the population of 2.7 million, which is considerably higher than the global average, according to a poll conducted by the Asia Pacific Foundation of Canada in 2007 (Zhang, 2007), with a recent estimated diaspora of 9% in 2017. Canadians abroad actively maintain and develop ties with Canada, whether abroad (such as through participation in bilateral chambers of commerce or social organisations; access to media about Canada) or through a high relative frequency of visits home to Canada (for work, family reasons or leisure) (Zhang, 2007). Analysis suggests there are multiple opportunities with regard to Canada's diaspora which include potential to increase Canada's competitiveness in global markets through facilitating trade links and championing the awareness of Canada's values and culture (Zhang, 2007). Recent research on the potential risks and opportunities which exist with regard to Canada's diaspora points to key strategic questions for the Government of Canada to consider such as how to strategically engage and interact with its diaspora (Welsh, 2011). The findings of a simple search of the Global Affairs Canada website readily point to Canada's intention to collaborate with the many foreign diasporas which collectively reside in Canada, however there is limited indication of a current focus on Canada's own diaspora. This primary focus on facilitating the support of incoming diasporas is a further positive indicator of Canada's inclusive national culture and closely held value of diversity. Canada's own diaspora worldwide may represent an important strategic and inimitable human capital resource to Canada as one component within its overall macro talent management system. Lack of readily available detailed analysis of Canada's diaspora (Statistics Canada 2014) may indicate that Canada's global diaspora is overlooked currently, a concern raised in recent literature (Welsh, 2011).

Second Level Outcomes

Talent Rankings/ Country Attractiveness

As introduced throughout this chapter, there are several cross-national indices of country level competitiveness which measure indicators related to the macro talent management system of a given country, including measures of context and environment, processes and functions and outcomes of competitiveness, both overall and with specific regard to talent. These published indices include: the World Economic Forum (WEF) Global Competitiveness Report 2016–2017 (Schwab & Sala-i-Martín, 2016b), the Economist's Global Talent Index (GTI) 2011–2015 published by Heidrick & Struggles (Heidrick & Struggles, 2015), IMD World Talent Report 2016 (IMD, 2016), the INSEAD Global Talent Competitiveness Index (GTCI) (INSEAD et al., 2017), and the World Bank Doing Business Index WorldBankGroup (2017). Each of these indices make observations about the outcomes of the macro talent management system in regards to Canada and report indicators of the extent to which the macro talent system is functioning for a given country, in this case Canada. For example, these indicators include assessment of a country's ability to enable, attract, grow and, retain talent; educational and workforce quality outcomes; and national attractiveness and competitiveness outcomes such as the extent of financial market development and the country's capability for innovation and readiness for technological advancement. As with any functional system whereby the outcomes influence the overall system via a feedback loop, these macro talent management and overall national country level outcomes are then argued to subsequently influence the strength of the context and environment of the macro talent system as it evolves.

Productivity

Canada's industry and workforce nationally are strong producers of national output, as measured in gross domestic product (GDP). Canada is ranked 16th globally in a study of 140 countries for its output of GDP per capita (DHL, 2016).

Innovation

Canada has been recognised as an innovator amongst international peers historically including the contribution of several key scientific discoveries and inventions to modern civilisation; such as notable invention of medicinal insulin by Banting, Best and Collip in 1922. Canadian inventors have also made contributions in technologies, such as the Blackberry smartphone, invented by Research in Motion Technologies in 1999 and the IMAX movie system developed in 1968 by Ferguson, Kroitor, and Kerr; and in sports, such as the sport basketball, a national favourite of Canada's neighbours in the United States, which was invented by Canadian James Naismith in 1891; and the ever-relied upon and often hotly-debated "instant replay" of film coverage of live sports in action, created in 1955 for Hockey Night in Canada©, the national Canadian hockey television program. In modern times, as the pace of innovation increases and the spread of technologies is inevitable (WEF, 2016), Canada's industry and business sectors recognise innovation as a key component of sustainable business as innovation drives growth and competitive advantage (Conference Board Canada, 2015) although some analysis indicates that the capacity for innovation within Canada varies by province with the strongest measures of innovation indicated in the province of Ontario (Conference Board Canada, 2015).

One outcome which indicates Canada's active development and innovation to participate in the global economy is the recognition of Toronto, one of Canada's major cities, located in the province of Ontario, which has been identified within the top 20 cities globally, at the position of 17th, by A.T. Kearney which ranks the world's cities in terms of their importunateness to the global economy based on their performance as a city according to a set of identified factors (A.T. Kearney, 2017).

Of particular note is Canada's ranking of 3rd of 85 countries ranked in the Global Connectedness Index (DHL, 2016), for information related measures including internet usership and bandwidth (DHL, 2016). As information is crucial to the knowledge-dependent ability to innovate, this recognised capability is expected to be highly relevant to Canada's future performance in technical and information-related sectors.

Canada's Competitiveness as a Country and Economic Development Outcomes

As with measures of a country's competitiveness and positioning for talent specifically, the multiple cross-national indices introduced in this chapter also provide overall levels of country competitiveness, which can be seen as second level outcomes of the country's macro systems, including some degree of contribution to that degree of competitiveness by the country's macro talent management system. These overall measures consider a range of factors as introduced in this chapter, including institutors, infrastructure, the macroeconomic environment, a country's technological readiness and innovation capability and the degree of development of their business structures and financial markets. Measures also investigate the extent of which there is press freedom and perceptions of corruption, which, in the case of Canada, are noted as high (press freedom) and low (perceptions of corruption).

Canada is recognised as one of the world's best places to do business, ranked 10th in the world of 139 countries assessed by Forbes in their 2016 report Best Countries for Business (Forbes, 2016). Consistent with this highly competitive standing are other rankings of Canada as 15th of 138 countries overall by the Economic Forum's Global Competitiveness Report (Schwab & Sala-i-Martín, 2016b), 13th of 188 countries reviewed in INSEAD's Global Talent Competitiveness Index 2017 (INSEAD et al., 2017), 22nd of 190 countries as reported in the World Bank's Doing Business Report (WorldBankGroup, 2017), and 12th of 61 countries as reported by IMD in the World Talent Report 2016 (IMD, 2016). In aggregate, the evidence from independent global rankings of Canada's positioning for overall readiness and competitiveness for future economic growth and attraction of talent to meet business and national requirements for organisational talent presents a positive national talent profile. Figure 2.4 presents a mini-case example of an MTM outcome: Economic Development and Competitiveness.

This section has reviewed the outcomes of macro talent management in Canada, resulting from the interaction of the national talent context and environment, together with the nation's core processes and functions for management of talent. The next and final section discusses opportunities for further development of MTM in Canada, after which the chapter is concluded.

Canada's cybersecurity sector ranked 4th in the world

Context

Cybersecurity risk has been identified as one of the top 4 commercial risks facing global businesses and society, along with geopolitical, environmental and economic risk, according to the World Economic Forum's Global Risk 2016 report (WEF, 2016).

Over the past several decades, together with the Government of Ontario, Canada together with its high-tech sector businesses have established a hub for emerging technologies development in the region known as the Toronto-Waterloo corridor in the province of Ontario. An early example of success was Research in Motion Technologies (RIM) which invented and launched the BlackBerry in 1999, an early leader in smart-phone technologies.

Activity

Following continuing sector-specific investment, today in Ontario approximately half of Canada's IT professionals work in the 20,000 IT firms based in the region such that the "Toronto and Kitchener-Waterloo regions are largely considered two of the largest start-up ecosystems in the world" (Ontario Investment, 2016).

Outcomes

Resulting from the world-class talent and expertise amassed in Canada's cybersecurity sector, the sector is now competitively ranked 4th in the world (Deloitte, 2016), for its demonstrated ability to attract venture capital deals and competitive positioning as a global hub for cybersecurity innovation, a sector predicted to grow 10% annually through 2020 (Deloitte, 2016).

Figure 2.4 Mini-Case: Canadian MTM Outcomes: Example of Economic Development and Competitiveness

Discussion

Limitations of This Review

This chapter has presented a review of talent management in Canada at the national level, illustrated by the Khilji et al. (2015) framework of MTM. While the framework is a helpful guide for the reader in considering MTM for a given country, further development of the framework is required to explain the interactions between the three components of MTM as theorised by Khilji et al. (2015) and to empirically examine the combined influences of national context with processes and functions in generating macro talent outcomes. Further clarification of the core components is also called for in order to further specify the model and its interactive components and to reduce current conflation of sub-factors in each. For example, macro talent outcomes such as high levels of educational achievement in the domestic talent pool may indeed also be considered as aspects of the current labour pool composition, a macro talent contextual factor.

Opportunities for Macro Talent Management in Canada

Overall, this chapter has provided evidence of the strength of Canada's positioning globally, in terms of both overall country competitiveness and competitiveness for talent. This review has illustrated the largely effective interaction of the Canadian MTM context with its MTM core processes and functions and associated this with high quality MTM outcomes such as competitiveness for talent, productivity and innovation-driven growth. While there is some evidence of effectiveness of the Canadian MTM system currently, opportunities for further improvement exist. Five opportunities are described next.

Accelerated National Labour Force Development and Growth

While Canada's labour force is recognised to be of high quality, such as in measures of language skills, technical skills and local management support (Heidrick & Struggles, 2015), labour force growth, as measured in percentage change in labour force size could be stronger to enable accelerated economic growth. Canada achieves a ranking of only 32nd of 61 countries in the IMD Global talent report 2016 (IMD, 2016) and only 33 of 60 countries in the Economist Global Talent Index (Heidrick & Struggles, 2015). As labour force growth rate is related to growth in trade and growth in national GDP and growth in overall availability of jobs, this presents an opportunity for improvement. However despite this potential limitation, Canada ranks exceptionally well in the Top 10 Countries for Global Talent (Heidrick & Struggles, 2015). Increasing engagement of Canada's diverse Indigenous Peoples and communities in the development of talent and opportunities for economic growth is a crucial component of the development of Canada's macro talent workforce and of Canada's unique and diverse talent pools.

Ease of Doing Business

Canada is recognised as one of the Top 10 Best Countries for Business (Forbes, 2016) and Toronto as one of the global Top 20 Cities in the World (A.T. Kearney, 2017). Canada and Canadian businesses undertake significant efforts to prevent corruption, associated with a reputation for very low perceived corruption (International, 2016). However, executives surveyed in Canada in the World Economic Forum Executive Opinion survey 2016 perceive insufficient capacity to innovate and inefficient government bureaucracy as the two factors most problematic for doing business (Schwab & Sala-i-Martín, 2016a). Addressing perceived or actual barriers to efficient business management practices could further enable Canada's ability to leverage economic development opportunities without undue constraints.

Personal Income

While Canada's quality of living is relatively very high and Canadians report life satisfaction more often on average than in all other OECD countries in the OCED's Better Life Index 2016 (OECD, 2016b), two factors may impact personal income. First, the effective rate of personal income tax is not highly competitive, ranking only 31st of 61 countries (IMD, 2016). Second, a gender pay gap, persisting in many countries worldwide, still remains unresolved in Canada. However, there are positive indicators that the pay gap is narrowing notably with increasing educational attainment in Canada (OECD, 2016a).

Innovation

Canada is recognised as strongly competitive for innovation (24th of 138), technical readiness (21st of 138) (Schwab & Sala-i-Martín, 2016b), and global connectedness (16th of 102) (DHL, 2016). The mini-cases presented examples of Canada's strategic sector-specific investment in technologies and talent (Ontario's investment as a cybersecurity hub; Alberta's investment in artificial intelligence). However a focused study by the Conference Board of Canada of a select group of only 16 peer advanced nations found that innovation varied by province and could be improved (Conference Board Canada, 2015; Schwab & Sala-i-Martín, 2016b). Increased industrial and government investment in innovation-focused development may offer talent attraction and development opportunities for future competitive advantage in Canada.

Canada's Worldwide Diaspora

Canada welcomes and values incoming diaspora from other nations as a long-standing and valued practice. However, a defined strategic position with regard to its own global diaspora of Canadians may, importantly, be overlooked or undefined. Active engagement of Canada's own diaspora could leverage economic and social opportunities for Canada's continuing development. (Economist, 2011; Welsh, 2011; Zhang, 2007). Table 2.4 summarises the five opportunities for further MTM effectiveness.

Table 2.4 Macro Talent Management: Opportunities for Canada

Facilitate accelerated growth of the national labour force
Further facilitate the "ease of doing business"
Further enable innovation-driven growth
Enable personal income growth
(via tax structures, gender pay gap)
Actively engage Canada's worldwide diaspora
(highly skilled, globally-experienced Canadian talent)

Implications for Stakeholders of the Canadian Macro Talent Management System

Following from the MTM opportunities presented previously, recommendations emerge for three central stakeholders of Canada's macro talent system, presented as follows.

Policy Makers

Given the ambiguity in global economies and the international political context, analysts identify that the future of today's global economy "depends critically on the choices of policymakers around the world" (DHL, 2016). This chapter's review sheds light on the importance of facilitating Canada's continued leadership in economic development nationally and globally and opportunities to reinforce Canada's investment in talent and innovation-driven economic development. For example, expanding investments in sector-specific capabilities such as cybersecurity, artificial intelligence and deep learning have the potential to accelerate Canada's continued competitive economic and social development while also building new dimensions within Canada's global "talent" brand in future. This chapter has presented only a few examples.

To facilitate the effectiveness and efficiency of Canada's MTM system going forward, four streams of enquiry are proposed for policy makers: First, what MTM context and environmental factors, if considered over time, may be indicators of ineffective long term trends which require nearer-term public policy intervention at a national level to mitigate future talent risk? Second, how can MTM core processes and functions be future-proofed to ensure the Canadian macro talent management system continues to adapt flexibly as global and national conditions and requirements change, to ensure Canada's ability to attract, develop and retain the talent Canada's advanced economy requires? Third, to what extent is Canada securing the talent needed for Canada's continued competitive positioning tomorrow and what current limitations can be used to inform future national planning to proactively sustain and further develop Canada's country competitiveness? Finally, how can Canada proactively engage its global diaspora to invest in Canada's future?

Organisations

Business leaders and executive management must consider how best to lead organisational talent management strategy and practices within the context of Canada's macro talent system while also seeking opportunities to nudge and influence the macro system to ensure it is positioned to generate the talent outcomes their businesses and Canada as a nation will benefit from. Management must reinvest in their capacity to lead and manage innovation (Conference Board Canada, 2015), continue to champion the diversity that has become so deeply valued as "Canada's advantage" (Trudeau, 2015) and to build on the national reputation for cultural fairness and inclusion which Canada is known for. Management's continued investment in Canada's global, regional and inter-organisational relationships, through which talented individuals, knowledge and ideas flow can create national future talent advantage. Collaboration across groups of stakeholders, such as regional groups of Canadian organisations, established with an aim to attract business to a specific region, may create shared benefit or distinct macro talent advantages.

Individuals

Individuals learning and developing their talent and skills in Canada's technical schools or universities and in today's Canadian workforces, each have an opportunity to contribute to the future of Canada's performance and development. Understanding how their talent and career aspirations can contribute to Canada's economic future is a micro-foundation of Canada's ability to innovate and create growth. Encouraging diversity of all types in work places and work teams, is an important path to innovation and growth, while maintaining Canada's advantage of diversity and inclusion. Finally, talented individuals who belong to Canada's own vast global diaspora each have an opportunity to consider how best to contribute their individual talent and international experience to Canada's continuing innovation-driven economic development for the benefit of Canadian business, culture and society in future years.

Future Research Directions

To deepen our understanding of the Canadian MTM system, three research priorities aligned to the three core MTM components are identified. First, as a "net talent importer" country, Canada is heavily reliant on a long standing set of high quality and effective immigration programs and the national, regional and local cultures which help make Canada home to new Canadians. Analysis of the effectiveness of Canada's macro talent context and institutional support for talent (both domestic and foreign incoming) is warranted to facilitate ongoing competitive talent environment for Canada at the national level. Second, assessment of the fit and functionality of Canada's current MTM processes and functions to continue to grow talent, enable high performance, offer competitive career opportunities and enable innovation-driven economic growth through talent and knowledge could inform further definition and refinement of processes. Third, analysis of the composition and global dispersion of the Canadian global diaspora could offer insight as to opportunities to engage and mobilise the diaspora for Canada's strategic advantage. Overall, a more defined strategic conceptualisation of MTM in Canada is warranted to plan forward to enable innovation-driven economic growth for Canada and Canadian organisations well into the future.

Chapter Conclusion

This chapter presented a review of talent management in Canada at the country level. Three core components of MTM in Canada were reviewed: the macro Canadian environment and context; functions and processes that influence MTM in Canada; and the outcomes of MTM in Canada. Five opportunities were presented for further enhancing the effectiveness of macro talent management in Canada, along with recommendations for key stakeholders.

Canada continues to be a strong champion and investor in talent and its development, both domestic and incoming international talent, in aspiration of desired outcomes for individuals, for companies and for the nation. Given the quality of macro talent outcomes which have been achieved, Canada and its cities have been recognised in their competitiveness and attractiveness in rankings globally as being a "place for talent". It appears that Canada and indeed its citizens are committed to the established national value of and investment in talent and diversity as the nation looks to the future. There are opportunities for Canada to continue to shape effective macro talent management and by doing so, Canada could further enable the effectiveness of talent management at the organisational level, which is an investment in the best interests of individuals, business and communities in Canada through the nation's continued innovation-driven economic development.

References

Alberta. (2017). Helping Indigenous students succeed in school [Press release]. Retrieved from www.alberta.ca/release.cfm?xID=483422FD516B3-F7CC-A9DD-ACAF8AA5918A2963.

Alfes, K., Truss, C., Soane, E. C., Rees, C., & Gatenby, M. (2013). The relationship between line manager behavior, perceived HRM practices, and individual performance: Examining the mediating role of engagement. *Human Resource Management, 52*(6), 839–859. doi:10.1002/hrm.21512.

A. T. Kearney. (2016). A.T. Kearney's Global Cities Report 2016. Retrieved from: www.atkearney.co.uk/documents/10192/8178456/Global+Cities+2016.pdf/8139cd44-c760-4a93-ad7d-11c5d347451a.

A. T. Kearney. (2017). A.T. Kearney's Global Cities Report 2017. Retrieved from: www.atkearney.com/global-cities/full-report.

Bartlett, C., & Ghoshal, S. (1986). Tap your subsidiaries for global reach. *Harvard Business Review, 64*(6), 87–94.

BBC. (2016, October 30). *Ceta: EU and Canada sign long-delayed free trade deal*. Retrieved from www.bbc.co.uk/news/world-europe-37814884.

Boudreau, J., & Cascio, W. (2017). Human capital analytics: Why are we not there? *Journal of Organizational Effectiveness: People and Performance, 4*(2). doi:10.1108/JOEPP-03-2017-0021.

Boulding, K. E. (1956). General systems theory: The skeleton of science. *Management Science, 2*(3), 197–208. doi:10.1287/mnsc.2.3.197.

Canada. (2017). *Prime Minister concludes successful week at the United Nations General Assembly* [Press release]. Retrieved from pm.gc.ca/eng/news/2017/09/21/prime-minister-concludes-successful-week-united-nations-general-assembly?utm_source=pm_eng&utm_medium=carousel_Can_ca&utm_campaign=UNGA.

Bank of England (2013). Governor of the Bank of England: Her Majesty the Queen has been pleased to approve the appointment of Mark Carney as Governor of the Bank of England from 1 July 2013. [Press release].

Conference Board Canada (2002). *Solving the skilled trades shortage: A feasibility report examining the barriers and solutions to youth participation in the skilled trades in Canada and proposing the development of pilot projects to increase the supply of youth into the skilled trades.* Canada. Retrieved from www.conferenceboard.ca/Libraries/EDUC_PUBLIC/Skilled_trades.sflb.

Conference Board Canada (2015). *How Canada performs.* Toronto, Canada. Retrieved from www.conferenceboard.ca/hcp/provincial/innovation.aspx.

Conference Board Canada (2017). *Conference board of Canada.* Retrieved from www.conferenceboard.ca/about-cboc/default.aspx.

Cappelli, P. (2008). Talent management for the twenty-first century. *Harvard Business Review, 86*(3), 74–81.

Cappelli, P. (2013). HR for neophytes. *Harvard Business Review, 91*(10), 25–27.

CityAir News, (2017). *The launching of Alberta school curriculum academic session 2017–18* [Press release]. Retrieved from cityairnews.com/content/launching-alberta-school-curriculum-academic-session-2017-18.

Collings, D. G. (2014). Toward mature talent management: Beyond shareholder value. *Human Resource Development Quarterly, 25*(3), 301–319. doi:10.1002/hrdq.21198.

Commonwealth, (2017). *About us.* Retrieved from thecommonwealth.org/about-us.

DeepMind. (2017). *DeepMind expands to Canada with new research office in Edmonton, Alberta* [Press release]. Retrieved from deepmind.com/blog/deepmind-office-canada-edmonton/.

Deloitte. (2014). *Diversity and inclusion in Canada: The current state 2014.* Retrieved from www2.deloitte.com/content/dam/Deloitte/ca/Documents/human-capital/ca-en-human-capital-diversity-and-Inclusion-in-canada.pdf.

Deloitte. (2016). *Harnessing the cybersecurity opportunity for growth. Cybersecurity innovation & the financial services industry in Ontario.* Retrieved from www.tfsa.ca/storage/reports/CyberInnovationReport2016.pdf.

Derry, K., & Douglas, P. H. (1922). The minimum wage in Canada. *Journal of Political Economy, 30*(2), 155–188.

DHL. (2016). *Global connectedness index 2016: The state of globalization in an age of ambiguity.* Bonn, Germany. Retrieved from www.dhl.com/en/about_us/logistics_insights/studies_research/global_connectedness_index/global_connectedness_index.html#.VvgijfkrJ1N.

Dries, N., & Pepermans, R. (2012). How to identify leadership potential: Development and testing of a consensus model. *Human Resource Management, 51*(3), 361–385. doi:10.1002/hrm.21473.

Economist Intelligence Unit. (2011). *The global talent index report: The outlook to 2015.* Chicago, IL: Heidrick & Struggles.

Economist Intelligence Unit. (2015). The global talent index report: The outlook to 2015. Chicago, IL: Heidrick & Struggles.

Economist. (2011, November 19). The magic of diasporas. *The Economist*.
Economist. (2017, July 12). Why Europe needs more migrants. *The Economist*. Retrieved from www.economist.com/blogs/graphicdetail/2017/07/daily-chart-6.
First Nations, Assembly of (2017). *About the assembly of First Nations*. Retrieved from www.afn.ca/home/.
Forbes. (2016). *Best countries for business 2016*. New York, USA. Retrieved from www.forbes.com/best-countries-for-business/list/#tab:overall.
GlobeProject. (2004). *Global leadership & organizational behavior effectiveness: Canada findings 2004*. Vancouver, Canada. Retrieved from globeproject.com/results/countries/CAN?menu=list.
Government of Canada (2011). First Nations people in Canada: Indigenous and northern affairs Canada. Retrieved from www.canada.ca/en/indigenous-northern-affairs.html.
Government of Canada (2017a). Canada's express entry system. Government of Canada. Retrieved from www.cic.gc.ca/english/immigrate/skilled/index.asp.
Government of Canada (2017b). Canada's health care system. Government of Canada. Retrieved from www.canada.ca/en/health-canada/services/health-care-system/reports-publications/health-care-system/canada.html.
Government of Canada (2017c). Canada's Red Seal Program: Support for apprentices. Retrieved from www.canada.ca/en/employment-social-development/services/apprentices.html.
Government of Canada. (2017d). Canada and the G7. Ottawa, Canada: Government of Canada. Retrieved from international.gc.ca/world-monde/international_relations-relations_internationales/g7/index.aspx?lang=eng.
Government of Canada. (2017e). Canada to host 2018 G7 Summit in Charlevoix, Quebec [Press release]. Retrieved from pm.gc.ca/eng/news/2017/05/27/canada-host-2018-g7-summit-charlevoix-quebec.
Government of Canada (2017f). International Experience Canada Program (IEC): Travel and work in Canada. Retrieved from www.cic.gc.ca/english/work/iec/index.asp.
Government of Canada (2017g). Jobs and the workplace. Retrieved from www.canada.ca/en/services/jobs.html.
Government of Canada. (2017i). Permanent mission of Canada to the United Nations. Ottawa, Canada: Government of Canada. Retrieved from www.international.gc.ca/prmny-mponu/index.aspx?lang=eng.
Government of Canada. (2017j). Work and travel abroad: International Experience Canada (IEC). Ottawa, Canada: Government of Canada.
Grant, T. (2017, March 6). *Gender equality. Who is minding the gap?* Retrieved from: www.theglobeandmail.com/news/national/gender-pay-gap-a-persistent-issue-in-canada/article34210790/.
Guest, D., & Conway, N. (2011). The impact of HR practices, HR effectiveness and a 'strong HR system' on organisational outcomes: A stakeholder perspective. *The International Journal of Human Resource Management*, 22(8), 1686–1702. doi:10.1080/09585192.2011.565657.
Heidrick, & Struggles. (2015). *The global talent index report: The outlook to 2015*. Retrieved from www.globaltalentindex.com/pdf/Heidrick_Struggles_Global_Talent_Report.pdf.
HSBC. (2016). *HSBC expat explorer survey*. Retrieved from www.expatexplorer.hsbc.com/survey/.
IMD. (2015). IMD World Talent Report 2015. Lausanne, Switzerland: IMD Business School. World Competitiveness Center.
IMD. (2016). *IMD world talent report 2016*. Lausanne, Switzerland. Retrieved from www.imd.org/globalassets/wcc/docs/talent_2016_web.pdf.
Mediacorp (2017a). Canada's Best Diversity Employers 2017. Toronto, Canada: Mediacorp Canada Inc.
Mediacorp (2017b). CANADA'S TOP 100 EMPLOYERS 2017. Toronto, Canada: Mediacorp Canada Inc.
INSEAD, Adecco, & HCLI. (2017). *INSEAD Global Talent Competitiveness Index (GTCI) 2017: Talent and technology*. Retrieved from www.insead.edu/global-indices/gtci.
International, T. (2016). *Corruptions perceptions index 2016*. Berlin, Germany. Retrieved from www.transparency.org/news/feature/corruption_perceptions_index_2016.
Javidan, M., Dorfman, P. W., De Luque, M. S., & House, R. J. (2006). In the eye of the beholder: Cross cultural lessons in leadership from project GLOBE. *Academy of Management Perspectives*, 20(1), 67–90. doi:10.5465/amp.2006.19873410.
Khilji, S. E., Tarique, I., & Schuler, R. S. (2015). Incorporating the macro view in global talent management. *Human Resource Management Review*, 25(3), 236–248. doi:10.1016/j.hrmr.2015.04.001.
King, K. A. (2015). Global talent management: Introducing a strategic framework and multiple-actors model. *Journal of Global Mobility: The Home of Expatriate Management Research*, 3(3), 273–288. doi:10.1108/JGM-02-2015-0002.
King, K. A. (2016). The talent deal and journey: Understanding how employees respond to talent identification over time. *Employee Relations*, 38(1), 94–111. doi:10.1108/ER-07-2015-0155.
Lanvin, B., Evans, P., & Rodriguez-Montemayor, E. (2016). *Attracting and mobilising talent globally and locally*. Fontainebleau. Retrieved from.

Lee, A. (2017, January 18). *Can RBC help stop Canada's brain drain in deep learning?* MacLeans.ca. Retrieved from www.macleans.ca/society/technology/can-rbc-help-stop-canadas-brain-drain-in-deep-learning/.

MLT Aikins (2017). Anti-Corruption Regulation in Canada: Why It Matters for Your Business. Retrieved from doi: www.lexology.com/library/detail.aspx?g=2fd007d9-f60d-4e5a-bdf2-ecde94f7f5a4.

Globe (2017). Changing history: Canada indigenous education. *Globe and Mail*. Retrieved from beta.theglobeandmail.com/news/national/education/history-canada-indigenous-education/article36157403/?ref=www.theglobeandmail.com&.

McBride, J., & Aly Sergie, M. (2017). *NAFTA's economic impact*. New York, USA. Retrieved from www.cfr.org/about.

McDermott, A. M., Conway, E., Rousseau, D. M., & Flood, P. C. (2013). Promoting effective psychological contracts through leadership: The missing link between HR strategy and performance. *Human Resource Management, 52*(2), 289–310. doi:10.1002/hrm.21529.

Milne, E. (2017). Implementing Indigenous Education Policy Directives in Ontario Public Schools: Experiences, Challenges and Successful Practices. The International Indigenous Policy Journal, 8(3), 2.

Mitacs. (2017). *Mitacs builds partnerships between academia, industry, and the world: To create a more innovative Canada*. Retrieved from www.mitacs.ca/en/about-mitacs.

Murphy, J. (2017, March 29). *Vector Institute is just the latest in Canada's AI expansion*. Retrieved from www.bbc.co.uk/news/world-us-canada-39425862.

Naylor, C. D. (2017). *Canada's fundamental science review: Final report: Investing in Canada's future: Strengthening the foundations of Canadian research*. Ottawa, Canada. Retrieved from www.sciencereview.ca/eic/site/059.nsf/eng/home.

Nishii, L. H. (2013). The benefits of climate for inclusion for gender-diverse groups. *Academy of Management Journal, 56*(6), 1754–1774. doi:10.5465/amj.2009.0823.Nye, J. S. (2009). Soft Power: The Means To Success In World Politics. New York, NY, USA.: Public Affairs.

OECD. (2012). *The ABC of gender equality in education: Aptitude, behaviour, confidence*. Retrieved from www.oecd.org/pisa/publications/pisa-2012-results-gender.htm.

OECD. (2014a). *Canada: Education at a glance: OECD indicators 2014*. Paris, France. Retrieved from www.oecd.org/edu/Canada-EAG2014-Country-Note.pdf.

OECD. (2014b). *Private spending on education*. oecd.org. Retrieved from data.oecd.org/eduresource/private-spending-on-education.htm#indicator-chart.

OECD. (2014c). *Public spending on education*. oecd.org. Retrieved from data.oecd.org/eduresource/public-spending-on-education.htm.

OECD. (2015a). *Consequences of corruption at the sector level and implications for economic growth and development*. Paris, France. Retrieved from www.oecd.org/publications/consequences-of-corruption-at-the-sector-level-and-implications-for-economic-growth-and-development-9789264230781-en.htm.

OECD. (2015b). *OECD health statistics 2015: At a glance*. Retrieved from www.oecd-ilibrary.org/social-issues-migration-health/health-at-a-glance-2015_health_glance-2015-en.

OECD. (2016a). *Canada: Overview of the education system (EAG 2016)*. Paris, France. Retrieved from gpseducation.oecd.org/CountryProfile?primaryCountry=CAN&treshold=10&topic=EO.

OECD. (2016b). *OECD better life index 2016: Canada*. oecd.org. Retrieved from data.oecd.org/eduresource/private-spending-on-education.htm#indicator-chart.

OECD. (2017a). *Employment database: Unemployment indicators*. Retrieved from www.oecd.org/els/emp/employmentdatabase-unemployment.htm.

OECD. (2017b). *OECD health statistics 2017*. Paris, France. Retrieved from www.oecd.org/els/health-systems/health-data.htm.

OECD. (2017c). The OECD Our Mission. 2017, from www.oecd.org/about/.

Ontario Investment. (2016). *Canada ranked 4th largest cybersecurity hub in the world*. Ontario, Canada: Queen's Printer for Ontario. Retrieved from www.investinontario.com/spotlights/canada-ranked-4th-largest-cybersecurity-hub-world.

Potter, E. H. (2009). Branding Canada: Projecting Canada's Soft Power Through Public Diplomacy. Kingston, Canada.: McGill-Queen's University Press.

Purcell, J., & Hutchinson, S. (2007). Front-line managers as agents in the HRM-performance causal chain: Theory, analysis and evidence. *Human Resource Management Journal, 17*(1), 3–20. doi:10.1111/j.1748-8583.2007.00022.x.

Schwab, K., & Sala-i-Martín, X. (2016a). *Executive opinion survey 2016, world economic forum global competitiveness report 2016–2017*. Geneva, Switzerland. Retrieved from www3.weforum.org/docs/GCR2016-2017/05FullReport/TheGlobalCompetitivenessReport2016-2017_FINAL.pdf.

Schwab, K., & Sala-i-Martín, X. (2016b). *The World Economic Forum global competitiveness report 2016–2017*. Geneva, Switzerland. Retrieved from www3.weforum.org/docs/GCR2016-2017/05FullReport/TheGlobal CompetitivenessReport2016-2017_FINAL.pdf.

Service, P. I. a. R. (2000). *Understanding the brain drain*. Parliamentary Information and Research Service. Retrieved from lop.parl.ca/Content/LOP/ResearchPublications/tips/tip5-e.htm.

Sikora, D. M., Ferris, G. R., & Van Iddekinge, C. H. (2015). Line manager implementation perceptions as a mediator of relations between high-performance work practices and employee outcomes. *Journal of Applied Psychology, 100*(6), 1908–1918. doi:10.1037/ap10000024.

Skills Canada. (2002). National skilled trades and technology week celebrates the history and importance of the skilled trades in Canada [Press release]. Retrieved from skillscompetencescanada.com/en/news-release/national-skilled-trades-technology-week-celebrates-history-importance-skilled-trades-canada/.

Statistics Canada. (2000). *Brain drain and brain gain: The migration of knowledge workers from and to Canada*. Retrieved from www.statcan.gc.ca/studies-etudes/81-003/feature-caracteristique/5018892-eng.pdf.

Statistics Canada. (2011a). *Aboriginal peoples in Canada: First nations people, Métis and Inuit*. Ottawa, Canada: Statistics Canada. Retrieved from www12.statcan.gc.ca/nhs-enm/2011/as-sa/99-011-x/99-011-x2011001-eng.cfm.

Statistics Canada. (2011b). *Immigration and ethnocultural diversity in Canada, National Household Survey (NHS)*. Ottawa, Canada: Statistics Canada. Retrieved from www12.statcan.gc.ca/nhs-enm/2011/as-sa/99-010-x/99-010-x2011001-eng.cfm.

Statistics Canada. (2011c). *Linguistic characteristics of Canadians*. Ottawa, Canada: Statistics Canada. Retrieved from www12.statcan.gc.ca/census-recensement/2011/as-sa/98-314-x/98-314-x2011001-eng.cfm.

Statistics Canada. (2012). *2012 Aboriginal Peoples Survey (APS)—Aboriginal peoples: Fact sheet for Canada*. Ottawa, Canada: Statistics Canada. Retrieved from www.statcan.gc.ca/pub/89-656-x/89-656-x2015001-eng.htm.

Statistics Canada (2014). *Canadians abroad*. Ottawa, Canada: Statistics Canada. Retrieved from www.statcan.gc.ca/pub/11-008-x/2008001/article/10517-eng.htm.

Statistics Canada. (2017). *Quarterly population estimate 2017*. Retrieved from www.statcan.gc.ca/eng/start.

Statistics Canada (2018). *Labour Force Survey*, December 2017. Retrieved from www.statcan.gc.ca/daily-quotidien/180105/dq180105a-eng.htm?HPA=1.

Strauss, K. (2017). Canada's Best Employers 2017. Forbes.com. Retrieved from Forbes.com website doi: www.forbes.com/sites/karstenstrauss/2017/02/08/canadas-best-employers-2017/#4c5282f922e2.

Tarique, I., & Schuler, R. S. (2010). Global talent management: Literature review, integrative framework, and suggestions for further research. *Journal of World Business, 45*(2), 122–133. doi:10.1016/j.jwb.2009.09.019.

Townsend, K., & Loudoun, R. (2015). The front-line manager's role in informal voice pathways. *Employee Relations, 37*(4), 475–486. doi:10.1108/ER-06-2014-0060.

Traxler, F., Blaschke, S., Kittel, B., & Publishing, E. (2001). National labour relations in internationalized markets: a comparative study of institutions, change, and performance. Oxford; New York: Oxford University Press.

Trudeau, J. R. H. (2015). *Address by the Right Honourable Justin Trudeau, Prime Minister of Canada*. London, UK: Government of Canada.

Trudeau, J. R. H. (2017). *Address by the Right Honourable Justin Trudeau to the 72th session of the United Nations General Assembly*. New York, NY: Government of Canada.

UAlberta (2017). UAlberta expertise brings DeepMind lab to Edmonton [Press release]. Retrieved from www.ualberta.ca/news-and-events/newsarticles/2017/July/ualberta-expertise-brings-deepmind-lab-to-edmonton.

United Nations. (2017). *United Nations: Overview*. Retrieved from www.un.org/en/index.html.

Von Bertalanffy, L. (1972). The history and status of general systems theory. *Academy of Management Journal, 15*(4), 407–426. doi:10.2307/255139.

WEF. (2016). *The global risks report 2016. 11th edition*. Geneva, Switzerland. Retrieved from www3.weforum.org/docs/GRR/WEF_GRR16.pdf.

WEF. (2017). The Global Competitiveness Report 2016–17: World Economic Forum. Retrieved from: www.weforum.org/reports/the-global-competitiveness-report-2016-2017-1.

Welsh, J. (2011). Our Overlooked Diaspora. Canada's millions of citizens abroad could be a national treasure—given the right strategy. LITERARY REVIEW OF CANADA. Retrieved from: reviewcanada.ca/magazine/2011/03/our-overlooked-diaspora/.

WorldBankGroup. (2017). *Doing business: Comparing business regulation for domestic firms in 190 economies 2017*. Washington DC, USA. Retrieved from www.doingbusiness.org/~/media/WBG/DoingBusiness/Documents/Annual-Reports/English/DB17-Full-Report.pdf.

Zhang, K. (2007). "Mission Invisible" – Rethinking the Canadian Diaspora (Research, Trans.) (Vol. 46). Vancouver, Canada: Asia Pacific Foundation of Canada. Retrieved from: www.asiapacific.ca/canada-asia-agenda/mission-invisible-rethinking-canadian-diaspora.

3
Macro Talent Management in the UK
Patterns of Agency in a Period of Changing Regimes

Paul Sparrow

Introduction

As noted in Chapter 1 which reviews macro talent management in the context of the USA, this chapter considers a series of macro or country factors of the global environment that serve TM at the individual and organizational levels specifically in the context of the United Kingdom, which is comprised of England, Scotland, Wales and Northern Ireland. Macro environmental factors, processes and outcomes can serve to both enable and accelerate talent management (Khilji, Tarique, & Schuler, 2015; Khilji & Schuler, 2017). As is made evident in each of the chapters in this section of the book, macro factors enable the management of talent by conditioning what might be desirable, relevant and possible at country level. As Global Talent Management (GTM) becomes an increasingly complex phenomenon, there are four essential functions of MTM at the country (also regional and local) level: talent planning, acquisition, development, and retention. The chapter develops the Khilji et al. (2015) model, by shedding light on, and explaining which processes appear to have most bearing upon three of their core talent processes (talent acquisition, growth and development, and retention), and the interplay between the factors involved.

The challenges facing the UK are stark, and will require new patterns of effective action. In order to understand which actions are likely to be the most effective, policy makers have to feel that they still have some agency in the situation. The chapter develops the notion of there being "*patterns of agency*" in the conduct of talent management at country level. A pattern of agency may be defined as those actions or interventions by which a result or an end may be achieved, or an effect created (there is a sense of *agency* in the situation), and the way in which these actions can be connected and woven together to help make sense of, and form, a bigger picture (the *patterns* that can be seen, and the web of connections across their actions). The analysis of these patterns in the UK (and the agency open to policy makers and

HRM actors that result from them) suggests that those who might seek to manage talent at a macro level have to:

1. see the connections that are occurring across these issues,
2. then organize these connections into a larger web of action that can be fitted into new patterns of agency.

Identifying useful actions that help national-level interventions in one area of policy (say vocational education and training or skills strategy) can help us understand why there needs to be linked sets of actions and behaviours in another area (say immigration). In other words, we need to understand how any new and observed patterns can help bring a sense of order to what needs to be de done across the piece—to build a picture of the larger pattern of agency that is open to us.

After this opening section, the chapter is structured into four further sections. In each of these subsequent sections, an attempt is made to signal why each topic is important for the study of macro global talent management, by noting the "agency" that the topic has on the conduct of talent management at the organizational level, and the situation as it is in the UK is explained. Through marshaling data and analysis of the UK context, this chapter draws attention to those generic factors that shape the conduct of macro global talent management and the agency through which they have a bearing.

The chapter first builds a picture of why UK talent management practice is as it is by examining the economic, technological and cultural context. The second section begins with a brief overview of the important macro environmental factors that serve to shape and set the conditions in which macro talent management occurs in a given country or region. It reviews evidence on four factors that set this overall context: the HRM philosophy and culture and the attitudes this creates towards talent management; country competitiveness and relative rankings of the UK's Human Capital; the openness of the UK economy to foreign direct investment; and the industrial structure.

Then, to better understand *how* macro factors condition the conduct of talent management, the chapter adopts a functional perspective on talent management looking at: growth and development of talent; attraction and retention of talent; and the enablement and acceleration of this management. The third section examines those macro factors that bear upon the growth and development of talent at national level. It examines the role of three factors: the link between skills and productivity; the country's vocational education and training (VET) strategy and future skills scenarios; and educational outcomes. The fourth section examines those macro factors (principally supply factors) that bear upon the ability of organizations to attract and retain talent. It examines the role of four factors in this regard: recent legislative and business climate changes impacting talent management; skills shortages and overeducation; immigration; and demographic changes, working age population and ageing. Finally, the fifth section examines the role of two macro factors that serve to enable and accelerate the effective management of talent at the national level: the role of global labour markets; and the role of global cities (in the instance of the UK, this is London).

The chapter concludes by summarizing the evidence reviewed to capture the ways in which talent management at the organization level in the UK is conditioned (in terms of success or not) by the series of macro institutional and cultural factors reviewed. The chapter reveals eight ways in which the economic, technological and cultural context *conditions* macro global talent management. It shows how a further three factors *shape* talent management activities that facilitate growth and development—and how another four factors bear upon the ability of organizations to attract and retain talent. Finally, it argues that two factors—globalized sector labour markets and the growing importance of global or large metropolitan cities—are serving to accelerate and amplify the impact of the other global talent management processes on large national employers and at the national level. The chapter concludes by suggesting a series of questions, driven largely by institutional theory, that should now form a useful future research agenda.

The Economic, Technological and Cultural Context

HRM Culture and Attitudes to Talent Management

The first macro environmental factors which serve to "shape" and "condition" the macro talent management debate is the HRM culture, and the resultant talent management philosophies. Such talent management philosophies can be detected at country level as a product of both national and business culture. The cultural assumptions that underpin them exert agency on typical talent management practice at the organizational level, by predisposing and shaping the activities that are felt to be legitimate within the field of practice. These cultural assumptions are embedded in tacit beliefs about what makes a manager effective. They differ across national systems. There are also a series of "enabling concepts", that need to be institutionalized before some of the precepts of talent management begins to garner professional support.

From the earliest days of research into comparative HRM it was evident that there were deep cultural differences both in the notion of what managers should be and models of their development, and in the way that national vocational education impacted subsequent resourcing, training and development practice (Sparrow & Hiltrop, 1994). Evans, Doz, and Laurent (1989) contrasted the elite cohort approach of countries such as Japan, with the Germanic functional approach to (what we would today call) talent management, or the political approach to elites in France and Latin European countries, and the Anglo-Dutch managed development approach to potential development.). They characterized the UK approach as being based on careful monitoring of high potentials, reviews to match up performance and potential with short term job requirements, an unmanaged and decentralized trial and error process over the first 5 to 7 years of a manager's development, some complimentary recruitment of high potentials rather than an elite cohort system, followed by the use of potential identification techniques via assessment centres and career development workshops that were designed to "predict" an individual's likely internal future mobility in the organization. Assumptions are embedded in beliefs about the predictability of individual career outcomes, rather than the more clinical assessment of risk that characterizes, say, a French selection system (Shackleton & Newell, 1991). The system was characterized then, and would still be described today, thus:

> . . . The British system . . . places a premium on personal experience, rather than the codified judgements of previous generations. Self-regulation in all things, rather than statutory control, are the preferred mechanisms of control, as is a liberal education

with less emphasis on vocational skills. The basis for selection . . . is therefore driven by assumptions about the basic character of the individual . . . These personality and behavioural assumptions are seen to underlie the most important skills, which are typically felt to be man-management, social, political and leadership skills.

(Sparrow & Hiltrop, 1994, p. 376)

UK HR professionals are then *culturally-predisposed* to receive the three intellectual drives that shaped conceptualizations of talent management in the 1990s (Sparrow, Scullion, & Tarique, 2014). Cultural and institutional traditions defined management capability as something built into the personal experiences of the people who filled leadership roles, rather than in their educational heritage or the structural capabilities built into organizational roles. Three "enabling concepts", all institutionalized in the 1980s, pre-dated the use of talent management, but later enabled both more rapid adoption and cultural acceptability:

1. a differentiated approach to talent management through what became known as the 9-Box model of performance versus potential;
2. the individualization of organizations through the adoption of management competencies, and the shift from a pay-for-the-job approach to pay-for-the-person approach selection systems; and
3. the assumption that informated workplaces were further enhancing the power and impact of talent.

Cranet data provides some insight into the comparative use of performance-potential matrices in talent management, the supporting adoption of performance management appraisal, and potential identification through assessment centres in the UK versus other countries. In 2004 this dataset showed that the proportion of organizations using assessment centres was 6.4 per cent in the UK, compared to 5.5 per cent in Germany, 3 per cent in the Netherlands, and 2.1 per cent in France (Brewster, Sparrow, & Vernon, 2007). By 2010 adoption had grown to 32 per cent in the UK by 2010, still ahead of the 8 per cent adoption in France, but lagging the by then 41 per cent adoption in Germany (Brewster, Houldsworth, Sparrow, & Vernon, 2016). Use performance appraisal for both clerical and management was 91 per cent and 92 per cent respectively, compared to between 75–81 per cent in France and 86–87 per cent in Germany.

The three enabling assumptions outlined previously made it easier for professionals to accept that organizations should design HR systems to forecast staffing needs to meet business needs, and manage staffing through succession planning and short-term development moves, and integrate previously separate resourcing and career development traditions into a life-cycle perspective, applied in the first instance to a small cadre of high-value managers. Structurally, Heads of Resourcing roles began to emerge in the 1990s and 2000s in larger organizations focused on the general stewardship of a senior manager and director cadres, typically the top 500 employees, and development of the senior cadre through role rotation and identification of potential (Sparrow et al., 2014). At the same time, organizations were exhorted to give renewed attention to the leadership models that underpinned their assessment of talent, creating linkage between talent management and efforts to foster specific brands of leadership, such as authentic leadership or sustainable leadership.

Reflecting such predispositions, professional guidance from the UK's Chartered Institute of Personnel and Development (CIPD) defined talent management as the systematic attraction, identification, development, engagement/retention and deployment of those individuals who through their potential have a positive immediate or long term impact on organizational performance (CIPD, 2008). As talent management is considered to be embodied in individuals, the role of HR systems is therefore to predict future internal mobility of such individuals. The most recent CIPD Resourcing and Talent Planning Survey shows that demand for HR specialists in talent and resourcing will increase in 46 per cent of organizations this year (CIPD/Hays, 2017). Over half of CEOs are prioritising talent management this year, with a third of organizations increasing their talent management budgets in 2017–18. The most significant challenges are increased competition for well-qualified talent (72 per cent of organizations), development of existing staff (68 per cent) and difficulties recruiting senior and skilled employees (61 per cent).

Country Competitiveness and Relative Rankings of the UK's Human Capital

The second environmental factor that serves to shape and condition the macro talent management debate is the level of competitiveness and the resultant quality of a country's human capital. In terms of agency, these considerations impact talent management through both macro- and micro-economic effects. At a macroeconomic level the accumulation of human capital is an important driver of output growth, with countries having higher levels of human capital also having greater potential for future growth, other things being equal. At a microeconomic level the labour market outcomes for any individual (such as earnings, levels of education, unemployment, social exclusion) are also linked to their human capital.

The UK is generally seen as one of the more competitive economies in global terms, despite being particularly hard-hit by the global financial crisis. On the World Bank *Doing Business* indicator (which measures business regulation and the protection of property rights, and their effect on businesses, especially small and medium-size domestic firms) the UK was 7th in 2016, down from 6th in 2015. It was ranked as the world's number 7 out of 138 counties in the World Economic Forum *Global Competitiveness Index* in 2017, moving up three places from the previous assessment (Schwab & Sala-i-Martin, 2016). Its strongest features include highly efficient goods and labour markets (9th and 5th, respectively); sophistication of business processes (7th), and a high level of digital readiness by both businesses and consumers (3rd). Its main weakness is the current macro-economic environment (data were collected before the decision to leave the EU).

In relation to a focus on talent management, the UK was ranked #3 in 2017 on the *Global Talent Competitiveness Index* (GTCI) out of 118 countries (Lanvin & Evans, 2017)—a ranking that hides some clear strengths as well as clear weaknesses. Whilst it ranks 2nd on global knowledge skills, it comes a poor 33th on vocational/ technical skills (see Table 1 in Chapter 7 on Finland for these data). The UK ranks 19th out of 130 on the World Economic Forum's (2016) *Human Capital Index*. Its score is 7 per cent lower than the top ranked country of Finland, 4.2 per cent lower than the 4th ranked country of Japan, 1.8 per cent lower than the 11th ranked country of Germany, but 1.4 per cent higher than the USA.

The UK government adopts the Organization for Economic Co-operation and Development (OECD) methodology to measure the value of its national stock of human capital. The OECD (2001) sees human capital as a measure of the knowledge, skills, competencies and attributes embodied in individuals that facilitate the creation of personal, social and economic well-being. Human capital is measured in monetary terms as the total potential future earnings of the working age population, based on current earnings, the overall skill level of workers and other relevant predictors such as the employment rate of those aged 16 to 64. The employment rate is relatively high in the UK compared with the EU average, and increased by 0.8 percentage points to 73.7 per cent in 2015 (Office for National Statistics, 2016a). It then uses a lifetime labour income model, drawing upon metrics for representative individuals in each classification category (i.e. by gender, age and educational attainment).

On this basis, the Office for National Statistics (2016b) estimates the value of employed human capital in the UK was £19.23 trillion in 2015 (its highest level since records began in 2004 and a 4.8 per cent increase from 2014) surpassing its pre-economic downturn peak for the first time at 0.2 per cent above the £19.19 trillion recorded in 2008. However, the study notes that the per head measure of human capital remains below pre-downturn levels.

Foreign Direct Investment

The third environmental factor that serves to shape and condition the macro talent management debate is the role of foreign direct investment (FDI). In terms of agency, studies of the processes through which multi-national enterprises (MNEs) globalize their HRM, show that as MNEs try to build skills and capabilities around the world, this increases the attention that they give to associated activities such as global capability transfer, strategic workforce planning and employer branding, and these activities themselves can serve to enhance, augment, and accelerate existing HR capabilities at any one country-level (Sparrow, Brewster, & Chung, 2017). FDI also plays in promoting skills and in improving productivity (the skills issue in the UK is outlined later in the chapter).

The latest UNCTAD report (UNCTAD, 2016) shows that global flows of FDI rose by 38 per cent in 2015, to $1.76 trillion, which was the highest level since the global economic and financial crisis began in 2008. The majority of this was down to corporate reconfigurations such as cross-border mergers and acquisitions rather than any new productive investment. The study notes that within this global picture the UK fell from the 7th to the 12th largest host of inward investment 2014–15, with an annual inflow of $40 billion, but its economy has for many years been open and built around high levels of FDI. Around a tenth of the UK's assets and liabilities are FDI, with foreign investors owning about £10.6 trillion of UK assets (Bank of England, 2015). This is more than five times the value of UK GDP. UK investors similarly own £10.2 trillion of foreign assets.

The Bank of England (2015) cites statistics reported by the UK's Department for International Trade on inward investment that suggest around 116,000 jobs were created or safeguarded in 2015 by FDI, with nearly 390,000 new jobs created through FDI since 2010. The USA remained the UK's largest source of inward investment, providing 570 projects in 2015, followed by China (including Hong Kong) with 156 projects and India with 140. Inward investment into the UK comes overwhelmingly from sectors and countries which have a technological advantage over the corresponding UK sector (Bank of England, 2015). At the time of writing, the future geographical balance of the UK's trading relationships remains uncertain after the decision to leave the EU, which was decided by a public referendum in 2015. UK exports and imports are together worth 60 per cent of UK GDP, and 44 per cent of that trade is with the rest of the EU (Bank of England, 2015). The EU is the source for 46 per cent of the UK's inward cross-border investments, and 43 per cent of its outward investment.

Industrial Structure and Talent Management

The fourth environmental factor that serves to shape and condition the macro talent management debate is the industrial structure and associated government policy. In terms of agency, at the European level it is argued that such policies create linkage by: fostering clusters, supporting innovation activity, building links between education providers and industry to strengthen market signals on industry skill demand, attracting foreign direct investment, and ensuring necessary access to finance (Department for Business Innovation & Skills, 2012). However, within EU frameworks different national policies exist. For example, France has focused on prioritising key sectors through clear national and sector level visions, whilst Finland has focused on building enablers, particularly in the ICT sector (Owen, 2012).

The UK government approach is still influenced by a strategic analysis it made of the sectors that could make the greater contribution to future economic growth and employment in the UK (Department for Business Innovation & Skills, 2012). From a talent management perspective, these are sectors in which investments should be expected to produce a greater return (though the analysis was not carried out for skills or investment purposes). In the UK, by 2011 knowledge intensive industries accounted for around a third of UK output and a quarter of total employment, whilst manufacturing contributed just over a tenth to UK output and slightly less to employment. From 1997–2011 the greatest changes in share of gross value added (GVA) came from financial services, then business services, health and social care and digital, creative and information services. The Department for Business Innovation & Skills (2012) analysis cites OECD data that shows compared to its major competitors, the UK's sectoral diversity is roughly the same as Germany's, and marginally higher than both the USA and France.

The analysis highlighted three strategic sectors: advanced manufacturing (including aerospace, automotive and life sciences); knowledge intensive traded services (including professional and business services, the information economy and traded aspects of higher and further education); and enabling sectors (such as energy and construction). The UK tends to perform well in terms of both the value of output generated per employee or hour worked, or the additional value of output generated after accounting for changes in the raw inputs used such as materials, capital, and labour, in highly skilled sectors such as financial services, publishing, R&D, utilities and construction (BERR, 2008). The UK performs less well in sectors such as mechanical engineering, electrical machinery and components, and precision instruments. Using Germany as a benchmark, the UK has a productivity advantage in sectors such as financial intermediation, communications, mining and food but lags behind Germany in a number of manufacturing activities.

The motivation of UK government has been to align policies—such as in technology, skills, tax and regulation—to support growth in particular sectors. Investments in basic skills such as funding for literacy and numeracy, knowledge transfer networks, and grants for collaborative R&D are seen as "horizontal" (addressing economy-wide market failures). Innovation funds and employer investment funds are more "sectoral" (where the country's research base collaborates with industry to solve business problems). Historically, prior to 1979 the UK gave greater emphasis on sectoral interventions with efforts to build national champions and promote industrial consolidation. After 1979, although there was some continuity in support for the aerospace industry, ". . . more use was made of horizontal instruments to encourage foreign investment, promote competition and liberalise markets" (Department for Business Innovation & Skills, 2012, p. 8). After Britain's forthcoming exit from the European Union, the environment will be characterised by deep debate about the most appropriate balance. It is worth noting that none of this debate had been undertaken or decided pre-referendum, hence the sense of turmoil and uncertainty in the UK at the time of writing. The challenges are systemic. The OECD's (2017) economic survey of the UK drew attention to the need to revive labour productivity, address deep regional divisions in productivity, and raise the competencies of low-skilled workers.

Finally, in terms of industrial structure, as in many countries, the small and medium sized enterprise (SME) sector (defined as businesses employing less than 250 people) is very important in the UK. Debates about talent management need to take into account this particular context. In the UK large businesses (those with more than 250 employees) account for less than 0.1 per cent of businesses but 40 per cent of employment and 53 per cent of turnover (Ward & Rhodes, 2013). In 2013 SMEs employed 14.4 million people in the UK, which the European Commission's SME Performance Review estimates to have a Gross value added (a productivity metric that measures the contribution to an economy, producer, sector or region by providing a financial value for the amount of goods or services that have been produced, less the cost of all inputs and raw materials attributable to that production) of €473 billion, or 50 per cent of the UK economy. Of all UK businesses, 96 per cent are in fact micro-businesses, employing less than 10 employees, although this sector only accounts for 33 per cent of employment and 19 per cent of revenue.

Talent management is seen as a challenge in the SME sector. A recent 2017 practitioner survey run by Vistage, called the UK SME Confidence Index, found that when the leaders of UK SMEs were asked to cite the biggest challenges facing their business in the forthcoming 12 months, almost half (47 per cent) cited talent management (Recruitment International, 2017). The study defined talent management as including hiring, retaining and training employees.

The Impact of Macro Factors on the Growth and Development of Talent at National Level

Skills and Productivity

Having outlined four important environmental factors that shape the overall talent management climate, the chapter now examines those macro factors that bear specifically upon the growth and development of talent at national level. The first of these macro factors is the relationship between skills and productivity. In terms of agency, the skills and productivity challenge means that MNEs find themselves collaborating with governments and other actors in the spheres of cross border flows of talent, diaspora mobility, and policies to attract, grow, develop and retain national talent in ways that facilitate their own GTM strategies and activities (Khilji et al., 2015). They need to develop and institutionalize their own capabilities (defined here as the skills, processes, tools and systems that enable improvements in employee learning). HR directors naturally focus on improving their organization's internal productivity. However, the ability of an organization to improve this is invariably dependent on external technical, and institutional, developments

UK governments first began to give serious attention to the role of skills in the economy by the mid-2000s, with a landmark study being the Leitch Report (2006). This landmark policy review brought the question of skills in the economy at a macro level to the fore. It demonstrated that, using the ILO distinction between *low skills* (below upper secondary), *intermediate skills* (upper secondary), and *higher skills* (tertiary), then productivity gains in the UK were largely associated with the ability to increase *intermediate* and especially *high level skills*, but also being able to improve skills at the *lower* level. At around the same time, a Bank of England analysis (Bell, Burriel-Llombart, & Jones, 2005) determined that around one fifth of the annual growth in the UK economy was due to improvements in workforce skills, but gaps in productivity with other countries were more to do with physical capital stocks per hour worked, and total factor productivity dimensions, rather than workforce skills levels.

In the UK, the then Commission for Employment and Skills (the Commission was disbanded in 2016) concluded that both MNEs and domestic employers face the challenge of balancing the opportunities for greater earnings with the need to both match skills and jobs more closely and ensure better opportunities for in-work learning:

> . . . given that productivity and earnings are positively linked to educational attainment, there is a general tendency to think in terms of a small proportion of low skills (relative to intermediate and high skills) and large proportion of high skills (relative to low and intermediate skills) as being 'good'.
>
> (Bosworth & Leach, 2015, p. 11)

This role of skills in improving productivity is then mainly seen in terms of the intangible benefits it has on knowledge transfer and innovation. Garrett, Campbell, and Mason (2010) draw attention to:

- transfer of knowledge between firms, sectors and countries, whether through collaboration on R&D and technical problem-solving by firms involved in supply-chains.
- mobility of highly-qualified talent between firms, such as engineers and scientists.
- effective use of knowledge, whereby ideas and technologies generated elsewhere can be enabled through an 'absorptive capacity' (a term that refers to a firm's ability to recognize the value of new information, assimilate it, and apply it to commercial ends).

Vocational Education and Training (VET) Strategy

The second macro factor that bears upon the growth and development of talent at national level is the VET strategy. Different countries have different strategies for growth, and much attention is given to high skill attainment. The OECD (2013) found that more than one half of the GDP growth in countries over the past decade is related to earnings growth among individuals educated to a high (tertiary) level. Its study uses an *International Skills Model* using data for the 10 years from 2003 to 2012 to identify trends in changes in educational attainment and project the educational attainment of the adult working-age population (aged 25–64) to 2020.

Given that the contribution and importance of high skilled individuals in the UK is significantly higher than the OECD average, the economic strategy requires that it improve qualification attainment levels (Bosworth & Leach, 2015). However, since the onset of the 2008 financial crisis, the Bank of England notes that UK labour productivity has been exceptionally weak, with whole-economy output per hour around 16 per cent below the level predicted from the pre-crisis trend (Barnet, Batten, Chiu, Franklin, & Sebastia-Barriel, 2014). Over the period 2003–2013 the UK improved attainment levels at the highest qualification levels. The proportion of the adult population qualified at this level increased from 27 per cent per to 38 per cent, whilst the proportion with 'no' or 'low-level' as their highest qualification fell from 34 per cent to 23 per cent. From 2013 to 2020 continued improvements are expected, with the proportion qualified to Level 4+ projected to rise to 47 per cent (an increase of 4 million individuals), while the proportion below Level 2 is projected to fall to 17 per cent. There are gender differences within this, with women expected to perform more strongly at both ends of the skills spectrum. The most pressing priority for a number of developed countries such as the UK is to accelerate the rate of reduction in the size of the long 'tail' of low skilled employees, by supporting the progression of those already in the labour force and helping them to move up into the intermediate band, and by minimizing the proportion of low-skilled new entrants to the labour market. However, in the international context this shift is still relatively limited (Barnet, Batten, Chiu, Franklin, & Sebastia-Barriel, 2014), and 19 out of 32 OECD countries already have lower proportions of low skilled employees in their workforces. There have been similar projected improvements in skill levels in many international labour markets. In terms of high skill levels the UK's projected increase by 2020 to 49 per cent being qualified at a higher (tertiary) level would elevate the UK's international ranking slightly from 11th to 7th (Bosworth & Leach, 2015).

One of the UK's key strengths, then, lies in the size of its pool of *high skilled labour*, whilst in countries such as Germany, the economic strategy is based on having a skills base weighted towards intermediate skills, with a relatively small proportion qualified at a higher level (but also only a small proportion of the population holding no qualifications or low level qualifications). Developing nations are increasingly investing in their skills base in order to exploit markets that have traditionally been dominated by developed nations.

However, as noted by the World Economic Forum (2016), whilst the UK exhibits a high tertiary attainment rate (33 per cent) and high-skilled employment share (48 per cent) for its 25–54 core working age group, it only ranks 46th on their incidence of overeducation indicator (overeducation is discussed a little later) and 33rd for its vocational enrolment rate. They conclude this indicates there is room for improvement in terms of recognising alternative education paths, a public debate that has returned within policy circles in the context of 're-balancing' the economy following the decision to leave the EU.

At the time of writing the impact of leaving the EU is as yet unknown (there are multiple variants across a spectrum of from 'hard' to 'soft' exit strategies, and different options might have different impacts on the skills profile), but the UK's Office for Budget Responsibility has made an assessment of another major system shock—the impact that the global financial crisis had on the UK's national productivity. By early 2015 output per hour was still 2 per cent below its pre-crisis peak and productivity in the rest of the G7 group was 5 per cent higher. French employees could take Friday off and still produce more than Britons do in a week, and confounding stereotypes, Italians were 9 per cent more productive (Economist, 2015). The UK also lags in infrastructure investments behind Canada, Japan, France and Germany. However, because of lower pay, poorer productivity was mitigated. The Economist (2015) estimates that of the initial 15 members of the EU, only Greece and Portugal had lower hourly wages. At that time, a British employee produced a fifth less than a French one but was more than a third cheaper to hire. When labour is widely available at very low cost, firms would rather hire than invest in machines or technology, and in the UK there has been a shift from capital to labour, with growth in the capital stock falling along with productivity.

Reflecting this, the UK skills bodies recently mapped out the future macro relationship between skills and productivity, especially in light of the concern over the future impact of digitalization and artificial intelligence. In the same way that business markets might in future begin to develop in different ways, there are also alternative ways in which the link between skills and productivity might also develop. In an innovative piece of work, the now disbanded UK Commission for Employment and Skills (UKCES) used the German Foresight Company to conduct an analysis of likely future pathways for the role of skills in the UK economy (Störmer, Patscha, Prendergast, & Daheim, 2014).

The study was premised on the assumption that the way we think about tomorrow influences what we do today and tried to systematically make sense of the direction of travel in the UK labour market. It examined the impact of the 13 most influential and plausible global trends (defined as empirically documented developments) through the lens of UK conditions and the realities of the UK labour market, and 10 disruptions that most probably could lead to significant deviations from the path of 'business-as-usual'. In so doing, it raised

> . . . the paradox where the emergence of a networked global talent pool seems to promise ever more intense competition for opportunities at all levels of the UK workforce, and at the same time we are also likely to face skills 'vacuums' where we are not fast enough at developing skills for newly emerging business fields.
> (Störmer et al., 2014, p. 1)

Störmer et al. (2014) plotted four anticipated scenarios—or development paths—based on plausible pictures of what the UK's job landscape might look like in 2030, and the skills required under each scenario (Figure 3.1 provides bullet point summaries of each scenario). Each scenario creates its own narrative.

The first business-as-usual scenario was called Enforced Flexibility. Here greater business flexibility and incremental innovation would be expected to lead to moderate growth in the economy, but the flexibility would result in fewer opportunities and weakened job security for the low skilled.

The second scenario, called Tiers: An Opportunity Divide, was one under which despite robust growth driven by strong high-tech industries, a two-tiered, divided society emerges, reinforcing the economic position of the 'haves' and 'have nots'.

The third scenario, called Skills Activism from Governments, was one in which technological innovation would drive the automation of white-collar work, bringing large-scale job losses and political pressure, which would have to lead to an extensive government-led skills programme.

Finally, the fourth scenario, called An Efficiency Imperative, was one in which in a stagnant economy, improved productivity would have to be achieved through the rigorous implementation of Information and Communications Technology (ICT) solutions.

The Störmer et al. (2014) study is discussed in this chapter, and is important to the chapter's broad argument, because it reminds us that new institutions have to form around the new patterns of agency that might emerge, and will have to evolve to deal with the nature of that agency.

Each scenario implied a different value that might be attached to human capital, pattern of industrial activity, and necessary institutional interventions in the labour market. The study also identified the factors that are expected to bear on the relationship between skills and productivity. They are many and broad—demographic change, growing diversity, income uncertainty, desire for better work-life balance, converging technologies and cross-disciplinary skills, digitalization of production, big data, artificial intelligence and robots,

ENFORCED FLEXIBILITY

- Volatile world economy with recovery from financial crisis through to 2020s
- Higher flexibility of work and employment contracts
- Hourglass labor market—high competition for low and high skilled workers, hollowing out of middle tiers
- Security of employment, work-life balance and autonomy as main drivers
- Wide variety of education channels for those who can afford it or are backed by employers

TIERS (AN OPPORTUNITY DIVIDE)

- Two tiers: Growth through innovative high tech flag bearer firm, low demand for intermediate level skills
- Liberal labor regulations, tax credits for intellectual property
- Boom conditions in London and SE of country, depressed regional economies
- Growing inequalities of earnings and opportunities for employees
- Higher skilled have more scope to negotiate own conditions, medium to low skilled have limited career options
- Technology and liberalization requires more marketized delivery of learning and training

MORE SKILLS ACTIVISM FROM GOVERNMENTS

- Technical innovation hollows out skills levels in professional and higher paid work
- Smart algorithms become more accurate and productive, replacing professional judgements in accountancy, law, accounting
- Response to the impact of IT becomes more regional and with more active interventions
- Government begins to intervene in the training market for the "battered middle"
- Shift towards a project-based economy, with opportunities for growth for sectors like healthcare and micropreneurship

AN EFFICIENCY IMPERATIVE

- Turbulent international environment with faltering trade and protectionist policies
- UK and Europe get stuck in a decade of slow growth and deflation in the 2020s
- Work designs continue to be lean managed
- Solutions push short term productive efficiency
- High earners also hit by lean management
- Growth in mobile and virtual workers to satisfy employer and customer demands at a lower market price
- Shift to online education and skills provision as education and training delivery is re-engineered

Figure 3.1 Alternative Futures for the Skills and Productivity Challenge

economic shifts to Asia and distribution of global centres of excellence, de-globalization, partial fragmentation of the EU, new business ecosystems, scarcity of resources, reverse migration, changing employee values, and decreased scope for political action.

Education Outcomes

The third macro factor that bears upon the growth and development of talent at national level can be considered to be the need to improve educational outcomes. In terms of relative educational achievement, on the Organization for Economic Co-operation and Development's (OECD) Programme for International Student Assessment (PISA) comparison of 72 countries, the UK's PISA score has remained largely static over the last decade, but has slipped down the league table as other nations, particularly those in East Asia, have rapidly improved (Organization for Economic Cooperation and Development, 2013).

In 2016 the UK came 15th in Science, 21st in Reading, but despite policy attempts to replicate the educational practices of East Asian countries, 26th in Maths. This latter area is recognised as problematic. Only 11 per cent of UK students rank as top performers compared to 35 per cent in the top performing country of Singapore, and there is a significant tail of poor performance, with 22 per cent of 15-year-olds in the UK not reaching the baseline level of achievement needed to solve problems "routinely faced by adults in their daily lives" (Level 2), compared to countries such as Korea and Singapore where the percentage of low-performing 15-year-olds was below 10 per cent. A similar picture emerges from the Trends in International Maths and Science Study (TIMSS, 2015) published by the International Association for the Evaluation of Educational Achievement (IEA). This shows that England has improved in both science and mathematics (maths), with the UK's maths results now at their highest point for 20 years in both age groups, but East Asian countries maintained their 20 year lead for pupils aged 10 and 14.

Where the UK has been undoubtedly successful is in its higher education sector. The UNESCO (2012) interactive map on global flows of tertiary-level students shows the UK's market share of global education is 13 per cent, second only to the USA which has a 16.5 per cent share. The number of students seeking a tertiary-level education more than doubled since 2000–12 from 2.1 million to over 4.5 million (Universities UK, 2014). However, the same study notes that the 30-year period of growth of international student numbers in the UK slowed after 2010, and began a slight decline since 2012–13. The market is becoming very competitive, and Universities UK (2014) uses the UNESCO (2012) data to show that the top five study destinations, as a whole, have seen their share decline since 2000 due to the emergence of rivals entering the market such as China and Malaysia in East Asia and the Pacific, and Egypt, Saudi Arabia and the UAE in the Middle East.

As an export industry, higher education was worth a total of £10.7 billion in 2012, and the global education market contributes more than £7 billion to the UK economy (Universities UK, 2014). The Universities UK (2014) report notes that statistics from the Higher Education Statistics Agency (the government body that collects and publishes information about the UK higher education sector) confirm the role that UK higher education plays in terms of global education. From 2015–16 there were over 438,000 overseas students at this level (19 per cent of all students in higher education in the UK), with 6 per cent coming from the rest of the EU and 14 per cent from the rest of the world. Universities UK (2014) note that the higher the education level, the more pronounced the globalization becomes. Of students studying at postgraduate level in the UK, 46 per cent are from outside the EU. The top seven sending countries in order are China, Malaysia, the USA, India, Hong Kong, Nigeria and Germany. The number of Chinese students far exceeds any other nationality at over 90,000—the only country showing a significant increase in student numbers. The number of Indian students coming to the UK to study continues to fall with a 44 per cent decrease in the last five years largely attributed to a result of visa changes (Universities UK, 2014).

Historically the debate was around the desirability of retaining educated talent within the countries that educate them, and in this regard the problem that the UK faced was that the majority of international students returned home after study, whereas in the USA more international students then stayed on in the country.

This debate has since receded, both because the structure of the labour market is changing, and there has been a conflating of higher education and immigration debates. First, in terms of structural changes, there has been considerable innovation in the UK's global education system (University of Oxford International Strategy Office, 2015). Although the

OECD projects increases in international student mobility to 8 million students per year by 2025, to counter the fact that such educated-talent is mobile and, given the changing topography of sending countries, talent (used here to refer to highly educated graduates) is returning increasingly to sending countries (University of Oxford International Strategy Office, 2015). The providers of education to globally mobile students are also themselves globalizing. There have been shifts in the UK higher education sector towards international campuses, online course delivery, knowledge hubs, academic engagement in industrial R&D, developing research capacity through inter-University collaborations and institution-industry partnerships. This has made academics themselves become part of an international talent pool. Universities UK (2014) cites data from the Higher Education Statistics Agency (HESA) that shows that EU nationals accounted for 12,635 of the 31,950 university lecturing and researcher jobs created in the UK in the past ten years, with the biggest increases coming from countries hit hard by the Eurozone crisis, including Portugal, Spain, Italy and Greece.

Second, Universities UK (2014) argues that the inadvertent politicization of international students and immigration is a direct result of the UK government's chosen measure of immigration flows, which is the Office for National Statistics (ONS) *Long-Term International Migration* (LTIM) estimate, based on the International Passenger Survey (IPS). By this measure, which has long been considered flawed (see Sparrow, 2008), it is estimated that 180,000 people entered the UK for the purpose of formal study in 2012, making international students the largest group of migrants from outside the EU (Universities UK, 2014). The size of this cohort has dragged the international student cohort into the immigration debate.

The Impact of Macro Factors on the Attraction and Retention of Talent at National Level

The chapter now examines those macro factors (principally these are supply factors) that bear upon the ability of organizations to attract and retain talent. The first of these is the role played by recent legislative and business climate changes.

Recent Legislative and Business Climate Changes Impacting Talent Management

Three recent pieces of legislation have impacted the talent management strategies of organizations in the UK (CIPD/Hays, 2017); the introduction of:

1. tax legislation in 2000, called IR35 intermediaries legislation, which was designed to combat tax avoidance by workers who supply their services to clients via an intermediary,
2. National Living Wage legislation in April 2016 for all working people aged 25 and over, and
3. an apprenticeship levy on UK employers in April 2017 to fund new apprenticeships.

The majority of UK organizations expect their recruitment to stay the same as a direct result of each piece of legislation (CIPD/Hays, 2017), but over a quarter expect the apprenticeship levy will lead to an increase in recruitment. Arguably, the largest impact on talent strategies of course has been the UK's decision to leave the EU. The CIPD survey (CIPD/Hays, 2017) was the first to explore the anticipated changes to organizational recruitment and talent strategies in light of this. Despite the decision to leave, the proportion of organizations anticipating that they will recruit EU migrants in 2017 was the same across all sectors compared to 2016 (CIPD/Hays, 2017). However, 26 per cent reported a renewed focus on practices to support the upskilling and development of existing staff, 90 per cent were investing more in building an attractive employer brand, 75 per cent anticipated a greater focus on developing more talent in-house, 68 per cent expected more recruitment for key talent and niche areas, and 63 per cent expected greater use of new media/technology to recruit (CIPD/Hays, 2017).

Skills Shortages and Overeducation

The second macro factor that bears upon the ability of organizations to attract and retain talent is the nature of skills shortages and the related issue of overeducation. As noted earlier, surveys of organizational practice consistently show that UK firms report problems with skills shortages. Skills shortages have been seen as one of the long-term structural trends in developed countries that can lead to a broadening of the scope of activity by MNEs, and other local actors, as organizations try to lessen them (Sparrow, Brewster, & Chung, 2017). In terms of agency, these skills shortages bear upon the choices that MNEs might make about the locating of certain operations, or the location of particular business models (which might be more or less value-creating in the broader local economy), within a particular market. Such discussion also has relevance to the topic of global sourcing and shoring. Sparrow et al. (2017) also point out that as a result of these macro factors, new functions and disciplines are emerging within MNEs, functions in which labour economists and operations expertise are being brought together with global talent management thinking. Labour economists, often now located within a global operations function, are being used to assist MNE to make judgements about the relative productivity of its plants or activities on a global basis, often establishing the metrics that might be used to monitor the performance of these operations and help make decisions on either initial locational decisions or further investment. In terms of global talent management, the management of intermediate-level skills across a national workforce, means that MNEs have to work with national governments and local education establishments to ensure sufficient levels of skill and speed to competence. Some MNEs are linking the work being done by their labour economists to that being done by people with more traditional talent management responsibilities (Sparrow et al., 2017).

In recent years a combination of solid job growth and weak working age population growth has led to declines in the unemployment rate in many mature economies. The ample supply of labour at relatively low cost during recent years has reduced the incentive for businesses to raise labour productivity (output per hour), which has meant that employers have had to expand their workforces even more to keep up with production demands (Sparrow et al., 2017).

This is true of the UK where, at the time of writing, the jobless rate was down to 4.3 per cent—its lowest level since 1975 (BBC, 2017). This compares to an unemployment rate of 7.7 per cent across the EU-28 group of nations and 9.1 per cent in the Eurozone (Office for National Statistics, 2016b). The employed population aged 16 to 64 grew 2.1 per cent between 2014 and 2015 (Office for National Statistics, 2016b). At 75.1 per cent, the proportion of people in work was the highest it has been since 1971—partly due to the introduction of a later state pension age for women (Office for National Statistics, 2016b).

In terms of recent policy debate, much of which is triggered by the decision to leave the EU, Dromey, McNeil, and Roberts (2017) found that employer spending on training is half (over £6 billion less) per employee per year than the EU average for continued vocational education. They argue that improvements in qualifications have not delivered economic benefits. Despite an 11 per cent increase in the proportion of the workforce with both basic and degree-level qualifications in the last decade, productivity has risen by just one per cent and average pay has fallen in real terms. Employers in England spend £5.1 billion less on training in real terms in 2017 compared to a decade ago, and public investment through the adult skills budget has been cut by 40 per cent in real terms between 2010/11 and 2015/16. They call for a £5.1 billion 'skills levy' to be introduced to boost employer investment and to enable skills devolution.

The Office for National Statistics (2016b) study notes that the effect of qualifications on the distribution of human capital shows the variation between the proportion of total employed human capital by qualification and the proportion of the population who hold that qualification. It shows that in 2015, a total of 37.3 per cent of the human capital stock was embodied in the 28.0 per cent of the working population whose highest educational attainment was a degree or equivalent. In contrast, only 5.1 per cent of the UK's human capital stock was embodied in the 8.8 per cent of the working age population who have no formal qualifications. In terms of employed human capital per person by qualification, on average in 2015, those with a degree or equivalent had human capital worth £628,000, which was £136,000 more than those with a highest qualification of GCE A-Levels or equivalent (£492,000 per head). In comparison, the average employed human capital stock for those with no qualifications was £274,000 (Office for National Statistics, 2016b).

The 2014 Hays Global Skills Index report (Hays/Oxford Economics, 2014) details the difficulties employers have in recruiting skilled labour across 30 countries, using indicators ranging from structural factors around education flexibility, labour market flexibility, and labour market participation, through to organization-level factors such as talent mismatches, overall wage pressure and pressure in high skills industries and occupations. This study shows that structural factors (around the flexibility of labour markets, education syllabi, and organizational policies aimed at the youngest and oldest segments of the labour market) have the greatest impact on the efficiency of the labour market. On its Index measure of the level of pressure being faced or skilled labour (with a higher score meaning that a country is experiencing more pressure than has historically been the case), the UK (before the advent of the decision to leave the EU and fears of a reduction in EU-labour inflows) faired relatively well. The 2014 Hays Global Skills Index reports the UK skills shortage index as 5.1, compared to Sweden at 6.6, Spain and Hungary 6.3, Germany 6.2, Russia 6.1, and Ireland 5.8. France and Poland had similar skills shortages. The Czech Republic and Netherlands at 4.8, Denmark and Switzerland at 4.5, Italy at 3.9, and Belgium at 3.8 had lower skills shortages pressure. The UK's situation was also better than that in the USA at 6.3, Japan at 6.0, and Brazil at 5.4, but slightly worse than in China at 5.0, India at 4.5, and Singapore at 4.1.

The 2015 Employer Skills Survey (UKCES, 2015) found that 86 percent of UK employers reported that they had a fully proficient workforce, but the 14 per cent of employers reporting skills gaps within their establishment meant that approximately 1.4 million UK workers lacked proficiency in their current role (five per cent of the UK workforce). The skills gaps that continue to exist are more prevalent in unskilled or semi-skilled occupations. Both the proportion of employers with any skills gaps, and the proportion of the workforce affected, decreased gradually at UK level between the 2011 and 2015 surveys.

However, this varied by nation. The density of skill-shortage vacancies remained at similar levels from 2013–15 in both England and Scotland, increased in Wales, and decreased in Northern Ireland.

At a macro level, there is a counter-side to skills shortages—and that is the problem of overeducation, and of skills underutilization, because of the increasing problem of qualification mismatches in recruitment, with more jobs being lower skilled (Sparrow, Brewster, & Chung, 2017). The 2012 Review of Employment and Social Developments in Europe (European Commission, 2012) showed this has become an issue across Europe, with the European Centre for the Development of Vocational Training (CEDEFOP) estimating at the time that mismatches between the level of education and jobs on offer affected around 36 per cent of the European population. The European Commission (2012) notes that between 2011 and 2012, the employment rate for the highest level of education attained increased in the major part of EU Member States. However, on average, it suggests that Eurostat data from 2012 show that nearly 15 per cent of European employees are classed as overeducated, while 19 per cent are undereducated. The figure for overeducation is 14 per cent in the UK. This compares favourably to a figure of 26 per cent in Greece, 22 per cent in Spain, 21 per cent in Portugal, and 18 per cent in Germany, but is worse than the figure of 12 per cent in France, 9 per cent in Poland, and only 5 per cent in Finland (European Commission, 2012).

Bosworth and Leach (2015) argue that data from the OECD Online Education Database shows wide variations in skills levels. The percentage of the labour force only qualified to low levels in 2015 averages 23 per cent for the EU21 countries and 24 per cent for the OECD countries (Bosworth & Leach, 2015). But they note the figures vary. Smaller proportions of low-skilled labour were found for example in Japan (6 per cent), with 10 per cent in Estonia and Poland, 11 per cent in the USA and Canada, 12 per cent in Sweden, 14 per cent in Germany, 15 per cent in Finland, and 18 per cent in Korea or Norway. The UK comes in at the average, along with Australia, Ireland and Denmark. France, the Netherlands, Belgium and Greece have between 27 per cent and 32 per cent low-skilled employees. But for Portugal and Mexico the figure is 63 per cent and it is 66 per cent for Turkey (Bosworth & Leach, 2015).

Bosworth and Leach (2015) note that the UK, along with countries such as Iceland, Ireland, Spain and Portugal, has a low level of intermediate skilled jobs, but would wish to improve attainment at this level. They suggest that countries that have high levels of intermediate level skills in their labour markets, often by design, include the Czech and Slovak Republics at 73 per cent, 65 per cent in Poland, 58 per cent in Germany, 52 per cent in Sweden and 48 per cent in Japan.

Using the International Labour Organization (ILO) statistical approach, the UK's Office for National Statistics (2016a) estimated that from 2002–15 the UK saw only a gradual increase in the proportion of workers who have a level of educational attainment matched to the average of those in their occupation—up from 67.4 per cent to 68.7 per cent. The proportion of the UK population with a degree or equivalent increased from 27.0 per cent in 2014 to 28.0 per cent in 2015. Those who had no formal qualifications fell from 9.0 per cent to 8.8 per cent (Office for National Statistics, 2016b). However, by 2015, there was a slightly higher percentage of overeducated workers in the UK (16.1 per cent of the workforce) than undereducated (15.1 per cent). In 2016, whilst 16 per cent of UK nationals were employed in jobs they were deemed to be overeducated for, the figure for non-UK nationals was almost 40 per cent (Office for National Statistics, 2017b).

Immigration

This brings us to the third macro factor that bears upon the ability of organizations to attract and retain talent, which is the role of immigration. Migration has become a central feature of international life as part of a multi-stranded process of globalization. Relating back to the discussion earlier of skills and productivity, in the UK immigration was one of the Sector Skills Development Agency's priorities and strategic objectives (this body oversees a network of 25 sector skills councils, each one being an independent employer-led organization), and one of the post-Leitch (2006) Report goals was to understand the link between skills issues and migration.

Until recently, government policy in the UK has been to drive a process of "managed migration" intended to attract skilled labour in job areas such as engineering, the financial sector, education and the health service, guided by a philosophy of voluntarism, but shaped through a package of legislative changes and reforms to the visa system. A review of the evidence around the role of migration conducted for the UK government's then Sectors Skills Development Agency by Sparrow (2008) concluded that longer term, mass migration carries complex benefits and costs. These include potential beneficial impacts on GDP growth rates, holding down wage inflation and by extension interest rates, and closing skills gaps and increasing firm-level productivity. It also has potential negative impacts such as: harming the indigenous population's employment prospects in specific sectors and regions, encouraging the employment of cheap labour, reducing incentives for long-term productivity-improving actions such as training and development, increasing social costs through unemployment and child benefit claims, and other usage of social services such as healthcare.

Official statistics data released in August 2017 present for the first time a worker's country of birth, and they reveal very different labour market outcomes for immigrants (Office for National Statistics, 2017b). Currently 3.4 million immigrants work in Britain, making up 11 per cent of the 30.3-million-strong workforce (Office for National Statistics, 2017b). There are an estimated 2.3 million EU citizens employed in the UK, and 1.2 million overseas nationals in employment from outside the EU. Just over one million of the EU nationals are from the 14 long-term member states (including Germany, Italy, Spain and France), a figure up around 6 per cent since the UK's referendum on EU membership and decision to leave. An estimated 997,000 employees are from the so-called EUA8 countries which joined the EU in 2004—Czech Republic, Estonia, Hungary, Latvia, Lithuania, Poland, Slovakia and Slovenia.

The non-UK workforce is almost evenly split between those who work in professional occupations and those in "elementary" occupations such as selling goods, cleaning or freight handling. Immigration is particularly important to the resourcing of Britain's health service, as well as its wholesale, retail, public administration and hospitality sectors, with more than 1.5 million immigrants working in these sectors. More than a quarter of immigrants work in the public sector, and 701,000 non-UK nationals work in public administration, education and health sectors. Immigrants make up 14 per cent of the workforce in the wholesale and retail trade and in hotels and restaurants, with more than 508,000 EU nationals working in these sectors.

There are very varied employment outcomes for immigrants (Office for National Statistics, 2017b). Whilst three-quarters of people migrating to the UK from these recent EU-joining countries end up working, 70 per cent of those who succeed in finding work end up in low-skilled jobs. Unemployed immigrants total 317,000 (one in five of the total number of unemployed), of which 98,000 were born in the EU and 219,000 born outside the EU. Immigrants from Eastern Europe are generally concentrated in agriculture and manufacturing sectors, are likely to work more hours (61 per cent complete more than 40 hours a week, compared to only 32 per cent of UK nationals) and earn lower wages than UK workers, partly reflecting their prevalence in lower skilled jobs. They are also likely to be over-educated for the jobs they do. In contrast, immigrants from Western European countries are concentrated in the financial and business service sectors. They are more likely to have a university degree, to be higher paid and to work in a job that matches their education. Western European EU immigrants, from countries such as France and Germany, earn more than the UK national average earnings (£12.59 an hour on average compared to £11.30 an hour) while those from Eastern Europe earn less (on average £8.33 an hour). This reflects education levels, with 56 per cent of Western European immigrants in the British labour force having degrees, compared to 29 per cent of immigrants from Eastern Europe.

Given these varied outcomes, it seems likely that inward migration, whilst supplying plentiful labour, has not in fact not been helpful to the UK's need to address its productivity issue. This is leading to debates about the relative role that labour market regulation should play in helping to better manage and benefit from free movement of labour.

Demographic Changes, Working Age Population and Ageing

The fourth macro factor that bears upon the ability of organizations to attract and retain talent is the extent of demographic change and changes in the working age population. These factors have pervasive impacts, but most notably impact the size and power of the domestic consumer market, the experience levels that can be attracted, and the requisite employee value propositions.

The latest official national population projection, at the time of writing, was published in 2015 by the UK's Office for National Statistics (ONS) (Office for National Statistics, 2015). This is a set of measures used for long-term fiscal projections, local resource allocations, policy decisions on benefits, pensions and the length of working lives, and future school populations and education needs. The ONS estimated the UK population at 64.6 million people in 2015, projected to increase by 4.4 million over the next decade, reaching 70 million in 2027—an increase roughly the size of the Irish Republic. Of the projected increase 51 per cent is accounted for by the positive balance of immigration over emigration.

This 14 per cent population rise puts the UK in a very different situation from Germany (which is expected to have a 3 per cent decrease by 2039, despite recent inflows), Spain (4 per cent decrease), Poland (6 per cent decrease), and Greece (13 per cent decrease). It is higher than other population-increase European countries such as the Netherlands (5 per cent increase) and Italy (9 per cent increase). However, more rapid population increases are foreseen in Sweden (21 per cent increase) and Belgium (23 per cent increase), although of course these percentage increases are on a much smaller base number.

Most developed countries have seen a slowing in the growth in the working-age population, and therefore a decline in the total labour force. However, the UK does not face this problem to quite the same extent. The United Nations (2015) has studied cumulative changes in the working-age population around the world, drawing on data from 2005–2015 and projections for 2015–2025 (their projections exclude future levels of immigration, but incorporate recent inflows). In the future, forecasts project that there will be small net increases in the working age population of just under 0.2 per cent in countries such as Mexico, India,

Indonesia, Turkey, Malaysia, Chile and Ireland, but the population of working age in the UK will shift from a recent increase to a slow decrease (the same is true of Singapore, Hong Kong, the USA, Canada, Belgium, South Korea and China). The UK population of working age is expected to remain broadly similar, increasing from 40 million in 2014 to 44.6 million by 2039 (Office for National Statistics, 2015). The UK population is also expected to continue to age, with an increase in the proportion of people aged over 60 from 23 per cent in 2015 to 30 per cent by 2039. National statistics show that this could be a growing problem particularly in the short term, as over the next seven years 14 million employees are expected to retire but just seven million people of working age will enter the market, leaving a deficit of seven million. By 2039 the people of pensionable age per 1000 people of working age will increase from 310 to 370. Therefore, the impact of demographic changes will be far less marked than the declines that will be seen in France, Spain, Netherlands, Finland, Italy, the Czech Republic, Poland, Portugal, Germany, the Russian Federation, Hungary and Japan.

Macro Factors That Serve to Enable and Accelerate the Management of Talent at National Level

Global Labour Markets

Finally, the chapter examines those macro factors that serve to enable and accelerate the management of talent at the national level. These, if you like, might be seen as amplifiers—forces that leverage the impact of those factors discussed in the third and fourth sections.

The first of these macro factors is the impact of specific globalized labour markets on large national employers. Sparrow, Brewster, and Chung (2017) note that as professional labour markets have themselves become highly globalized, they are trying to harmonize strategies designed to pick up potential talent in global cities with strategies aimed at attracting skilled immigrants from across the globe. As Khilji et al. (2015) demonstrate, MNEs now find themselves collaborating with governments and other actors in the spheres of cross border flows of talent, diaspora mobility, and policies to attract, grow, develop and retain national talent in ways that facilitate their own GTM strategies and activities.

As noted previously the healthcare sector can be used as an example of a globalized labour market that has an impact on the talent management strategies of national organizations. The UK's National Health Service (NHS) is the largest single employer within the UK. However, the healthcare sector has periodic episodes of skills shortages, during which it relies heavily on international recruitment. The healthcare sector is one of the highly globalized labour markets, making international recruitment a viable response to skills shortages. However, when excessive demands are made, then a macro-perspective to talent management generates debates about the ethics of stripping other healthcare systems, the transferability of skills and qualifications, failures of central workforce planning, forward investments in education and training, and the attractiveness or not of job conditions.

Through analysis of a prior period of global recruitment in the NHS, that of the early 2000s, Sparrow (2006) showed that the advent of globalized labour markets in specific sectors (such as healthcare) needs domestic employers to develop three kinds of strategy: active recruitment policies where specific skill groups and countries are targeted; passive recruitment policies where applicants take the initiative and organizations need to be able to capitalise on this, or where organizations may capture employees because of an increase in both the 'flow' and 'stock' of international employees through a hub within the domestic market; and longer term strategies to ensure the continued ability to compete in international labour markets.

In the UK the most recent episode of skills shortages in the sector began again in 2013–14, when one in five new nurses in UK hospitals came from abroad, a quadrupling from 2012–13 (NHS Employers, 2017). Of these nurses, 64 per cent came from just three national systems (the NHS has negotiated bi-lateral arrangements) of Spain, Portugal and the Philippines. In March 2016, following a review by the MAC on nursing supply and demand, the government announced that nursing remained on the national shortage occupation list. By 2015 shortages had spread to General Practitioners. Figures from the General Medical Council for January 2015 also showed that the number of foreign-trained doctors made up two-fifths of the year-on-year increase in the overall number of doctors, and of the 267,150 doctors of all types registered with the General Medical Council 36.6 per cent were foreign-trained, including 41.2 per cent of specialists (Royal College of General Practitioners, 2017).

As many professional labour markets have themselves become highly globalized, and MNEs or large domestic employers alike trying to pick up potential talent in global cities—such as London—with strategies aimed at attracting skilled professionals from across the globe, then MNEs and public service bodies alike try to build skills and capabilities, usually under the guidance of the need for global capability transfer, strategic workforce planning initiatives, or the dictates of the need to have a consistent employer brand (Sparrow et al., 2017).

Global Cities

Finally, the second of the macro factors that serve to enable and accelerate the management of talent at the national level is the role played by global cities, which in the instance of the UK is London. It was already evident in the UK by the early 2000s that London had become a market for the forward-brokerage of many skilled employees, both to other English-speaking countries and that UK organizations needed to develop strategies to ensure that they (and their location) could attract talented employees via this global city route (Sparrow, 2006).

The UK therefore is one of a small number of countries in which the talent management market is impacted by the presence of a global city. Much attention recently has been given to the role of London as a global city, but also the distorting effect this might be having on the broader UK's ability to survive and prosper. Economic geographers have started to study linkages between location for MNEs and the emergence and evolution of global cities (Dellestrand & Kappen, 2012; Sassen, 2012; Dickmann, 2012; Goerzen, Asmussen, & Nielsen, 2013). Global cities act as hubs in the broader web of global linkages, and there is a co-evolution between the two. The Brooking Global Cities Initiative reports that by 2014 just 300 metropolitan cities accounted for 47 per cent of all global economic output and nearly 40 per cent of global economic growth, while housing just 20 per cent of the global population (Brookings, 2014). One-third of the world's 300 largest metropolitan economies grew faster—in both GDP and employment growth—than their national economies. London's role as a global city has also seen it become the hub for "passive recruitment" activities in a number of global labour markets in the UK, such as for healthcare or IT professionals.

As global cities play an increasing role in these global strategies, MNEs are moving some specific roles closer to consumers in these cities. Countries and cities in both developed and developing nations are beginning to act like organizations, investing in niche areas of expertise, and using flexible local legislation to encourage investment, industry clusters and local centers of expertise to attract talent. These 'talent hubs', based around specific skills and industries, bring MNEs, cities and countries in direct competition with each other for those segments of talent that will work for the highest bidder or are seeking the most suitable cultural and physical environment. Cities are manipulating personal tax rates for expatriates, building international schools, and investing in arts and leisure facilities to increase their attractiveness. They also open up opportunities for new collaborations. MNEs will be induced or tempted to tap into talent pools that are physically located away from their operations, so will be tempted to locate portions of their work activity within these city states and also rely more on virtual global teams.

The concentration of economic resources and work means London recovered rapidly from the financial crisis of 2007–08. New experimental data from the Office for National Statistics (ONS) shows that by 2017 its economy generated a £26.5 billion surplus, recycled by the government to provide financial help to Britain's less well-off regions (ONS, 2017c). London had the highest net fiscal surplus per person, providing £3,070 more in tax revenues than they received in public spending, while people living in the south-east ran a surplus of £1,670 per head. The east of England turned a small deficit in 2014–15 into a surplus of £242 per head in 2015–16. By contrast, spending exceeded tax revenues by £5,440 per head in Northern Ireland and by £3,820 in the Northeast. Scotland, which has seen its public finances badly affected by the plunge in global oil prices, ran a deficit of £2,830 a head. Northern Ireland and Scotland attracted the highest expenditure per head, at £14,020 and £13,050 respectively.

A Deloitte (2016) study on global cities and global talent has tracked career movements of more than 50,000 executives and public sector leaders from 40,000 organizations across 160 countries, from the broader BoardEx repository of over 750,000 executive and director profiles. This shows that London's executive alumni are drawn from 95 nationalities that reach into 134 countries (the term alumni here is used for those individuals who at some stage in their career have attended university in London or have been employed by a business or public sector organization based in London) (Deloitte, 2016). In terms of high-skill, knowledge-based employment, Deloitte's work suggests that in a period of just three years, London has added 235,000 new high-skill jobs, making it the high-skills capital of the world as assessed in 2016, while equivalent employment in New York has declined marginally. London now employs approximately 1.7 million workers in highly skilled roles compared to 1.2 million in New York, the nearest rival. Hong Kong has 0.76 million high-skill jobs, Singapore 0.73 million, Paris 0.63 million, and Sydney 0.53 million. In addition to alumni effects, there is relatively high growth in London's three top economic categories—professional services, healthcare and education—owing to their competitive strength internationally (London Assembly, 2016). The jobs being created in London are also deemed to be more future-proofed than those of the rest of the UK. Although London jobs that pay £30,000 or less annually are eight times more likely to be automated than those that pay £100,000 or more (Deloitte, 2016), the sectoral balance is such that future automation is not expected to have a significant impact on the employment structure of London.

Conclusions: Implications of the UK Context for the Broader Study of Macro Talent Management

The previous analysis of the macro context for talent management in the UK should lead us to the following conclusions. First, it is evident that talent management at the organization level is conditioned in terms of success (or not) by a series of macro institutional and cultural factors. Moreover, we can discern some important patterns of agency in this, which are detailed next. By examining how each of these macro functions serves talent management, the chapter has suggested a range of processes that are in play. The research agenda now should help validate the proposed linkages. It also should help to broaden the education and role of HRM professionals and their understanding of how these macro factors need to be managed to improve the practical implementation and the values inherent in the conduct of talent management within organizations.

How do the 'patterns of agency' suggested in this chapter fit with, or contrast with, the Khilji et al. (2015) model of macro talent management? Khilji et al. (2015) grouped together a range of environmental contextual factors that intensified competition at the organizational and national levels and heightened the relevance of global talent management (GTM) at the macro level. They then argued that a series of important processes can be used to identify patterns and observe some relationships between talent management and outcomes such as competitiveness, innovation, economic development and the quality of the workforce. Each of these processes, they argued, could also be thought about in relation to the interplay between four core functions of GTM—talent planning, talent acquisition, talent development, and talent retention—which in turn both produce—and could also be facilitated by—three developmental events, which were seen to be talent flows, knowledge spillovers and learning. However, they cautioned that their model should not be viewed as being linear or simple relationships, and that ultimately we should think of macro talent management as a complex system that requires interactions between different partners, and advance the field by identifying and establishing those variables that should best be used to study talent mobility at a global scale.

The chapter has hopefully further developed their model, by shedding light on and explaining which processes appear to have most bearing upon three of the core talent processes, and the interplay between the factors involved. The key UK-specific conclusions can be explained through four observed patterns.

The first pattern that we can see from analysis of the UK is the way in which the economic, technological and cultural context can shape and condition the macro talent management debate at country level. The chapter has revealed eight ways in which this context *conditions* macro global talent management (see Figure 3.2).

Figure 3.2 is a further development of the Khilji et al. (2015) model in that it lays out some of the variables that they suggested we now need to identify. The eight variables, and their relevance to the first of Khilji et al.'s (2015) core functions of talent acquisition, can be explained as follows. The HRM culture and the tacit beliefs about what makes a manager effective predisposes and legitimizes activities within field of practice, and institutionalizes other enabling HRM activities. The level of competitiveness and the resultant quality of a country's human capital fosters macroeconomic outcomes such as output growth, and microeconomic outcomes such as earnings, education, unemployment and social exclusion. Foreign direct investment levels help globalize HRM capabilities in skills transfer, mobility, workforce planning, talent management and employer branding. Finally the industrial structure helps leverage domestic productivity through labour market skills transfers. It fosters talent clusters, innovation, education and industry links, it sends skill demand signals and enables resource access, and finally it signals the necessary strategic investments and shows how to link technology, skills, tax and regulation policy.

In relation to another of the core functions of growth and development, another pattern could be seen from analysis of the UK (see Figure 3.3) in which that there are clear agency

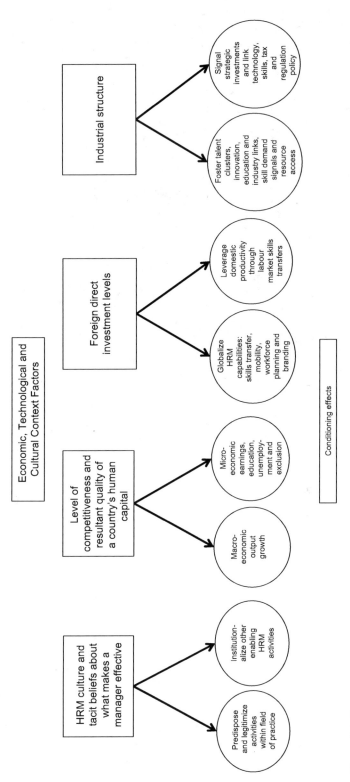

Figure 3.2 The Processes Through Which the Economic, Technological and Cultural Context Shapes and Conditions Talent Management Acquisition in the UK

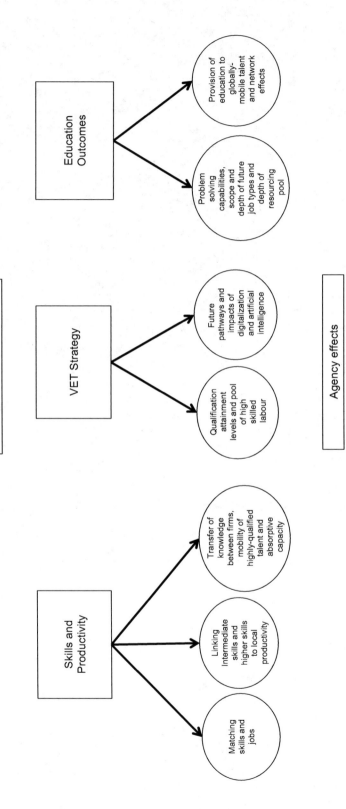

Figure 3.3 The Processes Through Which the Macro Context Shapes and Conditions Talent Management Growth and Development in the UK

effects exerted by a range of macro factors—notably skills and productivity, VET strategy, and education outcomes—on those talent management activities that facilitate growth and development.

As Figure 3.3 shows, understanding skills and productivity linkages helps match skills and jobs, creates links to local productivity through intermediate skills and higher skills, and brings tacit benefits of transfers of knowledge between firms, mobility of highly qualified talent and a general building of an organization's absorptive capacity. The VET strategy helps build necessary qualification attainment levels and develops a pool of high-skilled labour. It also helps broaden the options and future pathways to manage the impacts of digitalization and artificial intelligence. Finally, educational outcomes build the problem solving capabilities of local workforces, widen the scope and depth of future job types that become possible, and deepen the resourcing pool.

A third pattern that can be seen from analysis of the UK is that there are similar agency effects of a range of macro factors on those talent management activities that bear upon the ability of organizations both to attract and retain talent (see Figure 3.4).

These include legislative and business climate changes that can impact the conduct of talent management. Skills shortages, and the associated problem of overeducation and skills underutilization bear upon the choices that MNEs might make about the location of certain operations, or particular business models (which might be more or less value-creating to the broader local economy) within a particular market. They impact the incentives for businesses to raise labour productivity, and foster the creation of new functions and disciplines that are emerging within MNEs to manage the relative productivity of its plants or activities. Immigration can have beneficial impacts on GDP growth rates, levels of wage inflation, closing skills gaps and increasing firm-level productivity, but can also have negative impacts on the indigenous workforce's employment prospects in specific sectors and regions, incentives for long-term productivity-improving actions such as training and development, and increased social costs. In terms of agency, demographic changes, changes in the working age population and ageing all impact the size of the domestic consumer market, the experience levels, and the requisite employee value propositions.

Khilji et al. (2015) also suggested that there are some contextual factors that heightened the relevance of global talent management (GTM) at the macro level within national contexts. The fourth pattern that can be seen from analysis of the UK helps shed some light on what these factors are in a UK context. However, where the chapter builds on the Khilji et al. (2015) analysis is that it explains how this "heightening" takes place. The chapter shows that there are two macro factors that serve to *accelerate* and *amplify* the impact of all the aforementioned global talent management processes at the national level. There are two important factors here: the impacts that globalized sector labour markets have on large national employers, and the growing importance of global cities and large metropolitan cities. These developments are leading to the development of 'talent hubs', based around specific skills and industries, which in turn generates new insights into active and passive recruitment strategies, the transferability of skills and qualifications, the role of strategic workforce planning, the importance of forward investments in education and training, the attractiveness or not of locational value propositions, and the knock-on network effects that city cadres, such as executive alumni, can have on future business growth.

Finally, what are the implications of the prior conclusions for an audience of the policy makers or the managers of global and large domestic organizations? What are the future research questions and the future directions for policy makers and government? Although

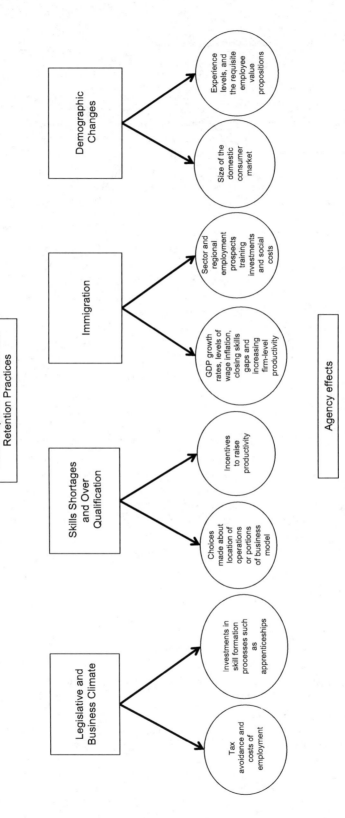

Figure 3.4 The Processes Through Which the Macro Context Shapes and Conditions Talent Management Attraction and Retention in the UK

the chapter has identified some of the important factors involved, it is of course still ultimately descriptive. We shall need to adopt broader theory to help guide the best policy interventions. The analysis has been conducted in a UK context, but arguably these conclusions, and the patterns of agency involved, are likely generic to all countries, and should inform the broad field of macro talent management.

But we do not know this. Indeed, if we draw upon institutional theory, then the next task, having presented a series of country-level analyses, is to determine what is generic, and what is country-bound. As a consequence of these new patterns of agency that the chapter suggests may now be opening up, new institutions will need to be formed and allowed to evolve around these emerging patterns of agency. In other words, by taking a macro talent management perspective, it might become evident that there may be a need for not merely new practices, but for changes in the structures in which these practices are embedded, and the regimes (the overriding expectations and planned way of doing things for a given issue-area around which actors tend to converge) in evidence.

Institutional theory argues that new institutions will form around the patterns of agency that have been suggested in this chapter, and that these institutions must evolve to deal with the nature of that agency (Ross, 1973). However, institutional theory argues that when faced with a new problem, individuals or organizations are drawn to accustomed solutions, whether or not these ever worked or could reasonably be expected to work (Meyer, 2008). A realist institutionalist view suggests there can be brief episodes of collective history (one might argue that macro global talent management is one such force of history), and these can create some crucial changes, but the tendency is for a stable equilibrium to ensue (again, in a UK context, the attempt to impose order subsequent to the decision to leave the EU is an example of this). Actors are constrained in their capacity, and have a picture of their institutional environment that is limited by the rules and regimes believed to be in force. Sociological institutionalism sees actors as being both more empowered but also constructed by their environment. They are controlled in more subtle ways, so in addition to more coercive influences, they are subject to professional norms and standards, and by a tendency to mimic what are considered to be taken-for-granted realities. They are constructed by the environment, and more scripted in their solutions.

From an institutional perspective, then, macro talent management researchers should now ask what must now be done in terms of managing, buffering and adapting (Mitnick, 1980, 2013) these new patterns of global talent management, and should also show what risks may become distorted in a dysfunctional manner by these factors if institutions and organizations are unable to do this. We need to raise questions about what incentives—monetary and behavioural—are needed to condition the behaviour of the key actors involved. We also need to consider the ways in which managers of organizations, and other actors such as policy makers, must now deal with the new uncertainties that are being created, and the levels of discretion that are in reality open to them. What new relations, exchanges and transactions (Williamson, 1964) need to be set up between those responsible for talent management within organizations, and the other agents involved?

There is a massive research territory now opening up, and the agenda needs to have an impact at national policy, MNE, sector, regional and domestic organization level.

References

Bank of England. (2015). *EU membership and the Bank of England*. London: Bank of England.
Barnet, A., Batten, S., Chiu, A., Franklin, J., & Sebastia-Barriel, M. (2014). The UK productivity puzzle, *Bank of England Quarterly Bulletin*, 2014 Q2, 1-15.

BBC. (2017). *Unemployment rate falls to 4.3% as wages stagnate.* Retrieved on September 13, 2017 from www.bbc.co.uk/news/business-41252976.

Bell, V., Burriel-Llombart, P., & Jones, J. (2005). *A quality adjusted labour input series for the United Kingdom (1974–2002).* Bank of England Working Paper No. 280. London: Bank of England.

BERR. (2008). *Cross country productivity performance at the sector level.* BERR Occasional Paper No. 1. Retrieved from www.bis.gov.uk/files/file44507.pdf.

Bosworth, D. L., & Leach, A. (2015). *UK skill levels and international competitiveness 2014.* London, UK: Commission for Employment and Skills.

Brewster, C., Houldsworth, L., Sparrow, P. R., & Vernon, G. (2016). *International human resource management* (4th ed.). London: Chartered Institute of Personnel and Development.

Brewster, C., Sparrow, P. R., & Vernon, G. (2007). *International human resource management* (2nd ed.). London: Chartered Institute of Personnel and Development.

Brookings. (2014). *Global metro monitor: An uncertain recovery.* Global Cities Initiative. Retrieved from www.brookings.edu/metro.

CIPD. (2008). *Talent management: Design, implementation and evaluation.* CIPD Online Practical Tool. London: CIPD.

CIPD/Hays. (2017). *Resourcing and talent planning survey report.* London: CIPD.

Dellestrand, H., & Kappen, P. (2012). The effects of spatial and contextual factors on headquarters resource allocation to MNE subsidiaries. *Journal of International Business Studies, 43*(3), 219–243.

Deloitte. (2016). *Global cities, global talent: London's rising soft power.* London: Deloitte.

Department for Business Innovation & Skills. (2012). *Industrial strategy: UK sector analysis.* BIS Economics Paper No. 18. London: BIS.

Dickmann, M. (2012). Why do they come to London?: Exploring the motivations of expatriates to work in the British capital. *Journal of Management Development, 31*(8), 783–800.

Dromey, J., McNeil, C., & Roberts, C. (2017). *Another lost decade? Building a skills system for the economy of the 2030s.* London: Institute for Public Policy Research.

Economist. (2015). The economy and productivity: Bargain basement. *Economist, 414*(8929), 29–30.

European Commission. (2012). *Employment and social developments in Europe 2012.* Brussels: European Commission.

Evans, P., Doz, Y., & Laurent, A. (Eds.). (1989). *Human resource management in international firms: Change, globalisation and innovation.* London: MacMillan.

Garrett, R., Campbell, M., & Mason, G. (2010). *The value of skills: An evidence review. Evidence report 22.* Wath-Upon-Dearne, UK: Commission for Employment and Skills.

Goerzen, A., Asmussen, C. G., & Nielsen, B. B. (2013). Global cities and multinational enterprise location strategy. *Journal of International Business Studies, 44,* 427–450.

Hays/Oxford Economics. (2014). *The perfect talent storm: The changing dynamics of the global skills landscape.* Hays global skills index 2014. London: Hays plc.

Khilji, S. E., & Schuler, R. S. (2017). Talent management in the global context. In D. Collings, K. Mellahi & W. Cascio (Eds.), *Oxford handbook of talent management.* Oxford, UK: Oxford Press.

Khilji, S. E., Tarique, I., & Schuler, R. S. (2015). Incorporating the macro view in global talent management. *Human Resource Management Review, 25*(3), 236–248.

Lanvin, B., & Evans, P. (2017). *The global talent competitiveness index 2017: Talent and technology.* Fontainebleau: INSEAD.

Leitch. (2006). *Prosperity for all in the global economy: Final report: World class skills.* London: HM Treasury.

London Assembly. (2016, February). *The hourglass economy: An analysis of London's labour market.* London Assembly, Economy Committee. Retrieved from www.london.gov.uk/sites/default/files/londonslabourmarketfinal.pdf.

Meyer, J. (2008). Reflections on institutional theories of organizations. In R. Greenwood, C. Oliver, R. Suddaby, & K. Sahlin (Eds.), *The Sage handbook of organizational institutionalism* (pp. 788–809). Thousand Oaks, CA: Sage.

Mitnick, B. M. (1980). *The political economy of regulation: Creating, designing, and removing regulatory forms.* New York: Columbia University Press.

Mitnick, B. M. (2013). Origin of the theory of agency: An account by one of the theory's originators. *SSRN Electronic Journal.* doi:10.2139/ssrn.1020378.

NHS Employers. (2017). *Shortage occupation list.* Retrieved on October 10, 2017 from www.nhsemployers.org/your-workforce/recruit/employer-led-recruitment/international-recruitment/shortage-occupation-list.

Office for National Statistics. (2015). *National population projections: 2014-based statistical bulletin*. London: Office for National Statistics. Retrieved on August 16, 2017 from www.ons.gov.uk/peoplepopulationandcommunity/populationandmigration/populationprojections/bulletins/nationalpopulationprojections/2015-10-29.

Office for National Statistics. (2016a). *Analysis of the UK labour market: Estimates of skills mismatch using measures of over and under education: 2015*. ONS Statistical Release 17 March 2016. London: ONS.

Office for National Statistics. (2016b). *Human capital estimates: 2015. Estimates of national and regional human capital in the UK from 2004 to 2015*. ONS Statistical Release 18 August 2016. London: ONS.

Office for National Statistics. (2017b). *International immigration and the labour market, UK: 2016*. ONS Statistical Release 12 April 2017. London: ONS.

Office for National Statistics. (2017c). *Country and regional public sector finances: Financial year ending March 2016*. ONS Statistical Release 23 May 2017. London: ONS.

Organization for Economic Cooperation and Development (OECD). (2001). *Measuring capital: OECD manual measurement of capital stocks, consumption of fixed capital and capital services*. Paris: OECD.

Organization for Economic Cooperation and Development (OECD). (2013). *Education at a glance 2013: Highlights*. OECD Publishing.

Organization for Economic Cooperation and Development (OECD). (2017). *OECD economic survey of the United Kingdom: Addressing Brexit and weak productivity*. Retrieved on October 24, 2017 from www.oecd.org/eco/surveys/economic-survey-united-kingdom.htm Accessed.

Owen, G. (2012). *Industrial policy in Europe since the Second World War: What has been learnt?* ECIPE Occasional Paper No 1/2012, Department of Management, London School of Economics. Retrieved from www.ecipe.org/publications/industrial-policy-europe-second-world-war-what-has-been-learnt/.

Recruitment International. (2017). *Half of UK SMEs face major talent management challenge in next 12 months*. Retrieved from www.recruitment-international.co.uk/blog/2017/07/half-of-uk-smes-face-major-talent-management-challenge-in-next-12-months-research-finds Accessed on 14th August 2017.

Ross, S. A. (1973). The economic theory of agency: The principal's problem. *American Economic Review*, 62(2), 134–139.

Royal College of General Practitioners. (2017). *RCGP welcomes international recruitment boost to ease GP shortages*. Retrieved on October 10, 2017 from www.rcgp.org.uk/news/2017/august/rcgp-welcomes-international-recruitment-boost-to-ease-gp-shortages.aspx.

Sassen, S. (2012). *Cities in a world economy*. Los Angeles: Sage.

Schwab, K., & Sala-i-Martin, X. (2016). *The global competitiveness report 2016–2017*. Geneva: World Economic Forum.

Shackleton, V., & Newell, S. (1991). Management selection: A comparative survey of methods used in top British and French companies. *Journal of Occupational Psychology*, 64(1), 23–36.

Sparrow, P. R. (2006). *International recruitment, selection and assessment*. London: Chartered Institute of Personnel and Development.

Sparrow, P. R. (2008). International recruitment, skills supply and migration. *Sector Skills Development Agency Catalyst Report*, 4, 1–20.

Sparrow, P. R., Brewster, C., & Chung, C. (2017). *Globalizing human resource management* (2nd ed.). London and New York: Routledge.

Sparrow, P. R., & Hiltrop, J. M. (1994). *European human resource management in transition*. London: Prentice Hall.

Sparrow, P. R., Scullion, H., & Tarique, I. (2014). Multiple lenses on talent management: Definitions and contours of the field. In P. R. Sparrow, H. Scullion, & I. Tarique (Eds.), *Strategic talent management: Contemporary issues in international context* (pp. 36–70). Cambridge: Cambridge University Press.

Störmer, E., Patscha, C., Prendergast, J., & Daheim, C. (2014). *The future of work: Jobs and skills by 2030. Evidence report 84*. London: UKCES.

Trends in International Mathematics and Science Study (TIMSS). (2015). Retrieved on October 10, 2017 from nces.ed.gov/timss/timss15.asp.

UK Commission for Skills and Employment (UKCES). (2015). *Employer skills survey 2015: Skills in the labour market*. Retrieved from www.gov.uk/ukces.

UNCTAD. (2016). *World investment report 2016*. New York: UNCTAD.

UNESCO. (2012). *Global flow of tertiary-level students*. Retrieved on October 10, 2017 from uis.unesco.org/en/uis-student-flow.

United Nations. (2015). *World population prospects: The 2015 revision*. New York: United Nations Department of Economic and Social Affairs, Population Division.

Universities UK. (2014). *International students in higher education: The UK and its competition*. London: Universities UK.

University of Oxford International Strategy Office. (2015). *International trends in higher education*. Oxford: Oxford University.

Ward, M., & Rhodes, C. (2013). *Small businesses and the UK economy*. House of Commons Statistical Note SN/EP/6078. London: House of Commons.

Williamson, O. E. (1964). *The economics of discretionary behavior: Managerial objectives in a theory of the firm*. Englewood Cliffs, NJ: Prentice-Hall.

World Economic Forum. (2016). *Human capital report 2016*. Geneva: World Economic Forum.

4

Macro Talent Management in Germany

A Strong Economy Facing the Challenges of a Shrinking Labor Force

Marion Festing and Katharina Harsch

Introduction

Germany is the largest economy in Europe with the largest population and the highest GDP (The World Bank, 2017) within the European Union. It is one of the founding members of the European Union and is located in the center of Europe with geographical boarders to eight European Member States (Tatsachen über Deutschland, 2017a). At the time of writing, it is characterized by an excellent economic situation associated with a historically low unemployment rate (Destatis, 2017c) and demographic developments leading to a shrinking population. The huge need for talent in many areas creates a severe "war for talent" (Festing, Schäfer, & Scullion, 2013; The World Bank, 2017). A recent example illustrates this situation: When the airline Air Berlin went bankrupt in October 2017, an employment fair was organized in the premises of Air Berlin, where various employers in need of talent such as the railway company Deutsche Bahn and the online retailer Zalando presented themselves in order to recruit the highly qualified but redundant employees from Air Berlin (Holecek, 2017).

While there is some empirical research on talent management in German companies (e.g., Festing et al., 2013; Festing, Kornau, & Schäfer, 2015; Festing & Schäfer, 2013; Ewerlin & Süß, 2016; Landwehr, 2017), the macro environment, to date, has not been the focus of academic talent management research. The impact of factors such as demographics and economic, educational, social, and political conditions in Germany, as well as governmental initiatives aiming at improving the quantitative and qualitative development of talent, have not been analyzed systematically from a national talent management perspective. According to Khilji, Tarique, & Schuler (2015), this perspective includes the core functions and processes involved in macro talent management and has an impact on the outcomes of these activities.

The aim of this chapter is to focus on macro talent management in Germany, by summarizing current information about the environmental factors that shape macro talent management in the country and discussing their impact on partly unique, country-specific macro talent management functions, processes, and outcomes through the provision of appropriate data.

Macro Talent Management Environmental Factors

The German Economy

With a gross domestic product (GDP) of 3,466,757 million USD in 2016, Germany is the largest economy in Europe and the fourth largest in the world (The World Bank, 2017). Almost 70% of this GDP is generated not by manufacturing but by services. Based on the GDP per capita, the economically strongest federal states are Hamburg, Bremen, and Bavaria (Statistische Ämter der Länder, 2017). Small- and medium-sized enterprises (SMEs) play a crucial role in the German economy and represent more than 99% of all national companies. Employment by SMEs has grown continuously and should have reached 30 million by the time of this writing, representing two-thirds of the German workforce. In addition, roughly 45% of corporate gross investments were accounted for by SMEs in 2015, which affords them enormous economic importance; the so-called "Mittelstand", i.e. the German small and medium-sized businesses, which are often still family businesses, is regarded as the backbone of the German economy (Söllner, 2014; KFW, 2015).

As Germany disposes of only a small amount of natural resources, the country is very dependent on foreign trade and innovation. In 2016, it was the world's third largest exporter, with an export value of almost 1,340 billion USD after China and the US (Statista, 2017c). In addition, Germany is responsible for 12% of the global trade volume in high-tech products, and thus it is 'export world champion' in this area (Tatsachen über Deutschland, 2017e). The strongest industries in Germany are automotive, engineering, electronics, and chemicals (Brodbeck & Frese, 2007), so the national economy concentrates more on technology, innovation, and services than on low-cost production, and "Made in Germany" is still a label for quality (Made in Germany, 2017).

The German economy is based on a social market economy model characterized by the conviction that economic prosperity and growth can best be achieved through cooperation between labor and capital. Therefore, in terms of the varieties of capitalism concept (Soskice & Hall, 2001) it represents a coordinated market economy, which has been stable for many years. Among others, this is reflected in a tight system of state regulations for industrial relations (Morley, 2004; Brodbeck & Frese, 2007). Two important features of this system include co-determination and collective bargaining. Co-determination provides workers with important rights, in order to involve their perspectives in decision-making on various levels and can be considered as '. . . the most influential labor market institution in Germany . . .' (Festing, 2012, p. 43). The collective bargaining system provides employers' associations and trades unions with the right to set a common framework for individual employment rights regarding, for instance, pay level and pay mix, working time, or holidays (Ferner & Varul, 1999). Within the framework of the social market economy, associations, trades unions, and enterprises should promote public welfare, social justice, and cooperative industrial relationships. The system, however, is also subject to criticism targeting costs and limitations for management action, thereby having a possible negative impact on the economic development of the country (Brodbeck & Frese, 2007).

The Education System

In Germany, which is known as the "land of poets and thinkers", the importance of knowledge and knowledge-work is still growing. Indicators include the increase in knowledge-based services or the decline in the production of less research-intensive products (OECD, 2012). In a country where labor costs are relatively high (Germany ranked seventh in the EU) and the private sector paid 30% more per working hour than the EU average (Destatis, 2017b), low production costs are difficult to achieve. Therefore, a focus on innovation is seen as the key for success. In 2014, the country invested 2.84% of its GDP into research and development, a percentage which is above the European average of 2.08% (Make it in Germany, 2017c). Education, which in this context plays a crucial role, is organized and controlled by individual federal states (Expatica, 2015). In order to allow access to education, regardless of the social background of students, public schools and universities are free of charge (Tatsachen über Deutschland, 2017b) and reflect a non-elitist perspective on education providing every individual with access to education regardless of the financial background. This is considered as one of the strengths of the German education system.

The school system is vertically organized on three levels, namely primary education and secondary levels I and II (Tatsachen über Deutschland, 2017b). On the primary education level, all children attend school, the so-called "Grundschule", from grade 1 through 4 or 6, depending on the federal state. Thereafter, parents usually decide on the basis of a child's performance and teachers' recommendations regarding the level of further education (Expatica, 2015). Again, depending on individual federal state regulations, there are mainly three types of secondary schools, namely the general school curriculum, applicable in the "Hauptschule" from grades 5 through 9 or 10 (depending on the individual regulations of the individual federal states); the intermediate school curriculum, valid in the "Realschule" from grades 5 through 10, and the grammar school curriculum, relevant in the "Gymnasium" from grades 5 through 12 or 13. The last option prepares students for their final examination, the so-called "Abitur", which is the prerequisite for studying at a German university (Tatsachen über Deutschland, 2017b; KMK, 2017; Expatica, 2015). In 2014, the distribution of pupils in grade 8 was as follows: 13.3% general school curriculum, 21.7% intermediate school curriculum, 35.8% grammar school curriculum, and the rest studied at other school types (KMK, 2017).

At secondary level II, vocational education is another avenue for education (Solga, Protsch, Ebner, & Brzinsky-Fay, 2014). Around two-thirds of all school graduates follow a dual vocational education program (Make it in Germany, 2017j), which includes theoretical and practical elements. Trainees receive, once or twice a week, classroom training organized by the individual federal state, and the rest of the week is taken up with on-the-job training within one company. The duration of a vocational education program lasts between two and three and a half years, depending on which of the more than 350 occupational profiles is chosen. During this time, trainees are employed as apprentices, receive a monthly salary and are covered by social security (Tatsachen über Deutschland, 2017d; Make it in Germany, 2017j). During the last few years, though, the demand for apprentices has been higher than the supply of positions, thereby indicating an emerging "war for talent". This was mainly due to decreasing birth rates in Germany and a higher valuation of higher education in German society. Vacancies have risen from nearly 37,000 in 2013 to more than 43,000 in 2016 (Make it in Germany, 2017j). The dual vocational training system still plays a crucial role in the German labor market and the economy, though, as it provides companies with skilled labor and prevents youth unemployment, which has increased enormously in other European countries over the last few years (Solga et al., 2014). Overall, 86% of adults in Germany have completed their education at secondary level II, which is higher than the OECD average of 75% (Tatsachen über Deutschland, 2017e). However, the educational success of students is still dependent on their social background. According to a PISA study from 2015, in Germany, 16% of differences in the performance of pupils can be traced back to their social origin, while the OECD average is only 13% in this regard (OECD, 2015d).

The tertiary education level in Germany includes a dense network of around 400 universities and other higher education institutions (bpb, 2013; Tatsachen über Deutschland, 2017f). The importance of tertiary education has increased over the past years, whereas in 2006, 35.6% of the relevant age group participated in tertiary education, and yet ten years later this percentage has now risen up to 55.5% (Statista, 2017a). German tertiary education has a strong focus on internationalization and fosters the mobility of students, graduates, and lecturers. Students from Germany are the largest group of international students in the OECD area, with the five most popular countries being Austria, the Netherlands, Great Britain, Switzerland, and the US. More than a quarter of the students enrolled in German universities stated in 2013 that they had completed a study-related stay abroad; most of them remain abroad for only half a year and less than 10% longer than a year (OECD, 2015b). Nearly 90% of all higher education courses in Germany now lead to Bachelor's or Master's degrees, to ensure the recognition of credits and degrees by different universities in different countries. Moreover, many courses are held in English. After the US and the UK, Germany is the most popular country for higher education among students from abroad (Tatsachen über Deutschland, 2017f). The country's excellent worldwide reputation can also be seen in various rankings, such as the QS World University Rankings or the Times Higher Education World University Rankings, where more than 10 German universities are listed in the Top 200 (Tatsachen über Deutschland, 2017c). The quality and the international orientation of the German education system can be seen as important roots of its success in the global economy.

Demographics

In 2014, Germany had a population of 81.2 million people, including 51% women and 49% men, and is thus the most populous country in Europe (Brodbeck & Frese, 2007; bpb, 2016). The population density of Germany is approximately 230 inhabitants per square kilometer, and whereas in the former West German states the number of inhabitants has risen up to its current 65.2 million people, the former states of East Germany are characterized by a demographic decline and represent around 12.5 million people today. This is on the one hand due to declining birth rates but also due to important rural depopulation and movements of the labor towards the economically stronger former West German states where wages and salaries were higher. The majority of the people (51%) live in North Rhine-Westphalia (17.6 million people), Bavaria (12.7 million people), and Baden-Wuerttemberg (10.7 million people). In addition, 31% live in big cities with more than 100,000 people, including Berlin, Hamburg, and Munich, which are the largest (bpb, 2016). The age distribution in Germany, as represented in Figure 4.1, shows that 18% of the population are younger than 20 years old, 61% are of working age between 20 and 64, and 21% are older than 65 (bpb, 2016). Due to the low birth rate of 1.47, the nation's population is shrinking (Make it in Germany, 2017a; bpb, 2016); furthermore, it is ageing, which, among other factors, is due to increasing life expectancy. The average age was 41.1 in 2010 and had risen to 44.7 by 2015 (Make it in Germany, 2017a). Despite an increasing retirement age from 65 to 67 till 2029 (OECD, 2015c), this development is associated with a decreasing number of working-age people, who carry the financial and social burden of an ever-larger number of people leaving the labor market (see Figure 4.1). The number of working-age people is supposed to decrease from 49 million in 2020 to 38 million in 2060, which it is thought will affect the productivity and competitiveness of the German economy, because especially in the fields of science, engineering, and health care, there is already a shortage of specialists (Make it in Germany, 2016c).

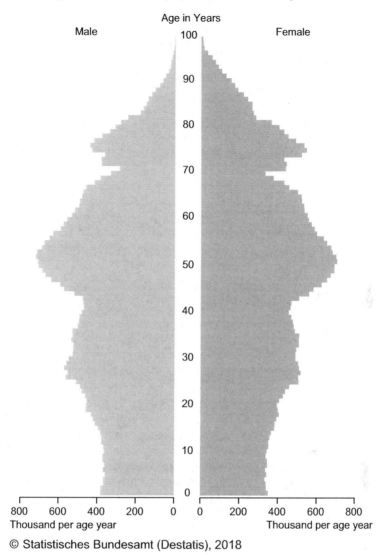

Figure 4.1 Population Pyramid Age Structure

(Destatis, 2016a)

Immigration Policies

The average age of migrants moving to Germany is below the average age of the German population (44.7 years), and so immigration is being discussed as one solution to closing the gap in workforce supply resulting from demographic change (Make it in Germany, 2017e). In 2015, the majority of immigrants came from Turkey, Italy, and Poland, with an average age between 37 and 43.3 years (Make it in Germany, 2017e). As stated by the Federal Institute for Population Research, if these young migrants had the right qualifications, they could help counteract the shortage of qualified workers and therefore contribute to prosperity and economic success (Make it in Germany, 2017e). Thus, labor-related immigration could affect economic development in Germany positively.

There are fundamental differences in rules and regulations concerning work permissions in Germany for various nationalities. People from EU countries as well as Switzerland, Liechtenstein, Norway, and Iceland do not need a resident title to work; however, people from non-EU countries do need a visa (Make it in Germany, 2016a).

In the last decade, conflicts in the Middle East triggered a refugee crisis, which in turn had an impact on the number of migrants entering Germany. In 2015, the peak of immigration was reached and a total of 1,810,904 people moved to the country, which was almost twice as many as in 2012 (Bundesamt für Migration und Flüchtlinge, 2016). In 2015, and as home to 36% of the EU's asylum seekers, Germany was the number one target country (Rietig & Müller, 2016), leading the German Chancellor, Angela Merkel, to proclaim in the same year: 'Germany is a country of immigration' (Deutsche Welle, 2015). When comparing the qualification structure of migrants and the total population, there are hardly any differences (Make it in Germany, 2017f). Therefore, the promotion of immigration seems to be a suitable approach to counteracting the decreasing population size, putting an end to the lack of skilled labor.

Talent Mobility—Diaspora and Returnees

The mobility of talent is important, as they can function as knowledge holders and therefore contribute positively to economic development (Khilji et al., 2015; Kuznetsov, 2006). If emigrants were once considered a loss to a country, it has now been recognized that they can be valuable assets as well, because they can have a positive impact on economic development (Kuznetsov, 2006; Sinning, 2007). Furthermore, they generate knowledge and skills and promote exchanges for the benefit of their country of origin. Previously, the flow of knowledge usually occurred only in one direction, i.e. the so-called "brain drain", but this has changed today to "brain circulation", as the knowledge circulates all around the world and global networks increase (Kuznetsov, 2006; Acosta Arcarazo & Wiesbrock, 2015).

Germany is a country of immigration rather than emigration, although over 15% of Germans indicate that they would like to move abroad. In 2010/11, 3.4 million Germans lived in another OECD country, which corresponds to an emigration rate of around 4% (OECD, 2015e). In 2015, almost 1 million people emigrated away from the country, which is an increase of 83,000 compared to the previous year. If this is compared with the number of migrants who travel to Germany, the result is a net immigration figure of 1,139,000 people in 2015. However, this was a special year and includes the largest number of immigrants in the history of the nation (Destatis, 2016c).

Almost 90% of German emigrants move to only 12 countries, the most popular of which are the US, with over 1.1 million, and Great Britain and Switzerland, each with about 270,000 (OECD, 2015e). On average, German emigrants are highly educated, with 40% of those who emigrated in 2011 holding a university degree and almost 50% having completed advanced secondary education (Sekundarstufe II) or vocational training. The best qualified German emigrants can be found in Switzerland and the US (OECD, 2015e).

According to the Gallup World Poll study, a quarter of 800 German emigrants who were interviewed between 2009 and 2013 stated that they were going to stay permanently abroad, while around 40% were planning to return to their home country (OECD, 2015a). However, the rate of returnees is difficult to determine. When asked for the reasons why German emigrants return to their home country, about two-thirds of the 900 surveyed Germans, who returned in 2013, moved back due to personal and family reasons, followed by work-related reasons (57%), dissatisfaction about their life situation (40%), and a limited stay abroad (40%). Compared to German emigrants, returnees are generally less well qualified, in that the share of highly qualified emigrants is 70%, whereas the proportion of highly qualified returnees is only 64%. As more Germans emigrate than return, and these are also better qualified, it can be concluded that emigration brings advantages regarding knowledge circulation, but it also reduces labor supply, especially with regard to highly qualified talents (OECD, 2015a).

Global and German Labor Markets

Overall, the global labor market faces several challenges. First, the International Labor Organization estimates the global *unemployment rate* for 2017 at 5.8%. Second, although *working poverty rates* have declined in recent years, this process is slowing down steadily, albeit in emerging and developing countries, the share of workers living in extreme or moderate poverty in 2016 was still 29.4% (ILO, 2017). Third, according to the recent ILO Global Wage Report, the *gender pay gap* has decreased, but in most countries, there is still no equal pay for women. For instance, women in France (16%), United Kingdom (21%) and Germany (22%) still earn less than men (Nier, 2017) and represent a situation that is below the OECD average (15%) (OECD, 2017; ILO, 2016). Furthermore, in order to understand the global labor market better, the supply and demand situation of *migrant workers* worldwide must be considered. For example, industrialized countries with a high wage level are home to only 16% of the total working population but also host 60% of the world's migrants, while developing countries with a lower wage level account for only about 1% of the workforce (ILO, 2015). It is noteworthy that countries with a comparable wage level and geographic proximity often enter into regional agreements, in order to simplify access to the labor market for these migrants and to achieve better economic integration (Beyer, 2016).

Looking at the German labor market, the working population was 42.71 million in July 2017, approximately 1.55 million of which was unemployed (unemployment rate of 3.6%) (Destatis, 2017a). According to the most recent available data, 69.5% of the female working population and 78.1% of the male working population were employed in 2014 (OECD, 2016c). In international comparison, Germany has one of the lowest unemployment rates in the world (Make it in Germany, 2017h). For instance, the average unemployment rate in the European Union in 2014 was 7.7%, which is more than twice as great as in Germany (Statista, 2017b). In terms of youth unemployment, Germany is also very well positioned when compared to other EU countries, the reason for which is often seen in its dual vocational training system; for instance, in 2015, in the EU-28 zone, more than 20% of young people aged between 15 and 24 were unemployed but the share in Germany was only 7.3% (Make it in Germany, 2017h).

In Germany, the social security system provides financial security for unemployment, illness, and old age, and social security contributions are paid by the employer as well as by the employee. Overall, wage deductions are quite high compared to other countries and include social security contributions, a solidarity surcharge (stemming from the times of reunification), and income tax (Make it in Germany, 2017d). In 2014, men earned an average of almost 4,300 euro gross per month while the average salary for women of 3,400 euro gross per month was considerably lower. (Make it in Germany, 2017d). An initiative taken against this injustice is "Equal Pay Day", which symbolizes how long women would have to work "for free" in the year to reach the same wage level as men. In 2017, this was the case on 18th March (Business & Professional Women, 2017).

As mentioned previously, the deficit of skilled workers poses a challenge for the German labor market. According to a study by EY (2015), more than half of German companies see the development of their business at risk, because there are not enough qualified workers available to fill vacancies. As a result, every second medium-sized company (51%) has reported sales losses (EY, 2017). However, when looking more closely at the deficit of skilled labor, it is striking that only certain regions and professions are affected, including the fields of science, engineering, and healthcare (Make it in Germany, 2017g). The regional analysis indicates a great demand for specialists particularly in Southern Germany. In 2015, Bavaria and Baden-Württemberg, the southern German states, were characterized by the lowest numbers of job seekers (Make it in Germany, 2017g). Overall, the deficit of skilled labor is a serious threat to the German economy, since the negative demographic development of the country cannot be stopped and progressive digitalization will lead to increasing demands in relation to workers' qualifications.

National Culture

There are many definitions of culture. We refer to the perspective of culture as the shared values of a group, which lead to similarities or differences as compared to other human communities (House, Hanges, Javidan, Dorfman, & Gupta, 2004; Hofstede, 1983; Schwartz, 1999). These are underlying cross-cultural management studies, for example the studies by Hofstede (Hofstede, 1980) and the GLOBE study (House et al., 2004). Despite serious criticism (see, for example, McSweeney, 2002), the dimensions identified in these studies are still often used to describe cultural differences. According to Hofstede's cultural dimensions, the German culture is characterized by low *power distance* and a rather high degree of *individualism*, which can be seen not only in direct, but also in participative communication. Furthermore, it is more *masculine* than *feminine*, meaning that competition and success are more important than caring for others. In addition, the German culture is characterized by a rather high degree of *uncertainty avoidance*, a good example of which is the German legal system, especially regarding the high level of labor regulation and legislation (Morley, 2004). The desire to avoid uncertainty and accompanying future prospects can probably be traced back to historical events such as the time of German National Socialism and the separation of East and West, which might be also be why Germans tend to feel uncomfortable with their identity (Make it in Germany, 2017b). The nation's culture is also characterized by a high score in *long-term orientation* (Hofstede, 2017), resulting in long-term financial investments rather than focusing on short-term success (Ferner & Varul, 1999; Dickmann, 2003). Consequently, human resources can be interpreted as a semi-fixed production factor and their management long-term-oriented (Streeck, 1995). The GLOBE report shows similar results and characterizes the German culture as strongly uncertainty avoiding, individualistic, power distant, assertive, and performance-oriented, with a low focus on interpersonal human orientation moderated by institutionalized welfare and strong labor rights (Globe, 2017; Brodbeck & Frese, 2007). However, cultural classifications by country have also been subject to strong criticism, e.g. from the perspective of poly-culturalism (Morris, Chiu, & Liu, 2015) or when considering archetypes of culture (Brodbeck & Frese, 2007; Venaik & Midgley, 2015).

Macro Talent Management Functions and Processes

As a result of demographic changes (see the Demographics section of this Chapter) and increased qualification requirements due to the progress of globalization and digitalization, there is a shortage of qualified workers, which makes it very difficult to fill vacancies with suitable talent (see the Talent Mobility – Diaspora and Returnees section). In order to cope with this "war for talent" in a globalized labor market, Germany engages actively in talent management. As knowledge work and innovation play an enormous role in the German economy, the topic of talent management is particularly important for the country. Talent management has been defined as activities and processes undertaken in order to fill strategically important positions with suitable human resources, or so-called "talents" (Collings & Mellahi, 2009), which means attracting, developing, and retaining talent in the long term, in order to gain competitive advantage (Stahl et al., 2007). However, as talent management is context-dependent, there is no "one-fits-all-approach" (Sparrow & Makram, 2015). Khilji et al. (2015) define macro talent management as 'the activities that are systematically developed by governmental and nongovernmental organizations expressly for the purpose of enhancing the quality and quantity of talent within and across countries and regions to facilitate innovation and competitiveness of their citizens and corporations' (Khilji et al., 2015, p. 237). In the following, we focus on the measures taken by Germany in order to attract, develop, and retain suitable talents.

Talent Attraction

To attract suitable talent to Germany—and thus fight the "war for talent"—several initiatives are currently underway. The Federal Ministry of Economics and Energy, the Federal Ministry of Labor and Social Affairs, and the Federal Employment Agency have launched the campaign "Qualified Professionals Initiative". This campaign aims to inform companies and qualified professionals and supports the federal government's concept of skilled workers. The two webpages "Website of the Qualified Professional Initiative" and "Make it in Germany" are central parts of the campaign. The first portal serves as an information platform for domestic qualified professionals and companies, while the second is a welcome portal for foreign qualified professionals thinking about immigrating to Germany and provides information about living in the country, career opportunities, and vacancies. Additionally, the portal provides information for companies, with the objective of recruiting qualified professionals from abroad (BMWI, 2017). This means that the German approach is based on the acquisition of domestic and foreign talents alike and aims at providing an attractive context for both target groups.

Looking at talent attraction from a domestic perspective, Germany has some untapped resources (BMWI, 2017). For instance, the majority of *women* of working age are very well educated (BMWI, 2017). Although the employment rate for women (75%) is above the European average (65.5%), they tend to work part-time and are frequently disadvantaged regarding career opportunities (European Commission, 2017). However, Germany has taken some measures to improve their access to and participation in the labor market. In 2015, an *Act for the equal participation of women and men* in leadership positions was adopted, requiring a quota of 30% of the underrepresented sex to sit on German supervisory boards. Since in most cases these are women, it is referred to as the so-called "women's quota". Today, about two and a half years after the introduction of the law, there is a clear change, as the share of women sitting on German supervisory boards has risen by 6.4 percentage points to 28.1% (BMFSFJ, 2017). Furthermore, Germany was one of the 10 European countries encouraged in 2016 by the European semester of economic co-ordination to improve conditions for women's participation in working life with regard to reconciling work and family life, for example through affordable full-time childcare or access to long-term care (European Commission, 2017). In this context, also the new *"Parental Allowance Plus"* was created, which encourages couples to distribute parental leave more equally to both parents. To date, the proportion of German fathers' parental leave is only around 34% with an average duration of 3.1 months (European Commission, 2017). Despite these measures, there is a need for further action.

The second still rather untapped talent pool includes *people with disabilities*. Companies in Germany with an average of more than 20 employees are required by law to employ at least 5% of severely disabled persons, and employers who fail to comply with this requirement must pay a countervailing charge (Bundesagentur für Arbeit, 2017b). There are also various labor market policies that aim at increasing the participation of disabled people in the labor market (Bundesagentur für Arbeit, 2017b). According to the Federal Agency for Employment, 177,000 people with severe handicaps are interested in pursuing a job (BMWI, 2017). Overall, the employment of severely handicapped persons has risen steadily in recent years, and unemployment in 2016 fell even more strongly than in the case of non-severely handicapped persons (Bundesagentur für Arbeit, 2017b). People with severe disabilities are often well above-average qualified, and their performance at work is hardly restricted by their disability (BMWI, 2017). Overall, it can be said that Germany has recognized the importance of untapped national talent pools in the fight against the skilled labor shortage (BMWI, 2017).

Another resource in this context includes *emigrants returning to Germany*. As already discussed, German emigrants are well-qualified and enjoy a top-class reputation abroad, but Germany could also benefit more from their knowledge and experience by better supporting returnees (BMWI, 2017). Currently, the Federal Office of Administration (BVA, 2017) lists on its website a good deal of important information for emigrants and returnees (BVA, 2017). In addition, the Federal Ministry of Education and Research provides financial resources, which are made available to German scientists abroad to help them return home within the framework of scholarships offered by the German Academic Exchange Service (DAAD, 2017a) and other scientific organizations (DAAD, 2017b). Moreover, the Federal Agency for Labor offers advice for migrants who want to return to Germany (Bundesagentur für Arbeit, 2017a). In addition, there are nongovernmental initiatives, such as the association "Deutsche im Ausland". The association provides the largest information platform for Germans abroad, including tips on emigration as well as some information for their return (DIA, 2017). Furthermore, networks, such as the German Academic International Network (GAIN), a group of German scientists in the US, maintain contacts with homeland scientific institutions and provide academic returnees with support, if required (GAIN, 2017). These measures provide good assistance, but a return to Germany could even be made more attractive, for instance, by increasing the transparency of offers and opportunities and by better supporting reintegration (BMWI, 2017).

In order to attract more international talent, the country changed its immigration reforms significantly in the early 2000s, which affected the Residence Law, the Right of Asylum, the Employment Ordinance, and the Integration Course Ordinance (Cerna, 2016). For instance, the Citizenship Law was liberalized by simplifying the process for immigrants to become German citizens (Oezcan, 2004). In 2009, the European Union launched the EU Blue Card, a resident title, to create better opportunities for qualified non-EU immigrants (Bundesamt für Migration und Flüchtlinge, 2016), and this was also adopted by Germany (Süssmuth, 2009). Requirements for obtaining a Blue Card are a university degree and an employment contract that meets the minimum gross salary requirement (Make it in Germany, 2016b). Furthermore, in 2012, the Recognition Act (Anerkennungsgesetz) was adopted, which allows immigrants the recognition of their foreign qualifications. This was an important change for non-EU migrants without a university degree as well as for EU nationals working in a regulated profession such as medicine or law and interested in working in Germany (Make it in Germany, 2017i). In summer 2013, new employment regulations promulgated by the Federal Ministry of Labor and Social Affairs came into force, the so-called "positive list", which lists all occupations for which there is a lack of qualified professionals. Immigrants are granted a residence and work permit if they are qualified in such a profession. The list contains over 50 occupations, mainly from the fields of health care, mechatronics, and electronics (BMI, 2017).

In addition, at the end of 2014, Germany improved access to the labor market for asylum seekers, first by increasing the number of job agency staff as well as of the agency concerned with asylum applications and integration problems, and second by creating training opportunities and improved access to the education system. As a consequence, the unemployment rate of immigrants has fallen steadily, and differences in the school performance of native-born and foreign-born youth have also declined significantly. However, as an OECD comparison indicates, there are still improvements that can be made for Germany to be viewed as an attractive country for highly qualified migrants (OECD, 2016a). Through the initiative "Research in Germany—Land of Ideas", the Federal Ministry of Education and Research has set itself the goal of promoting the international visibility of German top research by means of various network partners and activities at home and abroad, in order to strengthen innovation potential, arouse mobility interests, and promote cooperation (Research in Germany 2017).

Looking at the educational level of immigrants in Germany over the course of time, there is a clear change. In 2005, they were less well qualified than the local population, but 10 years later, they reached the same level. Therefore, attracting academics by simplifying immigration for this target group seems to be a promising initiative (Make it in Germany, 2017f).

Talent Development

As discussed earlier, the German economy is characterized by the high level of importance afforded to innovation, knowledge, and knowledge work. Therefore, especially in the context of the deficit of skilled workers, education is a major priority. According to the Federal Ministry of Education and Research, the key objective in the field of talent development at the macro level lies in the quality assurance of the education system. Due to current social and economic developments such as the increasing number of immigrants and growing digitalization, Germany faces various challenges in achieving this goal. To this end, it has steadily increased expenditure on education, research, and science over the last few years (Autorengruppe Bildungsberichterstattung, 2016), amounting to 129.2 billion euro in 2016, which corresponds to an increase of 5 billion euro compared to the previous year (Destatis, 2016d). Two major initiatives by the German Federal Ministry of Education and Research are the qualification initiative for Germany, "Advancement through Education," and an educational campaign for the digital knowledge society (BMBF, 2015b, 2016). The main actions and funding programs for the various areas of the German education system—school education, tertiary education, and vocational education—are outlined below.

School Education

The educational report[1] that provides an overview of current information on the various fields of education places special emphasis on education and migration in 2016 (KMK, 2016). According to this report, the educational participation of young immigrants seems to have improved, with the proportion of those having achieved a university entrance qualification, with or without an immigrant background, starting a university degree is roughly the same. However, young immigrants are still leaving the school system more than twice as often without a basic school certificate of secondary education (Hauptschulabschluss), and they are three times less likely to gain university entrance qualifications. Therefore, the challenge remains to integrate immigrants better into the school system, in order to provide equal opportunities for all students (Autorengruppe Bildungsberichterstattung, 2016). One of the joint initiatives of the Federal Ministry of Education and Research and the federal states to address this challenge is a quality campaign based on teacher training. The main aim of the program is to promote media and digital competencies as well as the cultural and intercultural skills of teachers, supporting them in addressing current challenges such as digitalization in all areas of life and the integration of migrants (BMBF, 2017b). In addition to this initiative, education spending per pupil has increased in recent years and was 6,500 euro per year above the OECD average in 2013. Furthermore, all-day courses were continuously expanded in all schools, and in 2014, a full-day rate of almost 60% of all schools was achieved (KMK, 2016; Destatis, 2016b).

Tertiary Education

As previously discussed, the importance of the tertiary education level has increased in recent years, as more than half of all young adults decide to pursue higher education (Statista, 2017a). Accordingly, there are many governmental and non-governmental initiatives and funding programs in this area. The government supports students financially through the "Bundesausbildungsförderungsgesetz" ("Bafög"), a combination of social benefits and a student loan, and allows them, regardless of their financial situation, to attend university and get an academic degree (Tatsachen über Deutschland, 2017c). In addition, there are numerous government-funded scholarship programs in Germany. For instance, the scholarship "Deutschlandstipendium" is funded by the federal government and private funding agencies and amounts to 300 euros monthly (BMBF, 2017a). Besides outstanding achievements in the course of study and social commitment, social background is also an important requirement in receiving this scholarship. Here, the needs of immigrants and other low income target groups are taken into account (BMBF, 2015b). Furthermore, the National Pact for Women in STEM (Science, Technology, Engineering, Mathematics) professions was created to combat the challenge of skilled labor shortages in the fields of STEM and the promotion of women. This initiative of the Federal Ministry of Education and Research is aimed at attracting young women to STEM courses and professions (Komm mach mit, 2017). Regarding the challenges of increasing digitalization and related threats to the shortage of skilled labor, the federal government and federal states have promoted education through the creation of open universities, which expand needs-based learning opportunities at universities for various target groups, usually with the aid of digital-based educational services such as MOOCs (Massive

Open Online Courses), virtual classrooms, virtual seminars, or online forums (BMBF, 2016). The German Academic Exchange Service (DAAD) has committed itself to the promotion of academic relations with foreign countries, especially through the exchange of students and academics. Its programs are usually open to all disciplines and countries and benefits both domestic and foreign applicants (DAAD, 2017b). In summary, talent development measures in the field of higher education in Germany promote international exchange, take account of digital developments, and promote the socially disadvantaged, immigrants, and women.

Vocational Education

Vocational education is of great importance in Germany, in order to meet the needs of the labor market for qualified professionals. In the 2017 vocational training report of the Federal Institute for Vocational Education and Training, the focus was on refugees and vocational training (BIBB, 2017). The Federal Ministry of Education and Research places the focus of its actions and support accordingly; for instance, increased advertising for companies that vocationally train young immigrants, or information and counseling for young immigrants, their relatives, and schools are emphasized (BMBF, 2015b). A further initiative of the Federal Ministry of Education and Research, in cooperation with the federal states and the Federal Ministry of Labor and Social Affairs is the initiative "Abschluss und Anschluss—Bildungsketten bis zum Ausbildungsabschluss", which includes an analysis of individual potential, measures regarding vocational orientation, and guidance when starting a career, and it is one of the key measures within the framework of the Alliance for Vocational Education and Training (BMBF, 2015b). In addition to the topic of integrating young immigrants, the subject of digitalization is a large area in the field of support measures and initiatives for vocational training in Germany. With the umbrella initiative "Berufsbildung 4.0", the ministry bundles various measures, such as the "Digital Media in Vocational Education and Training" program, which aims at anchoring learning with digital media in vocational education, or the joint initiative with the Federal Institute for Vocational Education and Training "Skilled worker qualification and competencies for the digitalized work of tomorrow", which aims at identifying changing requirements and taking them into account in vocational education and training (BMBF, 2016). Furthermore, the Federal Ministry of Education and Research is investing around 1 billion euro in the "Future of Labor" research program, to examine more closely the challenges, opportunities, and consequences of digitalization in relation to the working world (BMBF, 2015a).

Talent Retention

Within the scope of talent management at the macro level, it is not only about attracting talents or developing them, but also about keeping them in the country and promoting participation in working life. Measures in this context aim at primarily two target groups, namely migrants and elderly people. In order to retain qualified specialists from abroad in Germany, prerequisites must be created in a way that they can and will remain in Germany.

The topic of *integration* plays an important role in this context (Bundesregierung, 2016). In this respect, Germany takes certain measures, such as recognizing qualifications and improving the integration of immigrants into the German education system and its labor market (see sections on Talent Attraction and Talent Development). In addition, foreign specialists, who are employed in Germany and intend to stay for at least 12 months, are also given the opportunity to bring their spouse and children to the country.

In order to retain *international young talents*, Germany has increased the residence permits of students from abroad by 6 months to a total of 18 months after graduation. Once they have gained a foothold in the German labor market, they can remain permanently after two years. Similar regulations exist for foreigners who have completed vocational education programs, but they have only 12 months to find a job corresponding to their qualification, before they have to leave the country (BMI, 2017).

Older people also represent a resource that is often overlooked and should be retained in the labor market for a longer time. In addition, they should be taken into account when trying to find solutions to the deficit of skilled workers, as they have extensive expertise and many years of professional experience (BMWI, 2017). Just 20 years ago, the federal government was taking a different course in this context, since the law governing pre-retirement allowed older workers to make a sliding transition into retirement, in order to create vacancies for younger people. However, in 2009, respective subsidies were abolished (Budget, 2017) and the government recognized the importance of older people in combating the lack of qualified professionals. As such, it is important to secure their availability for the labor market for a longer time (BMWI, 2017).

Macro Talent Management Outcomes

Talent management outcomes in an international comparison reflect the competitiveness of the country in this area and show how successful the measures on macro-level have been in this regard. They also provide an indication of the extent to which the various challenges facing the country in this context, due to its environmental factors and the current global developments, can be addressed. Various international indices and rankings deal with the many different topics of macro talent management, but the following are the most important.

Global Talent Competitiveness Index

The Global Talent Competitive Index, produced by INSEAD, ranks countries via six categories, namely the input variables *enabling*, *attracting*, *growing*, and *retaining*, and the output variables *vocational and technical skills* as well as *global knowledge skills*. In the *enable* category, Germany occupies 14th place; however, it is outstandingly placed in the subcategory *market landscape* (third place), which can be attributed, for example, to significant expenditure on research and development and the predominant ICT infrastructure. *Labor market flexibility*, conversely, is rather limited, due to the country's strong labor rights. In the category *attraction*, Germany is ranked again 14th, but 51st place in the subcategory *business opportunities for women* shows a certain need for action. In the *grow* category, Germany is also ranked 20th. Although the quality of education is quite good (subcategories between 8th and 12th place), there is definitely still room for improvement for the use of virtual networks (subcategory places 52 and 66). In the area of *talent retention*, Germany ranks 11th, the only outlier being the fact that the tax burden is high and the country therefore is in this sub-category in 77th place. With regard to output variables, Germany is ranked first in the area of *vocational and technical skills*, which is attributable to the vocational education system. Overall, according to the Global Talent Competitiveness Index, Germany is ranked 17th out of 118 in the global ranking, with a score of 64.94, and in the European ranking it finds itself ahead of all southern European countries in 11th place (Lanvin & Evans, 2017).

Macro Talent Management in Germany • 115

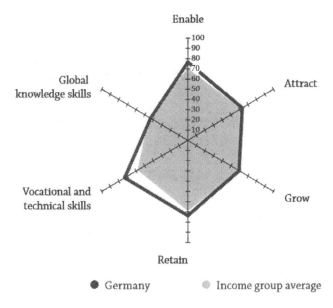

Figure 4.2 Global Talent Competitive Index—Germany
(Lanvin & Evans, 2017, p. 158)

Program for International Student Assessment (PISA)

The most well-known country ranking in the field of educational attainment is the OECD's PISA assessment, which is based on the achievements of 15-year-old students in the fields of math, science, and reading (OECD, 2016d). German students do very well in international comparison here and are above average in all three areas. However, despite the measures taken, 16% of the differences in school performance are due to the student's social background, which is above the OECD average of 13% (OECD, 2016d). Also, with regard to the achievement of pupils with a migration background, Germany scores worse than the OECD average (OECD, 2015d).

Human Capital Report

With regard to German talent management in its entirety, the current World Economic Forum's human capital report shows that the country's measures in this regard seem to be effective. Furthermore, Germany, after Japan and Canada, has improved most in comparison to the last evaluation period. Strong employee development, high rates of highly skilled employment, low youth unemployment, and the high quality of the education system as a whole have helped the country make up about 80% of the human capital potential (World Economic Forum, 2017).

European Lifelong Learning Index

The ranking of the Bertelsmann Foundation "European Lifelong Learning Index" is similarly positive, in that Germany is above-average in the field of lifelong learning and offers a good learning infrastructure (Bertelsmann Stiftung, 2010).

Global Competitiveness Report

The Global Competitiveness Report, on the other hand, does not focus on a single area but provides an overview of the competitiveness of 138 economies and gives an insight into the drivers of their productivity and prosperity. The index comprises more than 100 indicators, summarized in 12 pillars, which in turn are divided into the three areas of: Basic requirements (institution, infrastructure, macro-economic environment, health, and primary education), efficiency enhancers (higher education and training, goods market efficiency, financial market development, technological readiness, market size), and innovation and sophistication (business sophistication and innovation). Germany is one of the most innovation-driven countries in this respect and is ranked fifth overall after Switzerland, Singapore, the USA, and the Netherlands. This shows that, on average, Germany is quite well positioned on an international scale and is on the right track with the development of macro-level talent management to increase competitiveness.

Well-Being Index

The Well-being Index, compiled by the OECD, provides information on the well-being factors of a country. Overall, Germany is above the OECD average in almost all sectors (see Figure 4.3). However, the results also show that subjective educational success, health, and life expectancy are strongly dependent on the social background, while the overall results of well-being deteriorate with age. In contrast, income inequality is one of the lowest compared to the larger OECD economies, although the disposable income of the poorest households has not grown in real terms over the last decade despite low unemployment rates (OECD, 2016a).

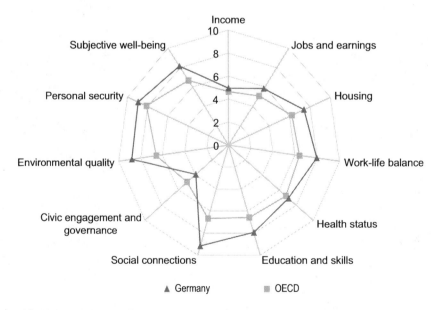

Figure 4.3 Well-being Index in Germany

(OECD, 2016b, p. 10)

Implications and Conclusion

This chapter has drawn a picture of macro talent management in Germany by investigating some important environmental factors affecting current talent management policies and activities on a national level that influence macro talent management on first- and second-level outcomes. Any analysis of environmental factors needs to make choices, which are at the same time limitations of the chapter. However, they also point to specificities within a country context.

To sum up, in the case of Germany, we focused on government policies, programs, and activities rather than on non-governmental activities. This reflects the strong role that the state takes in providing an educational context in the social market economy. As an economically strong country, Germany provides free education at the primary, secondary, and tertiary levels. Furthermore, the widespread dual vocational training system is the result of strong cooperation between the private and the public sector, and it is said that the overall high level of vocational qualifications is one of the backbones of the German economy. The demographic situation is characterized by a low birth rate and a shrinking population, which is typical for many developed countries. Together with the reported low unemployment rates, it requires measures that are supposed to lead to an increase in the workforce. Strong potential in this regard is seen in the cases of women, older people, immigration, and emigration. Here, a variety of measures concerning talent attraction (domestic and international), educational development, and retention regarding young and older people are taken. These measures should institutionally support macro talent management processes such as knowledge spillovers and sharing, learning in an excellent educational environment, and, eventually, corporate strategies.

Festing (2012) outlined the tight relationship between the national business system of Germany and human resource management on the corporate level. This notion also applies to corporate talent management, which reflects the culturally and institutionally explainable long-term and developmental orientation of the German economy in the context of strong cooperation between management and employees as a feature of the social market economy. Thus, macro talent management analysis helps understand and explain corporate talent management policies and practices in Germany as well. This underlines the importance of taking into account the broad context, in order to understand talent management better on all levels, including contextualization approaches (for the concept, see Michailova, 2011; for an application to talent management, see Muratbekova-Touron, Kabalina, & Festing, in press; or the impact of national business systems Festing et al., 2013).

The outcomes of macro talent management can be seen in this light and are important input factors for corporate talent management. In the case of Germany, we should stress the quality of education, innovation, research, and development activities, as well as support for the immigration of qualified professionals. Challenges such as providing better learning opportunities for students from environments with limited access to education, the better integration of females into the workforce, or educating for digitalization have at least been recognized and are subject to further action. This should eventually lead to improving further the second-level outcomes of macro talent management in Germany.

Note

1. Since 2006, the German Federal Ministry of Education and Research and the Conference of Ministers of Education and Cultural Affairs have supported the national report "Bildung in Deutschland," written by an independent expert group, which provides information on the status quo of all educational areas in Germany as well as funding programs and initiatives in this context. The report is published every two years (DIPF, 2016).

References

Acosta Arcarazo, D., & Wiesbrock, A. (2015). *Global migration issues: Myths and realities.* Retrieved from ssrn.com/abstract=2604184.

Autorengruppe Bildungsberichterstattung. (2016). *Bildung in Deutschland 2016—Ein indikatorengestützter Bericht mit einer Analyse zu Bildung und Migration.* Retrieved from www.bildungsbericht.de/de/bildungsberichte-seit-2006/bildungsbericht-2016/pdf-bildungsbericht-2016/bildungsbericht-2016.

Bertelsmann Stiftung. (2010). *ELLI Index Europe 2010—Indicators in Depth.*

Beyer, R. C. (2016). *The labor market performance of immigrants in Germany.* Frankfurt: International Monetary Fund. Retrieved from www.deutscher-lernatlas.de/fileadmin/Inhalte/Ergebnisse/Publikationen/Indicators_in_Depth.pdf.

BIBB. (2017). *Datenreport 2017.* Retrieved on September 12, 2017 from www.bibb.de/datenreport/de/aktuell.php.

BMBF. (2015a). *Bekanntmachung.* Bundesministerium für Bildung und Forschung. Retrieved on September 12, 2017 from www.bmbf.de/foerderungen/bekanntmachung.php?B=1017.

BMBF. (2015b). *Integration durch Bildung—Initiativen für Chancengerechtigkeit und Teilhabe.* Bundesministerium für Bildung und Forschung. Retrieved on September 21, 2017 from www.bmbf.de/pub/Integration_durch_Bildung.pdf.

BMBF. (2016). *Bildungsoffensive für die digitale Wissensgesellschaft—Strategie des Bundesministeriums für Bildung und Forschung.* Bundesministerium für Bildung und Forschung. Retrieved on September 21, 2017 from www.bmbf.de/pub/Bildungsoffensive_fuer_die_digitale_Wissensgesellschaft.pdf.

BMBF. (2017a). *Deutschland Stipendium.* Bundesministerium für Bildung und Forschung. Retrieved on September 12, 2017 from www.deutschlandstipendium.de.

BMBF. (2017b). *Qualitätsoffensive Lehrerbildung.* Bundesministerium für Bildung und Forschung. Retrieved on September 11, 2017 from www.qualitaetsoffensive-lehrerbildung.de.

BMFSFJ. (2017). *Quote für mehr Frauen in Führungspositionen: Privatwirtschaft.* Bundesministerium für Familie, Senioren, Frauen und Jugend. Retrieved on September 8, 2017 from www.bmfsfj.de/bmfsfj/themen/gleichstellung/frauen-und-arbeitswelt/quote-privatwitschaft/quote-fuer-mehr-frauen-in-fuehrungspositionen—privatwirtschaft/78562?view=DEFAULT.

BMI. (2017). *Arbeitsmigration.* Bundesminiterium des Innern. Retrieved on September 12, 2017 from www.bmi.bund.de/DE/Themen/Migration-Integration/Zuwanderung/Arbeitsmigration/arbeitsmigration_node.html.

BMWI. (2017). *Fachkräfte für Deutschland.* Bundesministerium für Wirtschaft und Energie. Retrieved on September 12, 2017 from www.bmwi.de/Redaktion/DE/Dossier/fachkraeftesicherung.html.

bpb. (2013). *Das Bildungssystem in Deutschland—Bildungseinrichtungen, Übergänge und Abschlüsse.* Retrieved on August 30, 2017 from www.bpb.de/gesellschaft/kultur/zukunft-bildung/163283/das-bildungssystem-in-deutschland.

bpb. (2016). *Ein Sozialbericht für die Bundesrepublik Deutschland.* Retrieved on September 21, 2017 from www.destatis.de/DE/Publikationen/Datenreport/Downloads/Datenreport2016.pdf?__blob=publicationFile.

Brodbeck, F. C., & Frese, M. (2007). Societal culture and leadership in Germany. In *Culture and leadership across the world: The GLOBE book of in-depth studies of 25 societies* (pp. 147–214). Mahwah, New Jersey: Lawrence Erlbaum Associates.

Budget. (2017). *In Altersteilzeit gehen.* Bundesministerium für Arbeit und Soziales. Retrieved on September 12, 2017 from www.budget.bmas.de/DE/StdS/Alter/Arbeit_Alter/Altersteilzeit/altersteilzeit_node.html.

Bundesagentur für Arbeit. (2017a). *Beschäftigung in Deutschland: Perspektiven für Rückkehrer.* Retrieved on September 8, 2017 from www3.arbeitsagentur.de/web/content/DE/service/Ueberuns/WeitereDienststellen/ZentraleAuslandsundFachvermittlung/Arbeit/ArbeiteninDeutschland/Detail/index.htm?dfContentId=L6019022DSTBAI524577.

Bundesagentur für Arbeit. (2017b). *Blickpunkt Arbeitsmarkt—Situation schwerbehinderter Menschen.* Retrieved on September 21, 2017 from statistik.arbeitsagentur.de/Statischer-Content/Arbeitsmarktberichte/Personengruppen/generische-Publikationen/Brosch-Die-Arbeitsmarktsituation-schwerbehinderter-Menschen-2016.pdf.

Bundesamt für Migration und Flüchtlinge. (2016). *Wanderungsmonitoring: Erwerbsmigration nach Deutschland.* Bundesamt für Migration und Flüchtlinge und Integration und Asyl Forschungszentrum Migration. Nürnberg. Retrieved from www.bamf.de/SharedDocs/Anlagen/DE/Publikationen/Broschueren/wanderungsmonitoring-2015.pdf?__blob=publicationFile.

Bundesregierung. (2016). *Zuwanderung allein ist keine Lösung.* Retrieved from www.bundesregierung.de/Content/DE/Artikel/2016/09/2016-09-01-demografiekongress.html.

Business and Professional Women. (2017). *Endlich partnerschaftlich durchstarten!* BPW Germany e.V. Retrieved on September 11, 2017 from www.equalpayday.de/startseite/.

BVA. (2017). *Informationen für Auswanderer und Rückkehrer nach Deutschland.* Bundesverwaltungsamt. Retrieved on September 8, 2017 from www.bva.bund.de/DE/Organisation/Abteilungen/Abteilung_ZMV/Bundesstelle_für_Auswanderer_und_Auslandstaetige/Länderinformationen/Europa/Deutschland/Deutschland_DE.html?nn=6167828.
Cerna, L. (2016). *Immigration policies and the global competition for talent.* London: Palgrave Macmillan.
Collings, D. G., & Mellahi, K. (2009). Strategic talent management: A review and research agenda. *Human Resource Management Review, 19*(4), 304–313. doi:10.1016/j.hrmr.2009.04.001.
DAAD. (2017a). *Deutsch Akademischer Austausch Dienst.* Retrieved on September 12, 2017 from www.daad.de/de/.
DAAD. (2017b). *Rückkehrstipendien für Deutsche aus dem Ausland.* Deutsch Akademischer Austausch Dienst. Retrieved on September 12, 2017 from www.daad.de/ausland/reintegration/stipendien/de/22184-rueckkehrstipendien-fuer-deutsche-aus-dem-ausland/.
Destatis. (2016a). *Age structure of Germany's population in 2015.* Retrieved on September 21, 2017 from www.destatis.de/EN/FactsFigures/SocietyState/Population/CurrentPopulation/CurrentPopulation.html;jsessionid=7748D4F763E59C16C9CC586227729448.InternetLive2.
Destatis. (2016b). *Bildungsfinanzbericht 2016.* Retrieved on September 21, 2017 from www.destatis.de/DE/Publikationen/Thematisch/BildungForschungKultur/BildungKulturFinanzen/Bildungsfinanzbericht1023206167004.pdf?__blob=publicationFile.
Destatis. (2016c). *Immigration and net immigration peaked in 2015.* Destatis, Statistisches Bundesamt. Retrieved on September 11, 2017 from www.destatis.de/EN/PressServices/Press/pr/2016/07/PE16_246_12421.html;jsessionid=9D97FF7B2F18405C78EC559543B2983E.cae2.
Destatis. (2016d). *Öffentliche Bildungsausgaben steigen 2016 auf über 129 Milliarden Euro.* Retrieved on September 1, 2017 from www.destatis.de/DE/PresseService/Presse/Pressemitteilungen/2016/12/PD16_454_217.html.
Destatis. (2017a). *Arbeitsmarkt—EU-Vergleich der Lohnnebenkosten—Statistisches Bundesamt.* Retrieved on September 1, 2017 from www.destatis.de/Europa/DE/Thema/BevoelkerungSoziales/Arbeitsmarkt/Hoehe Lohnnebenkosten.html.
Destatis. (2017b). *EU comparison 2017: Germany and the other member states.* Retrieved on September 12, 2017 from www.destatis.de/Europa/EN/Country/Comparison/GER_EU_Compared.html.
Destatis. (2017c). *Unemployment.* Statistisches Bundesamt. Retrieved on September 21, 2017 from www.destatis.de/EN/FactsFigures/NationalEconomyEnvironment/LabourMarket/Unemployment/Unemployment.html;jsessionid=EC7685B3FB1511764E47A667786A30FE.cae3.
Deutsche Welle. (2015). *Merkel: Germany is becoming a 'country of immigration'.* Retrieved on September 21, 2017 from www.dw.com/en/merkel-germany-is-becoming-a-country-of-immigration/a-18491165.
DIA. (2017). *Die größte Informationsplattform für Deutsche im Ausland.* DIA e.V. Retrieved on September 8, 2017 from www.deutsche-im-ausland.org.
Dickmann, M. (2003). Implementing German HRM abroad: Desired, feasible, successful? *International Journal of Human Resource Management, 14*(2), 265–283.
DIPF. (2017). *Bildung in Deutschland.* Deutsches Institut für Internationale Pädagogische Forschung 2016. Retrieved on September 11, 2017 from www.bildungsbericht.de/de/nationaler-bildungsbericht.
European Commission. (2017). *2017 Report on equality between women and men in the EU.* Retrieved from eeas.europa.eu/sites/eeas/files/2017_report_equality_women_men_in_the_eu_en.pdf.
Ewerlin, D., & Süß, S. (2016). Dissemination of talent management in Germany: Myth, facade or economic necessity? *Personnel Review, 45*(1), 142–160.
Expatica. (2015). *Education in Germany.* Retrieved on September 1, 2017 from www.expatica.com/de/education/Education-in-Germany-German-school-system_101611.html.
EY. (2017). *EY Mittelstandsbarometer Deutschland und Europa—Fokus: Fachkräftemangel.* Ernst & Young GmbH. Retrieved on September 21, 2017 from www.ey.com/de/de/newsroom/news-releases/20150225-ey-news-fachkraeftemangel-groesste-bedrohung-fuer-deutsche-unternehmen.
Ferner, A., & Varul, M. Z. (1999). *The German way: German multinationals and human resource management.* London: Anglo-German Foundation for the Study of Industrial Society.
Festing, M. (2012). Strategic human resource management in Germany: Evidence of convergence to the U.S. model, the European model, or a distinctive national model? *Academy of Management Perspectives, 26*(2), 37–54.
Festing, M., Kornau, A., & Schäfer, L. (2015). Think talent—think male? A comparative case study analysis of gender inclusion in talent management practices in the German media industry. *The International Journal of Human Resource Management, 26*(6), 707–732.
Festing, M., & Schäfer, L. (2013). Value creation through human resource management and talent management in clusters: A case study from Germany. In K. Brown, J. Burgess, M. Festing, & S. Royer (Eds.), *Resources and competitive advantage in clusters* (pp. 170–189). Munich and Mehring: Rainer Hampp Verlag.

Festing, M., Schäfer, L., & Scullion, H. (2013). Talent management in medium-sized German companies: An explorative study and agenda for future research. *The International Journal of Human Resource Management, 24*(9), 1872–1893.

GAIN. (2017). *German academic international network*. Retrieved on September 8, 2017 from www.gain-network.org/de/ueber-uns/.

Globe. (2017). *Germany*. Global Leadership & Organizational Behavior Effectiveness. Retrieved on September 11, 2017 from globeproject.com/results/countries/DEU?menu=list.

Hofstede, G. H. (1980). *Culture's consequences: International differences in work related values*. Beverly Hills, CA: Sage Publications.

Hofstede, G. H. (1983). National cultures in four dimensions: A research-based theory of cultural differences among nations. *International Studies of Management & Organization, 13*(1–2), 46–74.

Hofstede, G. H. (2017). *What about Germany?* Retrieved on September 11, 2017 from geert-hofstede.com/germany.html.

Holecek, A. (2017). *Jobmesse Deutsche Bahn wirbt um Air Berlin Mitarbeiter*. Berliner Zeitung. Retrieved from www.berliner-zeitung.de/28562882.

House, R. J., Hanges, P. J., Javidan, M., Dorfman, P. W., & Gupta, V. (2004). *Culture, leadership, and organizations: The GLOBE study of 62 societies*. Thousand Oaks, CA: Sage Publications.

ILO. (2015). *ILO global estimates of migrant workers and migrant domestic workers: Results and methodology*. Geneva: International Labour Office.

ILO. (2016). *Global wage report 2016/17: Wage inequality in the workplace*. Geneva: International Labour Office.

ILO. (2017). *World employment and social outlook: Trends 2017*. Geneva: International Labour Office.

KFW. (2015). *Profile the SME sector in Germany*. Frankfurt am Main.

Khilji, S. E., Tarique, I., & Schuler, R. S. (2015). Incorporating the macro view in global talent management. *Human Resource Management Review, 25*(3), 236–248.

KMK. (2016). *"Bildung in Deutschland 2016"Die Herausforderungen wachsen, aber die Leistungsfähigkeit des Bildungswesens steigert sich*. Kultusminister Konferenz. Retrieved on September 11, 2017 from www.kmk.org/aktuelles/artikelansicht/bildung-in-deutschland-2016-die-herausforderungen-wachsen-aber-die-leistungsfaehigkeit-des-bildungswesens-steigert-sich.html.

KMK. (2017). *Basic structure of the education system in the Federal Republic of Germany*. Berlin: Secretariat of the Standing Conference of the Ministers of Education and Cultural Affairs of the Länder in the Federal Republic of Germany.

Komm mach mit. (2017). *Kompetenzzentrum Technik-Diversity-Chancengleichheit e. V.* Retrieved on September 12, 2017 from www.komm-mach-mint.de.

Kuznetsov, Y. (2006). *Diaspora networks and the international migration of skills: How countries can draw on their talent abroad*. Washington: World Bank Institute.

Landwehr, J. (2017). The use of talent management instruments and procedures in Germany: A broad explorative study of effectiveness and success factors. *Journal of Human Resource Management, 4*(6), 77–99.

Lanvin, B., & Evans, P. (2017). *The global talent competitiveness index: Talent and technology*. Human Capital Leadership Institute. INSEAD and Adecco Group, Switzerland.

Made in Germany. (2017). *"Made in Germany": Historie einer Herkunftsbezeichnung*. Retrieved on September 8, 2017 from www.made-in-germany.biz/ueber-uns/made-in-germany.html.

Make it in Germany. (2016). *Plenty of room for growth: Granting of residence titles to qualified migrants*. Retrieved on September 8, 2017 from www.make-it-in-germany.com/en/for-qualified-professionals/discover-germany/facts-and-figures/immigration-development/granting-of-residence-titles.

Make it in Germany. (2016c). *Skilled labour shortages in German companies: Which occupations are in demand*. Retrieved on August 29, 2017 from www.make-it-in-germany.com/en/for-qualified-professionals/discover-germany/facts-and-figures/situation-of-qualified-professionals/skilled-labour-shortages-in-german-companies.

Make it in Germany. (2017a). */A continually shrinking and ageing population*. Retrieved on August 28, 2017 from www.make-it-in-germany.com/en/for-qualified-professionals/discover-germany/facts-and-figures/demography/a-continually-shrinking-and-ageing-population.

Make it in Germany. (2017b). *German society: A diverse population*. Retrieved on September 12, 2017 from www.make-it-in-germany.com/en/for-qualified-professionals/discover-germany/introduction-to-germany/society.

Make it in Germany. (2017c). *Germany as a country for research: Make it in Germany*. Retrieved on September 1, 2017 from www.make-it-in-germany.com/en/for-qualified-professionals/discover-germany/facts-and-figures/economy/germany-as-a-country-for-research.

Make it in Germany. (2017d). *Gross is not the same as net.* Retrieved on September 12, 2017 from www.make-it-in-germany.com/en/for-qualified-professionals/discover-germany/facts-and-figures/employment-and-earnings/gross-is-not-the-same-as-net.

Make it in Germany. (2017e). *Immigrants are frequently younger than the German population.* Retrieved on August 28, 2017 from www.make-it-in-germany.com/en/for-qualified-professionals/discover-germany/facts-and-figures/immigration-development/immigrants-are-frequently-younger.

Make it in Germany. (2017f). *Immigrants are increasingly well qualified.* Retrieved on August 28, 2017 from www.make-it-in-germany.com/en/for-qualified-professionals/discover-germany/facts-and-figures/immigration-development/immigrants-are-increasingly-well-qualified.

Make it in Germany. (2017g). *Labour shortages: Opportunities differ from region to region.* Retrieved on September 11, 2017 from www.make-it-in-germany.com/en/for-qualified-professionals/discover-germany/facts-and-figures/situation-of-qualified-professionals/labour-shortages.

Make it in Germany. (2017h). *Low unemployment rates in Germany.* Retrieved on September 11, 2017 from www.make-it-in-germany.com/en/for-qualified-professionals/discover-germany/facts-and-figures/employment-and-earnings/low-unemployment-rates.

Make it in Germany. (2017i). *Steady rise in number of recognised qualifications.* Retrieved on September 1, 2017 from www.make-it-in-germany.com/en/for-qualified-professionals/discover-germany/facts-and-figures/immigration-development/number-of-recognised-qualifications.

Make it in Germany. (2017j). *Vocational training in Germany.* Retrieved on August 30, 2017 from www.make-it-in-germany.com/en/for-qualified-professionals/training-learning/training/vocational-training-in-germany-how-does-it-work.

McSweeney, B. (2002). Hofstede's model of national cultural differences and their consequences: A triumph of faith—a failure of analysis. *Human Relations, 55*(1), 89–118.

Michailova, S. (2011). Contextualizing in international business research: Why do we need more of it and how can we be better at it? *Scandinavian Journal of Management, 27*(1), 129–139.

Morley, M. J. (2004). Contemporary debates in European human resource management: Context and content. *Human Resource Management Review, 14*(4), 353–364.

Morris, M. W., Chiu, C.-Y., & Liu, Z. (2015). Polycultural psychology. *Annual Review of Psychology, 66,* 631–659.

Muratbekova-Touron, M., Kabalina, V., & Festing, M. (in press). The phenomenon of young talent management in Russia: A context-embedded analysis. *Human Resource Management.*

Nier, H. (2017). *Wie viel Frauen in Europa weniger verdienen.* Statista 2017. Retrieved on September 21, 2017 from de.statista.com/infografik/11139/wie-viel-frauen-in-europa-weniger-verdienen/.

OECD. (2012). *Economic surveys: Netherlands 2012.* Retrieved from www.government.nl/documents/reports/2012/06/14/oecd-economic-surveys-netherlands-2012.

OECD. (2015a). Auswanderung aus und Rückkehr nach Deutschland: Muster und Beweggründe. In *Talente im Ausland: Ein Bericht über deutsche Auswanderer* (pp. 81–110). Paris: OECD Publishing.

OECD. (2015b). Deutsche Auswanderer, die im Ausland studieren oder forschen. In *Talente im Ausland: Ein Bericht über deutsche Auswanderer* (pp. 111–134). Paris: OECD Publishing.

OECD. (2015c). *Pensions at a glance 2015: Germany.* Retrieved on November 30, 2017 from www.oecd.org/germany/PAG2015_Germany.pdf.

OECD. (2015d). *PISA 2015 country note for Germany.* Retrieved on September 21, 2017 from www.oecd.org/pisa/PISA-2015-Germany.pdf.

OECD. (2015e). Zahl und Zielländer deutscher Auswanderer. In *Talente im Ausland: Ein Bericht über deutsche Auswanderer* (pp. 19–37). Paris: OECD Publishing. dx.doi.org/10.1787/9789264234055-de.

OECD. (2016). *OECD economic survey Germany.* Retrieved on September 21, 2017 from www.oecd.org/eco/surveys/2016%20Germany%20survey%20-%20Overview%20in%20ENGLISH.pdf.

OECD. (2016b). *Die OECD in Zahlen und Fakten 2015–2016. Wirtschaft, Umwelt, Gesellschaft.* Retrieved on September 21, 2017 from www.oecd-ilibrary.org/economics/die-oecd-in-zahlen-und-fakten-2015-2016_factbook-2015-de.

OECD. (2016c). *PISA 2015: Results in focus.* Retrieved on September 21, 2017 from www.oecd.org/pisa/pisa-2015-results-in-focus.pdf.

OECD. (2017). *Gender wage gaps.* Retrieved on September 21, 2017 from www.oecd.org/std/37964069.pdf.

Oezcan, V. (2004). *Migration policy institute.* Retrieved on September 21, 2017 from www.migrationpolicy.org/article/germany-immigration-transition/.

Research in Germany. (2017). *Kampagne & Beteiligung.* BMBF 2017. Retrieved on September 8, 2017 from www.research-in-germany.org/de/kampagne.html.

Rietig, V., & Müller, A. (2016). *The new reality: Germany adapts to its role as a major migrant magnet*. Berlin: Migration Policy Institute.

Schwartz, S. H. (1999). A theory of cultural values and some implications for work. *Applied Psychology, 48*(1), 23–47.

Sinning, M. (2007). *Determinants of savings and remittances: Empirical evidence from immigrants to Germany*. Bonn: The Institute for the Study of Labor (IZA).

Solga, H., Protsch, P., Ebner, C., & Brzinsky-Fay, C. (2014). *The German vocational education and training system: Its institutional configuration, strengths, and challenges*. Berlin: Wissenschaftszentrum Berlin für Sozialforschung.

Söllner, R. (2014). *Die wirtschaftliche Bedeutung kleiner und mittlerer Unternehmen in Deutschland*. Wiesbaden: Statistisches Bundesamt.

Soskice, D. W., & Hall, P. A. (2001). *Varieties of capitalism: The institutional foundations of comparative advantage*. Oxford: Oxford University Press.

Sparrow, P., & Makram, H. (2015). What is the value of talent management? Building value-driven processes within a talent management architecture. *Human Resource Management Review, 25*(3), 249–263. doi:10.1016/j.hrmr.2015.04.002.

Stahl, G., Björkman, I., Farndale, E., Morris, S., Paauwe, J., Stiles, P., . . . Wright, P. (2007). Global talent management: How leading multinationals build and sustain their talent pipeline. *INSEAD Faculty and Research Working Papers*. Fontainebleau.

Statista. (2017a). *Entwicklung der Studienanfängerquote* in Deutschland von 2000 bis 2016*. Retrieved on August 30, 2017 from de.statista.com/statistik/daten/studie/72005/umfrage/entwicklung-der-studienanfaengerquote/.

Statista. (2017b). *Europäische Union: Arbeitslosenquoten in den Mitgliedsstaaten im Juli 2017*. Retrieved on September 12, 2017 from de.statista.com/statistik/daten/studie/160142/umfrage/arbeitslosenquote-in-den-eu-laendern/.

Statista. (2017c). *Top 20 export countries worldwide in 2016 (in billion U.S. dollars)*. Retrieved on September 21, 2017 from www.statista.com/statistics/264623/leading-export-countries-worldwide/.

Statistische Ämter der Länder. (2017). *Gesamtwirtschaftliche Ergebnisse im Bundesländervergleich*. Stuttgart: Statistisches Landesamt Baden-Württemberg.

Streeck, W. (1995). *German capitalism: Does it exist? Can it survive?* MPIFG Discussion Paper. Köln: Max-Planck-Institut für Gesellschaftsforschung.

Süssmuth, R. (2009). *The future of migration and integration policy in Germany*. Bellagio: Migration Policy Institute.

Tatsachen über Deutschland. (2017a). *Advocate of European integration*. Frankfurter Societäts-Medien GmbH. Retrieved on November 15, 2017 from www.tatsachen-ueber-deutschland.de/en/chapter/foreign-policy/advocate-european-integration.

Tatsachen über Deutschland. (2017b). *Attraktives Schulsystem*. Frankfurter Societäts-Medien GmbH. Retrieved on August 30, 2017 from www.tatsachen-ueber-deutschland.de/de/rubriken/bildung-wissen/attraktives-schulsystem.

Tatsachen über Deutschland. (2017c). *Dynamic academic landscape*. Frankfurter Societäts-Medien GmbH. Retrieved on August 30, 2017 from www.tatsachen-ueber-deutschland.de/en/categories/education-knowledge/dynamic-academic-landscape.

Tatsachen über Deutschland. (2017d). *Endless opportunities: Open school system*. Frankfurter Societäts-Medien GmbH. Retrieved on September 1, 2017 from www.tatsachen-ueber-deutschland.de/en/young-people/endless-opportunities/open-school-system.

Tatsachen über Deutschland. (2017e). *Starker Wissensstandort*. Frankfurter Societäts-Medien GmbH. Retrieved on August 29, 2017 from www.tatsachen-ueber-deutschland.de/de/rubriken/bildung-wissen/starker-wissensstandort.

Tatsachen über Deutschland. (2017f). *Vibrant hub of knowledge*. Frankfurter Societäts-Medien GmbH. Retrieved from www.tatsachen-ueber-deutschland.de/en/chapter/education-knowledge/vibrant-hub-knowledge.

Venaik, S., & Midgley, D. F. (2015). Mindscapes across landscapes: Archetypes of transnational and subnational culture. *Journal of International Business Studies, 46*(9), 1051–1079.

The World Bank. (2017). *Gross domestic product 2016*. Retrieved on September 21, 2017 from databank.worldbank.org/data/download/GDP.pdf.

World Economic Forum. (2017). *Human capital report 2016*. Retrieved on September 21, 2017 from reports.weforum.org/human-capital-report-2016/.

5
Macro Talent Management in Spain
Is the Sun Rising Again?

Adoración Álvaro-Moya, Eva Gallardo-Gallardo and Jordi Paniagua

Introduction

An outlook of certain economic data, concerning the macroeconomic environment, would suggest that Spain is a talent magnet or has a great potential to be a talent magnet in the near future. For instance, in 2016 Spain had, for the first time since the start of the 2008 crisis, a positive net migration flow as a result of both an increase in the number of immigrants and a reduction in the number of Spaniards looking for a job abroad (INE, 2017a). A positive net flow of people is usually attributed to the country's relative social opportunities and economic prospectus, which also act as talent attraction factors (Parkins, 2010; Khilji & Schuler, 2016). In fact, according to the World Bank (2017), the Spanish economy ranked 13th by gross domestic product (GDP) in 2016, and the Spanish recovery, starting in 2013, has been one of the strongest in the OECD (OECD, 2017b). The job market is gradually improving, with employment annual growth rates of around 3% (OECD, 2017b). And in the OECD Well Being Index, the Spanish position has improved in most items since 2005, being above the average in terms of work-life, health status, social support and personal security (OECD, 2017e, pp. 45 and 295).

However, a more in-depth analysis of Spain's position in different dimensions of macro talent management (MTM) reveals possible weaknesses. For example, according to the Global Competitiveness Report (2017–2018) of the World Economic Forum (WEF), Spain ranks 34th, well below the largest European countries. Its position is particularly weak in relation to innovation and the macroeconomic environment. Although it is gathering pace, Spain's productivity growth in the last years (2008–2015) is well below the OECD average (around 0% and 0.5%, respectively) (OECD, 2017b), and there is still plenty of room to improve education attainment. Not surprisingly, Spain ranks 44th in the WEF's Human Capital Index.

The aim of this chapter is twofold. First, we seek to examine MTM in the Spanish context by providing current information about the environmental factors that shape current talent management (TM) policies and actions on a national level. Second, we are going to discuss the impact of such environment in terms of Spanish competitiveness and talent stock using a wide array of international indexes. The following section offers an overview of key facts about the Spanish economy in the last decades. Next, MTM environmental factors are analysed in order to look at their impact on Spanish competitiveness and talent outcomes in comparative perspective, and the final section concludes.

Spain's Economy Key Facts

With a gross domestic product (GDP) of USD 1,232,088 million in 2016, Spain is the fifth largest economy in Europe, ranking 13th at world level (World Bank, 2017). Real GDP posted a 3.2% growth in 2016 (World Bank, 2017). According to the most recent economic forecast for Spain (European Commission, 2017b), growth is set to remain robust but slow going forward. This report points to domestic demand as the main engine of growth, as strong job creation supports private consumption and residential construction investment has rebounded. Exports, furthermore, have accelerated and, since they are expected to continue growing faster than imports, net trade should make a significant contribution to sustain GDP growth (European Commission, 2017b).

"Spain is different" was a successful slogan aimed to attract tourism to Spain in the late 1960s that has endured as a sort of national motto (Afinoguénova & Martí-Olivella, 2008). Spain's long-term economic evolution, however, appears to be similar to that of Western nations, being characterized by sustained growth since mid-19th century (Prados de la Escosura, 2017). Although Spain has systematically ranked below other large Western European countries such as Britain, France or Germany, falling even farther behind between 1850 and 1950, this is common to other economies of the Mediterranean periphery, including Italy and Portugal (Tortella, 2000; Aldcroft, 2016; Prados de la Escosura, 2017). However, they were all able to grow fast and catch up with the Western leaders in the decades that followed (Figure 5.1).

A greater integration into the world economy and institutional change explain much of these countries' modernization. In the case of Spain, after autarky in the 1940s and, to a lesser extent, in the 1950s, foreign trade, capital and knowledge fuelled its definite industrialization

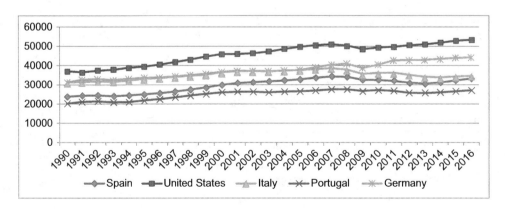

Figure 5.1 GDP per capita, (PPP constant 2011 international $) in Spain, United States (US), Italy, Germany and Portugal (1990–2016)

Source data: World Bank (data.worldbank.org/)

in the 1960s and early 1970s (Muñoz, Roldán, & Serrano, 1978). The United States and a handful of Western European countries (Britain, France and Germany) consolidated as main trade partners and foreign investors in the country at that time (Puig & Álvaro-Moya, 2016). Economic openness coincided with the definite rehabilitation of Spain in the international economic forum, after the diplomatic isolationism that characterized the first years of Franco's dictatorship (1939–1975), particularly during the aftermath of the second world war (Guirao, 1998; Powell, 2011). For instance, Spain joined the United Nations (UN) in 1955, the International Monetary Fund (IMF) in 1958, and the Organization for Economic Co-operation and Development (OECD) in 1961.

But the 1960s fast and technology-dependent growth, in the context of a still highly-intervened and protectionist economy but archaic Treasury and public sector, ultimately led to external deficit, poor industry competitiveness, institutional weakness and ultimately crisis and social unrest by the time of Franco's death in 1975 (Serrano & Pardos, 2002). Institutional reform, and economic stabilization and liberalization, then took place amidst the global oil crisis of the 1970s, to culminate with Spain's entrance into the European Economic Community (today the European Union [EU]), in 1986 (Rojo, 2002). Since then, Spain has enjoyed full membership, joining the European Monetary Union and adopting the euro as domestic currency in 2002. Although today Spain is a net contributor, for a long time the country was a net receiver from the EU budget, getting funds for regional investment policies, agriculture, rural development and the modernization of national infrastructure, which fuelled growth (Almunia, 2011).

As a member of the EU, the Spanish economy has followed the common expansion-recession cycle of other European countries, although with higher volatility levels (García Delgado, 2014; Jiménez & Martínez Serrano, 2014). Spain inaugurated the 21st century, for instance, with a strong expansion period, but to be more adversely affected by the 2008 crisis than most European countries. This resulted in a rapid increase of income inequality, which is still among the highest in the European context (European Commission, 2017c). The institutional reform of the late 1970s included the 1978 Constitution, which set up a parliamentary monarchy with separation of powers and a set of civil and social rights according to EU standards (Powell, 2016). The Constitution also stipulates legislative and executive powers for the 17 regions, or "autonomous communities", that comprise the country, and recognizes as official languages along with Spanish other spoken languages in the Basque Country, Catalonia, Valencia, Balearic Islands and Galicia communities (Constitución Española, 1978). By virtue of the "State of Autonomies", as this territorial organization is called, regional governments have jurisdiction to intervene in education, infrastructure and taxation issues, among others (López-Bazo & Motellón, 2017a). Although they also have financial autonomy, their revenue also depends on the central government, which mediates in an inter-territorial funding scheme that seeks to reduce regional economic disparity.

In the varieties of Capitalism literature, Spain has been characterized along with other Southern European countries as a "mixed market economy" (Molina & Rhodes, 2007) or "state-influenced mixed market economy" (Royo, 2007), a category that falls aside the traditional liberal market economies (such as the United States) and coordinated market economies (Germany and France, for example) (Hall & Soskice, 2001). In mixed market economies, the State plays a key role in facilitating the coordination of business actors (large firms, business associations and trade unions) to compensate for the lack of autonomous self-organization of business and labour (Molina & Rhodes, 2007). This coordination task takes place also at the regional level (Royo, 2009).

In Spain, as predicted by economic theory, economic growth and integration of national markets led to increasing income inequality in the early years of development (between 1850s and 1900s) to fall afterwards, particularly in the second half of the 20th century and the consolidation of Spain's modernization (Martínez-Galarraga, Rosés, & Tirado, 2015). Regional differences, however, were still notable in 2016, when only four Spanish regions (Madrid, the Basque Country, Navarre and Catalonia; all them in Northern Spain apart from Madrid, where the capital of the country is located) surpassed the European average in terms of per capita GDP according to Eurostat website (ec.europa.eu/eurostat). Regional disparity within Europe has been associated with the structure of labour markets, localization factors and the presence of a solid industrial base (Amendola, Caroleo, & Coppola, 2006). Regarding the latter, Catalonia is the region with the largest manufacturing sector and the largest share of manufacturing firms that pledged to innovate in product and process, followed by Madrid, the Basque Country and Navarre (López-Bazo & Motellón, 2017b). In fact, the share of firms performing R&D activities in a continuous way is between one quarter and one third in Catalonia, the Basque Country and Madrid, far beyond the numbers in low innovative regions, which are also specialized in the tourism sector (López-Bazo & Motellón, 2017a, 2017b). These differences are also related with regional cluster policy, explained later in the chapter. Spatial differences, finally, also concern population and thus talent concentration (Ayuda, Collantes, & Pinilla, 2010). High-skilled workers tend to concentrate in the most innovative regions (López-Bazo & Motellón, 2017b).

Nowadays, the Spanish productive sector is characterized by the marked influence of the tertiary sector and the low presence of the industrial sector, a common fact among developed countries). In fact, 74.1% of GDP in 2016 is generated by services, followed by industry and energy (17.8%), construction (5.6%) and agriculture (2.6%), according to Spain's National Institute of Statistics (INE). Correspondingly, 58.7% of the active companies belong to the service sector (excluding commerce at 23%), and services represent the majority of jobs. Only 6.1% of the companies are from the industrial sector while 12.3% belong to the construction sector (INE, 2017b). After six consecutive years of reduction, in 2014 the number of active firms started to grow again, rising from 3.1 million that year to nearly 3.3 in January 2017 (INE, 2017b). Micro SMEs are by far the most common type of companies in Spain, accounting for 94.5% of all enterprises (INE, 2017b). At the same time, Spanish companies have internationalized fast in recent times, inaugurating Spain's 21st century as a net exporter of capital, which contrasts with the country's historical position (Guillén, 2005). We will look more in-depth at these issues in the following pages.

The Macro Talent Management Environment Factors in Spain

Educational System

Economists have long linked human capital, understood as the stock of skills, abilities and knowledge embodied by individuals aimed at improving their job performance, with firm productivity and country competitiveness (Lucas, 1988; Barro, 1991). Human capital is also of great relevance when dealing with TM. Indeed, De Vos and Dries (2013) propose to refer to 'talent' as the human capital in an organization that is both valuable and unique. According to the economic mainstream, human capital is based on two pillars, education and training, and health (Goldin, 2015). Life expectancy at birth, usually considered as a proxy to population's health, in Spain is among the highest in the Euro area according to OECD data, and standards in education have greatly improved in the last years (Ministerio de Educación, Cultura y Deporte, 2017a). We focus on the latter here.

The Ministry of Education regulates education in Spain. However, regional governments are responsible for managing and financing schools in their territories. The structure of the educational system in Spain by age according to the International Standard Classification of Education of 2011 (UNESCO, 2011) is in Appendix 5.1. It is divided basically into five stages: Nursery and preschool (early childhood educational development and pre-primary), which is optional until age 6; primary and secondary education, both compulsory, until age 11/12 and 15/16, respectively; upper secondary education, optional, until age 17/18; and university/higher studies. After lower-stage secondary education, it is possible to follow alternative vocational training studies, which end at age 20 at its highest level (vocational training advanced level degree), and studies focus on music and dance. There are also mechanisms to facilitate students' transfer from vocational training to upper-stage secondary and university education.

Lessons in Spanish state schools are taught in Spanish, but also in the regional language, such as Catalan, Galician or Basque, when corresponding; and the study of, at least, a second language (namely English) is compulsory (www.expatica.com/es/education/Education-in-Spain_103110.html). As part of an initiative between Spain's Ministry of Education and the British Council, some state schools offer a bilingual integrated Spanish-British curriculum. Nearly 25% of children in primary education and 15% in secondary are following it (Ministerio de Educación, Cultura y Deporte, 2017b, p. 29). On average, 68% of children attend state schools, although the range varies from 51% to 83% by region (Ministerio de Educación, Cultura y Deporte, 2017b, p. 6).

Higher education in Spain dates back from mediaeval times. Today, there are 76 universities, most of them publicly funded. Undergraduate studies consist of four years and 240 ECTS, well above the 180 ECTS of most EU countries (Michavila, Martínez, & Merhi, 2015, p. 11). Masters degrees range from one to two years (60–120 ECTS) and PhD from three to five years. Concerning undergraduate studies, 26% of tertiary-educated individuals studied science, technology, engineering and mathematics (i.e., STEM studies) in Spain, one of the largest shares across OECD countries, followed by business, administration and law (around 25%) (OECD, 2017c). Women, however, are underrepresented in STEM studies, although they are predominant in education and health studies (Ministerio de Educación, Cultura y Deporte, 2017b, p. 22). Less than 3% of enrolled students are foreigners, most of them from the European Union, Latin America and the Caribbean (Michavila, Martínez, & Merhi, 2015, p. 28). This figure is far below the German (7%), French (11%), Swiss (16%), and British (17%) among others (Michavila et al., 2015, p. 29). But, at the same time, Spain is a very popular destination for those benefiting from European student exchange programs, as well as one of the largest countries sending students abroad under the Erasmus schedule (Michavila et al., 2015, p. 31). With the purpose of promoting not only student mobility, but also the attraction of talent at all levels (including staff) and the internationalization of research, the Spanish government has recently launched a very ambitious program to foster the internationalization of the Spanish university (Gobierno de España, 2014).

Different Spanish universities are highly ranked according to several rankings (Times Higher Education's World University Ranking, 2018; World University Rankings, 2018; Academic Ranking of World Universities, 2017). These are: Pompeu Fabra University,

University of Barcelona, University of Granada, Autonomous University of Barcelona, Autonomous University of Madrid, Complutense University of Madrid, University of Santiago de Compostela, Polytechnic University of Valencia, Universitat Jaume I, University of the Basque Country, University of Navarra, and University of Valencia.

Public spending on education in Spain has been around 4% of the GDP for the last several years, compared with the almost 5% European average (European Commission, 2016). According to the *Education and Training Monitor 2017* (European Commission, 2017a), public expenditure on education can be split into four categories of transactions: (a) 'compensation of employees' (i.e., gross salaries and social contributions for teaching and non-teaching staff); (b) 'intermediate consumption' (i.e., purchase of non-durable goods and services needed to provide education); (c) 'gross capital formation' (i.e., investment in acquiring fixed assets and durable goods and buildings); (d) 'other expenditure' (covers the residual variety of transactions, including subsidies in the form of transfers to households and payments to private schools; it reflects the organization of education provision). Spain ranks above EU average on 'compensation of employees' (almost 70%), and in 'other expenditure' (above 20%) categories. However, it ranks at the minimum in the 'intermediate consumption' (7,5%) and the 'gross capital formation' (5%) dimensions. Public spending per student is also below the European average: USD 6,970, USD 8,528 and USD 12,489 in primary, secondary and tertiary education, respectively, compared to the USD 8,803, USD 10,360 and USD 16,164 of EU-22 average (OECD, 2017a, p. 6). Note that public spending on education covered all stages of the educational scheme described previously, but concentrates in primary and secondary education, with 34% and 28.6%, respectively, of the total (Ministerio de Educación, Cultura y Deporte, 2017b, p. 10). Regarding university, public and private spending as percentage of GDP is comparable to the EU average (1.3% and 1.4%, respectively; Michavila et al., 2015, p. 35).

Data on educational attainment in Spain offers a rather contradictory picture. Early abandonment of education is higher compared to the European average (19 and 11%, respectively, in 2016); particularly in southern Spain, with rates over 20% (Eurostat, 2016; European Commission, 2017a, p. 60). The share of adults with only primary studies or low-stage secondary studies has decreased from 50.3% in 2006 to 47.7% in 2016, but it is still quite above the OECD average of 22.4% (Ministerio de Educación, Cultura y Deporte, 2017b, p. 7). A small percentage of young adults, furthermore, are enrolled in vocational education and training programmes, 12% compared to the 25% OECD average, despite the fact that those with a vocational qualification have a higher employment rate than those with a general qualification (74% and 63%, respectively) (OECD, 2017c). But, at the same time, the share of adults with tertiary studies is today 41%, around the OECD and EU averages (43% and 40.1%, respectively). Many experts conclude that Spain lacks vocational training professionals, while the country cannot offer enough job opportunities, not only due to circumstantial reasons such as the 2008 crisis, to people with tertiary studies (Dolado, 2015). Not surprisingly, emigration of talented nationals has increased in the last years, as explained in the following section.

Since 1980, when the Spanish education system was reorganized for the first time under democracy, there have been seven reforms, usually coinciding with changes in the political party ruling the country (Berengueras & Vera, 2015). In order to improve education results and enhance communication and cooperation among all the actors involved, the Spanish Parliament began in spring 2017 to draft a proposal for a Social and Political National Pact on Education, which set the terms for long-lasting education reform (Cervilla, 2017).

Demographics and Migration

By the end of 2017, Spain had a population of nearly 50 million people, which implies that it is the 28th most populated country in the world according to CIA World Factbook (2017). The intensive expansion period of the early 2000s had a significant impact on Spanish demography. As Figure 5.2 shows, Spanish population has been fairly constant until 2000, where the population was exponential and maintained high values until the 2008 economic downturn.

Most of the population growth during the expansion years is attributed to an increase in migration flows, as seen in Figure 5.3. In the last 20 years or so, Spain has passed from a country of emigrants to an attractive destination for foreigners. In the late 1990s, less of

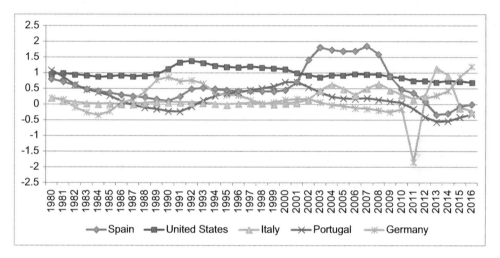

Figure 5.2 Population Growth (annual %) in Spain, US, Germany, Italy and Portugal (1980–2012)

Source data: World Bank (data.worldbank.org/)

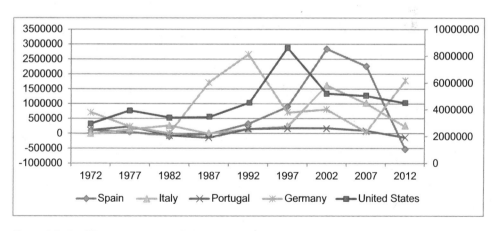

Figure 5.3 Net Migration in Spain, US, Germany, Italy and Portugal (1972–2012)

Note: the US data is on the right axis

Source data: World Bank (data.worldbank.org/)

2% of the residents were foreigners, while today this figure is 10%, similar to the European average (Delle Femmine & Alameda, 2017; INE, 2017a; Martin, 2013). Compared to other OCDE countries, migrants in Spain are more often of working age and have a low or middle educational attainment (OECD, 2017d, p. 5). Spain's ability to attract foreign labour and human capital during this period is unprecedented and superior to most advanced economies. Although there have been changes over these years, most of the immigrants have come from the north of Africa (Morocco particularly), Latin America and Eastern Europe (Delle Femmine & Alameda, 2017). A large part of migration flows is, however, within the country's territory. Particularly in the most recent years, the richest regions (such as Madrid, Barcelona and the Basque Country) have attracted many workers looking for job opportunities and better wages (INE, 2017a).

The increasing foreign-born population of the years before the 2008 crisis has not supposed a significant opposition against immigration like in other European countries. This is attributed to Spain's history as an 'emigrant country', particularly in the 1960s, when in the context of agriculture mechanization and rural flight many Spaniards left the countryside towards the country's largest industrial cities (such as Barcelona, Bilbao and Madrid) and Western Europe (Germany and Switzerland, among other) (De la Torre & Sanz Lafuente, 2008). Furthermore, in Spain's political culture immigration is understood as a vehicle to enhance democratic values and, compared to other countries, the low visibility of immigrants make them unperceived as a threat to national identity (Arango, 2013). Both immigrants and native-born, furthermore, show preference for assimilation of local values, rather than differentiation, in the process of adapting to other cultural framework, what it is related with low levels of conflict in intergroup relations and fewer prejudices (González López & Ramírez, 2016). Certainly, the 2008 crisis has moved the Spanish government, particularly under the rule of the conservative Popular Party which is very critical of the Socialist Party predecessor, to more restrictive policies (Ullán de la Rosa, 2016; Arango, 2013). But the economic situation, although it has promoted the emergence of new political forces and captured largely disgruntled voters, has not fuelled the rise of anti-immigration parties like in other European countries (Carbajosa, 2015; Buck, 2017).

The crisis of 2008, however, caused a significant percentage of immigrants to return home, particularly after 2013 (Parella & Petroff, 2014). The Spanish government, in fact, actively promoted this with return policies that financed part of the travel and relocation expenses. At the same time, a growing number of Spaniards have decided to look for jobs abroad, particularly young people with university studies, which has led to fears of brain drain (Lorca-Susino, 2011; González Ferrer, 2013). In fact, resident population increased 0.19% in 2016, but had been going down since 2011 (INE, 2017a). The migratory balance was indeed negative between 2009 and 2016 (INE, 2017a; Delle Femmine & Alameda, 2017). And between 2010 and 2014, Spain lost 10% of its researchers, who emigrated due to the lack of job and promotion opportunities, as well as 10% of its resources (INAECU, 2016).

The decrease in immigration rates along with the brain drain and returnees amplify one of the main threats to the Spanish economy in general and to its MTM potential in particular: population aging. As Figure 5.4 shows one of the challenges of Spain and most advanced economies is to cope with an aging population. A particularly simple solution is to attract young foreign talent. This remedy has the caveat of the short migration cycle, which follows closely the economic expansion-contraction cycle seen in Figure 5.1.

Changes in migration trends have also had an impact on migration policies. Migration policies in Spain had traditionally focused on the assistance to the national migrant

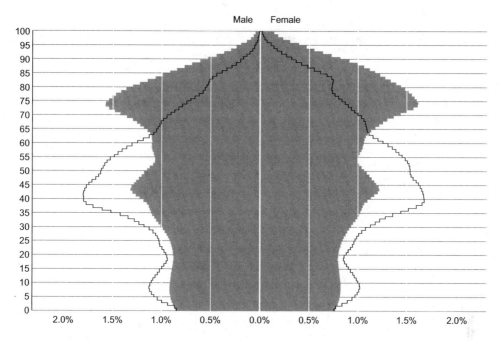

Figure 5.4 Population by Age in Spain

Note: The black line indicates population in 2016 and the grey area corresponds to 2050 projections.

Source data: Gapminder.org

(Sánchez-Alonso, 2011). This changed with Spain's entrance into the European Union and, above all, the impressive arrival of immigrants in the last decades of the 20th century. Since then, the migratory policy has focused on regulating the entry of foreigners. The first law to this respect, which was very restrictive and dictated by the EU in 1985, was liberalized in 2000. By doing so, social services (such as health and education) were ensured to both illegal and legal immigrants (Arango, 2000; Sánchez-Alonso, 2011). However, control of sea and land borders has been intensified over the last years, which can be linked not only to the global economic crisis but also to European guidelines.

National and regional governments in Spain have been at the same time pursuing policies aimed to palliate the brain drain, attracting foreign talent and aiding the return of expatriates. Most of these initiatives have been focused on young scientists like the national programs "Programa Severo Ochoa" and "Programa Ramón y Cajal", as well as regional initiatives in Catalonia, Madrid, Andalusia and Galicia, among others. These initiatives are making Spain more attractive for highly talented individuals from other countries (Martin, 2015).

Domestic Labour Market

> The structure of the labor market has changed more profoundly in Spain than in any other Western European country in the past twenty years [1975–1995]. No other country has seen its unemployment rate rise as dramatically and stay so persistently high.
>
> (Franks, 1997, p. 7, dates added)

In fact, the high and persistent level of unemployment is, unfortunately, one of the most relevant characteristics of the Spanish labour market even today (Andrés & Doménech, 2013).

During the dictatorship (1939–1975), Spain had a rigidly state-controlled labour market that was characterized by the prohibition of free trade unions, the setting of basic wages at a very low level, and the establishment of a quasi-tenured employment system that made it very difficult to fire workers by establishing a severance pay for dismissals (Ballester, 2005; Franks, 1997). Since 1975, the Spanish labour market policy has focused not only on deregulation and flexibility but also on a reduction of labour costs and, in the first years of democracy, the development of a collective bargaining system (Ballester, 2005). In fact, the last reform undertaken in 2012 promoted the internal flexibility of firms and reduced dismissal costs for permanent workers, which contributed to significant wage moderation and increased hiring on permanent contracts (OEDC, 2013). For a summary of the main labour reforms in Spain see Appendix 5.2. It is interesting to note here, however, that, during many years employment issues have been subordinated to macroeconomic stability (González-Calvet, 2002).

Along with the credit crunch and the trade collapse of 2008, structural weaknesses of the Spanish economy surfaced during the Great Recession. The global financial and economic crisis hit the Spanish labour market particularly hard in comparison with other European countries (Pérez Infante, 2016). The unemployment rate in Spain reached 26.7% in October 2013, which was more than three times the OECD average (7.9%) (OECD, 2017a). Even more serious is the fact that long-term unemployment, as a share of all unemployment rose from 19.1% in fourth quarter 2007 to 50.4% in third quarter 2013 (OECD, 2017a). Certain southern regions (i.e., Andalusia, Canary Islands, Ceuta and Extremadura) suffer long-term unemployment rates of more than 30%, according to Eurostat. Youth unemployment is even worse, with nearly 50% of the population under 25 unemployed.

Spain has paid a high price for an economic model excessively based on construction and real estate. In fact, the largest number of job losses was in the construction sector, the engine of the Spanish economy (Chislett, 2013). Job losses after 2008 also certainly hit temporary workers much harder than those on permanent contracts, which can be seen responding to economic crisis through adjustment of employment rather than through application of internal flexibility (Horwitz & Myant, 2015). Together with the increase in unemployment, wages in Spain have also had a negative trend. Since 2010 to 2014, the real wage has decreased in more than 7%, which means a considerable loss in purchasing power. Even the monetary wages have decreased since 2012; it should be said that this devaluation concentrates on those employees with lowest wages, whereas high salaries have been continuing to increase despite the economic crisis (Pérez Infante, 2016).

The labour market situation in Spain has continuously improved over the past three years: employment, as a share of the population aged 15–74 years, has increased by more than 4%, whereas the unemployment rate has decreased by more than 8% since 2013 (OECD, 2017a; European Commission, 2017b). In fact, at 17.8% in April 2017 the unemployment rate remains the second highest among OECD countries, and about 9% higher than its pre-crisis level (OECD, 2017a). Likewise, youth unemployment has decreased by almost 20% since September 2013 to October 2017. Despite this good news, unemployment remains stubbornly high and below its pre-crisis percentage.

The counterpart for all this is that Spain ranks in the bottom third of the OECD countries in terms of labour market security and job strain. The share of working-age persons living on less than 50% of the median income (16.5% of total) is the highest among OECD countries. Moreover, the employment gap of disadvantaged groups (such as mothers with children, youth, older workers, non-natives, and disabled people) is also worse than average in OECD countries (OECD, 2017a). But, according to the most recent Eurostat data on this issue (2015), the gender pay gap, that is, the difference in average wages between men and women, is in Spain similar to the EU-28 average (15%).

Foreign expatriates, however, perceive Spain, as an attractive destination. According to the Expat Explorer Global Report of HSBC, Spain is for the third consecutive year the second best country, after New Zealand, for foreign expatriates in terms of life experience (HSBC, 2017, p. 8). More than half of expats interviewed had chosen Spain as a destination to improve their personal lives in a wide array of aspects, including physical health, social life and climate (HSBC, 2017, p. 66). Around one third adapted easily to the new country and 66% felt right at home in less than one year. Furthermore, 24% consider Spain as a right market to start a new business (a percentage which has increased in the last years), which might lead to growing direct investment after the British Brexit.

Entrepreneurship

Employer's attractiveness matters to attract talented people (Collins & Kanar, 2013). This indeed explains the increasing attention to employer branding by human resource scholarship. Literature has long discussed the attributes related with companies' attractiveness, including economic and tangible aspects such as salary package and location, as well as subjective perceptions, such as prestige and reputation (Berthon, Ewing, & Hag, 2005; Srivastava & Bhatnagar, 2010). Large and global companies have had traditionally a greater potential of developing renowned brands than smaller firms. This is the reason why, dealing with MTM, we look at firm structure and entrepreneurship in the case of Spain.

The Spanish business fabric is characterized by a high weight of the services sector and a much lower presence of industrial activities. Correspondingly, as of January 2017 near 93% of firms in Spain were related somehow with services including transportation (data of January 2017; DIRCE database). Most of them are small and medium enterprises (SMEs), having less than 249 employees according to the EU standards (ec.europa.eu/growth/smes/business-friendly-environment/sme-definition_es). This predominance of SMEs is common to the largest countries in Europe, such as Germany and Great Britain (Fariñas & Huergo, 2015). What distinguishes Spain, and other Mediterranean countries such as Italy, from them is the much higher percentage over employment and value added that the smallest firms represent. For instance, microenterprises (less than 10 employees) count in Germany for 20% of employment, but 40% in the case of Spain. And while 37% of the working population in Germany work for big companies, the Spanish figure is only 23% (Fariñas & Huergo, 2015, pp. 7–8).

Interestingly, 52.67% of all active enterprises had 0 employees, which means that most Spanish firms are businesses run by self-employed individuals (INE, 2017b). However, Spain is very alike to the EU-28 in which 93% of all enterprises are micro SMEs, and 56% of all active enterprises had 0 employees (European Commission,2017d). Several factors affect both the supply and demand for self-employment, such as the increasing importance of the 'gig' economy, and the 'sharing' or 'collaborative' economy; a change in attitude from Millennials towards operating as independents in the labour market, rather than entering into a long-term employer-employee relationship; and downsizing and outsourcing to independent workers of activities previously undertaken in-house by companies (European Commission, 2017a, pp. 48–49).

This growth in self-employment can be seen as stimulus for entrepreneurship and increment of the economy's dynamism and flexibility to changing circumstances. However, a recent report by Eurofound (2017) shows that while 54% of self-employed chose to, 26% self-employed because they had no other alternative to work. In fact, in Spain more than a quarter of full-time self-employed people are at risk of poverty and social exclusion (Eurofound, 2017). This lack of job alternatives we have referred to is related to the effects of the 2008 crisis and the slow economic recovery, but also to self-employees' qualifications. A recent report highlighted that 42% of those self-employed have basic compulsory education (double the average of the UE-28), and, despite the fact that training has advanced significantly in recent years, only 24.8% have university studies (Fundación BBVA-Ivie, 2016).

Regarding ownership, 89% of Spanish firms are family firms, representing 57% of GDP and 67% of total employment (data for 2013; Instituto de la Empresa Familiar, 2015). In Europe, family businesses account for around 60% of all firms, and 40–50% of all jobs (according to European Family Businesses), but, in the United States, 80–90% of firms are family businesses, generating 63% of GDP and representing 57% of employment (Instituto de la Empresa Familiar, 2015). Although most family firms are small or microenterprises, there are also many examples of large multinationals.

One of the most remarkable outcomes of Spain's liberalization has been the rise of multinational firms, particularly after 1986 (Durán & Sánchez, 1981; Guillén, 2005; Guillén & García-Canal, 2011). We look at this phenomenon as an indicator of corporate entrepreneurship (Zahra & George, 2002). At the end of 2016, Spain has the EU's sixth-largest stock of direct investment abroad (UNCTAD, 2017). Outward foreign direct investment stock was of more than USD 500,000 million, around four times more than in the year 2000 (UNCTAD, 2017, p. 226). The Spanish firms that have led this process are to a large extent either former public or private monopolies and state-owned firms (Telefónica, Repsol, Iberdrola, Gas Natural Fenosa, Iberia and Endesa, to name a few included in Forbes' World's Biggest Public Companies ranking); banks (Santander, BBVA-Banco Bilbao Vizcaya and Caixabank, for instance); or family firms (Inditex, Ferrovial, Grifols, FCC and Acciona, among others). Spanish investment abroad initially focused on Latin American and Western Europe, due to geographical and cultural factors and the opportunities brought about by massive privatization in 1990s Latin America (Durán, 1999; Toral, 2001; Martín & Toral, 2005), but the United States and Asia have received increasing attention in recent years (Observatorio de la Empresa Multinacional Española, 2015; Datainvex). Recent studies explain the fast rise of Spanish multinationals by a combination of relational, networking, management and project execution capabilities (Guillén & García-Canal, 2011) and the ability to internalize foreign knowledge historically acquired through partnerships and other alliances (Puig & Álvaro-Moya, 2016; Fernández Pérez & Díaz Morlán, 2015).

To what extent is the Spanish government promoting entrepreneurship? A comprehensive way to deal with such a broad issue is the World Bank's *Doing Business Index* (World Bank, 2016). The relevant aspects are shown in Table 5.1. Spain ranks 28th; far below the US although around the average of the OECD high-income countries. Spain performs particularly well regarding "Trading Across Borders" —this factor includes time to export and cost to export across borders, and it is related to the country's transportation infrastructures; "Protecting Minority Investors"; and "Taxes". The country's weaknesses are related above all with legal procedures, like "Dealing with Construction Permits", "Getting Electricity" and "Registering Property". In general, however, Spain performs like other high-income countries.

Table 5.1 Spain, Italy, France, Germany and US Rank (out of 190) According to the DB 2018 Rank World Bank's Doing Business Index*

Area	Spain Rank	Italy Rank	France Rank	Germany Rank	US Rank
Overall: Ease of Doing Business	28	46	31	20	6
Starting a Business	86	66	25	113	49
Dealing With Construction Permits	123	96	18	24	36
Getting Electricity	42	28	26	5	49
Registering Property	53	23	100	77	37
Getting Credit	68	105	90	42	2
Protecting Minority Investors	24	62	33	62	42
Paying Taxes	34	112	54	41	36
Trading Across Borders	1	1	1	39	36
Enforcing Contracts	26	108	15	22	16
Resolving Insolvency	19	24	28	4	3

Note: This index looks at 10 areas and examines the extent for local entrepreneurs to start and run a small to medium-size business when complying with relevant regulations. Countries are ranked on their ease of doing business, from 1 (the most supportive environment to establish a new business) to 190 (the least supportive).
Source: www.doingbusiness.org/rankings

Regional governments also play an important role in enhancing entrepreneurship. The best examples of this are the policies developed to promote clusters in two of the most traditional industrial regions, the Basque Country and Catalonia. Clusters are understood as a geographic concentration of interconnected manufacturers, suppliers and associated institutions in a particular industry (Porter, 1990). By driving innovation, productivity gains and the creation of new businesses, clusters make companies compete in some aspects (market share, for instance) while cooperating in others, such as R&D and training programs. Clusters, furthermore, have proved to improved competitiveness, so not surprisingly the last EU Cohesion Plan (2014–2020) aims to innovate by exploiting the knowledge, skills and assets that regions, rather than nations, possess (European Commission, 2013).

As early as 1991, and as a response to industrial crises in the late 1970s and 1980s, the Basque Country government decided to adapt its industrial policy to create a supportive environment for the development of clusters and firm internationalization (Valdaliso, Elola, Aranguren, & López, 2011; Royo, 2009). This has led to remarkable growth since then. The success of the export-oriented Electronics, IT and Telecommunications Cluster of the Basque Country (one of the largest and oldest), and the Basque aeronautical and space cluster, for instance, relies on domestic firms' capabilities and accumulated experience, the regional government's financial support, and knowledge sharing within related sectors (López García, Elola, Valdaliso, & Aranguren, 2013; López García & Valdaliso, 2011). Similar examples can be found for the motor and agricultural industry in Catalonia and the shoe sector in Islas Baleares (Catalan, Miranda, & Ramon, 2011). Catalonia launched in 1993 its first cluster initiatives, followed soon by other regions and, since 2009, all supported by the National Federation of Innovative Business Groups (Novo, 2014). However, it was not until 2006 that the Spanish central government developed the first national program to support clusters, including the creation of a national registry for "Innovative Business Groups".

National Culture and Country Image

Cultural norms, values and beliefs are considered powerful forces shaping the dominant decision makers' perceptions, disposition and behaviours, which in turn affect those choices made regarding the intended HRM strategy (Paauwe, 2004; Paauwe & Boselie, 2003), and so TM strategy. In fact, there is evidence of the need for companies to tailor their programs for managing talent with sensitivity to local country culture conditions (e.g., Cooke, Saini, & Wang, 2014; Sidani & Al Ariss, 2014). Indeed, both national and organizational culture is seen as of increasing importance for the management of talent (see Thunnissen & Gallardo-Gallardo, 2017), since they provide explanations to attitudinal and behavioral variation between human communities that can help to delineate the appropriateness of TM policies and practices in a particular context. When considering cross-cultural dimensions the two best known frameworks are: the 6-D model by Hofstede (1980), Hofstede, Hofstede and Minkov (2010) and the GLOBE CEO study (House, Hanges, Javidan, Dorfman, & Gupta, 2004). According to Hofstede's cultural dimensions, the Spanish culture is characterized by *high power distance*, and *short-term* orientation. In other words, Spain is a hierarchical, normative and *restrained* society. Indeed, hierarchies are very clear and are respected, people do not expect power or rewards to be distributed evenly among the society, and actions are restrained by social norms. Moreover, traditions and norms are sacrosanct and family life is guided by imperatives. In comparison with other European countries (except for Portugal), it is *collectivist* (i.e., people belong to strong, cohesive in-groups, often extended families, that take care of them in exchange of loyalty). In other words, Spaniards have a 'we' consciousness, stress on belonging and try to maintain harmony. That is why teamwork is considered as something natural, and could explain why there is low mobility. Furthermore, it is more *feminine* than masculine, meaning that caring for others and quality of life are more important than competition and success. The *uncertainty avoidance* dimension clearly identifies Spain. It is considered the 'second noisiest country in the world' in which people like to have rules for everything; confrontation is avoided; and changes, ambiguous and undefined situations cause stress and scale up to the personal level very quickly (Hofstede Insights). Thus, it explains why most Spanish students want to work in civil service (i.e. a job for life, no concerns about the future) or in multinationals rather than in SMEs (which are the type of firms that define Spanish productive system) or that aim to create their own business (Jaurégui, Carmona, & Carrión, 2016). The GLOBE study of CEO Leadership Behavior and Effectiveness (House, Dorfman, Javidan, Hanges, & Sully de Luque, 2014) shows similar results. Spain belongs to the Latin Europe cluster together with France, Israel, Italy, Portugal and Switzerland. Spaniards are characterized by high power distance, short-term orientation, in-group collectivism, low assertiveness, performance orientation, and uncertainty avoidance. Moreover, it is a male-dominated society.

A term connected with national culture and, in particular, with the perceptions about national culture, is 'country image', or people's beliefs, ideas and impressions about a certain country (Kotler, Haider, & Rein, 1993). Country image, therefore, also affects talent attraction and retention. As a relatively backward country within Europe, Spain has traditionally dealt with a poor country image. This is the leitmotif for initiatives such as "Marca España" (Spain's brand). In 2012, the Spanish government launched this program to improve the perception of Spain abroad as well as within. The initiative of the 'Marca España' project responds to the need to coordinate the different public and private actions on the Spain brand, to convey to companies and institutions the importance of having a good image of the country, and to inform them about how to communicate and "sell" the new reality of Spain (Nicolás, 2003).

In the last report of *Observatorio Marca España* (the Spanish Observatory for the country brand), Spain had a mark of 7.1 (out of 10), similarly to the United States and slightly lower than Japan and the European leaders, but much better than the Asian, Latin American and African countries considered in the sample. This position has improved in the last years. Although country image differs among countries, in general the Spanish language and culture is very positively perceived, but Spanish products still lack a reputable 'Made in Spain' brand (Real Instituto El Cano, 2017). Spanish goods are indeed perceived as of low-quality and low technological content, to a lesser extent in the case of traditional agrarian exportations, such as wine and olive oil. From the point of view of foreign investors, Spain still needs to promote professional training and foreign languages.

The main cause of most of these negative aspects seems to be attributed to the absence of a State policy, in the sense that in Spain there is a notable deficit, especially at the public or institutional level, regarding the need to export the 'Made in Spain' brand, which contrasts with the enormous concern of other countries (ICEX, 2003; Real Instituto El Cano, 2017).

Macro Talent Management Outcomes

To assess the outcomes of macro talent management in Spain, we consider in this section a wide array of comprehensive and well-known international indexes, which include key variables connected with talent. We follow here a comparative perspective, evaluating the Spanish position in relation to the United States, the largest European economies (Germany and France) and other Mediterranean countries (Italy). In a globalized world, to what extent a country attracts or repels talent depends on what competitors (other countries) are doing to catch talent, which justifies the comparative perspective. The choice of countries to be compared to, on the other hand, responds to Spain's historical economic evolution. As explained previously, Spain and the Mediterranean periphery have traditionally lagged behind the US and the economic centre of Western Europe. We want to address to what extent this is also reflected in these countries' relative position in international indexes.

How we approach talent management outcomes entailed a relevant limitation. As the indexes we look at are at a national level, we put aside regional differences, which, at least in the Spanish case, seem to be wide. Spanish regions not only have historically enjoyed a different level of development, and business and job opportunities, but also regional governments have a great autonomy in education policy and other issues closely related with talent management.

The World Economic Forum's "Global Competitiveness Index"

The Global Competitiveness Index (GCI) elaborated by the World Economic Forum (WEF) measures the economic micro and macroeconomic foundations of national competitiveness, looking at the set of institutions, politics and factors that determine the productivity level (and potential growth) of a given country (World Economic Forum, 2017a). In the latest report (2017–2018), Spain ranks 32nd of 138, being better positioned than other Mediterranean countries like Italy (44th), but far below Germany (5th) and US (3rd). Spain's relative position has not changed significantly in the last years.

The GCI comprises 12 pillars. The pillars that relate the most to MTM are the 3rd Pillar (Macroeconomic Environment), 4th Pillar (Health and Primary Education); 5th Pillar (High Education and Training); 7th Pillar (Labour Market Efficiency); and 12th Pillar (R&D Innovation). As shown in Table 5.2, in general Spain does not outrank any apart from Italy.

Table 5.2 Spain, Italy, France, Germany and US Rank (out of 138) According to the Global Competitiveness Index 2016–2017

INDEXES		Spain Rank	Italy Rank	France Rank	Germany Rank	US Rank
Overall Index		34	43	22	5	2
Sub-indexes	Basic Requirements	33	51	26	11	25
	Efficiency Enhancers	30	43	20	6	1
	Innovation and Sophistication factors	38	28	17	3	2
PILLARS	**Description**	Spain Rank	Italy Rank	France Rank	Germany Rank	US Rank
Institutions*	Examines the institutional environment which includes the legal and administrative framework	54	95	31	21	20
Infrastructure*	Looks at the infrastructure of a country (i.e., available modes of transport, electricity supplies, telecommunication networks)	12	27	7	10	9
Macroeconomic environment*	Examines the stability of the macroeconomic environment of a country	90	96	63	12	83
Health and Primary Education*	Examines investments in the provision of health services, and the quantity and quality of basic education	32	25	24	13	29
High Education and Training**	Measures secondary and tertiary enrolment rates, and the extent of staff training	28	41	22	15	3
Good Market Efficiency**	Analyses efficiency of the goods markets	49	60	36	11	7
Labour Market Efficiency**	Looks at the efficiency and flexibility of the labour market	70	116	56	14	3
Financial Market development**	Examines the well-being of financial and economic activities	68	126	33	12	2
Technological readiness**	Looks at the agility with which an economy adopts existing technologies	28	41	21	8	6
Market size**	Examines the size of the markets by considering both domestic and foreign markets	17	12	8	5	2
Business sophistication***	Looks at the quality of a country's overall business networks and the quality of individual firms' operations and strategies	29	25	16	5	2
Innovation***	Looks at the investment in research and development (R&D), especially by the private sector; the presence of high-quality scientific research institutions; extensive collaboration in research and technological developments between universities and industry; and the protection of intellectual property	42	34	17	5	2

Note: *Those pillars belong to the *Basic Requirements* sub index;
**Those pillars belong to the *Efficiency Enhancers* sub index;
*** Those pillars belong to the *Innovation and sophistication factors* sub index.
Source: World Economic Forum (2017a)

Only regarding Health and Primary Education, Spain outranks a leading country, the United States, like the other Europeans, which also enjoy a public and universal healthcare system. Spain has historically had a very weak position in terms of innovation (López García & Valdaliso, 2001; Sáiz, 2005). According to World Bank data (World Bank, 2017), research and development expenditure (as % of GDP) was 1.2% in 2015, which contrasts with the nearly 3% of Germany and the United States, and the 2.14% of the Euro area. The number of researchers in Spain has also gone down in the last years as highlighted earlier. But, at the same time, research productivity in Spain increased between 2010 and 2014 according to a wide array of indicators (IUNE, 2016).

The Institute of Management Development's 'World Talent Report'

The World Talent Report published by the Institute of Management Development (IMD) compares and ranks countries on three factors: (a) Investment and Development; (b) Appeal; and (c) Readiness. According to this report, the overall Spain ranking in 2017 is 30 out of 63 economies (table 5.3). Note that Spain has improved 9 points since 2015. Table 5.3 shows that, again, Spain usually lags behind US, German and French benchmarks, but it is particularly well positioned in 'Appeal', that is, regarding the ability to attract and retain talent.

INSEAD's "Global Talent Competitiveness Index"

INSEAD's Global Talent Competitiveness Index (GTCI) allows us to focus on core MTM processes which include knowledge spill overs, learning and knowledge sharing, institutional support, educational leadership, corporate strategy and leadership. Specifically, the GTCI ranks countries on 6 pillars to determine their ability to grow, attract and retain talent. As shown in Table 5.4, differences between the United States and the rest of the sample are significant for most items. If we look now within Europe, Spain and Italy rank again worse than the others (particularly regarding vocational skills), but the Spanish position is comparable to the largest European economies in terms of 'Growth', that is, the opportunities for formal education, lifelong learning and access to growth. However, the participation of adults in lifelong learning in Spain is only close to the European average, around 47% according to the PIAAC's Survey of Adult Skills elaborated by the OECD (data of 2013; OECD, 2016b; Felgueroso, 2016; INE, 2017b). Spain is situated better than France and Italy (less than 40% in both cases), and not significantly below Germany (51%).

Table 5.3 Spain, Italy, France, Germany and US Rank (out of 63) According to the IMD World Talent Ranking 2017

Factor	Description	Spain Rank	Italy Rank	France Rank	Germany Rank	US Rank
Investment and Development	Measures the investment in and development of home-grown talent	30	33	20	10	29
Appeal	Evaluates the ability of a country to attract and retain talent	25	41	29	8	2
Readiness	Quantifies the quality of the available skills and competencies in the talent pool	41	34	28	15	24

Source: IMD (2017, pp. 29–31)

Table 5.4 Spain, Italy, France, Germany and US Rank (out of 118) According to the Global Talent Competitiveness Index (GTCI) 2017

GTCI	Spain Rank	Italy Rank	France Rank	Germany Rank	US Rank
Overall Position	35	40	24	17	4
PILLAR *Sub-pillars*	Spain Rank	Italy Rank	France Rank	Germany Rank	US Rank
ENABLE	43	62	34	14	11
Regulatory Landscape	36	57	31	12	22
Market Landscape	32	30	18	3	5
Business and Labour Landscape	96	102	99	45	7
ATTRACT	41	64	26	20	16
External Openness	50	82	19	22	21
Internal Openness	32	45	36	18	12
GROW	23	28	18	20	2
Formal Education	25	22	18	13	2
Lifelong Learning	28	57	18	32	8
Access to Growth Opportunities	29	31	23	33	3
RETAIN	30	41	25	11	8
Sustainability	51	48	36	12	4
Lifestyle*	7	31	19	14	33
VOCATIONAL and TECHNICAL SKILLS	48	31	7	1	20
Mid-level Skills	63	19	7	4	28
Employability	34	60	29	3	11
GLOBAL KNOWLEDGE SKILLS	32	39	24	26	3
High-level Skills	26	45	22	27	2
Talent Impact**	49	32	25	27	12

Note: *Lifestyle is measured by taking into consideration 'environmental performance', 'personal safety', physician density', and 'sanitation'.
**Talent impact is measured considering 'innovation output', 'high-value exports', 'new product entrepreneurial activity', and 'new business density'.
Source: Lanvin and Evans (2017, pp. 156, 158, 170, 220, 232)

Program for International Student Assessment

The OECD ranks countries on their levels of educational attainment for many age categories. One of its most famous rankings is the Program for International Student Assessment (PISA), which ranks 15-year-old students on the basis of their achievement in math, sciences and reading. Both Spain and the United States do relatively poorly on the PISA scores with respect to the OECD average as shown in Table 5.5. The only subject where Spain has a greater score than the United States is math, but both are behind the OECD average.

Table 5.5 Spain, Italy, France, Germany and US Rank According the *Programme for International Student Assessment* (PISA) * 2015

	Mean Score in Mathematics[a]		Mean Score in Reading[b]		Mean Score in Science[c]	
	PISA 2015	PISA 2012	PISA 2015	PISA 2012	PISA 2015	PISA 2012
Spain	486	484	496	488	493	496
Italy	490	485	485	490	481	494
Germany	509	514	506	508	509	524
US	470	481	497	498	496	497
OECD Average	490	494	493	496	493	501

Note: * PISA examines the extent to which 15-year-old students have acquired important knowledge and skills that are essential for full participation in modern societies.
[a] In 2012, the highest ranked country (Shanghai-China) achieved 613 and the lowest (Peru) 368; whereas in 2015 were 564 (Singapore) and 328 (Dominican Republic).
[b] In 2012, the highest ranked country (Shanghai-China) achieved 570 in Readiness and the lowest (Peru) 384; whereas in 2015 were 535 (Singapore) and 358 (Dominican Republic).
[c] In 2012, the highest ranked country (Shanghai-China) achieved 580 in Science and the lowest (Peru) 373; whereas in 2015 were 556 (Singapore) and 332 (Dominican Republic).
Source: OECD (2014, 2016a)

The World Economic Forum's Human Capital Index

The Global Human Capital Index assesses how well countries are developing their human capital according to different dimensions and differentiating by age group. Spain ranks 44th, and is behind most EU countries (Table 5.6). This is also the case for the four sub-indexes included, with differences particularly striking in terms of 'Development'. The Spanish position is influenced there by the relatively poor vocational education enrolment rate and quality of the education system in the age group 15–24, and low extent of staff training for the age group 25–64 (World Economic Forum, 2017b, p. 167), which is consistent with the educational prospectus provided in a previous section. Deficiencies in vocational training also help to understand why the score regarding know-how in medium-skilled workers is relatively low regarding other countries.

The overall Spanish position is also explain by relative high unemployment and underemployment rates, particularly among the younger people, which are included in the 'Deployment' sub-index. While unemployment refers to the share of active people jobless, underemployment considers to what extent workers use all their skills, education, or availability at their jobs. Spain, therefore, is not taking enough advantage of its workforce's human capital potential, particularly in the case of the youngest, and high-qualified, professionals. The Deployment sub-index, however, also takes into account the labour force participation rate in the age group 65 years and over. Retirement age in Spain is 65 (extended recently to 67), which explains the low score obtained there.

Spain, however, is one of the high-income OECD countries. This is reflected in the human capital indexed with high scores in terms of 'Capacity', which includes literacy rates and attainment rates at the different stages of education. Included in 'Development', Spain is very well positioned regarding enrolment rates at primary, secondary and tertiary education; as well as skill diversity of graduates. It even ranks 1st in secondary enrolment gender gap (0–14 age group).

Table 5.6 Spain, Italy, France, Germany and US Rank (out of 130) According to the Global Human Capital Index 2017

INDEXES		Spain Rank	Italy Rank	France Rank	Germany Rank	US Rank
Overall Index		44	35	26	4	6
Sub-index	**Description**	Spain Rank	Italy Rank	France Rank	Germany Rank	US Rank
Capacity	Level of formal education of younger and older generations as a result of past education investment	66	41	39	22	29
Deployment	Skills application and accumulation among the adult population	30	28	20	4	12
Development	Formal education of the next-generation workforce and continued upskilling and reskilling of the current workforce	101	107	86	43	40
Know-How	Breadth and depth of specialized skills use at work	31	23	14	13	7

Note: This index ranks countries according to how well they are developing their human capital. Although not included here, the index differentiates by age group (0–14 years; 15–24 years; 25–54 years; 55–64 years; and 65 years and over).
Source: World Economic Forum (2017b, pp. 3 and 8)

Conclusion

In this chapter we have provided information about the main environmental factors that deal with the creation, attraction and retention of TM in Spain. Moreover, we have discussed the result of such environment in terms of Spanish competitiveness and talent stock using a wide array of international indexes. Thus, the following interrelated questions arise: *Is Spain able to create, attract and retain talent? And to what extent is Spain able to compete with others for talent?*

It is not possible to give an answer to these questions without defining and measuring talent first. At some point in this chapter, inspired by economic theory and in line with Makram, Sparrow and Greasley (2017), we have used the term 'human capital' as a synonym of talent resources. In fact, according to Cappelli (2008), 'at its heart, talent management is simply a matter of anticipating the need for human capital and setting out a plan to meet it' (p. 1). When looking at talent through the human capital lens we are referring to the unique stock of knowledge, capabilities, skills, competencies, social and personality attributes possessed by a person, and embodied in the ability to perform labour so as to produce economic value (Farndale, Scullion, & Sparrow, 2010; Sparrow & Makram, 2015). In fact, economists have long linked human capital to those personal attributes aimed to improve individuals' job performance along with firms' productivity and countries' competitiveness (Lucas, 1988; Barro, 1991).

In order to measure Spanish talent on a macro level, and going with the economic mainstream, we should focus on two pillars (Goldin, 2015): education and training, and health. Starting with the latter, and as mentioned before, Spain ranks at the top of the European Union in terms of life expectancy at birth, which is considered a proxy to a population's health; and a bit lower regarding perceived health and coverage of the publicly funded healthcare system according to the OECD data. However, Spanish data on education is not so positive. Although enrolment and attainment rates are comparable to the European average, particularly for the youngest (see, for instance, the Global Human Capital Index), Spain still has plenty of room to improve in terms of adult and vocational education. The results in the PISA analysis suggest that learning effectiveness needs to progress as well. Hence, Spain still has issues about generating talent, compared with the leading world countries, although much less than in the past. Note that, for instance, the share of adults with only primary studies or low-stage studies has decreased over the last decade and that several Spanish universities are highly ranked according to different World University rankings. Indeed, increasing public spending on education would help to achieve better improvements. Moreover, providing better learning opportunities for students from environments with limited access to education, educating for digitalization, and helping with the integration of females in STEM degrees are interesting subjects for further action that can also help to improve the achievements on developing talent in Spain.

But, what about attracting and retaining talent? If we measure this as job opportunities and job quality, in both cases Spain fails compared to top economies. Apart from the structural unemployment problem, the 2008 crisis affected Spain more negatively than central Europe countries, which clearly limited job opportunities over the last decade. Although growth and recovery is giving pace, job quality has deteriorated in the last years leading to an increasing income inequality within the Spanish society. Despite these facts, and as we have discussed in previous sections, Spain is a very popular and attractive destination for not only those benefiting from the European student exchange programs, but also, for expatriates. In fact, Spanish language, local culture and, above all, quality of life are very positively perceived for foreign talent. Within the country, however, there are few regions that act as talent magnets. Specifically, Madrid, Barcelona and the Basque Country regions have historically attracted many qualified Spanish workers looking for job opportunities and better wages. Indeed, Madrid, Bilbao, and Barcelona rank among the top twenty world cities considered key players on the global talent scene according to the Global City Talent Competitiveness Index 2017. Note that national and regional governments in Spain have been at the same time pursuing policies aimed to palliate the brain drain, attracting foreign talent and aiding the return of expatriates. Although these initiatives are improving Spanish position on the global talent scene, much still remains to be done.

To sum up, two main conclusions can be drawn. First, at present, Spain is able to create, attract and retain talent significantly more than in the past. All the indicators used in this chapter have dramatically improved in the long term, particularly after Spain's entrance into the European Union. Second, the national picture hides important regional differences. Although this chapter does not deal with MTM at regional level, in the previous pages we have highlighted several times how a few regions are better positioned than the national average in different indicators related to talent management, acting as talent pools at least at the national level. This is largely the result of industrial policies designed by regional institutions, but also promoted at national and even EU levels. In fact, the EU Cohesion Policy for the next years (2014–2020) spins around regions as sources of national and global competitiveness. Indeed, an interesting further research avenue would be to analyse macro talent management in a long-term and regional perspective.

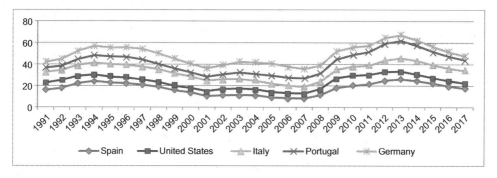

Figure 5.5 Unemployment, Total (% of total labour force) (modelled ILO estimate) in Spain, US, Germany, Italy and Portugal (1991–2017)

Source data: World Bank (data.worldbank.org/)

144 • Adoración Álvaro-Moya et al.

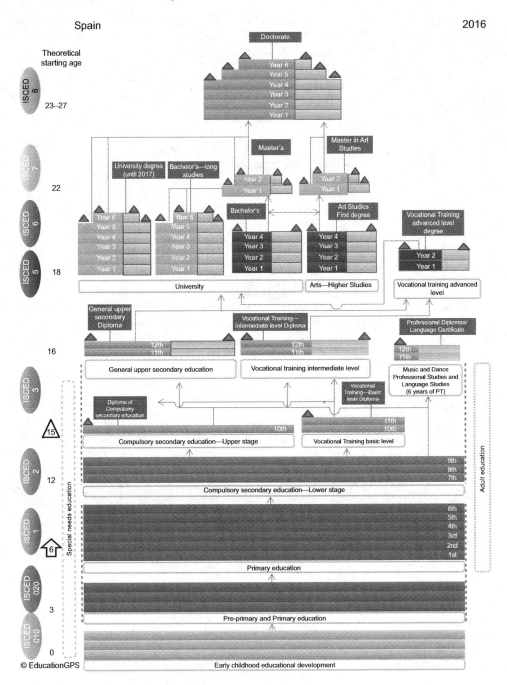

Appendix 5.1 Structure of the Spanish Education System

Source: OECD. Education GPS (gpseducation.oecd.org/CountryProfile)

Key

⇧/△ Starting/ending age of compulsory education

▲ Recognized exit point of the education system

↑ Typical student flow

⇡ Transfer from one programme to another

▨ Programme designed for part-time attendance

☐ Vocational/Professional orientation (according to national definition at the tertiary level)

☐ Single structure education (integrated ISCED levels)

⋮ May be provided within one school structure

⩍ Transfer at crossing lines is not possible

Diploma Name of diploma, degree of certificate

2016 Reference year (school year 2015/2016 in the northern hemisphere)

* **Theoretical starting ages** refer to the ages as established by law and regulation for the entry to a programme, actual starting ages may vary depending on the programme.

Appendix 5.1 (Continued)

Appendix 5.2 Summary of Main Spanish Labour Market Reforms

Year	Main objective	Some effects
1984	Introduction of temporary contracts in order to increase flexibility; young people and long-term unemployed were the main targets of the reform	Small, though non-negligible, effect on employment growth
		Importance rested in the increase of turnover
		Led to the creation of a gap between the cost of dismissal of temporary and permanent contracts, and the widening of the scope of temporary contracts
		Temporary contracts increased
1994	Enhance the role of collective bargaining; a deregulatory reform.	Elimination of the fixed-term employment promotion contract, which led firms to use other forms of temporary employment (low-cost or high-flexible)
		Reduction of dismissal costs in order to recognize the rights of firms to dismiss workers for economic reasons
		Eased labour mobility and working hour flexibility, and temporary work agencies were introduced
1997	Enhance the competitiveness of Spanish firms by reducing both temporality and rotation, whilst promoting continuous training	Decrease in the number of temporary contracts
		Changes in the role of the temporary work agencies
		Augment the reasons for objective dismissals
	Linked to the Tripartite Agreement on Continuous Training	Introduction of a new permanent contract, with lower dismissal costs than the existing one, and with tax benefits
		Positive effects: 80% of net employment created after the reform was permanent employment

(Continued)

Year	Main objective	Some effects
2001	Promote stable and indefinite contracts Limit abuse in the use of temporary contracts Promote female, part-time and groups with special difficulties employment	Increased flexibility by widening the applicability and scope of the new permanent contracts, by reducing dismissal costs for normal permanent contracts, and by making the working times for part-time and discontinuous permanent workers more flexible
		Introduced a limited compensation for the sacking of temporary workers
2002	Reduce the number of unemployed receiving unemployed benefit for lengthy periods	Unemployed people were forced to sign a written commitment with the employment office and the definition of suitable job was altered
		Unemployment protection was reduced for discontinuous permanent contracts, and interim wages were to be abolished
2010	Reduce labour market dualism and increasing flexibility; 'align pay with productivity' (i.e., to reduce wages)	Modification of multi-employer agreements through bargaining at company level
		Conditions for fair dismissal were merely clarified by the inclusion of explicitly economic, organizational, technical and production-related reasons as grounds for fair dismissal
		Increased severance pay for temporary contracts and generalized the severance pay subsidy scheme to all employers and types of dismissal for permanent contracts signed after the date of approval of the reform
2012	Restore competitiveness by aligning labour costs more closely to productivity and allow employers to exploit more easily internal flexibility measures Make the labour market more dynamic and less segmented	Gave absolute priority to enterprise-level agreements over those established at the sector or regional level, and made it easier for firms to opt-out of a collective agreement and implement internal flexibility measures (e.g., introducing changes to working conditions, such as working hours or wages) as an alternative to job destruction
		Redefined the conditions for a fair dismissal (i.e., a dismissal is always justified if the company faces a persistent decline in revenues or ordinary income; moreover, the firm does not have to prove that the dismissal is essential for the future profitability of the firm)
		Reduced monetary compensation for unfair dismissal and eliminated the requirement of administrative authorization for collective redundancies
		A new permanent contract for full-time employees (*Contrato de Emprendedores*) in small firms was introduced, entailing and extended trial period of one year. During this trial period, workers can be dismissed for no reason and without compensation. Moreover, the use of such contracts allows firms to claim several tax benefits

Source: Ballester (2005), Bertelsmann (2004), Horwitz & Myant (2015), Laparra & García (2003), Martín (2004), OCDE (2013) & Toharia (1997).

References

'A guide to education in Spain'. (2015, July). Retrieved from Expatica website www.expatica.com/es/education/Education-in-Spain_103110.html.

Afinoguénova, E., & Martí-Olivella, J. (2008). *Spain is (still) different: Tourism and discourse in Spanish identity*. Lanham, MD: Lexington Books.

Aldcroft, D. H. (2016). *Europe's third world: The European periphery in the interwar years.* New York, NY: Routledge.
Almunia, J. (2011). Spain's membership in the EU: Assessment of a success story. In J. Roy & M. Lorca-Susino (Eds.), *Spain in the European Union: The first twenty-five years (1986–2011)* (pp. 1–4). Retrieved from aei.pitt.edu/32455/1/SPAIN-EU-25-allPDF.pdf.
Amendola, A., Caroleo, F. E., & Coppola, G. (2006). Regional disparities in Europe. In F. E. Caroleo & S. Destefanis (Eds.), *The European labour market* (pp. 9–31). AIEL Series in Labour Economics. Heidelberg: Springer International Publishing AG.
Andrés, J., & Doménech, R. (2013). *Budget balance, structural unemployment and fiscal adjustments.* Economic Watch, BBVA Research. Retrieved from goo.gl/Xq2sr9.
Arango, J. (2000). Becoming a country of immigration at the end of the twentieth century: The case of Spain. In R. King, G. Lazaridis, & Ch. Tsardanidis (Eds.), *El Dorado or fortress? Migration in Southern Europe* (pp. 253–256). Londres: Macmillan.
Arango, J. (2013, March). *Exceptional in Europe? Spain's experience with immigration and integration.* Migration Policy Institute Report. Retrieved from www.migrationpolicy.org/research/exceptional-europe-spains-experience-immigration-and-integration.
Ayuda, M. I., Collantes, F., & Pinilla, V. (2010). From locational fundamentals to increasing returns: The spatial concentration of population in Spain, 1787–2000. *Journal of Geographical Systems, 12*(1), 25–50.
Ballester, R. (2005). *Employment strategy and Spanish labour market policies.* Working Papers No. 14, Department of Economics, University of Girona, 1–31. Retrieved from www3.udg.edu/fcee/economia/n14.pdf.
Barro, R. (1991). Economic growth in a cross section of countries. *The Quarterly Journal of Economics, 106*(2), 407–443.
Berengueras Pont, M., & Vera Mur, J. M. (2015, October). Las leyes de educación en España en los últimos doscientos años. Supervisión 21. Revista de Educación e Inspección, 38. Retrieved from www.usie.es/SUPERVISION21/2015_38/SP_21_38_Articulo_Leyes_educacion_ultimos_200_anyos_Berengueras_y_Pont.pdf.
Bertelsmann, S. (2004). International Reform Monitor-Social Policy. Labour Market Policy and Industrial Relations, Issue 9. Verlag Bertelsmann Stiftung, Gütersloh.
Berthon, P., Ewing, M., & Hag, L. L. (2005). Captivating company: Dimensions of attractiveness in employer branding. *International Journal of Advertising, 24*(2), 151–172.
Buck, T. (2017, January 17). No right turn for Spanish politics. *Financial Times.* Retrieved from www.ft.com/content/414246f6-dbe4-11e6-86ac-f253db7791c6.
Cappelli, P. (2008). *Talent on demand: Managing talent in an age of uncertainty.* Boston, MA: Harvard Business School Press.
Carbajosa, A. (2015, July 13). Why Spain has resisted the rise of the far right. *El País.* Retrieved from elpais.com/elpais/2015/07/06/inenglish/1436183846_250471.html.
Catalan, J., Miranda, J. A., & Ramon, R. (2011). *Distritos y clusters en la Europa del Sur.* Madrid: LID Editorial.
Cervilla, P. (2017, June 13). El Pacto de Estado por la Educación empieza a negociarse en el Senado. *ABC.* Retrieved from www.abc.es/sociedad/abci-pacto-estado-educacion-empieza-negociarse-senado-201706132023_noticia.html.
Chislett, W. (2013). *Spain: What everyone needs to know.* Oxford: Oxford University Press.
Collins & Kanar. (2013). Employer brand equity and recruitment research. In K. Yu, D. Cable (Eds.), *The Oxford Handbook of Recruitment.* Oxford: Oxford University Press.
Constitución Española. (1978). Retrieved from www.congreso.es/consti/constitucion/indice/index.htm.
Cooke, F. L., Saini, D. S., & Wang, J. (2014). Talent management in China and India: A comparison of management perceptions and human resource practices. *Journal of World Business, 49*(2), 225–235.
De la Torre, J., & Sanz Lafuente, G. (Eds.). (2008). *Migraciones y coyuntura económica del franquismo a la democracia.* Zaragoza: Prensas Universitarias de Zaragoza.
Delle Femmine, L., & Alameda, D. (2017, March 1). La metamorphosis de España. *El país.* Retrieved from elpais.com/internacional/2017/02/27/actualidad/1488194732_820452.html.
De Vos, A., & Dries, N. (2013). Applying a talent management lens to career management: The role of human capital composition and continuity. *International Journal of Human Resource Management, 24*(9), 1816–1831.
Dolado, J. (Ed.). (2015). *No country for young people? Youth labour market problems in Europe.* London: Centre for Economic Policy Research (CEPR) Press. Retrieved from voxeu.org/sites/default/files/file/No_Country_Young_People_VoxEU.pdf.
Durán, J. J. (1999). *Multinacionales españolas en Iberoamérica: valor estratégico.* Madrid: Pirámide.
Durán, J. J., & Sánchez, P. (1981). *La internacionalización de la empresa española: inversiones españolas en el exterior.* Madrid: Ministerio de Economía y Comercio.

Eurofound (2017), *Exploring self-employment in the European Union*, Publications Office of the European Union, Luxembourg. Retrieved from www.eurofound.europa.eu/publications/report/2017/exploring-self-employment-in-the-european-union.

European Commission. (2013, Winter). Cohesion policy 2014–2020. *Panorama*, 48. Retrieved from ec.europa.eu/regional_policy/sources/docgener/panorama/pdf/mag48/mag48_en.pdf.

European Commission. (2016). *Monitor de la Educación y la formación de 2016—España*. Luxembourg: Office of Publications of the European Union. Retrieved from ec.europa.eu/education/sites/education/files/monitor2016-es_es.pdf.

European Commission. (2017a). *Education and training. Monitor 2017*. Luxembourg: Office of Publications of the European Union. Retrieved from ec.europa.eu/education/sites/education/files/monitor2017-country-reports_en.pdf.

European Commission. (2017b, November). *European economic forecast Autumn 2017*. Institutional Paper 063. Report of the Directorate-General for Economic and Financial Affairs. Retrieved from ec.europa.eu/info/business-economy-euro/economic-performance-and-forecasts/economic-performance-country/spain/economic-forecast-spain_en.

European Commission. (2017c). *2018 European semester: Draft joint employment report*. Luxembourg: Office of Publications of the European Union. Retrieved from ec.europa.eu/info/publications/2018-european-semester-draft-joint-employment-report_en.

European Commission. (2017d, November). Annual Report on European SMEs 2016/2017: Focus on self-employment. Report of the Directorate-General for Internal Market, Industry, Entrepreneurship and SMEs. Retrieved from ec.europa.eu/docsroom/documents/26563/attachments/1/translations/en/renditions/native.

Eurostat, the Statistical Office of the European Union. (2016). *Labour force survey in the EU, candidate and EFTA countries: Main characteristics of national surveys, 2015*. Statistical Working Papers. Luxembourg: Office of Publications of the European Union. Retrieved from ec.europa.eu/eurostat/documents/3888793/7751652/KS-TC-16-021-EN-N.pdf/8475c2e2-c037-4ba2-9029-93db1ade41fe.

Fariñas, J. C., & Huergo, E. (2015). *Demografía empresarial en España: tendencias y regularidades*. Madrid: FEDEA, Estudios sobre la Economía Española—2015/24. Retrieved from documentos.fedea.net/pubs/eee/eee2015-24.pdf.

Farndale, E., Scullion, H., & Sparrow, P. (2010). The role of the corporate HR function in global talent management. *Journal of World Business*, 45(2), 161–168.

Felgueroso, F. (2016). *Lifelong learning in Spain: A challenge for the future*. Madrid: FEDEA. Retrieved from www.fedea.net/nsaw/descargas/NSAW02en.pdf.

Fernández Pérez, P., & Díaz Morlán, P. (2015). Entre el poder y el mercado. Aproximación a la evolución histórica de los grandes grupos empresariales familiares en la España del siglo XX. In P. Fernández Pérez & A. Lluch (Eds.), *Familias empresarias y grandes empresas familiares en América Latina y España. Una visión de largo plazo*. Bilbao: Fundación BBVA.

Franks, J. (1997). *Labor market policies and unemployment dynamics in Spain*. Banco de España-Servicio de Estudios, Documento de Trabajo nº9708. Retrieved from www.bde.es/f/webbde/SES/Secciones/Publicaciones/PublicacionesSeriadas/DocumentosTrabajo/97/Fic/dt9708e.pdf.

Fundación BBVA-Ivie. (2016). *El capital humano de los emprendedores. La formación de los emprendedores españoles mejora, pero el peso de los que solo tienen educación obligatoria es el doble que en la Unión Europea*. Esenciales Fundación BBVA-Ivie, nº12/2016. Retrieved from w3.grupobbva.com/TLFU/fbin/FBBVA_Esenciales_12_tcm269-627367.pdf.

García Delgado, J. L. (2014). Economic modernisation. In J. L. García Delgado (Ed.), *The Spanish economy: An introduction* (pp. 15–25). Madrid: Civitas.

Global Leadership & Organizational Behavior Effectiveness (GLOBE). (2004). *Globe culture and leadership study*. Retrieved from globeproject.com/study_2014.

Gobierno de España. (2014). *Estrategia para la internacionalización de las universidades españolas, 2015–2020*. Madrid: Gobierno de España. Retrieved from www.mecd.gob.es/educacion-mecd/dms/mecd/educacion-mecd/areas-educacion/universidades/politica-internacional/estrategia-internacionalizacion/EstrategiaInternacionalizacin-Final.pdf.

Goldin, C. (2015). Human capital. In C. Diebolt & M. Haupert (Eds.), *Handbook of cliometrics* (pp. 55–86). Berlin, Heidelberg: Springer. doi:10.1007/978-3-642-40406-1_23.

González-Calvet, J. (2002). Employment policies in Spain: From flexibilisation to the European employment strategy. In P. Pochet & C. De la Porte (Eds.), *Building social Europe through the open-method of co-ordination* (pp. 177–221). Brussels: PeterLang.

González Ferrer, A. (2013). *La nueva emigración española. Lo que sabemos y lo que no.* (n°18/2013). Madrid: Fundación Alternativas. Retrieved from www.fundacionalternativas.org/laboratorio/documentos/zoom-politico/la-nueva-emigracion-espanola-lo-que-sabemos-y-lo-que-no.

González López, B., & Ramírez, M. A. (2016). La sensibilidad intercultural en relación con las actitudes de aculturación y prejuicio en inmigrantes y sociedad de acogida. Un estudio de caso. *Revista Internacional de Sociología, 74*(2), e034. doi:10.3989/ris.2016.74.2.034.

Guillén, M. (2005). *The rise of Spanish multinationals: European business in the global economy.* New York: Cambridge University Press.

Guillén, M., & García-Canal, E. (2011). *The new multinationals: Spanish firms in a global context.* Cambridge, MA: Cambridge University Press.

Guirao, F. (1998). *Spain and the reconstruction of Western Europe, 1945–57: Challenge and response.* London: Macmillan Press Ltd.

Hall, P., & Soskice, D. (2001). *Varieties of capitalism: The institutional foundations of comparative advantage.* Oxford: Oxford Press.

Hofstede, G. (1980). *Culture's consequences: International differences in work-related values.* Beverly Hills, CA: Sage.

Hofstede, G., Hofstede, G. J., & Minkov, M. (2010). *Cultures and organizations: Software of the mind* (3rd ed.). New York: McGraw-Hill.

Hofstede Insights. (n.d.). *What about Spain?* Retrieved from www.hofstede-insights.com/country-comparison/spain/.

Horwitz, L., & Myant, M. (2015). *Spain's labour market reforms: The road to employment—or to unemployment?* Working Paper 2015.03. European Trade Union Institute. Retrieved from www.etui.org/Publications2/Working-Papers/Spain-s-labour-market-reforms-the-road-to-employment-or-to-unemployment.

House, R. J., Hanges, P. J., Javidan, M., Dorfman, P.W., & Gupta, V. (Eds.). (2004). *Culture, leadership, and organizations: The GLOBE study of 62 societies.* Thousand Oaks, CA: Sage.

House, R. J., Dorfman, P.W., Javidan, M., Hanges, P. J. & Sully de Luque, M.F. (Eds.). (2014). Strategic Leadership across cultures: The GLOBE study of CEO Leadership Behavior and Effectiveness in 24 countries. Thousand Oaks, CA: Sage.

HSBC. (2017). *Expat explorer: Broadening perspectives.* Global Report. Retrieved from www.expatexplorer.hsbc.com/survey/.

IMD. (2017). *IMD world talent ranking 2017.* Retrieved from www.imd.org/wcc/world-competitiveness-center-rankings/talent-rankings-2017/.

INAECU. (2016). *Informe IUNE 2016: Actividad investigadora de la Universidad Española.* Retrieved from www.informes.iune.es/Informe%20IUNE%202016.pdf.

Instituto de la Empresa Familiar. (2015). *La empresa Familiar en España.* Barcelona: Instituto de la Empresa Familiar y Red de Cátedras de Empresa Familiar. Retrieved from www.iefamiliar.com/upload/documentos/la-empresa-familiar-en-espana-2015.pdf.

Instituto Nacional de Estadística (INE). (2017a, June 29). *Estadística de Migraciones 2016. Notas de Prensa.* Retrieved from www.ine.es/prensa/cp_2017_p.pdf.

Instituto Nacional de Estadística (INE). (2017b, July 1). *Estructura y dinamismo del tejido empresarial en España.* Directorio Central de Empresas (DIRCE) a 1 de enero de 2017 Retrieved from www.ine.es/prensa/dirce_2017.pdf.

IUNE. (2016). *Informe IUNE 2016. Actividad investigadora de la universidad española.* Retrieved from www.informes.iune.es/Informe%20IUNE%202016.pdf.

Jauŕegui, F., Carmona, L., & Carrión, E. (2016). *Universidad y empleo: manual de instrucciones.* Córdoba: Almuzara.

Jiménez, J. C., & Martínez Serrano, J. A. (2014). Spain in the economic and monetary union. In J. L. García Delgado (dir.), R. Myro Sánchez (dir.), M. E. Álvarez López, C. M. Fernández-Otheo Ruiz, & J. Vega Crespo (Eds.), *The Spanish economy: An introduction* (pp. 45–59). Madrid: Editorial Civitas.

Khilji, S. E., & Schuler, R. (2016). Talent management in the global context. In D. Collings, K. Mellahi, & W. Cascio (Eds.), *Oxford handbook of talent management* (pp. 399–420). Oxford: Oxford Press.

Kotler, P., Haider, D., & Rein, I. (1993). *Marketing places: Attracting investment and tourism to cities, states and nations.* New York: The Free Press.

Lanvin, B., & Evans, P. (Ed.). (2017, November). *The global talent competitiveness Index: Talent and technology 2017.* Human Capital Leadership Institute. INSEAD and Adecco Group, Switzerland. Retrieved from www.gtci2017.com/documents/GTCI_2017_web_r3.pdf.

Laparra, M., & García, R. (2003). *Labour reform for flexibility: Imposition or social agreement*. Paper presented at the 1st ESPAnet Conference: Changing European Societies—the role for social policy, Copenhagen. 13–15 November 2003.

López-Bazo, E., & Motellón, E. (2017a). Firm exports, innovation and the regional dimension in Spain. *Regional Studies*, 52(4), pp. 490–502. doi:10.1080/00343404.2017.1332406.

López-Bazo, E., & Motellón, E. (2017b). Innovation, heterogeneous firms and the region: Evidence from Spain. *Regional Studies*, 52(5), pp. 673–687.doi:10.1080/00343404.2017.1331296.

López García, S., Elola, A., Valdaliso, J. M., & Aranguren, M. J. (2013). *El clúster de la industria aeronáutica y espacial del País Vasco: orígenes, evolución y trayectoria competitiva*. Donostia: Eusko Ikaskuntza; Instituto Vasco de Competitividad—Fundación. Retrieved from www.euskomedia.org/PDFAnlt/mono/book_cluster_aero/cla001173.pdf.

López García, S., & Valdaliso, J. M. (2001). Cambio tecnológico y crecimiento económico en España en la segunda mitad del siglo XX: Indicadores y polémicas existente. *Revista de Historia Industrial*, *19–20*, 319–337.

López García, S., & Valdaliso, J. M. (2011). Del acero y el cobre al silicio, del mercado nacional al mercado mundial. Orígenes y evolución de GAIA, el cluster de las TICs en el País Vasco. In J. Catalan, J. A. Miranda & R. Ramon (Eds.), *Distritos y clusters en la Europa del Sur* (pp. 317–336). Madrid: LID Editorial.

Lorca-Susino, M. (2011). Spain and the brain drain in the 21st CENTURY: It is not only what you can do for your country, but also what your country can do for you. In J. Roy & M. Lorca-Susino (Eds.), *Spain in the European Union: The first twenty-five years (1986–2011)* (pp. 211–228). Miami: The Miami-Florida European Union Center of Excellence. Retrieved from aei.pitt.edu/32455/1/SPAIN-EU-25-allPDF.pdf.

Lucas, R. E. Jr. (1988). On the mechanics of economic development. *Journal of Monetary Economics*, *22*, 3–42.

Makram, H., Sparrow, P. R., & Greasley, K. (2017). How do strategic actors think about the value of talent management? Moving from talent practice to the practice of talent. *Journal of Organizational Effectiveness: People and Performance*, 4(4), 259–378.

Martín, C. (2004). El empleo en España: su evolución de 1996 a 2003 y los efectos de las reformas laborales. *Cuadernos de Información Sindical*, *52*.

Martín, F., & Toral, P. (Eds.). (2005). *Latin America's quest for globalization: The role of Spanish firms*. Hampshire: Ashgate Publishing Limited.

Martin, H. (2015, Summer). Top 10 investment locations. *New European Economy*, pp. 90–94.

Martin, P. (2013). The global challenge of managing migration, *Population Bulletin*, *68*(2). Retrieved from www.prb.org/pdf13/global-migration.pdf.

Martínez-Galarraga, J., Rosés, J. R., & Tirado, D. A. (2015). The long-term patterns of regional income inequality in Spain, 1860–2000. *Regional Studies*, 49(4), 502–517.

Michavila, F., Martínez, J. M., & Merhi, R. (2015). *Comparación Internacional del sistema universitario español*. Monografias CRUE Universidades Españolas. Retrieved from www.crue.org/Documentos%20compartidos/Publicaciones/Monograf%C3%ADas/Monografia_Web_Comparacion.pdf.

Ministerio de Educación, Cultura y Deporte. (2017a). *Panorama de la educación 2017: Indicadores de la OCDE*. Retrieved from www.mecd.gob.es/dctm/inee/eag/2017/panorama-de-la-educacion-2017-def-12-09-2017red.pdf?documentId=0901e72b8263e12d.

Ministerio de Educación, Cultura y Deporte. (2017b). *Educación. Datos y cifras. Curso 2016/2017*. Madrid: Ministerio de Educación, Cultura y Deporte. Retrieved from www.mecd.gob.es/servicios-al-ciudadano-mecd/dms/mecd/servicios-al-ciudadano-mecd/estadisticas/educacion/indicadores-publicaciones-sintesis/datos-cifras/Datosycifras1718esp.pdf.

Molina, O., & Rhodes, M. (2007). The political economy of adjustment in mixed market economies: A study of Spain and Italy. In B. Hancké, M. Rhodes & M. Thatcher (Eds.), *Beyond varieties of capitalism: Conflict, contradictions, and complementarities in the European economy* (pp. 223–252). Oxford: Oxford University Press.

Muñoz, J., Roldán, S., & Serrano, A. (1978). *La internacionalización del capital en España, 1959–1977*. Madrid: Edicusa.

Nicolás, J. D. (Director). (2003). *Informe Proyecto Marca España*. Edited by Asociación de Directivos de Comunicación (DIRCOM), Foro de Marcas Renombradas Españolas, Instituto Español de Comercio Exterior (ICEX) and Real Instituto Elcano de Estudios Internacionales y Estratégicos. Retrieved from www.marcasrenombradas.com/wp-content/uploads/2017/02/Informe_Proyecto_Marca_Espana.pdf.

Novo Guerrero, A. (2014). *Clusters, engines of business innovation in Spain*. Spanish Federation of Innovative Business Groups and Clusters. Retrieved from www.fenaeic.org/wp-content/uploads/2014/05/Clusters-in-Spain-PDF.pdf.

Observatorio de la Empresa Multinacional Española. (2015). *Estrategias de globalización de las multinacionales españolas.* Retrieved from itemsweb.esade.es/research/oeme/informes/cuarto-informe/OEME_4%20 informe_Capitulo%202.pdf.

OECD. (2013, December). *The 2012 labour market reform in Spain: Preliminary assessment.* Retrieved from www.oecd.org/employment/spain-labourmarketreform.htm.

OECD. (2014). Resultados de PISA 2012 en Foco: Lo que los alumnos saben a los 15 años de edad y lo que pueden hacer con lo que saben. Retrieved from www.oecd.org/pisa/keyfindings/PISA2012_Overview_ESP-FINAL.pdf.

OECD. (2016a). PISA 2015 Resultados Clave. Retrieved from www.oecd.org/pisa/pisa-2015-results-in-focus-ESP.pdf.

OECD. (2016b). Skills matter: Further results from the survey of adult skills. Paris: OECD Publishing. Retrieved from www.keepeek.com/Digital-Asset-Management/oecd/education/skills-matter_9789264258051-en#.WjgMSt_iaUk.

OECD. (2017a). *OECD employment outlook 2017.* Paris: OECD Publishing. Retrieved from www.keepeek.com/Digital-Asset-Management/oecd/employment/oecd-employment-outlook-2017_empl_outlook-2017-en#.Wjb2l1SdVxg#page4.

OECD. (2017b). *OECD economic surveys: Spain.* Paris: OECD Publishing. Retrieved from www.oecd.org/eco/surveys/Spain-2017-OECD-economic-survey-overview.pdf.

OECD. (2017c) *Education at a glance 2017: OECD indicators.* Paris: OECD Publishing. Retrieved from www.keepeek.com/Digital-Asset-Management/oecd/education/education-at-a-glance-2017_eag-2017-en#.Wjb42VSdVxg.

OECD. (2017d). *Spain—Economic forecast summary.* Paris: OECD Publishing. Retrieved from www.oecd.org/eco/outlook/spain-economic-forecast-summary.htm.

OECD. (2017e). *How's life? 2017. Measuring well-being.* Paris: OECD Publishing. Retrieved from www.keepeek.com/Digital-Asset-Management/oecd/economics/how-s-life-2017_how_life-2017-en#page47.

Paauwe, J. (2004). *HRM and performance: Achieving long term viability.* Oxford: Oxford University Press.

Paauwe, J., & Boselie, P. (2003). Challenging strategic HRM and the relevance of the institutional setting. *Human Resource Management Journal, 13*(3), 56–70.

Parella, S., & Petroff, A. (2014). *Migración de retorno en España: Salidas de Inmigrantes y programas de retorno en un contexto de crisis.* Retrieved from www.cidob.org/en/articulos/anuario_de_la_inmigracion_en_espana/2014/migracion_de_retorno_en_espana_salidas_de_inmigrantes_y_programas_de_retorno_en_un_contexto_de_crisis.

Parkins, N. C. (2010). Push and pull factors of migration. *American Review of Political Economy, 8*(2), 6–24.

Pérez Infante, J. I. (2016, Febrero) *Mercado de trabajo y devaluación salarial.* Retrieved from www.aeet.eu/index.php/es/tribuna-abierta/266-mercado-de-trabajo-y-devaluacion-salarial.

Porter, M. (1990). *The competitive advantage of nations.* Cambridge, MA: Harvard University Press.

Powell, C. (2011). The long road to Europe: Spain and the European community, 1957–1986. In J. Roy & M. Lorca-Susino (Eds.), *Spain in the European Union: The first twenty-five years (1986–2011)* (pp. 21–44). Miami: The Miami-Florida European Union Center of Excellence. Retrieved from aei.pitt.edu/32455/1/SPAIN-EU-25-allPDF.pdf.

Powell, C. (2016). Revisiting Spain's transition to democracy. In S. Florensa (Ed.), *The Arab transitions in a changing world. Building democracies in light of international experiences.* Retrieved from charlespowell.eu/revisiting-spains-transition-to-democracy/.

Prados de la Escosura, L. (2017). *Spanish economic growth, 1850–2015.* London: Palgrave.

Puig, N., & Álvaro-Moya, A. (2016). The long-term impact of foreign MNEs in Spain: New insights into an old topic. *Journal of Evolutionary Studies in Business, 2*, 14–39.

Real Instituto El Cano. (2017, Febrero–Marzo). *Barómetro de la Imagen de España (BIE).* Retrieved from www.realinstitutoelcano.org/wps/wcm/connect/7cb3a69f-1f93-4dd3-b0dd-0b7c0d7d6672/7BIE_Informe_mayo2017.pdf?MOD=AJPERES&CACHEID=7cb3a69f-1f93-4dd3-b0dd-0b7c0d7d6672.

Rojo, L. A. (2002). La economía española en la democracia. In F. Comín, M. Hernández, & E. Llopis (Eds.), *Historia económica de España. Siglos X–XX* (pp. 397–436). Barcelona: Crítica.

Royo, S. (2007). Varieties of capitalism in Spain: Business and the politics of coordination, *European Journal of Industrial Relations, 13*(1), 47–65.

Royo, S. (2009). *The politics of adjustment and coordination at the regional level: The Basque country.* Center for European Studies, Working Paper Series, 171. Retrieved from ces.fas.harvard.edu/publications/000016-the-politics-of-adjustment-and-coordination-at-the-regional-level-the-basque-country.

Sáiz, P. (2005). Investigación y desarrollo: patentes. In A. Carreras & X. Tafunell (Coords.), *Estadísticas Históricas de España, Siglos XIX–XX* (Vol. II, pp. 835–872). Bilbao: Fundación BBVA.

Sánchez-Alonso, B. (2011). La política migratoria en España Un análisis de largo plazo. *Revista Internacional de Sociología, 69*(M1). doi:10.3989/ris.2011.iM1.393.

Serrano, J. M., & Pardos, E. (2002). Los años de crecimiento del franquismo (1959–1975). In F. Comín, M. Hernández, & E. Llopis (Eds.), *Historia económica de España. Siglos X–XX* (pp. 369–396). Barcelona: Crítica.

Sidani, Y., & Al Ariss, A. (2014). Institutional and corporate drivers of global talent management: Evidence from the Arab Gulf region. *Journal of World Business, 49*(2), 215–224.

Sparrow, P. R., & Makram, H. (2015). What is the value of talent management? Building value-driven processes within a talent management architecture. *Human Resource Management Review, 25*(3), 249–263.

Srivastava, P., & Bhatnagar, J. (2010). Employer brand for talent acquisition: An exploration towards its measurement. *Vision: The Journal of Business Perspective, 14*(1–2), 25–34.

Thunnissen, M., & Gallardo-Gallardo, E. (2017). *Talent management in practice: An integrated and dynamic approach*. Bingley, UK: Emerald Publishing Limited.

Toharia, L. (1997). *Labour market studies: Spain*. Employment & Labour Market Series N°1. Luxembourg: Office for Official Publications of the European Communities.

Toral, P. (2001). *The reconquest of the new world: Multinational enterprises and Spain's direct investment in Latin America*. Hampshire: Ashgate Publishing Limited.

Tortella, G. (2000). *The development of Modern Spain: An economic history of the nineteenth and twentieth centuries*. Cambridge, MA: Harvard University Press.

Ullán de la Rosa, F. J. (2016). Immigration and immigration policies in Spain. In D. Leal & N. Rodríguez (Eds.), *Migration in an era of restriction and recession: Immigrants and minorities, politics and policy* (pp. 175–210). Cham: Springer.

UNCTAD. (2017). *World investment report 2017*. Washington, DC: UNCTAD. Retrieved from unctad.org/en/PublicationsLibrary/wir2017_en.pdf.

UNESCO. (2011). *International Standard Classification of Education (ISCED) 2011*. UNESCO Institute for Statistics. Retrieved from uis.unesco.org/sites/default/files/documents/international-standard-classification-of-education-isced-2011-en.pdf.

Valdaliso, J., Elola, A., Aranguren, M., & López, S. (2011). Social capital, internationalization and absorptive capacity: The electronics and ICT cluster of the Basque Country. *Entrepreneurship & Regional Development: An International Journal, 23*(9–10), 707–733World Bank. (2016). *Doing business*. Retrieved from www.doingbusiness.org/rankings.

World Bank. (2017). *Gross domestic product 2016*. Retrieved from databank.worldbank.org/data/download/GDP.pdf.

World Economic Forum. (2017a). *The global competitiveness index 2017–2018*. Retrieved from reports.weforum.org/global-competitiveness-index-2017-2018/.

World Economic Forum. (2017b). *The global human capital report 2017*. Retrieved from weforum.ent.box.com/s/dari4dktg4jt2g9xo2o5pksjpatvawdb.

Zahra, S. A., & George, G. (2002). International entrepreneurship: The current status of the field and future research agenda. In M. A. Hitt, R. D. Ireland, S. M. Camp, & D. L. Sexton (Eds.), *Strategic entrepreneurship, creating a new mindset* (pp. 255–288). Oxford: Blackwell Publisher.

Website Links Referred to in This Chapter

Academic Ranking of World Universities (ARWU, 2017). Retrieved from www.shanghairanking.com/ARWU2017.html.

CIA World Factbook. Retrieved from www.cia.gov/library/publications/the-world-factbook/geos/sp.html.

Comunidad de Madrid. (2017). *Ayudas para la atracción del talento investigador*. Retrieved from www.madrid.org/cs/Satellite?c=CM_ConvocaPrestac_FA&cid=1354591154440&definicion=BaseReguladora&language=es&pagename=ComunidadMadrid%2FEstructura&pid=1109265444835&segmento=1&tipoServicio=CM_ConvocaPrestac_FA.

European Family Businesses. Retrieved from www.europeanfamilybusinesses.eu/family-businesses/facts-figures.

Eurostat, the Statistical Office of the European Union. Retrieved from ec.europa.eu/eurostat.

Family Firm Institute data. Retrieved from www.ffi.org/page/globaldatapoints.

Gobierno de España. *Spain and the Spanish Administration*. Retrieved from en.administracion.gob.es/pag_Home/espanaAdmon/comoSeOrganizaEstado/ComunidadesAutonomas.html.

Instituto Nacional de Estadística (INE). Retrieved from www.ine.es/.
Junta de Andalucía. *Programa retorno del talento*. Retrieved from www.extenda.es/retorna/intranet/index.htm.
Observatorio Imagen de España *7ª Oleada Barómetro Imagen de España*, febrero-marzo 2017. Retrieved from www.realinstitutoelcano.org/wps/portal/rielcano_es/encuesta?WCM_GLOBAL_CONTEXT=/elcano/elcano_es/observatoriomarcaespana/estudios/resultados/barometro-imagen-espana-7.
OECD Data. Retrieved from data.oecd.org/.
Times Higher Education World University Ranking 2018. Retrieved from www.timeshighereducation.com/world-university-rankings/2018/world-ranking#!/page/0/length/25/sort_by/rank/sort_order/asc/cols/stats.
The World Bank. *Data*. Retrieved from data.worldbank.org.
World University Rankings, 2018. Retrieved from www.timeshighereducation.com/world-university-rankings.
Xunta de Galicia. (2017). Retrieved from emigracion.xunta.gal/es/actividad/retorno.

6
Macro Talent Management in Denmark
The Origins of Danish Talent Paradox

Dana Minbaeva, Torben Andersen, Nikolaj Lubanski,
Steen Erik Navrbjerg and Ronja Marie Torfing

Introduction

Did you know that Denmark was the best European country for doing business in 2016?[1] Denmark beat 127 other countries in terms of making exceptional social and environmental progress across all dimensions of the 2017 Social Progress Index.[2] The country ranks second in English proficiency among the world's non-English speaking countries[3] and offers one of the most innovation-friendly environments in the EU.[4] According to the 2017 Global Talent Competitiveness Index (GTCI),[5] Denmark excels in its ability to enable and grow talent internally. It scored highest in the areas of formal education, growth opportunities, the labor market, and the business landscape. More importantly, the GTCI highlighted the Danish approach to the workplace, with first-place rankings in labor-market flexibility, the delegation of authority, and the freedom of expression, as vital for growth. Denmark's high ranking confirms that the country has a solid platform for growing talent internally.

Interestingly, the fact that Denmark enables and grows internal talent does not translate into a strong ability to attract and retain foreign talent (DI, 2016). According to Kristian Jensen, the Danish Minister of Finance, "the country faces a number of challenges in persuading highly skilled professionals to bring their much-needed expertise to an economy now facing labor shortages".[6] This is problematic because, without foreign talent and given the projected economic growth,[7] Denmark will experience talent shortage. A report published by the Confederation of Danish Industry in September 2015 predicted that Danish companies will lack 44,000 skilled workers by 2025 (DI, 2016). Figure 6.1 illustrates the gap between the extent to which attraction and retention of talent is a priority for Denmark and the extent to which highly-skilled foreign workers are attracted to the country (compared to other countries in the same income group).

In this chapter we argue that certain macroeconomic factors allow Denmark to grow its home talent base. Moreover, the Danish business environment is clearly attractive for foreign talent in numerous respects.[8] However, at the same other characteristics of the Danish

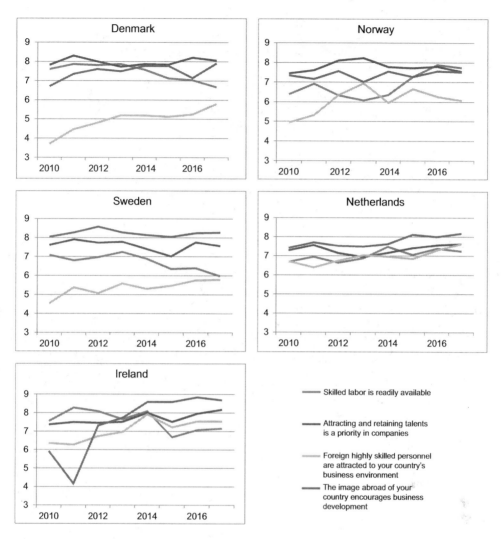

Figure 6.1 Skills, Talent Attraction and Image of the Selected Countries

(Based on the Survey Done by IMD, Scale 1–10)

macro environment make it difficult for companies to attract and retain talent. This gives rise to what we label the *Danish talent paradox*:[9] to maintain continuous growth and attract more FDI to Denmark, the country needs to attract, develop, and retain talent. However, the fact that Danish companies and society in general consider internal talent growth a top priority does not translate into a strong ability to attract and retain talent (DI, 2016), especially the global talent.

The rest of the chapter is structured in the following way. First, we provide a brief introduction to Denmark. Then we present and discuss three macro-level forces that are shaping the Danish talent paradox. Finally, we present implications for research and practice of talent management, both in Denmark and more generally.

Denmark

Denmark is a small country in Scandinavia (43,560 square kilometers) with a population of 5.7 million and GDP per capita of DKK 344,000 (approximately USD 55,000). Denmark is often recognized as a country characterized by equality, social balance, a low level of corruption, and a high level of transparency. The Danish economy relies heavily on a high-tech agricultural sector; the pharmaceutical industry, the maritime shipping sector, and the renewable energy industry. It is highly dependent on foreign trade. Denmark is a net exporter of food, oil, and gas, and it enjoys a comfortable balance of payments surplus. However, it depends on imports of raw materials for the manufacturing sector.[10]

The total work force in Denmark is approximately 2.8 million. Knowledge-intensive, service-oriented and high-tech production companies form the core of the Danish economy, while Denmark's competitive strength is its ability to attract and develop human capital. This is particularly important because more than 97% of Danish organizations have less than 100 employees and more than 80% have less than 50 employees.

From a cultural perspective, Denmark scores high on egalitarianism and low on power distance. At workplace, great emphasis is placed on equality and consensus. "In the typical Danish workplace, everyone is encouraged to contribute with ideas and professional opinions regardless of title or status.[11]" Danish workplaces are characterized by flat hierarchies, teamwork, participative leadership and open communication (considered a low context culture by Hall (1976), where blending in should be relatively straightforward).

Denmark is a coordinated market economy (CME) (Hall & Soskice, 2001; Gooderham & Nordhaug, 2011). Collective institutions prevail, and formal representation and work are carried out by committees and secretariats in support of political initiatives. Small in size and early in globalization, Denmark has long had a small open economy in which cooperation has been the human capital theme at home and abroad. This is true on every level, from the Danish state-run primary schools to the Sino-Danish Center for Education and Research in Beijing (SDC), which is run by all Danish universities in concert. Finally, similarly to Finland (see chapter seven), Denmark has a long tradition of making high demands on its own education system.

Despite the relatively high wages and high taxes, MNCs are attracted to Denmark (Minbaeva & Navrbjerg, 2016). According to the American Chamber of Commerce in Denmark, the country's main attraction is the availability and quality of human capital. The majority of these companies are headquartered elsewhere in Europe, especially in other Scandinavian countries. As such, MNCs operating in Denmark tend to come from countries that are similar.[12] Nordic companies account for 47% of the foreign MNCs operating in Denmark. However, around 20% of foreign MNCs originate from outside Europe. Of these, US-based companies dominate (16%). Only 6% of the MNCs are based outside Europe and the US. In other words, a large proportion of MNCs operating in Denmark come from countries with similar business models.

Nevertheless, Denmark is not a top expat destination. In the Expat Insider survey,[13] Denmark's rating fell by eleven spots, making it one of the survey's "biggest losers." Much of the decline was driven by the challenges foreigners face when attempting to "fit in." In general, foreigners find it difficult to settle into the Nordic countries. Denmark, for example, is ranked fiftieth in this regard (Sweden: 42, Norway: 43). Furthermore, Expat Insider claims that the ruling government, led by the Venstre party along with the anti-immigration Danish People's Party, is "locking every door possible to keep foreigners out."[14] This way Denmark is characterized by very opposing standpoints at the political level, with conflicting interests on who should occupy the future (knowledge) jobs in the country, and this is an important element in the framing of the Danish talent paradox.

Due to the fact, that there is not (yet) a well-established and -integrated talent management system in Denmark, work is carried out by a variety of actors at many different levels and in many contexts in Danish society. There is not one shared definition of the concept, and therefore no rigorous, commonly accepted framework. Many initiatives are labelled talent work and/or talent management. For the purpose of this chapter we define talent management as a nested phenomenon centered on the systematic use of practices to attract, develop and retain individuals who possess, or are in the process of acquiring, high levels of human capital required for the strategic priorities of the business (see other chapters in this book). The nested nature of talent management comes from macro-level factors such as demographics, the economic, educational, social and political conditions as well as "the activities that are systematically developed by governmental and nongovernmental organizations expressly for the purpose of enhancing the quality and quantity of talent within and across countries and regions to facilitate innovation and competitiveness of their citizens and corporations" (Khilji, Tarique, & Schuler, 2015, p. 237).

In the context of Denmark, we argue that three macro-level forces are most influential in shaping the macro talent management in Denmark, contributing to the Danish talent paradox and consequently determining talent management at the company level. These forces are (1) the labor market, (2) education, and (3) policy interventions (see Figure 6.2). In the following, we describe each of them in detail.

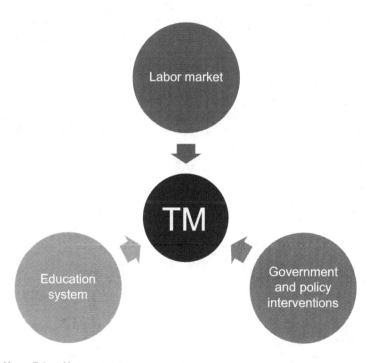

Figure 6.2 Macro Talent Management

1. The Danish Labour Market: Building a Context for Talent Management

The Danish labor market is characterized by a high level of regulation through collective agreement. The most important labor-market issues are regulated through collective agreements signed by the social partners—trade unions and employers' organizations. As such, the Danish industrial-relations system is dominated by a high degree of voluntarism (Galenson, 1952; Due, Madsen, Jensen, & Petersen, 1994; Andersen, Dølvik, & Ibsen, 2014): trade unions and employers negotiate solutions to various challenges through collective agreements lasting two to four years.

The Danish labor market model was established in 1899 in the so-called September Compromise. After 19 weeks of industrial conflict, the peak organizations on the employers side (back then the Employers' Confederation of 1896, today DA—The Confederation of Danish Employers) and on the employee side (back then DsF, The Co-Operating National Trade Unions in Denmark, today LO—The Danish Confederation of Unions) made an agreement that (a) secured managements prerogative, (b) workers' right to form organizations, (c) the peace obligation, i.e. the obligation on the part of the unions to secure peace in the labor market as long as the collective agreements are running, and (d) the right to strike or lock-out while collective agreements are negotiated.

The September Compromise laid the fundament for a centralized bargaining system that became gradually established in the following decades. In 1908, the August Committee was established by the government with the purpose to establish an arbitration system to resolve industrial disputes. The result was the Permanent Arbitration Court, which has ever since been a cornerstone in the Danish labor market model and is an important sign of the institutionalization of disputes. The fact that the government established the August Committee is furthermore a proof that the voluntaristic system, where the social partners themselves close agreements on labor market issues, was accepted by the political system already at this early stage (Due et al., 1994).

One prerequisite for such a high level of regulation by social partners is legitimacy in the political system. In other words, the government acknowledges that the social partners are responsible supporters of the Danish welfare system. In return, employers expect access to a steady flow of talented young people, who have graduated from state-run education institutions. Furthermore, over the years the *flexicurity* model has developed as a cooperation between the state and the social partners. Flexicurity entails a high level of *flexibility* regarding hiring and firing, i.e. relatively limited notice (and more recently also a high level of flexibility regarding working time), combined with a high level of *security*, when individuals are laid off—in the form of relatively high unemployment benefits and a rather advanced system for further education in case the job function has been made obsolete due to new technology and/or international completion.

Another prerequisite for having collective agreements as a decisive regulator of the Danish labor market is that the collective agreements must cover the majority of employees on the labor market. In other words, high collective-agreement coverage, high union density, and a high level of membership in employers' organizations are necessary. This prerequisite appears to be met. Overall, 75% of the Danish labor market was covered by collective agreements in 2010 (80% in 2007 and 84% in 1997; Larsen, Navrbjerg, & Johansen, 2010; Due, Madsen, & Pihl, 2010), although the coverage rates vary considerably from 100% in the public sector to 71% in the private sector (Larsen et al., 2010). However, most of the rules defined in the collective agreements apply to the non-covered parts of the labor market. Thus far, the collective agreements have not included talent elements, but the employment contracts signed by young people participating in talent programs and their employers cannot depart from the relevant collective agreement.

Sectoral agreements prescribe national standards, and establish procedural and economic guidelines for local negotiations on pay and working conditions. The social partners are also involved in the policy-making process when the government considers new legislation. While decisions on wages and working conditions are basically left to social partners, legislation covers such areas as vacation time, and health and safety. Therefore, the regulation of the labor market is not left entirely to social partners. Instead, the state, unions, and employers' associations collaborate and coordinate their activities to ensure that government-led initiatives do not clash with the agreements signed by social partners. As such, relations among the parties are based on the premise of mutual respect for their diverging interests and on a drive for consensus when attempting to resolve conflicts (Madsen & Due, 2008, p. 517).

Since circa 1990, collective agreements have increasingly involved issues that were traditionally mainly considered within the sphere of the political system. These issues include, among others, pension, holiday, parental leave, and vocational training thereby contributing to the Danish welfare system. The continuous development of welfare services has benefited a very broad variety of Danish population, paving the way for individual development and mobility.

Over the years, education has been an area of interest for the social partners and the government alike. While basic education (i.e., primary schooling, high school, and university) has been only of interest to the social partners from a lobbying perspective, they have been more directly involved in technical-education and continued-education programs. The social partners are represented on the boards of universities and vocational-education institutions. As such, they are involved in the longer-term, more strategic development of the programs, including talent initiatives. This makes the institutions relatively strong, provides them with legitimacy, and helps them respond to market changes.

Continued education and training are high on the social partners' agendas. Employers are interested in increasing the pool of highly-skilled employees, who understand and can utilize new technologies. For unions and employers, the aim is to move people up the education ladder, and to ensure that as many people as possible are employable, especially when technological changes mean that the need for traditional skills declines (Navrbjerg & Minbaeva, 2009). A world-leading company today might become redundant tomorrow due to new technologies and fierce international competition. However, the Danish structure of small and medium size enterprises entails relatively high flexibility. Although about 60,000 Danish companies close every year, almost as many are established. Therefore, one company's end might be another company's beginning, but the movement up the value chain can only continue *if* talent is constantly managed and nurtured through regular training.

Continued training has been a priority in collective bargaining over the years. By setting funds aside and including incentives in the collective agreements, the social partners also send a signal to the government that they are reliable partners not only in relation to this important labor issue but also with regard to other key issues.

In the industrial sector, the collective agreement has traditionally been one of the most important signals of the responsibilities for further training held by the social partners. The industrial-sector agreement is characterized by a high level of decentralization. In other words, the sector agreement outlines the frame within which local actors can establish local agreements. Over the years, collective agreements have encompassed numerous initiatives aimed at motivating local social partners to focus on continued education.

Since 2013, the debate among social partners has focused on estimates indicating that Denmark will lack 100,000 skilled workers by 2020. Of these, an estimated 30,000 will be skilled workers who have completed some type of advanced education. If these skills cannot be found in Denmark, the jobs will be outsourced. Furthermore, if no steps are taken to address this issue, then an estimated 140,000 unskilled workers without any continued training will find themselves without a job. The actors all agree on the numbers and the challenges, which serve as a good starting point for dealing with the issue. The question is how these challenges can best be resolved and who should pay for their resolution.

In the 2014 growth plan, the Confederation of Danish Employers (DA), the Danish Confederation of Trade Unions (LO), and the government agreed to allocate DKK 1 billion to strengthen continued training. The fact that the responsibility is shared on the macro level is perhaps best illustrated by the statement released by the trade union, the Central Organization of Industrial Employees in Denmark (CO-industry), which argued for a shift in the way education is perceived among skilled and unskilled workers. The union made it clear that no one can expect their education to remain relevant forever. Therefore, each worker must view education as an ongoing part of the work required to stay employable. In fact, the statement indicates that, at some point in the future, a job and the education it entails might only be relevant for a decade. This implies that employees will have to continually prepare themselves to take on new kinds of jobs.

This rhetoric, which was partly based on the discussion that began in 2013, was intended to fertilize the ground for including a new view on education in the 2017 collective agreement for the industrial sector—a view that embraces the prediction of the Industry 4.0 scenario. When the draft of the collective agreement was presented on February 12, 2017, CO-industry emphasized that it included a "historical enhancement of education within the industrial sector".[15] The aim was to deal with the challenges posed by new technologies (Industry 4.0), particularly in terms of ensuring that Danish employees could work with new technologies rather than being made obsolete by them.

Prior to the 2007 collective agreement, continued training had been challenged by an inherent conflict—if an employer decided to pay for an employee's continued training, the employer made that employee more employable, which gave rise to the risk of employee mobility (e.g., the employee could accept a position in another company). The 2007 collective agreement encompassed two tracks: (a) company-related education and (b) individually chosen education. The latter was financed using education funds paid by employers as part of the overall concession scheme in the collective agreement. However, the funds were difficult to use owing to a highly bureaucratic process, which meant that typically only larger companies took advantage of the funding. Furthermore, there was little coherence between the two tracks, as employers and employees seemed to have different interests in continued training. These problems reflected the fact that numerous initiatives had been introduced over the years to ensure that continued training would be relevant and systematic.

To address these problems, the 2017 collective agreement introduced the concept of "negotiated training." Under the new agreement, it is easier to obtain funding for continued training if upper management and the shop steward apply in concert, and if the employee has developed a plan for that training. The agreement creates an incentive for management, shop stewards, and employees to enhance the education of both unskilled and skilled workers and, thereby, educate workers out of the Industry 4.0 threat.

Undoubtedly, talent management in the form of vocational training is on the minds of social partners and politicians alike. This is particularly true given the challenges posed by globalization and, more recently, Industry 4.0. However, establishment of a coherent framework for systematic continued training to ensure that skilled and unskilled workers are ready to take on new challenges still seems problematic. In Denmark, the highly voluntaristic system also means an ongoing fine-tuning of efforts and aims among the social partners. Tripartite negotiations—between The Danish Confederation of Unions (LO), The Confederation of Danish Employers (DA) and the Government—is an important tool in this tuning, and there is no doubt that further vocational training is high on the agenda in these negotiations. It still remains to be seen if it will be possible to reach some kind of overarching, long-term agreement that can solve the talent-related challenge. Talent management has the magnitude and potential to be a groundbreaking issue, but it requires that talent management can be covered by the collective bargaining system and the agreements coming out of that system.

2. The Education System: Providing Internal Supply

Talent management regained momentum after the Danish economy returned to growth (fueled with the Industry 4.0 race). The demand for talented labor is increasing again. At the same time, the strategic focus in the education system has shifted from growth per se towards the development of education programs directed at sectors in which demand for employees is likely to be profound (often emphasizing STEM—Science, Technology, Engineering and Math—skills). This strategic shift reflects the fact that bottlenecks are already evident in some parts of the labor market. On all education levels, the major changes relate to an increasing focus on talent initiatives. In fact, talent management seems to be cascading through the education system.

In primary schools, the focus is on the identification and development of talent, and this focus is introduced at a very early stage. In this regard, research shows that talent is not stable and resilient (Meyers & van Woerkom, 2014)—it can increase or decrease over time. Therefore, it requires nurturing at the early stages (see Nissen, Kyed, & Baltzer, 2011). Moreover, educators on this level recognize that the relationships in which children are involved are important for maintaining their talent. As such, primary schools have become an important arena for the initial development of talent. Research also shows that many "gifted" children generally need more, and different, attention and challenges than their peers. At the same time, many of these gifted individuals represent untapped potential that could help Denmark ensure that its human resources are among the world's best. Questions about how schools should support gifted children and the best ways for teachers to accommodate talented children in the classroom have emerged. Such considerations were basically non-existent just a decade ago. Notably, despite the hostile atmosphere between the employers' association and the teachers' trade union due to the reform of the primary-school system, talent-oriented initiatives have been introduced in many schools. In line with the emergence of a broader, more complex talent-development system, master classes, innovation camps, and other network activities have been set up across schools, where they are carried out by relatively new institutions. Many of these institutions are project-based organizations financed by large private funds or single projects financed by the Ministry of Education.

In the vocational education and training (VET) area, talent tracks were introduced in 2013 as a consequence of the VET-reform initiated by the Danish government. As of 2017, 12 of the largest schools in Denmark are participating in an EU-funded talent-development program. Participants are presented with more difficult assignments with the goal of stimulating their creativity and to encourage innovative solutions (on a practical level). This leads to significantly higher levels of self-confidence among the students (see Holsbo & Secher, 2015). Moreover, participants are not isolated in their own classes—they all take part in "normal" classes on a daily basis, as an important part of the project is to develop general and personal competences. In other words, the program does not aim to attract the "elite" from the collective and isolate them in their own classes, but to attract students who have the potential to grow by participating in the program, even if they are not generally considered to be the best in their classes. In addition, as much of the program is based on group work and master classes, social skills are an important prerequisite. This way talent work seems to follow a very long tradition for egalitarianism and generalism as stressed in the Grundtvigian tradition in the nineteenth century, where Danish identity construction heavily relied on further education of the masses (see Cambell, Hall, & Pedersen, 2006). Generalism at a high quality level has for a very long time characterized skilled labor, and it has been reinforced in the further development of the VET system and by the collective bargaining system, carried by the social partners (see previous section on labor market).

In 2007 a special track, known as The Academy of Talented Youth, was introduced across the Danish high-school ("gymnasium") system. Participants in this track take part in lectures and meetings that are held in the late afternoons and evenings. The program enrolls around 2,000 students every year in three geographical regions in Denmark, and graduates of the program receive a special diploma in addition to their high-school diploma. The goal is to attract highly motivated, talented youth in order to maintain their interest as they move into their work lives. The program aims to strengthen the links among gymnasiums, corporate life, and higher education. Participants meet researchers and scientists from a variety of organizations and companies at an early stage, and the emphasis is on network building. The approach is broad, as it covers the social sciences, the humanities, technical sciences, and natural science. The program was initiated and is financed by the high schools themselves, and it works through local talent coordinators all over the country.

Finally, a number of talent initiatives have been introduced at Danish universities. In this regard, the talent focus has entered new sectors. For example, in 2015, the first talent awards were presented to recipients of kindergarten teaching degrees and primary-school teaching degrees. Other talent initiatives have been developed for Ph.D. programs run by various faculties, including prizes for outstanding (young) researchers. More recently, Danish universities have introduced special honors programs. Other major initiatives to develop a more talent-oriented mindset among students have also been initiated (e.g., specialized master classes conducted in close cooperation with leading companies) on the department and faculty levels. In addition, since 1954 (with the establishment of the Nordic Passport Union), students from other Nordic countries have been able to travel freely and to live and study in Denmark without applying for residence or work permit (see also Textbox 6.1). This has huge implications in particular in the health sector in terms of a net talent inflow in Denmark. Finally, the Danish universities have been working to build up their career-counselling and support functions for graduates, including internships and shared talent programs with larger companies, where time is spent on universities as well as in companies over a certain time period.

On the collective level, the Consortium for Global Talent, which is situated in the Confederation of Danish Industry, promotes cooperation between companies and Danish universities, especially in terms of attracting (young) foreign talent (i.e., professionals and students). In this regard, the focus is on knowledge sharing, establishment of a stronger platform, and visibility for Denmark and Danish companies abroad. However, it can be difficult to establish cooperation between universities (and their collective institutions) and the individual MNCs (and their executives). One key challenge is the need to address both the public sector's long-term oriented administrative approach and the shorter-term focus common among private companies.

In general, the education system has gone through a series of significant developments with regard to talent initiatives. On many levels in the education hierarchy, there is an increasing focus on talent identification and development. The education institutions have supported the buildup of broader talent pools from which companies can choose candidates for their own talent programs. An increasing number of would-be future managers of both public as well as private organizations are expected to arrive in company pipelines in following years. In addition, talent have most likely become more aware of their market value, which could in the longer run create pressure on pay level and a retention problem for Danish companies (see Björkman, Ehrnrooth, Mäkelä, Smale, & Sumelius, 2013).

In many respects, the increasing focus on talent development appears to be giving rise to a more competitive environment in education institutions, where social acceptance of being different, gifted and having a higher potential is increasing. However, it also seems to represent a continuation of the dominant democratic logic, that there should be specialized programs for all groups in education institutions, including the most talented young people. So the educational system as such, even though it is still not so integrated when it comes to talent work, does provide a thorough outcome on identification and development of talent in Denmark.

3. Policy Interventions: Affecting global Supply

Changes in the political climate for attracting and retaining talent have been evident for several years in Denmark. As countries and cities are forced to compete for talent due to shifts in technology and innovation, and the increase in globalization, several initiatives both governmental and private were introduced that favored global talent management. For example, it seems that in the past the Danish government addressed this issue with more favorable immigration policies and talent strategies that were preparing the country for globalization or more favorable education policies (see previous section). However, a recent report from the Human Capital Analytics Group indicates that many Danish companies, especially in the engineering and IT sectors, are experiencing an acute skills gap[16] and are dependent on foreign talent. One might wonder whether Danish companies are failing to allocate the resources needed to establish HR architectures relevant for successful talent management. However, even if this is the case, it might not be the full story since several external factors could be contributing to this situation (DI, 2016).

Among the immediate stakeholders interested in talent management in Denmark are businesses, civil society, governments, and academia. Success in the battle for the world's talented professionals requires a joint effort across these stakeholder groups in the areas of education and immigration policies. For example, in 2006, Denmark introduced a strategy entitled "Progress, Innovation and Cohesion,"[17] which was designed to prepare Denmark for the challenges and opportunities arising from globalization. At that time, the government was under the leadership of the Liberal Party and the Conservative People's Party, which aimed to prepare the country for further globalization by introducing 350 initiatives, reforms, and policies focused on two main areas: human development (education) and immigration. More specifically, the initiatives centered on helping universities compete and reach a world-class level, and on attracting and maintaining highly qualified labor.

Discussions of talent shortages in Denmark continued. In 2014, the socio-democratic government addressed this challenge by launching reforms to ease the recruitment of highly skilled foreign labor (see Textbox 6.1 for the overview). This international recruitment reform had four main targets: to enable companies to easily recruit international workers; to retain international students who had completed their education at a Danish university; to welcome and retain international workers; and to establish equal conditions for international workers. In addition, new immigration laws and entrepreneurial initiatives were introduced, including a fast-track system and the start-up Denmark program. These reforms were intended to herald a promising future for companies operating in Denmark and for Danish companies' international competitiveness.

Textbox 6.1   Obtaining a Work Permit in Denmark

Nordic Citizens

Nordic citizens are free to live and work in Denmark. Consequently, they do not need a residence or work permit.

EU/EEA Citizens

EU/EEA citizens and Swiss citizens can live and work in Denmark under the EU regulations on freedom of movement. Consequently, they do not need a residence or work permit.

Non-EU/EEA/Swiss citizens: As a general rule, non-EU/EEA/Swiss citizens must have a residence and work permit in order to reside and work in Denmark. However, a number of schemes have been introduced in order to make it easier for highly qualified professionals to obtain a residence and work permit:

- *The Positive List* is a list of professions currently experiencing a shortage of qualified personnel. People who have been offered a job in one of these professions and who have completed the required education can easily gain access to the Danish labor market.
- *The Pay-limit Scheme* gives persons who have been offered a job with an annual pay above a certain limit easy access to the Danish labor market.
- *The Fast-track Scheme:* A residence permit under the fast-track scheme is contingent upon the company in Denmark (the employer) being certified by the Danish Agency for International Recruitment and Integration. The scheme enables certified companies to quickly hire certain types of highly qualified foreign professionals.
- *Researchers and Guest Researchers:* Researchers can easily gain access to the Danish labor market.
- *The Start-up Denmark Scheme* enables entrepreneurs to operate a company in Denmark.
- *The Establishment Card* enables foreign nationals who complete a Danish Master's degree or a Danish Ph.D. degree to obtain a residence permit in order to establish themselves in Denmark after graduating.
- *Trainees* can work for a Danish company for a period of time for education and training purposes.

Read more about the schemes: www.nyidanmark.dk/en-us/coming_to_dk/work/work.htm

Several public-private organizations were established for FDI promotion and deal with the potential talent shortage. One of them is Copenhagen Capacity, which is the official organization for promoting investments and economic development in Greater Copenhagen. In its efforts to help Danish companies attract and retain highly skilled international talent, Copenhagen Capacity makes use of various communication channels to assist businesses in Denmark in attracting foreign talent (see Textbox 6.2 for description). A good example is a Targeted Talent Attraction Campaign and the most recent one was the Fintech campaign. It ran 10 weeks from February to April 2017 and focused on attracting senior software developers to 36 jobs in 13 Fintech companies placed in Greater Copenhagen. The campaign resulted in more than 19 million views, but more interesting it inspired 175,481 international candidates (unique) to visit the Fintech Campaign. The campaign received more than 1,400 applications, and 31% of the candidates went on to interviews in the participating companies. In the campaign period of 8 weeks, 5 candidates were hired, and resulted in more than 400 new motivated and mobile IT profiles in our Talent Pool, but many more have been inspired to look to Greater Copenhagen for career opportunities, making these campaigns a long-term effort to brand Greater Copenhagen as an interesting career destination and creating a pipeline of relevant candidates in our IT Talent Pool for future jobs in Greater Copenhagen.

Until recently, Denmark seemed to be approaching the changing global environment in a strategic manner. However, with the emergence of the European refugee crisis, the Danish

---

Textbox 6.2   Copenhagen Capacity

Copenhagen Capacity was established in 1994 as an independent organization with the mission to support foreign companies, investors and talent in identifying and capitalizing on business opportunities in Greater Copenhagen. It offers a broad range of services around setting up a business in the region for all foreign-owned companies. One of these services is to attract foreign talent for businesses in Denmark e.g. via the projects "Talent Attraction Denmark" (ended in 2015) and "Vækst gennem udenlandske højtuddannede" ("Growth through high-educated foreigners") (ongoing). Through various initiatives within this project, Copenhagen Capacity aims to assist companies in attracting foreign talent, in strengthening their reputation as a workplace or to provide free marketing material to promote life as an expat in Denmark to foreign talent. For instance, participating in various conferences and campaigns organized by Copenhagen Capacity exposes a company and its open positions to a worldwide talent pool that is otherwise difficult to reach. Being the best-connected network and expert in the region has further allowed Copenhagen Capacity to develop several best-practice solutions for various industries and companies of all sizes. Another strength of Copenhagen Capacity lies in its expertise to promote Denmark as a preferred location for expats to work and live. Since attracting foreign talent is not only about the company as an employer but also about the new country as a home to the international employees, using the free marketing materials about Denmark's attractiveness is an important way to enhance the companies' recruitment strategies. Overall, Copenhagen Capacity not only assists companies in recruiting international talent, but also ultimately promotes the Danish economy by bringing the talent into the country.

Read more: www.copcap.com/how-we-help/finding-talent; www.talentattractiondenmark.dk/en/

government implemented several "harsh" changes in its immigration policy that had serious consequences for talent management. For example, the Green-Card scheme was scrapped and the minimum annual salary in the Pay-Limit Scheme[18] was increased. These moves had direct consequences for foreigners in terms of obtaining work and residence permits. These changes, together with the tightened immigration laws, mean that Denmark is likely to continue facing talent shortages (DI, 2016). Moreover, estimates indicate that the gap between education institutions and employer demands will continue to widen.

In summary, despite the fact that a number of schemes have been implemented in order to make it possible for highly qualified workers to come to Denmark, this still remains an area in need of improvement. The advantages of the flexicurity system (flexibility and security for all Danish citizens) have in this light not been developed further into the foreign talent attraction domain, ie. the smooth adaptive processes, which are an important element in the Danish model, are not present here.

Conclusion

In general, Denmark appears to be quite successful in growing internal talent. It excels in certain areas, such as formal education, market landscape, and growth opportunities, all of which are internal factors, i.e. the talent management system has been able to energize and renew itself for a long time. However, Denmark is not doing as well in attracting and retaining foreign talent. Although Denmark is a leader in terms of education and internal growth, some external, macro-level factors act as obstacles for talent attraction. Indeed, although Danish companies view talent attraction as a key part of their business, foreigners do not find Danish businesses highly attractive.[19] According to DI (2016), there are several reasons for this lack of attractiveness: high taxation and high costs of living, i.e. factors typical for Scandinavian countries. But according to the report, another crucial obstacle is a lack of openness to foreign cultures and people. In fact, compared to Sweden and Norway, Denmark ranks very low in terms of its attractiveness for global talent.[20] According to the head of the Danish Green Card Association, Naqeeb Khan, foreign talent may choose another destination because Denmark is "constantly making life more difficult for skilled foreigner workers."[21] As Khan explains, foreign professionals who have lived and worked in Denmark for more than four years have the possibility to invest in real estate and settle in Denmark. Although many of them would like to do so, they refrain from settling down because of the uncertainties and the constant changes in immigration rules.[22]

Several crucial aspects need to be considered when thinking about talent management in Denmark. Regardless of how much a Danish company invests in global talent management, the country has its own established laws, policies, and culture, where the latter encompasses a general lack of openness to foreigners. Therefore, in order to become a leader in all areas of talent competitiveness, Denmark must address these issues in the coming years, especially as digitalization and globalization are accelerating. As DI (2016, p. 17) states, "Denmark needs to improve its general appeal and external openness in order to accommodate the talent shortage and be attractive for foreign talents."

Implications for Research

The emerging contours of a Danish talent system and the presence of a Danish talent paradox described in this chapter highlight the importance of including country-level activities (governmental and non-governmental) in discussions of talent management. Historical-dependent system descriptions of developments offer good insight in the scope of and framework within which talent management is carried out. As Khilji et al. (2015) argue, in order to fully comprehend the complexities of attracting, developing, and retaining talent in today's globalized world, we need to go beyond "an individual and organizational analysis to incorporate a contextualized macro view" (p. 237). To be able to do so, future conceptualization of global talent management must be understood from a "nested systems" perspective (Reeves, Levin, & Ueda, 2016). Nested systems encompass inward (emergence) and outward (feedback and selection) influences. In this regard, we have begun to shed some light on the adaptive processes and micro-foundations of inward influence in talent management.

However, we still know very little about the outward influences. They are generative, in that they enable and maintain the emergent quality of the enclosed system, but they can also negatively affect that emergent quality. The latter occurs in in social systems in which emergent cultural and political systems continuously change (Walloth, 2016). Given the high degree of contextualization, the forces driving outward influences will vary by country. In other words, the elements of the "macro environment" in Khilji et al. (2015) will differ among the countries and go beyond the identified three areas (e.g. the other elements may be global mobility, integrated human development agenda, and the diaspora effect/brain circulation). For Denmark, we identified three factors (i.e., labor market, education system, and policy interventions) in the macro environment that shape talent management at the company level. Without implying any generalization, we would expect these factors to also be relevant for other CMEs with multi-party governmental structures (see other chapters in this book).

Additional research is needed to help us fully understand the inward and outward influences in talent management, as well as the interplay between those influences. This understanding is crucial, as "neither the enclosed systems nor the enclosing system stand alone" (Walloth, 2016: 25). These influences do not exist independently: "There is mutual influence between the enclosing system and the enclosed ones, i.e., between the whole and its parts" (Walloth, 2016: 25). Such research can directly respond to the call for greater contextualization in international management research, as it can incorporate both individual heterogeneity and the heterogeneity of the immediate contexts in which individuals are embedded (Minbaeva, 2016).

Implications for Talent Management in MNCs

The inclusion of a macro view in talent management will significantly affect the ways in which multinational corporations design and administer their talent-management programs. We have spent years trying to persuade managers to build talent strategies that encompass a "workforce differentiation" approach (Becker, Huselid, & Beatty, 2009: 3). In the talent management literature, this approach has been labelled "exclusive" (i.e., it focuses on the A players, high potentials, high performers, or strategically important employees) rather than "inclusive" (i.e., directed towards the whole workforce) (Iles, Preece, & Chuai, 2010; Lewis & Heckman, 2006; Stahl et al., 2012). However, the debates related to macro-level talent management point to another basis for differentiation—the characteristics of the context in which individual talent is embedded. For MNCs, the crucial issue in building their differentiated approach to talent management is ongoing evaluation of the macro environmental factors shaping talent management in the specific context. The specific factors will vary between the countries and regions. The true challenge for MNCs, therefore, is whether they could identify and how they can best use this source of differentiation in building their talent strategies to ensure a competitive advantage.

Overall, the macro aspects of global talent management—such as those three macro-level forces considered in this chapter—will continue to evolve and transform the way talent is being managed in companies. More direct theorizing about the macro level influences as opposed to post hoc contextualizing will advance future research on global talent management.

Notes

1. eucham.eu/charts/193-2016-07-best-european-countries-for-business-2016
2. www.socialprogressimperative.org
3. www.ef-danmark.dk/epi/
4. ec.europa.eu/growth/industry/innovation/facts-figures/scoreboards_da
5. www.insead.edu/news/2017-global-talent-competitiveness-index-davos
6. www.bloomberg.com/news/articles/2017-06-26/world-s-best-place-to-live-is-now-looking-for-brainy-foreigners
7. www.oecd.org/economy/denmark-economic-forecast-summary.htm
8. www.insead.edu/news/2017-global-talent-competitiveness-index-davos
9. Inspired by DI's (2016) Danish Competitiveness Paradox.
10. www.forbes.com/places/denmark/
11. www.workindenmark.dk/Working-in-DK/Working-culture-in-Denmark
12. www.cbs.dk/files/cbs.dk/useful_link/report_on_employment_practices_of_mcs.pdf
13. www.internations.org/expat-insider/2016/the-best-and-worst-places-for-expats
14. www.thelocal.dk/20160831/denmark-is-locking-every-door-to-immigrants
15. www.co-industri.dk/DA/Nyheder/Pages/Default.aspx?NewsItemId=328
16. www.cbs.dk/files/cbs.dk/skills_gap_in_denmark.pdf
17. Fremgang, Fornyelse og Tryghed, Strategi for Danmark i den globale økonomi, Regeringen, April 2016.
18. This scheme gives persons who have been offered a job with an annual pay above a certain limit particularly easy access to the Danish labour market.
19. www.internations.org/expat-insider/2016/the-best-and-worst-places-for-expats
20. www.internations.org/expat-insider/2016/the-best-and-worst-places-for-expats
21. www.thelocal.dk/20161014/denmark-is-shooting-itself-in-the-foot-with-treatment-of-foreign-workers
22. www.thelocal.dk/20161014/denmark-is-shooting-itself-in-the-foot-with-treatment-of-foreign-workers

References

Andersen, S. K., Dølvik, J. E., & Ibsen, C. L. (2014). *Nordic labor market models in open markets*. Brussels: European Trade Union Institute.

Becker, B., Huselid, M., & Beatty, R. (2009). *The differentiated workforce: Transforming talent into strategic impact*. Boston, MA: Harvard Business Press.

Björkman, I., Ehrnrooth, M., Mäkelä, K., Smale, A., & Sumelius, J. (2013). Talent or not? Employee reactions to talent identification. *Human Resource Management, 52*(2), 195–214.Campbell, J., Hall, J., & Pedersen, O. (2006). National identity and varieties of capitalism: The Danish experience. McGill-Queen's University Press. Retrieved from www.jstor.org/stable/j.ctt818c9.

DI. (2016). *Talent shortage in Denmark: Key challenges and recommendations on how to address current and future skills gap*. Retrieved from di.dk/SiteCollectionDocuments/Arbejdskraft/analyser/Udenlandsk%20arbejdskraft/Global%20Talent%20Report%20(05.10.16).pdf.

Due, J. J., Madsen, J. S., Jensen, C. S., & Petersen, L. K. (1994). *The survival of the Danish model: A historical sociological analysis of the Danish system of collective bargaining*. Copenhagen: Djøf/Jurist- og Økonomforbundet.

Due, J. J., Madsen, J. S., & Pihl, M. D. (2010). *Udviklingen i den faglige organisering: Årsager og konsekvenser for den danske model*. Kbh.: Landsorganisationen i Danmark. (LO-dokumentation; Nr. 1/2010).

Galenson, W. (1952). *The Danish system of labor relations: A study in industrial peace*. Cambridge, MA: Harvard University Press.

Gooderham, P., & Nordhaug, O. (2011). One European model of HRM? Cranet empirical contributions. *Human Resource Management Review, 23*(1), 27–36.

Hall, E. T. (1976). *Beyond culture*. New York: Anchor Books.
Hall, P. A., & Soskice, D. (Eds.). (2001). *Varieties of capitalism*. Oxford: Oxford University Press.
Holsbo, A., & Secher, J. O. (2015). *Afsluttende evaluering*. Slagelse: Selandia. Retrieved from www.talentvejen.nu.
Iles, P., Preece, D., & Chuai, X. (2010). Talent management as a management fashion in HRD: Towards a research agenda. *Human Resource Development International, 13*, 125–145.
Khilji, S., Tarique, I., & Schuler, R. (2015). Incorporating the macro view in global talent management. *Human Resource Management Review, 25*, 236–248.
Larsen, T. P., Navrbjerg, S. E., & Johansen, M. M. (2010). *Tillidsrepraesentanten og arbejdspladsen*. Kbh.: Landsorganisationen i Danmark. (Tillidsrepræsentantundersøgelsen 2010; Nr. rapport 1).
Lewis, R. E., & Heckman, R. J. (2006). Talent management: A critical review. *Human Resource Management Review, 16*(2), 139–154.
Madsen, J. S., & Due, J. J. (2008). The Danish Model of industrial relations: Erosion or renewal? *Journal of Industrial Relations, 50*(3), 513–529.
Meyers, M., & van Woerkom, M. (2014). The influence of underlying philosophies on talent management: Theory, implications for practice, and research agenda. *Journal of World Business, 49*, 192–203.
Minbaeva, D. (2016). Contextualizing the individual in international management research: Black boxes, comfort zones and a future research agenda. *European Journal of International Management, 10*(1), 95–104.
Minbaeva, D., & Navrbjerg, S. (2016). The (un)predictable factor: The role of social capital in subsidiaries' takeovers. *Journal of Organizational Effectiveness, People and Performance, 10*(1), 95–104.
Navrbjerg, S., & Minbaeva, D. (2009). HRM and IR in multinational corporations: Uneasy bedfellows? *International Journal of Human Resource Management, 20*(8), 1720–1736.
Nissen, P., Kyed, O., & Baltzer, K. (2011). *Talent i Skolen*. Copenhagen: Dafolo Forlag.
Reeves, M., Levin, S., & Ueda, D. (2016). The biology of corporate survival. *Harvard Business Review, 94*(1), 46–55.
Stahl, G., Björkman, I., Farndale, E., Morris, S., Paauwe, J., Stiles, P., . . . Wright, P. (2012). Six principles of effective global talent management. *MIT Sloan Management Review, 53*(2), 25–32.
Walloth, C. (2016). *Emergent nested systems: A theory of understanding and influencing complex systems as well as case studies in urban systems*. Basel: Springer International Publishing.

7

Macro Talent Management in Finland

Contributing to a Rapidly Evolving Knowledge Economy

Paul Evans, Adam Smale and Ingmar Björkman[1]

Introduction

Finland? Why study how talent management (TM) has contributed to the development of a country that few people visit, that has only 5.5 million people, that lies near and within the arctic circle, and where they speak a strange language? Finland was a largely agrarian country in 1950—and within those seventy years it has transformed itself into a prosperous service economy with a burgeoning high tech sector, and a degree of prosperity that equals the UK and approaches that of the United States.

Today, Finland is ranked 8th out of 140 countries in the World Economic Forum Global Competitiveness Index, 3rd after Denmark and New Zealand on Transparency International's Corruption Index, and 4th in terms of freedom of speech as measured by the World Press Freedom Index.[2] Closer to our talent focus, Finland is 9th on the Global Talent Competitiveness Index (GTCI) out of 118 countries, and it is the top country on World Economic Forum (WEF) survey measures of how easy it is for companies to find skilled employees.[3] Indeed, in terms of talent competitiveness, defined as a country's ability to attract, develop and retain the human capital that contributes to its productivity (Lanvin & Evans, 2017; Khilji, Tarique, & Schuler, 2015), four Nordic countries are in the top ten (see Table 7.1). There are thus important learning points to draw from the Nordic region where the similarities between Finland and the Scandinavia countries of Sweden, Denmark and Norway outnumber the differences. Although our focus in this chapter is on Finland, we will draw relevant comparisons underway.

What are some of the key learning points from Finland's rapid evolution from an agrarian to a knowledge economy that today is being transformed by digitalization and rapid technological change? Based on data presented in this chapter, Finland appears to be well positioned in this societal transformation, and our analysis explores some of the talent aspects of this disruptive transformation. Focusing on the role of TM, we start by outlining the historical background, which leads us then to an assessment of the pillars of TM at the societal level. To frame this, we use the six-pillar model of the GTCI (Lanvin & Evans, 2017; Evans,

Table 7.1 GTCI Rankings of Top Ten Countries (out of 118): Overall and by Pillar

Country	GTCI rank	ENABLE	ATTRACT	GROW	RETAIN	VT SKILLS*	GK SKILLS*
Switzerland	1	2	5	5	1	3	7
Singapore	2	1	1	13	7	8	1
UK	3	8	11	7	5	33	2
USA	4	11	16	2	8	20	3
Sweden	5	9	13	8	4	10	11
Australia	6	17	6	9	14	25	5
Luxembourg	7	21	2	17	3	24	12
Denmark	8	3	15	3	15	17	14
Finland	**9**	**6**	**21**	**4**	**9**	**2**	**18**
Norway	10	13	14	10	2	6	22

* VT Skills = Vocational/Technical skills; GK = Global Knowledge skills

Rodriguez-Montemayor & Lanvin forthcoming)—four input pillars (Enable, Attract, Grow, Retain) and two output pillars (Vocational and Technical skills based on expertise, and Global Knowledge skills that underlie leadership, entrepreneurship and innovation/creativity).

Using these pillars we identify the positive features that differentiate TM in Finland from other countries—the emphasis on social mobility and egalitarian development as well as the close collaboration around TM between key stakeholders. We will also discuss some of the country's main drawbacks, notably the constraints of Finland's relatively rigid labor market and its challenges in external talent attraction. We conclude by examining Finland's future TM prospects through the lens of Industry 4.0. Throughout the chapter we highlight the educational and development dimension as being critical to understanding Finland's impressive evolution towards a knowledge economy.

Building the Modern Finland

Finland celebrated its 100 years of independence in 2017. Since the Napoleonic era, it had been a Grand Duchy in the Tsarist Russian Empire that collapsed in 1917. Upon becoming independent, Finland remained a relatively poor, largely agrarian society until well after WW2. In 1950, 46% of Finnish workers worked in agriculture and only a third of the population lived in urban areas. During the 1960s, some 200,000 Finns fled the country in search of blue-collar jobs in neighboring Sweden—a country that had already successfully built a modern industrial economy and was in search of labor.

However, during the latter half of the 20th century the economy developed rapidly as the country built a strong manufacturing sector and expanded into services. In a 2004 comparison, with its star company Nokia attracting worldwide attention, high-technology manufacturing in Finland ranked second largest after Ireland among OECD countries (OECD, 2004). The industrial sector was export oriented, dominated by large companies such as forest industry companies Stora Enso, UPM and the Metsä Group, elevator and escalator giant Kone, and diesel engine producer Wärtsilä. Like other OECD countries, the service sector had become by far the biggest part of the economy, with the new jobs in manufacturing and services quickly attracting people to the cities.

In what follows, we briefly paint a history of Finland's development into a knowledge economy, drawing on indicators relating to the two output pillars of GTCI—Vocational and Technical skills, and Global Knowledge skills.

Education as the Talent Motor

From the perspective of human capital, the most important driver of this growth was education, with the emergence of the modern system in the 1970s. In the new educational system that was put in place in 1972–77, there was no kindergarten preschool—formal schooling started at age 7 and still does. One of the features of striking relevance to today's debates on how to prepare children for our rapidly changing society is that almost all young children went to the new playschools that were available in all urban areas, seen as being the subjective right of the child rather than as a place to park the kids on the way to work. The philosophy of playschools was that you were not taught—you learnt how to play with others. This quickly evolved into a **learning-how-to-learn** orientation that child psychologists claim is instilled at this age (Hautamäki et al., 2002). The aim of preschool education was not "school readiness" but rather the development of thinking, and to promote children's growth into responsible members of society with an appreciation for other people (Sahlberg, 2015). Early childhood education became a formal part of the Finnish education system in 2013.

Other features of the evolving educational system to be highlighted are the emphasis on **egalitarianism** and the importance of **vocational education**. From age 7, formal schooling from grades 1–9 is mandatory. But there is no streaming of students and standardized testing is absent, reflecting egalitarian Nordic values—the strong students were expected to help out the weak. After the age of 15, the system bifurcates into academic (*lukio*) and vocational tracks (*ammattikoulu*). About 40% of the students continue on the vocational track (*cf.* Switzerland, the GTCI world talent leader, where the figure is 70%), and such technically trained people fuel the demands of industry. In the mid-2000s the Finnish education system suddenly attracted worldwide attention when the OECD's PISA ranking of student skills in maths, reading and problem solving put Finland at number 1 in the world (4th in 2015).

Even in comparison with its Scandinavian neighbors, Finland's education system provided a stable and high-quality supply of vocational and technical talent that fueled industrial growth. The country has invested heavily in the training of engineers at universities and universities of applied sciences, contributing to Finland today being number 1 in the world in terms of the availability of scientists and engineers.

Based on GTCI's assessment, Finland's education system helped propel it to 2nd in the world in terms of vocational/technical skills. This should be contrasted with concerns about the skills gap and the employability of people that worry governments and corporations in many Western countries—and even more so in China, South Korea, South Africa, and Russia.[4] Whilst unemployment in Finland today is still relatively high (8.7% in September 2017), the country has risen to become one of the model nations in matching talent to work needs, ranking number 1 on the GTCI measures of employability (4th on the 'relevance of the educational system to the country', and as noted the top nation on 'ease of finding skilled employees').

The Rise and Fall of Nokia

After 20 years of growth, Finland entered a crisis in the early 1990s as its role in bridging the grey zone between the Soviet Union and Western nations ended with the collapse of the Soviet regime in 1991. One of the foundations supporting the Finnish economy disappeared. With an over-indebted business sector and an overvalued currency, the country went into a banking crisis, leading to a deep recession that saw unemployment jump from 4% to 18%, with public debt mounting to become over 60% of GDP.

As discussed later in this chapter, the strength of collaboration between key stakeholders—government, municipalities, business, unions, and educational institutions—and the high levels of trust between these social partners helped significantly in developing a new vision and plans for economic recovery. Amongst other things, this involved a move away from bureaucratic central administration to a more decentralized system that empowered local authorities to make some of the difficult decisions, particularly in an educational arena that should place more emphasis on high-skilled tertiary competencies. Finland joined the European Union in 1995, following a referendum, and this opened up new markets for exports.

It was the rise of Nokia, one of the largest Finnish companies since the 1960s, which played a major role in Finland's transition towards becoming a technology-driven knowledge economy. Up until the recession of the early 90s, Nokia was a highly diversified corporation involved in businesses such as car tyres and consumer electronics, but it also had a foot in the mobile phone market that had been pioneered in Scandinavia. After a successful gamble on GSM becoming the mobile standard, Nokia grew rapidly, and by the end of the 1990s Nokia had become a pioneer in mobile telephones and the global market leader.

Finland's rise in mobile telephony was soon viewed as a success story of coevolution—sound government policy in areas such competition, deregulation and innovation working in tandem with education and government-supported research, supported by the effective development of firm-level capabilities and strategic leadership. In short Nokia became a synonym for superior management in Finland (Laamanen, Lamberg, & Vaara, 2016); and a defining symbol of Finland's entry onto the world stage. To illustrate its significance, by 2000 Nokia accounted for 4% of Finnish GDP, 70% of Helsinki's stock exchange market capital, 43% of corporate R&D, 21% of total exports and 14% cent of corporate tax revenues (Kelly, 2013). Whilst Finland invested heavily in Nokia's R&D projects, Nokia repaid this in tax revenues. This enabled developments within the Finnish education system to meet the rapidly growing demands for high-skilled workers. Nokia's success, especially overseas, provided the much-needed impetus for other ambitious Finnish companies to internationalize. It also served as a talent incubator for corporate Finland with many engineers, managers and soon-to-be top executives having spent part of their careers at Nokia.

Nokia's rapid fall from top spot began in 2007–8 when Apple launched the first iPhone, quickly followed by the first phone models using Google's Android operating software—just before the global economic crisis. Various studies have assessed the lessons of this rapid decline, pointing to the problematic implementation of a matrix structure that resulted in a lack of internal integration, and an emotionally charged attention gap between top and middle management (Doz & Wilson, 2018; Vuori & Huy, 2015). Nokia's deteriorating financial performance led to the appointment of Stephen Elop as CEO in 2010, who oversaw the sale of Nokia's mobile phone business to Microsoft in 2013.

Since key stakeholders in Finland could see this coming, the coordinated response to job losses at Nokia came in the form of significant investments in the creation of small businesses. Tekes (The Finnish Funding Agency for Technology and Innovation) had its annual budget for funding new and innovative businesses increased to €550 million, and the Finnish Ministry of Employment and Economy launched a start-up accelerator in 2009 (Kelly, 2013). Nokia, too, created an incubator program (Nokia Bridge) that offered grants to departing employees who had a good start-up idea. At the same time, a vibrant entrepreneurial eco-system started to develop around Aalto University, which was formed in 2010 through a merger of the leading Finnish universities in the areas of technology, business, and art and design. A new start-up event embedded in the Aalto University eco-system, Slush, largely run by students, grew rapidly into a major event that in 2016 attracted some 17,500 participants, 2,336 companies, 1,146 investors, and 610 journalists from 124 countries.

Finland was severely hit by the combination of the rapid decline of Nokia's handset business, the worldwide recession that began in 2008, and the Russian trade sanctions introduced in 2014; but by 2016 the country's economy was growing again. Over 10,000 ex-Nokia R&D experts released into a job market built around a thriving high-tech sector had provided a significant stimulus. In a similar fashion to Nokia's stardom being born out of the ashes of the recession in the early 1990s, new stars are today being born. These include unicorns in the mobile gaming applications industry—Supercell (the creator of Clash of Clans) and Rovio (the creator of Angry Birds).

Assessing Macro Talent Management in Finland With the GTCI Framework

Having presented the historical backdrop to Finland's development as a knowledge economy, we now take a more systematic look at Finland today from a macro talent management (MTM) perspective. To do this, we use the model provided by the Global Talent Competitiveness Index (GTCI) that was developed for this purpose (Lanvin & Evans, 2013, 2017; Evans, Rodriguez-Montemayor & Lanvin forthcoming).

The Global Talent Competitive Index Framework

GTCI is a composite index where six pillars are measured by 65 variables from reliable sources (World Bank, World Economic Forum, OECD, UNCTAD, etc.), covering 118 countries (a beta version of a parallel City Competitiveness Index was also pioneered in 2016, comprising 45 cities across the world) (Lanvin & Evans, 2017).[5,6] The model goes through an annual audit by the world's leading statistical authority on such composite indexes, the Joint Research Council of the EU, and it has been certified as being robust, parsimonious, and reliable (Saisana, Becker, & Dominiquez-Torreiro, 2017).

According to the GTCI framework, Talent Competitiveness is defined as the set of policies and practices that enable a country or a city to attract, develop and retain the human capital that contributes to its productivity, where productivity is viewed as output per unit of input. Based on the assumption that there is a close relationship between talent and economic prosperity (an assumption since validated by GTCI research), the model has four input pillars or parameters of talent management, and two output pillars.

Input Pillars of GTCI

The first input pillar captures the wider context of the country or city, namely the factors that **ENABLE** talent competitiveness, which are classified into three groups: ***regulatory context***—encompassing government effectiveness, anti-corruption, and the quality of business-government relations; ***market landscape***—which includes the intensity of competition, the ease of doing business, the ICT infrastructure, the strength of industrial clusters, and the investment in R&D; and ***business and labor landscape***—which has two components that are particularly relevant to MTM, namely the flexibility of the labor market and adoption of professional management practices.

The second input pillar is **ATTRACT**. A country has to attract talent from one of two pools—internal and external—that vary in terms of openness. ***Internal openness*** refers to the talent pool within a country's own borders; access to the talent pools may be restricted by factors such as gender, ethnic background, parental class or wealth. *External openness* refers to whether organizations in that country have an international orientation (which they do not have in North Korea, to use an extreme example), and whether policy and practice facilitates immigration as well as the integration of migrants into society.

The third pillar is **GROW**, focused on how a country develops talent. Economists tend to focus on the *formal educational system* since it is measurable, but talent development does not end there. *Lifelong learning* throughout adulthood is also important, encompassing both the investment of companies and organizations in training and career development as well as national systems of continuous education. GTCI also tries to capture a third source of learning, learning through experience *(access to growth opportunities)*; this is often acknowledged as being important but typically ignored because it is more difficult to measure.

Lastly, since capable individuals will always have opportunities elsewhere, a country's ability to **RETAIN** talent is the fourth input pillar of GTCI. *Sustainability* is one component, encompassing pay, taxation and pensions. The other is *lifestyle,* which includes indicators such as environmental performance and personal safety.

While the four input pillars are conceptually distinct, they are obviously related. For instance, factors that make a country attractive to skilled immigrants are also likely to contribute to talent retention. Therefore, although personal safety and environmental attractiveness appear in the GTCI model as part of the retention dimension they are also likely to influence the perceived attractiveness of the country from the point of view of potential skilled immigrants.

Output Pillars of GTCI

In terms of output pillars, how is "talent" conceptualized in this framework? The academic debate on this is far from over (see e.g. Lewis & Heckman, 2006; Gallardo-Gallardo, Dries, & González-Cruz, 2013; Cappelli & Keller, 2014). GTCI has a broad view of talent as being skilled human capital, leaving unskilled labor out of the talent equation. With its measures, GTCI attempts to assess the quality of those skills across countries, but its two output pillars make an important distinction between two types of talent that an economy needs.

The first is **VOCATIONAL AND TECHNICAL SKILLS**, specialized expertise in a particular domain (*mid-level skills*) that makes an individual employable, fostered by secondary education and in particular by vocational and polytechnic education, as well as by experience within a trade or function. As reliable data became available, the GTCI model was extended to include an *employability* component—the extent to which a country is able to match supply and demand for expertise, avoiding the skills gaps and youth unemployment problems that have captured so much attention in recent years.[7]

The second output pillar and type of talent is **GLOBAL KNOWLEDGE SKILLS.** Linked to professional knowledge, these *high-level skills* involve analytic capacity, social and project skills, and the ability to work across fields. They are the underpinnings of entrepreneurship and creativity, leadership, and innovation. Higher institutes of learning aim to foster these skills, even in specialized domains. Whereas technical skill/expertise helps a company, city or country to run effectively, it is global knowledge skills that help it to grow and expand.

Assessing Finland's Talent Competitiveness

We now turn to this model more analytically in order to assess Finland's current talent competitiveness against the backcloth of its rapid transformation to a diversified knowledge economy, as outlined earlier. For this we use GTCI 2017 data, typically presented as

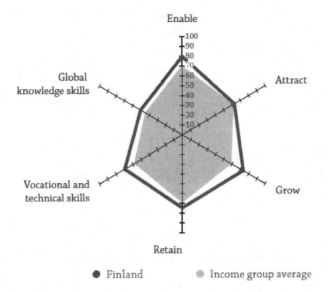

Figure 7.1 Finland's GTCI 2017 Country Profile by Pillar*

* Income group used to compare a country with its income group peers. Income group (in this case the 'high income' category) is based on the UN classification.

Source: Lanvin and Evans (2017).

a country ranking, with raw data where that is meaningful.[8] Figure 7.1 presents the overall profile of Finland on the GTCI in comparison with the average of high income countries, showing its comparative strengths on vocational/technical skills and on growing talent. The full table with indicators for each of the six pillars is provided in Appendix 7.1.

The Enabling Context

Perhaps unsurprisingly, Finland has a highly favorable enabling context for talent with an overall ranking as 6th out of 118 countries. Its *regulatory landscape* is exemplary, with an effective government (3rd out of 118 countries), close relationships between government and business (5th), and an environment that is largely free of corruption (2nd).

The Finnish economy and labor markets are strengthened by relatively clear and developed clusters (concentrations of interconnected firms, suppliers and specialized institutions, 15th), including the electro-mechanical industrial sector, software development, and the gaming industry that potentially act as talent magnets. But Finland struggles because the intensity of competition is much lower (82nd) than in its Scandinavian neighbors—also notably less than in dynamic Estonia next door.

A major disabling factor in Finland concerns the *business and labor landscape*—in particular, a relatively rigid labor market that handicaps start-ups as well as organizational change in established companies. Business leaders and entrepreneurs grumble about the difficulties in hiring and firing staff (70th and 46th respectively out of 118 countries in the GTCI rankings), complaining about the cumbersome procedures and consultations that they must go through. Indeed, labor legislation makes it virtually impossible to fire staff for under-performance, and unions have resisted linking pay too closely to performance, as is generally true across the Nordic countries. This is a real challenge in Finland since union membership is very high (65% overall, but is even higher among those employed in industry, where 81% of wage and salary earners belong to a union).

Further, labor-employer cooperation is relatively weak (20th), with often strained relationships between unions and employers. The Finnish government has made significant efforts in recent years to get employers and unions to agree on measures to cut unit labor costs and strengthen the competitiveness of Finland. This has culminated in, for example, a recent 'competitiveness pact' within the public sector that includes a wage freeze, a requirement for staff to work 24 hours more each year for the same compensation, and a temporary reduction of the holiday bonus pay (a so-called 'thirteenth salary' month) for over half a million municipal and state workers.

The less flexible Finnish labor market makes adaptation to changing circumstances more difficult for organizations—notably the disruptive adaptation to digitalization and algorithms discussed later. This contrasts sharply with nearby Denmark, where employers have greater freedom to hire and fire when necessary (number 1 in the world, alongside Singapore). But flexibility is only one element of a three-sided Danish policy mix that was put in place in the 1990s, known as Flexicurity, that is upheld by the European Commission as a model for employment policy in the EU. Along with labor market flexibility goes the right of people who lose their job to generous compensation for up to two years. But the third pillar is distinctive, namely the obligation of these individuals to retrain, change career, create a start-up or go freelance—or lose those benefits, replaced only by minimal financial aid. Accompanied by training, counseling and support, such "active labor market policies", as labor economists call them, are less deeply rooted in Finland. They are important at a time of deep societal transformation.

Attracting Talent Externally

With its small population of 5.5 million and location far from big global hubs, Finland is not a leading magnet for direct foreign investment (FDI). The value of FDI to Finland has been stable at around EUR 70 billion over the last ten years, most of this originating from neighboring Scandinavian countries, the UK and the US. Whilst this has lagged behind outward FDI (averaging around EUR 100 billion), the gap is closing and the number of new foreign-owned firms in Finland has been growing year on year.

However, Finland cannot hope to supply all the specialized talent that its now diversified and globalized economy requires. Moreover, as in many other developed countries, Finland's population is aging—all age groups of the population are declining except for the 65+ age group (Heikkilä, 2012). Finland until the 1980s was traditionally a land of emigration, but the tide has turned; its multinational companies are strong advocates for importing talent, especially in the technology-driven domain. There is evidence to suggest that immigrants are more likely than locals to be innovative and entrepreneurial, and that migrants bring new perspectives and thereby creativity to teams (Litan, 2015; see Evans & Rodriguez-Montemayor, 2016 for a review of such research).

Attracting skilled immigrants has become a concern across Europe, particularly in the Nordic region (see European Migration Network, 2013, 2017). However, external attraction is a problematic area of MTM for Finland. While 5% of the population is Swedish speaking (Finland was part of Sweden for 600 years and the constitution anchors Swedish as an official language alongside Finnish), only 6% of its citizens are foreign-born (compared to 9% in Denmark and

16% in Sweden). Compared with other small countries that are high in the GTCI talent league, 43% of the population of Singapore were born abroad, as were 27% in Switzerland.

Finland is not a particularly attractive country to talent from abroad, captured by a brain gain ranking of 52 out of 118 countries. Lanvin, Evans and Rodriguez-Montemayor (2016) assess the factors associated with country attractiveness. At the head of the list is language. Finnish is very different from all other languages except Estonian, and also difficult to learn. That Finns are generally fluent in English partly compensates for this, although the fact remains that fluency in Finnish is often a pre-requisite for employment. For young talent, opportunity comes next while lifestyle also counts, particularly for those with families. As any recent visitor to Helsinki knows, the Finns take city design and architecture seriously, trying to compensate for the long arctic winter in making the venue more seductive. Indeed, Helsinki ranks 3rd out of 45 global cities, including London, Paris, Singapore and Shanghai, on INSEAD's new City Talent Competitiveness index.[9] The introduction of a flat 35 percent tax rate for foreign "key employees" during their first four years in the country has been one measure to make Finland more attractive to international talent. Further, a number of English-speaking schools have been established, and public services are offered in English. Nonetheless, its remote location and the dark, harsh winters are additional factors that make attracting talent to Finland a challenging endeavor.

Countries such as the US with world-class institutes of higher education are at an advantage in attracting creative talent, and here Finland also tries hard to capitalize on the solid quality of its universities (17th in its university ranking and 23rd in the world on the number of international students), where an increasing share of the programs are taught in English. The quality of management practices is a less widely recognized factor of attraction and retention, sharply acting in favor of Finland (and indeed other Nordic countries), because of their merit-based professionalism in management and their attention to employee development. As described in the next sub-section, our blurb for capturing this is that "if you want to live the American dream of rags to prosperity, then go Nordic".

Attracting Talent Internally

An essential dimension of MTM is the openness of the talent pool in terms of gender, ethnic background or religion, and social mobility. In some countries, if one is born female or from a poor family within an ethnic minority, there is a very low probability of ever receiving an education that will permit entry in the talent pool. The inclusive-exclusive dimension of TM (Collings & Mellahi, 2009) is particularly salient at the country level of analysis.

Like other Scandinavian countries, Finland upholds strong egalitarian values. One of the Nordic hallmarks is an explicit value attached to *social mobility and equal opportunity*. People should be able to enter the talent pool, to go from rags to prosperity (if not riches) regardless of their birth, social origins, gender or ethnic background. This lies deeply engrained in the design of the Finnish educational system (which is free from first grade through to a university Master's degree), and in other artifacts of Finnish culture. Indeed, Finland is the top country in the world on World Economic Forum measures of social mobility. This is a salient issue for analysis at a time when deep divisions between the haves and have-nots exist, which reflect widening inequalities in wealth and opportunity in virtually all countries of the world (Piketty, 2014).[10]

Finland has for a long time done well in various aspects of gender equality. It was the first country in Europe to give women universal voting rights and today ranks 4th for business opportunities for women in the GTCI. Finland is closing the difference in earnings between men and women, moving from number 20 to 8 in a recent 2017 WEF Report.

The Three Elements of Growing Talent

As mentioned previously, developing talent has three dimensions: *formal education* (which receives a lot of attention since it is most easily measurable in ways that facilitate comparison and analysis), *lifelong learning* (that becomes important in a rapidly changing world of innovation), and *learning through experience* (often ignored since it is difficult to measure).

FORMAL EDUCATION

We discussed earlier some of the features of the formal educational system in Finland—number 1 in the world on the GTCI (though the Netherlands excels more on overall talent development). Its performance on the OECD's PISA assessment positions Finland's approach to education as one of the world's benchmark models. In a comprehensive review of the Finnish education system and why it has become so successful, Sahlberg (2015) identifies a number of areas where Finnish education reform has taken a different direction from mainstream global trends. The main differences are collaboration rather than competition between schools, personalized as opposed to standardized learning, a focus on the whole child instead of on literacy and numeracy, trust-based responsibility instead of test-based accountability, and equity of outcomes over school choice. We extract from this three distinguishing features that we believe hold important lessons for MTM.

The first, as discussed earlier, is the **education system's inclusive emphasis on opportunity for all**, in a country where equity and egalitarianism has been a cornerstone of education policy since the early 1970s. Equity in education is reflected in the high degree of individual guidance, personalized help, and teaching support for all students (particularly those who struggle and those who have learning disabilities), facilitated by small class sizes of 20–30. Further, performance differences between schools in Finland are among the smallest in the world (Sahlberg, 2007).

The second is **teacher professionalism**. The teaching profession enjoys a high status in Finnish society, and teachers are paid reasonably well at just above the national average salary. The standards are high: teachers need to hold a Master's-level degree before securing a permanent position in a Finnish school. However, the competition for places is tough and has been getting tougher. In 2014, there were 8,400 applications for schoolteacher university programs and only 800 study places on offer.[11] If accepted, the student gets to benefit from a high-quality teacher education program. Another feature that makes the teaching profession attractive (and the education system itself so effective) is that teachers in Finland are allowed—even expected—to exercise their professional judgment independently and collectively in determining the curriculum, student assessment and school improvement. There is also a strong emphasis on the continuous professional development of teachers all the way down to kindergarten level.

The third feature is the attention to **maintaining an attractive vocational educational system** in parallel with the generalist academic track. In many countries, vocational education becomes the route for those that failed. Students and families will be put off vocational education if it is seen as a cul-de-sac, a one-way street with no return (one of the keys to the success of vocational education in Switzerland is the multiple cross-over paths between vocational and generalist or higher education at different age levels (see Lanvin, Evans, & Rasheed, 2014).

In Finland it is formally possible to enter tertiary education with a vocational degree, although this is difficult in practice since the vocational study path does not prepare the student for the university entrance exams. It is also possible for the best graduates of the universities of applied sciences to pursue university Master's and even doctoral degrees. As in Switzerland there is close collaboration between schools, trade unions, and employees—another critical element in ensuring that formal education is turned into employability, supplying the short- and long-term job needs. Indeed, Finland ranks 4th in terms of the relevance of its education system to the needs of the economy.

When it comes to tertiary or higher education, Finland is also high on the scoreboard. In terms of tertiary enrolment Finland ranks 3rd in the world on the GTCI, and in tertiary education expenditure it is 8th. The country has chosen to focus heavily on engineers in its university-level training, with 21% of the total number of master's graduates majoring in engineering or technology.[12] It has also graduated a sizeable number of PhDs during recent years, considerably more per capita than its Nordic neighbors. These investments are evident in Finland's positioning in the GTCI: it is the world leader on the availability of scientists and engineers, doing very well in terms of the number of researchers (3rd) as well as on the quality of its scientific institutions (10th). Finland also ranks well on its universities (17th). Overall, public investments in the university system increased until 2015 when, in the light of a weakened economy and amidst other austerity measures, the Finnish government announced that basic funding to the country's 15 universities and 25 universities of applied sciences would be reduced and research funding cut.

The establishment of Aalto University in 2010 through a merger of the Helsinki University of Technology, the Helsinki School of Economics, and Helsinki's University of Art and Design is an example of public-private initiative to strengthen the innovation ecosystem in Finland, along with its competitiveness. Established with generous financial support from both public and private funds, the vision of the University is "*an innovative society*", while its mission is "*shaping the future: science and art together with technology and business.*" Multidisciplinarity in both research and teaching is at the core of the university's strategy, with experiential challenge-based learning key to how Aalto University strives to develop 'game changers' for the future.

The eco-system of entrepreneurial activities in and around Aalto University—exemplified by the start-up event Slush, the Aalto student entrepreneurship society, and the Aalto Start-up Sauna accelerator program—has recently spread to other universities and universities of applied sciences in Finland. These changes have led to a gradual increase in Finnish entrepreneurial intentions and greater start-up activity, as measured by Total Early-stage Entrepreneurial Activity (TEA).[13]

CONTINUOUS EDUCATION AND DEVELOPMENT

In the 20th century factory age, one could learn a trade or domain of expertise at school, along with the basics literacies, that would then serve for progression through a lifelong career; but no longer. In our fast-moving age of knowledge-based innovation, people can be expected to change careers many times during their adult lives (emerging spiral careers are described by Gratton, 2011; see Evans & Rodriguez-Montemayor, 2017 for a review). For example, the German apprenticeship system has come under critique because skilled technicians are not adequately equipped to adapt and reskill themselves when technologies change (Hanushek, Woessman, & Zhang, 2011). Continuous adult development becomes critically important.

Finland performs reasonably well when it comes to continuing education, adult learning and development, and learning through experience, although by Scandinavian norms it is the follower and not the leader. It ranks 11th on continuous education, albeit some distance behind Switzerland—the model in this arena of MTM. When it comes to learning through experience (what the GTCI calls *access to growth opportunities*), the Nordics are the clear global benchmark, with Denmark as the exemplar—but Finland trailing at 16th. Learning through experience is measured indirectly with indicators of delegation of authority,[14] use of networks (learning from each other), and voice or freedom of expression.

Retaining Talent

Finland is doing reasonably well in terms of talent retention, judging by its GTCI scores. Its environmental performance is stellar by international comparisons, and it does well in terms of sustainability (10th) and personal safety (12th), having recently come out as the safest country in the world according to the 2017 Travel and Tourism Competitiveness Report. While it does very poorly when it comes to taxation (88 out of 118 countries), this is an integral element of the welfare model that characterizes the Nordic countries. Nonetheless, the comparatively small salary differences in Finland and the high taxation may be viewed as potential challenges when it comes to retaining top performers with ample international opportunities. Indeed, cuts in the university sector (as well as in the partially publically funded research institutes in Finland) have triggered some scholars to relocate to universities in other countries, with their decisions being highly publicized in Finnish media.[15]

Finland Through the Lens of Industry 4.0

The work scene is undergoing significant, potentially massive, change that may be transforming talent management. What has been happening during the last 15 years in a largely invisible way is that machines (digitalization, algorithms, robots, AI) have been replacing work, a trend headlined recently as Industry 4.0 or the fourth industrial revolution (Schwab, 2016).[16] What is clear from research is that most routine work can be better done by machines (Autor, 2015; Brynjolfsson & McAffee, 2014; Frey, Osborne, & Holmes, 2016; see Evans & Rodriguez-Montemayor, 2017 for a research review)—not just manual work but also work in professions such as law, accountancy, journalism and consulting (Suskind & Suskind, 2015).

This has already resulted in a hollowing out of work in the economies of developed nations (Holmes & Mayhew, 2014)—the disappearance of mid-skill jobs. Our recent research commentary comes to the conclusion that it is important to think beyond automation, to understand the way in which organizations are changing in the platform economy, and the way that free agents replace salaried employment (over 30% of the population in Europe and North America earn all or part of their income as freelancers, in a world where getting a mortgage, car loan or unemployment benefit is typically dependent on being a salaried employee) (see Evans & Rodriguez-Montemayor, 2017). Work will not disappear, contrary to some dire forecasts such as Ford (2015). While certain less skilled jobs will remain (the hairdresser is the prototypical example, as is the medical assistant), countries have to help their adult populations understand that their children will have three, four, five or more different careers during their lives (the US Department of Labor estimates that 63% of children going into high school today will graduate in 2025 into jobs like drone manager and human technology integration facilitator that do not exist today).

Educational systems must be reformed to facilitate an up-skilling of the population—mastering literacy, math and scientific understanding at primary school, and then developing the knowledge/skills that will make them employable through secondary and university education, together with project skills and the interpersonal skills for the teamwork that collaborative innovation and entrepreneurship requires, complemented by broad interdisciplinary understanding.[17] We hear many debates on the respective virtues of a broad liberal education *versus* a specialized education that makes people employable (GK versus vocational/technical skills in GTCI terms). But the mindset required by our globalized technology-driven 21st century world is not *either/or* thinking but *both/and* duality (Evans, 2000; Pucik, Evans, Björkman, & Morris, 2017)—people in the job market need both the technical skills that makes people employable AND the broad project and collaborative skills that allow them to contribute to a world of innovation and entrepreneurship.

These are immense challenges for **educational systems**. The traditional school classroom looks like a fast disappearing 20th century factory, while scholars point out that a good playschool looks more like a modern workplace. Higher education must make people employable (too many graduates in too many countries cannot find jobs), but graduates must also be equipped for cross-disciplinary and cross-functional collaboration. States need to expand and fund continuous education. Another challenge is changing **employment systems** so that they reflect the realities of a world when many people are free agents; countries have to learn how to facilitate the necessary transitions, job/career changes, and mobility of people through "active labor market policies" such as those exemplified by the Danish Flexicurity system described earlier (Kristensen, 2016).

The overall implication of all of this is that adaptation will require **strong ecosystem partnerships** between government or municipalities, business and employer federations, educational institutions, and labor as represented by social partners such as unions.

The GTCI 2017 Report assessed the Talent Readiness for Technology of its 118 nations on indicators of these three challenges, along with measures of various technological competencies such as virtual work, collaboration, and personal innovativeness (see Evans & Rodriguez-Montemayor, 2017 for details). On these criteria, ten out of 118 countries are relatively well positioned in terms of talent readiness for technology—but not Finland.[18]

Finland is the world's leading country, along with Singapore, on INSEAD's sister index, the Global IT Readiness Index or GITR,[19] which focuses on infrastructure and capability dimensions of the digital economy as well as talent considerations. But the glaring weakness of Finland as it faces up to the disruptive challenges of Industry 4.0 is the rigidity of its labor market, as discussed earlier, coupled with the difficulties that it faces in attracting and retaining the specialized talent that its burgeoning technology industry requires—in addition to its lag behind the other Nordic countries in continuous education and learning through experience. Consequently it trails behind Denmark on talent readiness for technology, both as measured by the GTCI and by EU comparisons (EurActiv, 2016). Consultants forecast that Finland may take a lead in the emerging technology-driven economy of the 21st century, building on its technology initiatives, the strength of its educational system, and the larger size of its firms than Denmark—but we would add only *if* it can overcome these hurdles.[20,21]

The Importance of Ecosystem Collaboration

Will Finland overcome these hurdles? This is not just a crystal ball question—we have substantive grounds to be cautiously optimistic. The evolution of TM in a society requires more than sound models backed up by solid research. As noted earlier, it requires close partnership between the different stakeholders that constitute a society—between the government and/or municipalities, business and their representatives, labor representatives such as trade unions, and educational institutions.

Consider for example the vocational educational system that is one of the powerhouses of GTCI's talent leader, Switzerland. Vocational education in Switzerland is not just a policy issue of starting to think about one's vocation at age 12, as Swiss schoolchildren are required to do. "Thinking of one's vocation" between ages 12 and 15 means carefully organized visits to factories, research labs, banks and hospitals so that "vocation" becomes tangible for school children—and aligned with realistic industrial policy scenarios. Seventy per cent of Swiss school children choose the vocational apprenticeship track at age 15 (three days of work and two days of schooling). The vocational visits, the design of apprenticeship programs, the work and salary conditions and accompanying teaching are constantly evolving and changing, requiring close on-going collaboration between businesses, industry sectors, local schools, cantons and government, carefully steered and orchestrated by the Swiss Federal Institute for Vocational Educational and Training (SFIVET) that is chaired by a former Swiss minister of education. The devil lies in such granular details that have a 90-year history in Switzerland.

Close collaboration between stakeholders underlies the success of Swiss vocational education, resulting in high employability. Indeed such collaboration between the stakeholders in national or city ecosystems underlies most successful national policies linking talent management to short and long term prosperity (Williamson & De Meyer, 2012).[22] Finland leads the Nordic countries in terms of government-business relations (5th out of 118 countries), and this is backed up by our experience.[23] A group encompassing government ministers, university vice chancellors, military generals, CEOs and bishops—all sectors of society—visited INSEAD and other European organizations in the mid-90s on a study tour to weld agreement on how to get Finland out of the crisis that the demise of the Soviet Union had brought on. And for many decades, an exclusive invitee-only National Defense Course has brought together leaders from different sectors of society. On the other hand, the quality of labor-employer cooperation is the lowest among the Scandinavian countries (20th), perhaps helping to account for disappointing progress in terms of employment policy in Finland.

Conclusion

With this assessment of macro talent management (MTM) in Finland, we have focused on a country that over seventy years went from being a predominantly agricultural nation to a high-tech service economy that leads the world on many indicators of economic prosperity and civic sophistication. The Global Talent Competitiveness Index (GTCI) provides us with a useful lens for analysis of a country's ability to enable, attract, develop and retain human capital, and we have used this index to assess the lessons from Finland's evolution.

This analysis highlights three features of MTM in Finland. The first is the role of education as a talent motor—notably paying attention to the balance between technical/vocational education and the global knowledge skills associated with leadership, entrepreneurship and innovation. Second, egalitarian values permeate education and most other aspects of Finnish MTM, from social mobility to gender equality. Third, close collaboration between social partners in the state also helps explain Finland's successful development, and notably how the country surmounted various times of turmoil, from the mid-90s through to the crisis brought on by Nokia's decline at a time of global recession. Balanced education, emphasis on egalitarianism, and close ecosystem collaboration help explain why Finland is a country where companies find it easy to find skilled employees.

We have also highlighted two main challenges that Finland confronts today—that of building and consolidating the technology sector as well as the entrepreneurial ecosystem that came into being with the decline of Nokia's mobile phone business; and confronting the technology transformations in the talent and work scene that are underway today as machines take over routine work. Despite Finland's strengths, it faces three risks to its prosperity in the MTM domain. The first is the risk of slow responsiveness due to a comparatively inflexible labor market. The second is the need to direct more attention to continuing education and life-long learning, and to active labor market practices that will help people adapt to accelerating change. And the third is the difficulty that Finland faces in attracting specialized talent from abroad, at a time when many nations are waking up to the fact that the declining local populations cannot staff all the talent needs. Such talent considerations have important implications for policy makers as well as labor economists and TM scholars interested in shedding light on factors contributing to long-term country competitiveness.

Appendix 7.1 Finland's Profile on the GTCI 2017 (Lanvin & Evans, 2017)

Indicator (score)	Rank
1 ENABLE (79.76)	**6**
1.1 Regulatory Landscape (94.39)	*2*
1.1.1 Government effectiveness (94.88)	3
1.1.2 Business-government relations (91.67)	5
1.1.3 Political stability (94.68)	5
1.1.4 Regulatory quality (92.07)	3
1.1.5 Corruption (98.65)	2
1.2 Market Landscape (75.56)	*11*
1.2.1 Competition intensity (62.65)	82
1.2.2 Ease of doing business (87.86)	9
1.2.3 Cluster development (65.10)	15
1.2.4 R&D expenditure (78.57)	4
1.2.5 ICT infrastructure (78.52)	28
1.2.6 Technology utilisation (80.63)	10
1.3 Business and Labour Landscape (69.33)	*29*
Labour Market Flexibility	
1.3.1 Ease of hiring (55.67)	70
1.3.2 Ease of redundancy (80.00)	46
Management Practice	
1.3.3 Labour-employer cooperation (68.98)	20
1.3.4 Professional management (86.44)	3
1.3.5 Relationship of pay to productivity (55.58)	38
2 ATTRACT (63.05)	**21**
2.1 External Openness (42.59)	*40*
Attract Business	
2.1.1 FDI and technology transfer (56.55)	70
2.1.2 Prevalence of foreign ownership (64.86)	45
Attract People	
2.1.3 Migrant stock (12.51)	52
2.1.4 International students (36.78)	23
2.1.5 Brain gain (42.24)	52
2.2 Internal Openness (83.52)	*4*
Social Diversity	
2.2.1 Tolerance of minorities (96.67)	3
2.2.2 Tolerance of immigrants (76.76)	32
2.2.3 Social mobility (89.98)	1
Gender Equality	
2.2.4 Female graduates (78.00)	33
2.2.5 Gender earnings gap (81.27)	20

Indicator (score)	Rank
3 GROW (73.53)	**4**
3.1 Formal Education (75.59)	*1*
Enrolment	
3.1.1 Vocational enrolment (100.00)	1
3.1.2 Tertiary enrolment (82.07)	3
Quality	
3.1.3 Tertiary education expenditure (49.14)	8
3.1.4 Reading, maths, science (85.43)	4
3.1.5 University ranking (61.32)	17
3.2 Lifelong Learning (72.13)	*11*
3.2.1 Quality of management schools (74.02)	12
3.2.2 Prevalence of training in firms (n/a)	n/a
3.2.3 Employee development (70.24)	10
3.3 Access to Growth Opportunities (72.86)	*16*
Networks	
3.3.1 Use of virtual social networks (89.41)	10
3.3.2 Use of virtual professional networks (36.65)	26
Empowerment	
3.3.3 Delegation of authority (76.99)	5
3.3.4 Personal rights (88.40)	12
4 RETAIN (74.44)	**9**
4.1 Sustainability (66.80)	*10*
4.1.1 Pension system (89.90)	18
4.1.2 Taxation (38.26)	88
4.1.3 Brain retention (72.25)	7
4.2 Lifestyle (82.08)	*15*
4.2.1 Environmental performance (100)	1
4.2.2 Personal safety (93.70)	12
4.2.3 Physician density (37.36)	35
4.2.4 Sanitation (97.27)	35
5 VOCATIONAL AND TECHNICAL SKILLS (69.91)	**2**
5.1 Mid-Level Skills (59.93)	*17*
5.1.1 Workforce with secondary education (61.70)	26
5.1.2 Population with secondary education (54.35)	31
5.1.3 Technicians & associate professionals (80.20)	13
5.1.4 Labour productivity per employee (43.47)	20
5.2 Employability (79.90)	*1*
5.2.1 Ease of finding skilled employees (76.79)	1
5.2.2 Relevance of educational system to the economy (78.57)	4
5.2.3 Availability of scientists & engineers (84.33)	1
5.2.4 Skills gap as major constraint (n/a)	n/a
6 GLOBAL KNOWLEDGE SKILLS (50.69)	**18**
6.1 High-Level Skills (63.54)	*5*
6.1.1 Workforce with tertiary education (65.37)	14
6.1.2 Population with tertiary education (38.26)	25
6.1.3 Professionals (64.55)	12
6.1.4 Researchers (86.78)	3
6.1.5 Senior officials and managers (29.21)	46
6.1.6 Quality of scientific institutions (79.30)	10
6.1.7 Scientific journal articles (81.34)	7
6.2 Talent Impact (37.84)	*30*
6.2.1 Innovation output (70.20)	10
6.2.2 High-value exports (20.77)	46
Entrepreneurship	
6.2.3 New product entrepreneurial activity (40.67)	52
6.2.4 New business density (19.73)	32

Notes

1. We gratefully acknowledge the input of Kati Hagros.
2. The Central Statistical Office of Finland provides a comprehensive list of measures where Finland is among the best in the world (e.g. society, equality, environment, education). See: www.stat.fi/ajk/satavuotiassuomi/suomimaailmankarjessa_en.html.
3. Malaysia, Ireland and Norway are other countries where companies report it to be easy to find skilled employees, as evaluated by the WEF Opinion Survey.
4. When it comes to the skills gap in the West, there were 15 million unemployed people in North America and Western Europe in 2013, including youth unemployment exceeding 25% in countries such as Spain (McKinsey Global Institute, 2012; see also Cappelli, 2012). On the other hand, there were more than 5 million vacant jobs in industry and the service sector—jobs going vacant because people did not have the required skills (Lanvin, Mettgenberg-Lemière, & Merdikawati, 2013).
5. A full account of the conceptual reasoning and empirical basis for GTCI can be found in Evans and Rodriguez-Montemayor (forthcoming).
6. The conceptual framework behind the Global City Talent Competitiveness Index (GCTCI) is outlined by Lanvin (2017), along with the pilot ranking of 45 cities on four continents. While this index will be improved with better measures and broader coverage, the beta version results suggest that mid-sized well-connected cities may have advantages in terms of talent competitiveness over the metropolises that hitherto have captured attention. Copenhagen is ranked #1 out of 45 cities, and Helsinki is #3 (more or less equal to San Francisco and well above New York and London).
7. See the discussion and references in the section Education as the Talent Motor on page 172.
8. The definitions of variables, sources, as well as data tables and country profiles can be found in the full GTCI report (Lanvin & Evans, 2017); also available online at: www.gtci2017.com.
9. Lanvin (2017). See earlier discussion on this beta index at the outset of the section The Global Talent Competitiveness Index.
10. This was the theme of the WEF Annual Meeting in Davos in January 2018: "Creating a shared future in a fractured world".
11. The University of Helsinki publishes data on the number of applicants to schoolteacher university programs in Finland, see www.helsinki.fi/fi/verkostot/vakava/vakava-koe/tilastoja.
12. Eurostat reports that 20.7% of Finnish students graduated in 2013 in engineering, manufacturing and construction, the highest proportion in Europe and ahead of Germany (20.1%)(ec.europa.eu/eurostat/statistics-explained/index.php/File:Distribution_of_tertiary_education_graduates_by_field,_2013_%28%25%29_ET15.png
13. Global Entrepreneurship Monitor (Global Report 2016–17), www.gemconsortium.org.

    This recent ecosystem development is not yet seen in the GTCI data on 'New product entrepreneurial activity' (Finland is #52), operationalized as the percentage of revenues coming from products/services introduced in the last 4 years. We predict that Finland will improve on this measure in the years ahead, though the rigidity of the labor market may act as a brake.
14. The rationale for this proxy is that with high delegation people are more likely to learn from experience, especially if it accompanied by training and coaching, which the GTCI also measures. With low delegation, people simply follow orders and rules and learn little. There is wide variation on this variable across countries.
15. Figures from Statistics Finland show that the number of PhD-educated Finns who have moved abroad increased by 37% between 2011 and 2015 (compared to a 38% decrease in PhD-educated immigrants over the same period).
16. The other three industrial revolutions, as viewed by Schwab (2016), were the mechanical production revolution of the late 18th century, the mass production revolution of the late 19th century, and the computer revolution of the 1960s.
17. The OECD's PISA recently announced the extension of its student assessment on math, literacy and problem solving to include collaborative problem solving (see www.oecd-ilibrary.org/education/collaborative-problem-solving_cdae6d2e-en).
18. These ten countries (listed in order of their overall GTCI ranking) are Switzerland, Singapore, the United Kingdom, Denmark, the Netherlands, Ireland, Canada, New Zealand, the United Arab Emirates, and Bahrain. The United States does not appear on this list because of the variance in this large and complex country, comprising cities that are clear technology-talent leaders and states that are ill prepared (see discussion on ecosystems in the next sub-section).
19. For GITR, see Baller, Dutta, and Lanvin (2016).
20. See BCG (2016).

21. It is worth drawing the parallel with another country, namely South Korea, that scores high on technological sophistication but which fails to capture the prosperity benefits because MTM, including education, lags far behind. South Korea ranks as the world leader on, for example, broadband availability but only #29 on the GTCI.
22. The importance of ecosystem collaboration is evidenced in Asia by the success of the Indian IT/business process outsourcing industry (which built partnership with NIIT's (national institutes of information technology) across the provinces of India to supply its growing needs for skilled labor; and by the success of Singapore in building competence in aircraft engine servicing through a partnership (see Kwan & Siow, 2013).
23. The fact that Scandinavia in general and Finland in particular is largely free of corruption is important to note in this context. Whenever business and government get together, there is a danger that money passes under the table. This fear of corruption blocked close relationships between business and government for many decades in Denmark, in the experience of one of the authors.

References

Autor, D. (2015). Why are there still so many jobs? The history and future of workplace automation. *Journal of Economic Perspectives, 29*(3), 3–30.

Baller, S., Dutta, S., & Lanvin, B. (2016). *The global information technology report 2016: Innovating in the digital economy.* Geneva: World Economic Forum. Retrieved from www3.weforum.org/docs/GITR2016/WEF_GITR_Full_Report.pdf.

BCG (2016, August). *Digitizing Denmark: How Denmark can drive and benefits from an accelerated digitized economy in Europe.* Retrieved from di.dk/SiteCollectionDocuments/DI%20Business/Google%20Denmark%20Report%2006%20.

Brynjolfsson, E., & McAfee, A. (2014). *The second machine age: Work, progress, and prosperity in a time of brilliant technologies.* New York: W.W. Norton.

Cappelli, P. (2012). *Why good people can't get jobs: The skills gap and what companies can do about it.* Philadelphia, PA: Wharton Digital Press.

Cappelli, P., & Keller, J. R. (2014). Talent management: Conceptual approaches and practical challenges. *Annual Review of Organizational Psychology and Organizational Behavior, 1*(1), 305–331.

Collings, D. G., & Mellahi, K. (2009). Strategic talent management: A review and research agenda. *Human Resource Management Review, 19*(2), 304–313.

Doz, Y., & Wilson, K. (2018). *Ringtone: Explaining the rise and fall of Nokia.* Oxford: Oxford University Press.

EurActiv. (2016, February 26). EU countries issue mea culpas for poor marks on internet connectivity. *EurActiv. com.* Retrieved from www.euractiv.com/section/digital/news/eu-countries-issue-mea-culpas-for-poor-marks-on-internet-connectivity.

European Migration Network. (2013). *Attracting highly qualified third country nationals: National contribution from Finland.* Retrieved from www.emn.fi/files/822/EMN_study_Attracting_highly_qualified_third_country_nationals_Finland_FI_EN_2013.pdf.

European Migration Network. (2017, September). *The EU in the global race for talents: Challenges and solutions in strengthening the EU's competitiveness.* Tallinn Conference. Retrieved from www.eu2017.ee/political-meetings/eu-global-race-talents-challenges-and-solutions-strengthening-eus.

Evans, P. (2000). The dualistic leader: Thriving on paradox. In S. Chowdhury (Ed.), *Management 21C.* New York and London: Prentice Hall-Financial Times.

Evans, P., & Rodriguez-Montemayor, E. (2016). International mobility and talent attraction: A research commentary. In B. Lanvin & P. Evans (Eds.), *The global talent competitiveness index, 2015–16: Talent attraction and international mobility.* Fontainebleau: INSEAD. Retrieved from www.insead.edu/global-indices/gtci.

Evans, P., & Rodriguez-Montemayor, E. (2017). Are we prepared for the talent overhaul induced by technology? A GTCI research commentary. In B. Lanvin & P. Evans (Eds.), *The global talent competitiveness index, 2017: Talent and technology.* Fontainebleau: INSEAD. Retrieved from www.gtci2017.com.

Evans, P., Rodriguez-Montemayor, E., & Lanvin, B. (forthcoming). The global talent competitiveness index: An empirical assessment and lessons for MTM. In I. Tarique (Ed.), *The Routledge companion to talent management.* New York: Routledge.

Ford, M. (2015). *The rise of the robots: Technology and the threat of mass unemployment.* New York: Basic Books.

Frey, C. B., Osborne, M. A., & Holmes, C. (2016). *Technology at work 2.0: The future is not what it used to be.* Citi GPS Report, Oxford Martins School. Retrieved from www.oxfordmartin.ox.ac.uk/downloads/reports/Citi_GPS_Technology_Work_2.pdf.

Gallardo-Gallardo, E., Dries, N., & González-Cruz, T. F. (2013). What is the meaning of 'talent' in the world of work? *Human Resource Management Review*, 23(4), 290–300.

Gratton, L. (2011). *The shift: The future of work is already here*. London: Collins.

Hanushek, E. A., Woessmann, L., & Zhang, L. (2011). *General education, vocational education, and labor-market outcomes over the life-cycle*. NBER (National Bureau of Economic Research) Working Paper 17504, Cambridge, MA.

Hautamäki, J., Arinen, P., Eronen, S., Hautamäki, A., Kupiainen, S., Lindblom, B., . . . Scheinin, P. (2002). *Assessing learning-to-learn: A framework*. Helsinki: National Board of Education.

Heikkilä, E. (2012). *Labour market participation of immigrants in Finland and its regions*. Institute of Migration, Turku. Retrieved from www.migrationinstitute.fi/files/pdf/artikkelit/labour_market_participation_of_immigrants_in_finland_and_its_regions.pdf.

Holmes, C., & Mayhew, K. (2014). The winners and losers in the hourglass labour market. In L. Archer, A. Mann, & J. Stanley (Eds.), *Understanding employer engagement in education: Theories and evidence*. London: Routledge.

Kelly, G. (2013). Finland and Nokia: an affair to remember. *Wired Magazine*. Retrieved on March 29, 2017 from www.wired.co.uk/article/finland-and-nokia.

Khilji, S. E., Tarique, I., & Schuler, R. S. (2015). Incorporating the macro view in global talent management. *Human Resource Management Review*, 25(3), 236–248.

Kristensen, P. H. (2016). Constructing chains of enablers for alternative economic futures: Denmark as an example. *Academy of Management Perspectives*, 30(2), 153–166.

Kwan, C. W., & Siow, R. (2013). Business ecosystems: Developing employable talent to meet Asia's needs. In B. Lanvin & P. Evans (Eds.), *The global talent competitiveness index 2013*. Fontainebleau: INSEAD. Retrieved from www.insead.edu/global-indices/gtci.

Laamanen, T., Lamberg, J.-A., & Vaara, E. (2016). Explanations of success and failure in management learning: What can we learn from Nokia's rise and fall? *Academy of Management Learning & Education*, 15(1), 2–25.

Lanvin, B. (2017). Benchmarking cities as key players on the global talent scene. In B. Lanvin & P. Evans (Eds.), *The global talent competitiveness index 2017: Talent and technology*. Fontainebleau: INSEAD. Retrieved from www.gtci2017.com.

Lanvin, B., & Evans, P. (2013). *The global talent competitiveness index 2013*. Fontainebleau: INSEAD. Retrieved from www.insead.edu/global-indices/gtci.

Lanvin, B., & Evans, P. (2017). *The global talent competitiveness index 2017: Talent and technology*. Fontainebleau: INSEAD. Retrieved from www.gtci2017.com.

Lanvin, B., Evans, P. & Rasheed, N. (2014). Growing Talent for today and tomorrow. In B. Lanvin & P. Evans (Eds.), *The global talent competitiveness index 2014: Growing talent for today and tomorrow*. Fontainebleau: INSEAD. Retrieved from www.insead.edu/global-indices/gtci.

Lanvin, B., Evans, P., & Rodriguez-Montemayor, E. (2016). Attracting and mobilising talent globally and locally. In B. Lanvin & P. Evans (Eds.), *The global talent competitiveness index, 2015–16: Talent attraction and international mobility*. Fontainebleau: INSEAD. Retrieved from www.insead.edu/global-indices/gtci.

Lanvin, B., Mettgenberg-Lemière, M., & Merdikawati, N. (2013). Global and mobile: Talent is reshaping the world economy. In B. Lanvin & P. Evans (Eds.), *The Global Talent Competitiveness Index 2013*. Fontainebleau: INSEAD. Retrieved from www.insead.edu/global-indices/gtci.

Lewis, R. E., & Heckman, R. J. (2006). Talent management: A critical review. *Human Resource Management Review*, 16(2), 139–154.

Litan, R. (2015, January–February). How the United States can regain its entrepreneurial edge. *Foreign Affairs*.

McKinsey Global Institute (2012). *The world at work: Jobs, pay and skills for 3.5 billion people*. MGI Report. Retrieved from www.mckinsey.com/global-themes/employment-and-growth/the-world-at-work.

OECD. (2004). *OECD economic survey Finland* (Vol. 2004/14). Paris: OECD.

Piketty, T. (2014). *Capital in the twenty-first century*. Cambridge: Harvard University Press.

Pucik, V., Evans, P., Björkman, I., & Morris, S. (2017). *The global challenge: International human resource management* (3rd ed.). Chicago: Chicago Business Press.

Sahlberg, P. (2007). Education policies for raising student learning: The Finnish approach. *Journal of Education Policy*, 22(2), 147–171.

Sahlberg, P. (2015). *Finnish lessons 2.0: What can the world learn from educational change in Finland?* New York: Teachers College Press.

Saisana, M., Becker, W., & Dominiquez-Torreiro, M. (2017). The JRC statistical audit of the global talent competitiveness index 2017. In B. Lanvin & P. Evans (Eds.), *The global talent competitiveness index, 2017: Talent and technology*. Fontainebleau: INSEAD.

Schwab, K. (2016). *The fourth industrial revolution*. Colligny and Geneva: World Economic Forum.
Suskind, R., & Suskind, D. (2015). *The future of the professions: How technology will transform the work of human experts*. Oxford: Oxford University Press.
Vuori, T. O., & Huy, Q. N. (2015). Distributed attentions and shared emotions in the innovation process: How Nokia lost the smartphone battle. *Administrative Science Quarterly, 61*(1), 9–51.
Williamson, P. J., & De Meyer, A. (2012). Ecosystem advantage: How to successfully harness the power of partners. *California Management Review, 55*(1), 24–46.

8

Macro Talent Management in the Netherlands

A Critical Analysis of Growing and Retaining Talent in the Netherlands

Marian Thunnissen, Joop Schippers and Paul Boselie

Introduction

The growing awareness of the impact of contextual factors in the shaping of the employment relationship and HRM (Paauwe, 2004; Collings, 2014) is largely neglected in academic Talent Management (TM) research. Up until now most studies investigate talent and TM on the individual and organizational level (Khilji & Schuler, 2017; Thunnissen & Gallardo-Gallardo, 2017). The focus in empirical TM research is on explaining a specific TM issue or research topic, and the studies often fail to use the context of the organization to explain the specific conceptualization of talent and TM (Gallardo-Gallardo & Thunnissen, 2016). Yet, several authors—in particular from the field of international HRM or Global TM—called for more research on TM in a variety of countries and sectors of industry, and advise to contextualize TM in both theoretical frameworks and in research designs (e.g., Collings, Scullion, & Vaiman, 2011; Thunnissen, Boselie, & Fruytier, 2013). The scarce TM studies which include environmental factors indeed illustrate that both institutional factors (such as legislation, politics, country culture and the educational system) and market mechanisms (in particular the labor market) seem to affect the shaping of a TM approach (e.g., Boussebaa & Morgan, 2008; Cooke, Saini, & Wang, 2014; Shi & Handfield, 2012).

Around 2013 a new topic in the field of TM arose: Macro TM (MTM) (e.g., Khilji & Schuler, 2017). MTM is about the broader organizational context which is often forgotten in TM research. Like TM, MTM is focused on the attraction, development, engagement/retention and deployment of talents (e.g., Scullion, Collings, & Caligiuri, 2010), but on a regional or country level instead of the usual individual or organizational level. More specifically, MTM is aimed at assessing the interplay between external mechanisms and actors in the regional or national context, as well as the effects on a regional level (Khilji, Tarique, & Schuler, 2015; Schuler, Tarique & Khilje, Chapter 1 in this book). Despite the newness of the topic, there are already two leading longitudinal empirical studies on MTM: the Global Talent Competitiveness Index (GTCI) by INSEAD and partners (e.g., Lanvin & Evans, 2013, 2014, 2016, 2017) and the Human Capital Index (HCI) of the World Economic Forum (WEF) (e.g., WEF, 2013, 2016). The GTCI uses 65 variables (ordered in 14 sub pillars) to assess in 118 countries what countries do to produce and acquire talents, and the kind of skills that are available to them as a result. The HCI covers 46 indicators (ordered in 7 categories) to rank 130 countries on how well they are developing and deploying their human capital potential. The indices make use of quantitative, secondary data, made available by international organizations such as the World Bank, the WEF, the International Labor Organization, and UNESCO.

Both benchmark studies show that some countries are a better 'breeding ground' for talent or a stronger 'talent magnet' than others. The top ten countries are dominated by high income countries, and in particular European countries are in the top of the rankings (7 out of 10 countries). The leaders of these rankings have placed importance on high educational attainment and putting a correspondingly large share of their workforce in high-skilled occupations (WEF, 2016), where they use their (human) capital for innovation, entrepreneurship and collaboration (Lanvin & Evans, 2017).

This chapter is about MTM in the Netherlands. In the annual rankings of the GTCI and HCI the Netherlands is in or close to the top 10 (11th position in the 2017 GTCI and 8th position in the 2016 HCI), which indicates that the Netherlands belongs to the 10% of countries that offers organizations and individuals an excellent context to attract, identify, develop and deploy their talents. Both indices show that the Netherlands excels in developing or growing talent through its educational system, its accent on lifelong learning, the quality of its scientific research institutions and closeness of links between universities and the private sector (Lanvin & Evans, 2017; WEF, 2016). The latter also illustrates the innovation driven economy of the Netherlands, which—together with the stable regulatory landscape—makes the Netherlands a pleasant country for doing business for organizations (Lanvin & Evans, 2017; WEF, 2016). Regarding the attraction and retention of talent the rankings for the Netherlands are slightly behind the top countries, because of some inconsistencies of the labor market (Lanvin & Evans, 2017).

Despite the comprehensiveness of the indices—in content and in the amount of countries involved—and the quality of the data used, both studies mainly paint an abstract and overall picture of the talent attractiveness of a country. In this chapter we aim to present an in-depth and more qualitative description of the way the Netherlands attracts and retains talent on a national level. This overview is based on primarily Dutch publications and data of, for example, Netherlands Bureau for Economic Policy Analysis (CPB), Rathenau Institute, Dutch Social and Economic Council (SER), and Statistics Netherlands (CBS). We start with some information about macro environmental factors (*cf.* Khilji et al., 2015), i.e. the circumstances in the market, business and regulatory landscape in the Netherlands. According to the GTCI, these circumstances can accelerate or impede the MTM processes of attracting, growing and retaining talent in a country (Lanvin & Evans, 2017). Subsequently, we turn to the MTM process of 'growing and developing talent', and discuss the strengths and weaknesses of the Dutch educational system. After that we present information about the Dutch workforce and (un)employment of the labor market as we focus on the processes of 'attracting and retaining talent' in the Netherlands. The chapter ends with a discussion and recommendations for future research.

The Netherlands: The Market, Business and Regulatory Landscape

The Netherlands is a small country (41.500 km^2) situated in West-Europe and is with a population of 17 million people one of the most densely populated countries in the world. Most people (around 40%) live in or around cities in the western part of the country. Less than a quarter of the Dutch population (22% in 2016) are immigrants from inside (10%) and outside (12%) of Europe (Huijnk & Andriessen, 2016). The majority of them are from families that have been in the Netherlands for several generations.

According to EPTA (2014), the Netherlands traditionally has derived much of its wealth from trade and other international transactions. The country is tightly integrated in the global economy through trade and foreign investment. The EPTA study (2014) indates that Dutch exports have grown rapidly in recent decades corresponding to the expansion of EU and world trade. Up until now the largest sectors of industry are services, retail and trade (Chamber of Commerce, 2017), with Schiphol Airport and the economic activity around it and the Port of Rotterdam being the two main drivers of the Dutch economy (EPTA, 2014). Although the majority of the Dutch companies (99%) are small and medium enterprises (SME's) with less than 250 employees (Bijl, Boelhouwer, Pommer, & Andriessen, 2015), the Netherlands is the home base for several multinational corporations (MNC), such as Heineken, Unilever and Royal Dutch Shell. The MNC's are accountable of 40% of all jobs in the country (CBS, 2015).

The Dutch government and business community have invested significantly in infrastructure—in roads, water management (half of the Netherlands lies below sea level), international (air)ports and in ICT infrastructure—to keep ahead of the international competition (EPTA, 2014). For the same reason the Dutch government also stimulates knowledge development, innovation and cooperation between knowledge institutes and the business community (Ministry of Education, Cultural Affairs and Science, 2011). Dutch organizations themselves—in particular large organizations—also invest in research and development (R&D), yet a study by Deuten (2015) shows that since 2007 the investments in R&D activities abroad surpass the investments in local R&D activities. For research activities Dutch companies choose regions where they have access to excellent knowledge institutes and researchers and where they find good opportunities to cooperate, while for development activities they choose regions with attractive market opportunities such as Asia (Deuten, 2015). Deuten (2015) warns against these increasing outward R&D investments, suggesting that the Netherlands is losing its position in science and technology (research) and that Dutch-based MNCs are stepping up their operations in foreign markets (development).

The GTCI (Lanvin & Evans, 2017) states that labor market flexibility is a hindering factor for doing business in the Netherlands. Other studies, however, have labeled the Dutch labor market as one of the most flexible labor markets within the European Union (e.g., Euwals, De Graaf-Zijl, & Van Vuuren, 2016). The country is famous for its 'polder-model' (EPTA, 2014), and traditionally the labor unions are powerful stakeholders and involved in the negotiation of collective labor agreements. Of the Dutch labor force, 80% are covered by a collective labor agreement. In line with the values of solidarity and inclusiveness Dutch labor law is known for its strong protection of employee's rights, but in 2015 the Work and Security Act was introduced to increase the ease of hiring and resignation staff for organizations (WEF, 2016). According to EPTA (2014) and the OECD (2016) the overall labor productivity in the Netherlands is high, but shows less growth than in other OECD countries.

The previously discussed market and business landscape—both enablers in the GTCI—highlight the talent context from an organizational perspective and mainly focus on the ease of doing business in a county. However, being attractive for organizations is one side of the 'talent magnet'. A country or a region must also be attractive for the talent or employees themselves. The presence of attractive and excellent performing organizations is important to make a region economically sustainable, but the literature on smart cities also shows that these regions take good care of their citizens by offering *all* a good place to live (e.g., Deloitte, 2015). Therefore, we add offering and protecting a good quality of life as an enabler. Several studies show that the Netherlands is good place to live (Bijl et al., 2015). The standards of living are high, with a good education and health care system and low criminality rates (OECD, 2016). The citizens of the Netherlands score their quality of life with a 7.38 on a 1 to 10 scale, which is close to 7.54 given by the Norwegian inhabitants who rank number 1 in happiness studies (Helliwell, Layard, & Sachs, 2017). Comparable to other countries the income inequality in the Netherlands is relatively low, but the gap between the lowest and the highest incomes has increased since 1985 (Kremer, Bovens, Schrijvers, & Went, 2014). In particular households with a single breadwinner and people with flexible contracts are becoming vulnerable groups on the labor market, and the government tries to prevent an increasing income gap by implementing several redistributive (tax) regulations and social security measures (Kremer et al., 2014). In general the Netherlands offers a stable governmental and political climate. Even during difficult times, such as the recent economic crisis, the refugee crisis and the announced exit of Britain from the European Union (Brexit), the Netherlands has proven to be stable and resilient (EPTA, 2014; OECD, 2014). For many years the country can be described as liberal but social, which is reflected in the parties represented in the Dutch parliament and government. The country has evolved from a Christian-conservative welfare state towards a more neo-liberal welfare state, where the sharp edges are softened by Christian and social-democratic influences (Hemerijck, 2013),

The GTCI (Lanvin & Evans, 2017)—from a strong neo-liberal perspective—hints that the solidarity and inclusiveness which are deeply embedded in the Dutch culture and the regulatory landscape are at odds with innovation and entrepreneurship (which are also a traditional values of the Netherlands) in the market landscape, and can hinder the attraction and retention of talent. Research by the Dutch Social and Economic Council (SER, 2017) shows that regional cooperation between educational and knowledge institutes, the business community and local government can have a significant effect on the wellbeing of *all* citizens in that region. It is beneficiary for developing talent (via learning), attracting and retaining talent (via employment) and productivity and innovation (via entrepreneurship). One of the examples in the SER-report is the cooperation in and around Eindhoven: Brainport. The starting point of Brainport was the closing of the DAF automobile factory and the re-organization of Philips in the 1990s, which cost the region 36,000 jobs. Local government leaders decided to start a new style of co-operation to accelerate economic and social growth for individuals, organizations and society. Together with the Technical University Eindhoven and the Chamber of Commerce they initiated a close Triple Helix collaboration between government, industry, and research and educational institutions (SER, 2017) aimed at achieving high tech innovation. Since that start in the 1990s the Brainport region—expanded to the city of Eindhoven and 21 municipalities around Eindhoven—has made a grand transition, from a region of shrinking industry and high unemployment to an international high-tech hotspot in a global network. All participants are focused on one thing: contributing to a sustainable, healthy and secure society with prosperity and wellbeing for all people by the means of collaboration. The local Triple Helix collaboration has proven to be successful: in the GTCI Report 2017 Eindhoven is the top 10 (8th position) of most talent minded cities in the world, illustrating that a region that invests in entrepreneurship, innovation and inclusiveness can be a true 'talent magnet' for both organizations as talents. Even though this is just one single example it shows that—in line with the previously mentioned SER (2017) findings—cooperation sometimes may be more rewarding than competition.

Growing and Developing Talent

The Netherlands is valued for its investments and successes in growing talent. In general the level of education is high in the Netherlands. The percentage of people with only primary or low level secondary education has decreased from around 30% in 2004 to less than 25% in 2014, while the percentage of people with a bachelor or master degree keeps growing gradually (around 30% in 2014) (Bijl et al., 2015). In this section we discuss the strengths and weaknesses of the Dutch educational system, and the implications for growing and developing talent.

Strengths of the Dutch Educational System

The high level of education is the result of the rather egalitarian educational system that aims to offers children from all socio-economic and ethnical backgrounds equal opportunities to develop their talents through high level education. Primary and secondary education are completely publicly funded, and parents do not have to pay a financial contribution. Also the larger part of higher education is funded by the government, but students, or their parents, have to contribute a relatively small part of 2,000 euro per year. For those who cannot afford this, there is an extensive loan system with soft conditions on payback.

Both in primary and secondary education there is extensive public supervision on all dimensions of the educational process to secure the quality of educational institutes and programs. This supervision concerns the safety of the buildings, class hours, teacher quality, pupils' and students' educational success, etc. All rules are laid down in a large set of laws and regulations and the compliance to these rules and regulations is frequently monitored by the Inspectorate for Education. In addition to the requirements concerning the educational process there is also public supervision on the level of the final exams of primary and secondary schools (although this has been delegated to an NGO with public authority) through a national, central exam. Although higher education institutes also have to give accountability of the quality of the educational standards every four to six years (through an accreditation by an authorized review committee), both universities (academic education) and universities of applied science (higher vocational education) independently determine their own educational standards. If the accreditation ends in a negative judgement, they have some time to improve their program, under penalty of the discontinuation of the program at hand.

The Dutch educational system has been relatively successful over the past decades in stimulating and facilitating upward social mobility (De Graaf, De Graaf, & Kraaykamp, 2000) and high skills levels (OECD, 2016). In particular female educational participation has increased significantly since the second World War (Portegijs & Van den Brakel, 2016). While older generations show men to accomplish higher educational results than women, recent generations show the opposite: women complete their initial education with higher degrees, better marks and faster than their male counterparts (Bijl et al., 2015; Portegijs & Van den Brakel, 2016). Also, educational participation as well as the education level of immigrants increased, although there still is a considerable gap between non-western immigrants and the native Dutch population (Bijl et al., 2015; Huijnk & Andriessen, 2016).

Weaknesses in the Dutch Educational System

The way the Dutch educational system 'manages' talent is not only a success story. The development of skills and talents of some groups are lagging behind (OECD, 2016). Also the Dutch Inspectorate for Education (Onderwijsinspectie, 2017) warns for not fully developing all potential talents in the Netherlands, and even wonders whether the country will be able to maintain its high educational level. Next we elaborate on some weak spots.

First, despite the intensive governmental supervision on the quality of the educational programs in primary and secondary education, the Inspectorate of Education (Onderwijsinspectie, 2017) states that the differences in educational quality can differ between schools, which affects the educational success of students significantly (Bijl et al., 2015).

A second weak spot concerns the early age children (and their parents) have to make a decision about their future education. After primary education—which is equal for all children between four to twelve years old—secondary education is divided into a complex system of multiple levels and routes, and when children reach the end of primary education they have to make a choice between a career in general secondary education or a career in vocational training. The problem with the young age at which the stream of pupils is divided, is that many children are still going through so much development that it is still not clear at all where their real talents lie. Once shunt into the siding of vocational training it is difficult to get back to the general educational track again, and some students remain in vocational training although this is not the optimal match from the perspective of their talent development (Onderwijsinspectie, 2017). Once you have chosen vocational training it is difficult to find your way back to general education, and if you succeed it usually takes a detour of at least some years. That and the fact that general secondary education is the main road towards the university causes a lot of parents to push their child to reach for general secondary education. Although the admittance to the various forms and levels of secondary education is in part based on the scores of a central exam in the 8th (final) grade, often parents put pressure on primary school teachers to advise that their child is capable of general secondary education. As a consequence some children are allocated to a school that demands too much of them, while others—whose parents are less committed or less successful in 'promoting' their children—are allocated to schools where they are likely to underperform, given their talents (Onderwijsinspectie, 2017). All in all, a situation has grown where Dutch children go to general secondary education if they possibly can, and only 'opt' for vocational education if the road towards general education is closed (Onderwijsinspectie, 2017). To some extent this has made secondary vocational training a repository of disappointed young people with low self-esteem for whom this type of education is more or less second best (Kloosterman, 2010).

The third problem concerns the bias against talents from children with an immigrant background, which is partly related to the aforementioned problems. As we mentioned before, the general level of education increased for children from immigrant families, yet education inequalities remain (Onderwijsinspectie, 2017; Huijnk & Andriessen, 2016). Parents who belong to the first generation of immigrants especially have little knowledge about the (relatively complicated) Dutch educational system. Often they even have to depend on their children when it comes to the communication with the children's teachers, as these parents do not master the Dutch language (Huijnk & Andriessen, 2016). But also often the children start their educational career already behind in the mastery of the Dutch language as the language at home is Turkish or Moroccan. This implies that part of their learning energy will not be devoted to the content of the topic they have to study, but to dealing with language problems (apart from cultural differences they have to bridge). For their part teachers may find it hard to get a 'true' picture of the capacities of the boy or girl originating from abroad. And as it is unlikely that these children's parents put much pressure on reaching for the highest level of education—the opportunity of learning for a job like that of a nurse or a lorry or bus driver is already a big step forward—teachers in primary education may go for the safe choice and advise their immigrant pupils to opt for the vocational road (Van Grinsven, Van der Woud, & Elphick, 2016; Onderwijsinspectie, 2017). Once again, talent may be lost.

The final deficiency we want to address concerns the limited interests of young Dutch students for educational programs in STEM (Science, Technology, Engineering and Mathematics). The GTCI (Lanvin & Evans, 2017) points at the impact of technology on our way of living and working and the necessity of technical skills for future talent. Yet, the performances of the Dutch pupils regarding mathematics and sciences is lagging behind other high income countries and need more attention (Onderwijsinspectie, 2017). Moreover, in 2016 just a quarter of all students in higher education opted for a study in Nature or Science at a Dutch university (VSNU, 2017). The share of females in STEM educational programs in secondary and higher education is even lower than that of males, although it is steadily growing (Portegijs & Van den Brakel, 2016). Looking for explanations for this lack of interest in studying technology experts usually come up with a twofold answer. The first part of the answer is that since the Golden Age the Netherlands has a strong tradition in trade and commerce, and even currently the Netherlands is not primarily an industrialist country (although several large multinational companies originate from the Netherlands). So, traditionally tradesmen, lawyers, economists and even clergymen have been held in higher regard than engineers and technicians. So far, the educational system has not been able to change this image. Recently, the government initiated several programs to stimulate youngsters—in particular girls—to choose for STEM-programs in higher education, and with some growing success (Portegijs & Van den Brakel, 2016). The second part of the twofold explanation of the low participation of the Dutch in STEM-programs at all educational levels is the little attention for technology and science in primary schools. Much of the attention in the educational programs is paid to learning language and mathematics (Bijl et al., 2015), and teachers have little knowledge on how to teach technology and science to young children (Verkenningscommissie Wetenschap en Technologie primair onderwijs, 2013). Up until recently technology and engineering have not been part of the curriculum of Dutch academies for teaching, and many current teachers—nowadays almost all teachers in primary education are female—do not have a particular interest in technology and have a rather traditional view of technology, so there was little chance that primary school pupils got involved with STEM (Verkenningscommissie Wetenschap en Technologie Primair onderwijs, 2013).

Developing Talent in Higher Education

To complete this part of the chapter on the role of the Dutch educational system in spotting and developing talent we pay some explicit attention to higher education. In general, higher education in the Netherlands is very good. As a matter of fact, all Dutch universities are within the top 200 of the Times Higher Education rankings for 2018 (THE, 2017) and in many disciplines Dutch scientists are among the most productive ones in the world (Rathenau Instituut, 2017). Still, no single Dutch university can compete with Harvard, Oxford or Cambridge. The Dutch university system has been characterized as "a plateau without peaks", because there are hardly any differences between the profiles and performances of the higher education institutes, but this characterization also applies to the performances of Dutch students. In Dutch society as a whole, a lot of effort goes to keeping the slow developers and those at risk of staying behind connected to the bunch, and to give them the same opportunities to get a bachelor or master degree as the more brilliant students (Onderwijsinspectie, 2017). The latter group received far less attention, because of the assumption that they would be able to find their way anyway, so there is no need to worry about them. Lately, this approach is changing. Within higher education we see institutes organizing special classes for top talents and developing talent programs for the most promising young scholars (Onderwijsinspectie, 2017). It seems like the traditional Dutch saying "act normal; then you are special enough" is losing its strength, and in higher education the talent concept is increasingly referring to the best performing students instead of all students.

Attracting and Retaining Talent

In general the Dutch labor force is well educated and highly productive (EPTA, 2014; OECD, 2016). Moreover, it seems that in 2017 the Dutch labor market is recovering from the economic crises with a decreasing unemployment rate (July 2017: 4.7%) and increasing numbers of jobs available on the labor market (CBS, 2017b). Yet, we see some frictions which affect the attraction and retention of talent. Next we discuss these frictions.

Talent Attraction Through Formal Recruitment

After completing their studies most young people start looking for a job, and most of them succeed in finding one within a reasonable period of time. Although youth unemployment has peaked during the economic crisis, it has never exceeded the level of about 15 percent and remained much lower than the alarming levels of thirty or forty percent in some Mediterranean countries. Yet, many young people making the transition to the labor market find it hard to deal with the detailed requirements in terms of qualifications at the demand side of the labor market. The high degree of specialization and segmentation in the Dutch educational system is also reflected in the labor market and employers' behavior. Often (vacant) jobs are described in large detail, including the specific qualifications and diplomas the applicant needs to have. If an applicant does not have the proper diploma, the chance of him/her passing the first round of selection is very small. Dutch employers take the whole diploma system very seriously and are not inclined to 'experiment' too much with candidates that seem to have the proper talents, but lack the formal qualifications to prove this. In many cases this is quite logical. Legal rules require, for example, hospitals only to employ nurses who have a certificate for specific medical actions in order to protect the patients. The same holds for teachers to guarantee the quality of education, bus drivers to guarantee the safety of the passengers, etc. Also in cases where there are no legal requirements employers tend to look for applicants from particular educational segments only, and often ignore the talents of those who do have the competences, but lack the diplomas. So, contrary to, for instance, the UK one will hardly find any philosophers or historians within the ranks of high civil servants.

Underemployment of Female Talent

According to the GTCI the lower labor participation of females, together with those of immigrants, is one of the causes of the relatively lower scores of the Netherlands on the talent attraction and retention pillar (Lanvin & Evans, 2017). Yet, female labor market participation in the Netherlands has risen considerably over the past decades (from 44% in 1986 to 70% in 2014), and is now right behind the Scandinavian countries in the European rankings (Van Echtelt, Croezen, Vlasblom, & De Voogd-Hamelink, 2016; Portegijs & Van den Brakel, 2016). Nonetheless, a major problem with female labor market participation in the Netherlands is that most women work part time (Van Echtelt, Schellingerhout, & De Voogd-Hamelink, 2015). Although there is a positive correlation between women's educational level and the number of hours they work, even many high educated women work less hours (e.g. 32 hours/week) than their male counterparts; low educated women often work 12–20 hours per week (Van Echtelt et al., 2015). This long standing part time culture is not beneficial for women's economic independency, nor does it help them to break the so-called 'glass ceiling'. The share of women in the boardrooms of large Dutch companies is only 10 percent, while women only make up 18 percent of the full professors at Dutch universities (Portegijs & Van den Brakel, 2016). These figures imply an enormous waste of female talent. This is more striking if one realizes that for almost two decades women have been outperforming men in terms of educational attainment (see previous section). The 'returns on investments' in female talent could be much higher if women would work more hours and would have access to the top of organizations, politics, and science. Of course, the hours spent outside the labor market have 'returns' too: Dutch children are among the happiest in the world (UNICEF, 2013) and that may be partly due to the large amounts of care provided by women with part-time jobs. It is very common for Dutch female workers to shift from a full time job to a part-time job once their children are born, while the young father continues to work in a full time job and tries to 'mold his job' to take care of the children occasionally (Portegijs & Van den Brakel, 2016). Research even shows that the majority of the Dutch male workers prefer a full time job while most female workers show a preference for a part-time position (Van Echtelt et al., 2015). This points at a suboptimal use of talent, because female talent is underutilized in the labor market and male talent is underutilized in the domain of care. Despite the many public campaigns and policy measures to promote a more equal division of work and family tasks between women and men, the unbalanced division of tasks is deeply rooted in Dutch society and organizations and still rules the lives of many families in the Netherlands (Portegijs & Van den Brakel, 2016).

Dealing With an Ageing Workforce

Just like in most other European countries the population in the Netherlands is ageing due to increasing longevity on the one hand and low birth rates on the other. According the OECD the ageing population in the Netherlands is going to put serious constraints on the labor market and labor productivity (EPTA, 2014). In order to strengthen the financial foundations of the welfare state the Dutch government has taken several measures since the start of the 21st century to discourage early retirement and to increase the official retirement age (Klosse & Schippers, 2008). This age rises to 67 in 2021 and from then on it will be linked to the development of life expectancy in the Netherlands. This institutional rearrangement raises the question of how to retain the talents of older workers. Over the last decade the average actual retirement rate in the Netherlands has risen from below 60 to somewhere between 63 and 64 (which is still below the official retirement age that the Netherlands has known since 1957) (Van Echtelt et al., 2016). Research shows that Dutch organizations employ what may be called a 'permissive' strategy towards the older workers within their company (Van Dalen, Henkens, Henderikse, & Schippers, 2006; Van Echtelt et al., 2015). Older workers are being spared. They are for instance exempted from night shifts, have additional holidays or shorter working hours to grant those older workers who have contributed to the company's fortunes for a long time a decent and pleasant way to the end of their labor market career. Contrary to this permissive strategy is the broad reluctance of Dutch employers to hire older workers once they have become unemployed (Van Dalen, Henkens, & Schippers, 2010). More than in many other European countries employers in the Netherlands think there is an unbalance between older workers' productivity and labor costs (Conen, 2013; Van Echtelt et al., 2015), and complain that older workers' talents are worn and outdated. For their own older workers with a limited scope of competences they still have some tasks available, often tasks these workers have been performing for ages and tasks that will eventually disappear, but hiring older workers is considered a bridge too far for most employers (Van Dalen et al., 2010). Consequently, the share of older workers within the group of long term unemployed has grown significantly (CBS, 2017c). For those long term unemployed older workers the increase in the official retirement age does not imply an extension of working life, but an extension of the period they will be on social benefits. So, despite the institutional changes the Dutch labor market has not found a way yet to deal properly with the remaining talents of older workers. Moreover, the traditional focus of employers/managers on young workers to fill job openings may be outdated, because it neglects the changes in the modern, much more service oriented economy in which many customers are ageing too. An older employee can be more appealing or trustworthy to these customers than a young employee.

The Selective Use of Talents of Immigrants

In the 1950s and 1960s the Dutch government encouraged immigrants to come to work in the Netherlands in order to fill in the many hard to fill vacant low skilled positions in Dutch industry (Ooijevaar & Verkooijen, 2015). These workers were mainly men from Spain, Italy, Turkey and Morocco who came to the Netherlands without their families. Due to the economic crisis (and its effects on the labor market) this stream of low skilled and low educated immigrants was brought to an end in the 1970s and 1980s. Since then migration is mainly based on family reunification and refugees asylum. During the past decade labor immigration increased again (Ooijevaar & Verkooijen, 2015). On the one hand a lot of workers from Middle and East-European countries (Poland, Bulgaria and Romania) came to the Netherlands to work in low skilled jobs in, for example, agriculture and construction (CBS, 2017a). On the other hand there is an increasing inflow of highly educated workers from abroad who are attracted by organizations to fulfill jobs that require specific skills and knowledge that are not available on the Dutch labor market (Ooijevaar & Verkooijen, 2015). Many of those expats are males working in high income jobs in business services and trade, in health care organizations and higher education institutes (Ooijevaar & Verkooijen, 2015). The assumption is that these migrant workers—both the low and high skilled ones—only contribute to the Dutch labor market and economy for a short period of time, because they do not have the intention to stay in the Netherlands for long. However, there is hardly any empirical evidence available to ground this hypothesis (Ooijevaar & Verkooijen, 2015).

So, where the 'new immigrants' are explicitly recruited for their specific talents and unique skills, the talents of the immigrants that came to the Netherlands in the 20th century (and their children) are underused. Their position on the Dutch labor market is particularly vulnerable. Despite the aforementioned rising education level of children from non-Western migrant groups, research on the labor market position of migrants shows that the talents and skills immigrant youngsters developed at school are not sufficiently used in the world of work. In particular access to (permanent) work remains a key stumbling block, with unemployment—including youth unemployment—almost three times as high as in the native Dutch population (Huijnk & Andriessen, 2016). The migrant unemployment rate is heavily influenced by the economic climate: in a weak economic climate migrant unemployment rises rapidly and the gap relative to Dutch natives widens, while the unemployment gap narrows when the economic climate improves (Huijnk & Andriessen, 2016). Because employers have more choice in times of economic weakness, the person's origin counts for more. Discrimination of immigrant workers by Dutch employers still exists and has a negative effect on their opportunities to find a job (Huijnk & Andriessen, 2016). The weak labor market position of migrants is also reflected in the high proportion of flexible jobs in this group. Nowadays a permanent job is scarce for all young people, but migrants more often end up in a non-permanent job than native Dutch people (37% versus 24% among Dutch natives) (Huijnk & Andriessen, 2016). Research also shows that, despite the rising occupational level of second generation migrants, income differentials are still considerable and have widened slightly over the last decade, again emphasizing the vulnerable position of migrants in the Dutch labor market (Huijnk & Andriessen, 2016).

Maintenance of Talent: Lifelong Learning

The increasing global competition and the rapid speed of technological innovation present a major challenge to the Dutch economy: how do we keep the competences of the labor force up to date? For almost two decades the necessity to invest in lifelong learning—i.e. all post-initial activities aimed at the maintenance and renewal of human capital that allows people to be productive in the labor market—has been on the agenda of both employers' organizations and unions (Van Echtelt et al., 2015). Although the GTCI praises the Netherlands for its lifelong learning investments, reality shows that there is not much action yet. Lifelong learning activities are well below the level most employers and policy makers consider necessary to keep up with technological progress and to keep up with the increasing demand for ICT-competences. A major problem in this field, and an explanation for the relatively low level of investments in lifelong learning, is the high degree of contract flexibility in the Dutch labor market (Van Echtelt et al., 2015). While a job for life with one employer was more or less the rule in the 1960s, this job for life has become the exception. The proportion of employees with a fixed-term contract, a job with a temporary agency or in self-employment increased from 13% in 2004 to 19% in 2014 (Van Echtelt et al., 2016). This growing share of non-permanent jobs seems to be detrimental for investments in lifelong learning and the maintenance of human capital, as both employers and employees avoid the risk of investing in learning activities with uncertain returns. Research shows that many Dutch employers do not or only to a limited extent invest in the training of employees, and especially those with a temporary contract are deprived from formal learning opportunities (Van Echtelt et al., 2015), as the returns will probably go to another company. In a similar way, just a very small portion of the Dutch workers (6% in 2014) think that their skills and knowledge are obsolete and require improvement via training (Van Echtelt et al., 2016). In particular employees with fixed-term contracts refrain from investing in training activities when they do not know whether they will have a job where they can use their new knowledge and skills in the future (Van Echtelt et al., 2016). Despite the necessity to invest in higher levels of lifelong learning and maintenance of human capital, successive Dutch cabinets—both left wing and right wing—have been reluctant to take serious and substantial initiatives to develop a proper institutional framework for lifelong learning. All in all, government, employers and unions are looking at each other wondering who is going to take the initiative here.

Fortunately, when it comes to the maintenance of talent it is not all doom and gloom. Although the level of investment may be suboptimal, there is still a large number of workers (especially those with a permanent contract) who do frequently participate in training activities (OECD, 2016). But also within this group one may question the division between those who do and those who do not participate. Systematic research is not available, but some studies illustrate that participation in training activities is subject to the so-called Matthew effect: employers grant training opportunities to employees who perform well (as a kind of secondary benefit), while those whose productivity lags behind (and would benefit from additional human capital investment) are not entitled for these 'benefits' (Van Echtelt et al., 2015; Van Echtelt et al., 2016). So, once again the conclusion must be that there is still room for improvement when it comes to the optimal use of talents in the Dutch economy.

To Conclude

We come to the conclusion that, from a macro perspective, there is no optimal use of talents in the labor market and within organizations in the Netherlands. There are differences between people of different educational levels and streams, between flexible workers and individuals with a permanent contract, etc. Older workers may lack some necessary talents, but the talents they do have are not always fully recognized and optimally used. Also female talents are not optimally used in the labor market, while male talents are not optimally used when it comes to care and activities outside the labor market. We also pointed out the suboptimal use of the talents of migrants. All talents would benefit from more systematic attention for the maintenance and renewal of human capital throughout the life course.

Discussion and Recommendations

As we stated in the introduction, the Netherlands belongs to the 10% of countries that offer organizations and individuals an excellent context to attract, identify, develop and deploy their talents (Lanvin & Evans, 2017). Our in-depth and qualitative description of the way the Netherlands attracts and retains talent indeed shows that the country excels in the development of talent. In particular education offered at young citizens is good: the quality is high (due to strict regulations and high quality standards) and up until the master degree education is available for all young people, reflecting the principles of equality and solidarity. However, regarding the development of talent we pointed at several deficiencies, which indicate that not all skills and talents, such as the talents of young people originating from immigrant families, are not fully recognized and developed. Also the development of workers through (formal) lifelong learning activities is limited. The latter is in contrast to the findings of the GTCI (Lanvin & Evans, 2017). In the long term these deficiencies will result in the underuse of the talents of some groups on the Dutch labor market, and an obsolescence of knowledge and skills. More investments in the Dutch educational system are required to boost the skills and talents of all (OECD, 2016) if the Netherlands wants to keep its top position regarding the development of talent.

The Netherlands has a strong profile regarding the attraction and retention of talent on the Dutch labor market. Although the workweek is rather short in the Netherlands, productivity of those working is high (OECD, 2016). Yet, this productivity is delivered by a select group of workers. We detected an underutilization of the talents of immigrant, female and older workers—the 'outsiders'—while the talents of many young, highly educated and male workers—the 'insiders'—are overutilized. We do not agree with Lanvin and Evans (2017) who claim that the lack of labor market flexibility is a problem. Increasing labor market flexibility, as the GTCI suggests, can even have a hindering effect on lifelong learning activities, and worsen the already vulnerable labor market positions of the 'outsiders'. We state that the tension between insiders and outsiders seems to cause more difficulties than the lack of labor market flexibility detected by the GTCI. The question even arises whether this gap between insiders and outsiders is the cause for the Netherlands not being in the top 10 countries in the talent indices and can be a threat for the future.

We want to point out a discrepancy regarding the talent concept in developing and in retaining and deploying talent. One of the core debates in TM at the organizational level is whether to conceive TM as an inclusive approach (aimed at all employees) or an exclusive approach (aimed at a select group of high performers or high potentials) (e.g., Dries, 2013). When we make a parallel to the MTM approach of the Netherlands we see that in the educational system an inclusive approach prevails as all young Dutch citizens are offered equal chances to learn and develop their talents. Nonetheless, once on the labor market this inclusive approach shifts towards a more exclusive orientation in which organizations are mainly interested in employing the highly productive 'insiders'. Yet, this tension is changing. In education there is more attention for special programs for highly gifted children and students (a shift towards a more exclusive talent approach), while in organizations—regardless of governmental policies on this matter—the awareness of their role as an employer in society grows as they put effort in developing and deploying the strengths of all employees, including the talents of those with a weaker position on the Dutch labor market. The question is how this blurry and confusing talent concept is going to work out in the future. It definitely demands a more differentiated approach to manage talent at both the macro and the organizational level, in which society and organizations adapt to the different talents available. Yet, this is something many organizations and governmental entities are not used to do and find difficult to achieve.

Another finding in our chapter is that—in line with the GTCI—the Dutch regulatory and market landscape is focused at making the Netherlands a pleasant country to live, work and do business in. The quality standards are high, and based on the principles of equality vs. entrepreneurship and innovation the Dutch government together with national and local stakeholders aims to create a breeding ground for talent. Although these values can be at odds with each other—which can cause tensions again—the chapter illustrated that some local communities exploit those circumstances in a beneficiary way. Especially in regions where local government organizations collaborate with private and public sector organizations—such as in the Brainport region of Eindhoven—the talents of all people are recognized and deployed. Together with the broad embracement of technology and the good (ICT) infrastructure in those regions a true breeding ground for talent arises, which makes the region also interesting for innovative organizations. In the Brainport Region in Eindhoven there was a real sense of urgency to work together, but what about the regions that don't find that sense of urgency? Are they going to feel the need to cooperate with competitors to win the battle for talent? The previously discussed example of Brainport shows that a good regulatory landscape creates the necessary basics, but active actor involvement at a local level and creating possibilities to establish an innovative and sustainable (labor) market landscape at the regional level is essential to make a change.

This chapter is one of the first attempts to give an in-depth and qualitative picture of the talent mindedness of the country. Although there is a lot of research on the several aspects of MTM in the Netherlands, most of that is quantitative or highlights just one part of MTM. We therefore encourage scholars to continue this exploration and complement our analysis with more details and information. We also recommend more research on a regional level. It would be interesting to develop a regional ranking for the Netherlands, but that would require developing reliable pillars to measure MTM at the local level. Additionally, we also noticed that at the regional level not all required information is available, or scattered between different databases. A regional ranking implies that several regions have to gather the same data and provide this data for research. Open access of data is something to strive for.

Besides improving local measures of MTM, we noticed that the GTCI and HCI implicitly emphasize the economic value of developing and attracting talent at a macro level, while our review of local activities also shows that inclusiveness can go hand in hand with entrepreneurship and innovation. We therefore encourage the indices to include some non-economic societal outcomes such as quality of life and well-being. Finally, in the discussion we pointed at some tensions in MTM in the Netherlands. It is interesting to do more research on those tensions—how and to what extend do they exist—and to elaborate on how to deal at a national and organizational level with these tensions. After all, this data presented suggests that the way the Netherlands deals with inclusiveness, exclusiveness and innovation in MTM will make a great difference in keeping the country's position in the top 10% or the slide down to a position in the middle of the rankings.

References

Bijl, R., Boelhouwer, J., Pommer, E., & Andriessen, I. (2015). *De sociale staat van Nederland (2015)*. Den Haag: Sociaal en Cultureel Planbureau.

Boussebaa, M., & Morgan, G. (2008). Managing talent across national borders: The challenges faced by an international retail group. *Critical Perspectives on International Business, 4*(1), 25–41.

Centraal Bureau voor de Statistiek (CBS). (2015). *Internationaliseringsmonitor 2015* (3e kwartaal). Retrieved from www.cbs.nl/nl-nl/publicatie/2015/30/internationaliseringsmonitor-2015-derde-kwartaal.

Centraal Bureau voor de Statistiek (CBS). (2017a). *Meer personen uit Oost-Europa aan het werk in Nederland*. Retrieved on October 12, 2017 from www.cbs.nl/nl-nl/nieuws/2017/05/meer-personen-uit-oost-europa-aan-het-werk-in-nederland.

Centraal Bureau voor de Statistiek (CBS). (2017b). *Totaalbeeld arbeidsmarkt*. Retrieved from www.cbs.nl/nl-nl/achtergrond/2017/38/totaalbeeld-arbeidsmarkt.

Centraal Bureau voor de Statistiek (CBS). (2017c). *Langdurige werkloosheid daalt ook onder 55 plussers*. Retrieved from www.cbs.nl/nl-nl/nieuws/2017/07/langdurige-werkloosheid-daalt-ook-onder-55-plussers.

Chamber of Commerce. (2017). *Bedrijfsleven 2016. Jaaroverzicht ondernemend Nederland*. Retrieved from www.kvk.nl/download/Jaaroverzicht%20Bedrijfsleven%20Nederland%202016%20versie%20US7_tcm109-433766.pdf.

Collings, D. G. (2014). Integrating global mobility and global talent management: Exploring the challenges and strategic opportunities. *Journal of World Business, 49*(2), 253–261.

Collings, D. G., Scullion, H., & Vaiman, V. (2011). European perspectives on talent management. *European Journal of International Management, 5*(5), 453–462.

Conen, W. (2013). *Older workers: The view of Dutch employers in a European perspective*. Amsterdam: Amsterdam University Press.

Cooke, L., Saini, D., & Wang, J. (2014). Talent management in China and India: A comparison of management perceptions and human resource practices. *Journal of World Business, 49*(2), 225–235.

De Graaf, N., De Graaf, P., & Kraaykamp, G. (2000). Parental cultural capital and educational attainment in the Netherlands: A refinement of the cultural capital perspective. *Sociology of Education, 73*(2), 92–111.

Deloitte. (2015). *Smart cities*. Retrieved from www2.deloitte.com/content/dam/Deloitte/nl/Documents/public-sector/deloitte-nl-ps-smart-cities-report.pdf.

Deuten, J. (2015). *R&D goes global: Policy implications for the Netherlands as a knowledge region in a global perspective*. The Hague: Rathenau Instituut.

Dries, N. (2013). The psychology of talent management: A review and research agenda. Human Resource Management Review, 23(4), 272-285.

European Parlementary Technology Assesment (EPTA). (2014). *Productivity in Europe and the United States. Technology Trends and Policy Measures.* Retrieved from epub.oeaw.ac.at/0xc1aa500e_0x0031e598.pdf.

Euwals, R., De Graaf-Zijl, M., & Van Vuuren, M. (2016). *Flexibiliteit op de arbeidsmarkt. CPB policy brief 2016/14.* Den Haag: Sociaal en Cultureel Planbureau.

Gallardo-Gallardo, E., & Thunnissen, M. (2016). Standing on the shoulders of giants? A critical review of empirical talent management research. *Employee Relations, 38*(1), 31–56.

Helliwell, J., Layard, R., & Sachs, J. (2017). *World happiness report 2017.* Retrieved from worldhappiness.report/ed/2017/.

Hemerijck, A. (2013). *Changing welfare states.* Oxford: Oxford University Press.

Huijnk, W., & Andriessen, I. (2016). Integratie in zicht? In *De integratie van migranten in Nederland op acht terreinen nader bekeken.* Den Haag: SCP.

Khilji, E., & Schuler, R. (2017). Talent management in the global context. In D. Collings, K. Mellahi & W. Cascio (Eds.), *Oxford handbook of talent management.* Oxford: Oxford University Press.

Khilji, S. E., Tarique, I., & Schuler, R. S. (2015). Incorporating the macro view in global talent management. *Human Resource Management Review, 25*(3), 236–248.

Kloosterman, J. (2010). *Social background and children's educational careers: The primary and secondary effects of social background over transitions and over time in the Netherlands.* Nijmegen: Radboud Universiteit.

Klosse, S., & Schippers, J. (2008). The integration of older workers in European labour markets: Between macro desires and micro reality. In F. Pennings, Y. Konijn, & A. Veldman (Eds.), *Social responsibility in labour relations* (pp. 391–411). Alphen aan den Rijn: Kluwer Law International.

Kremer, M., Bovens, M., Schrijvers, E., & Went, R. (Eds.). (2014). *WRR-Verkenning 28 Hoe ongelijk is Nederland? Een verkenning van de ontwikkeling en gevolgen van economische ongelijkheid.* Amsterdam: WRR.

Lanvin, B., & Evans, P. (2013). *The global talent competitiveness index.* INSEAD Business School, Adecco Group and Human Capital Leadership Institute.

Lanvin, B., & Evans, P. (2014). *The global talent competitiveness index 2014: Growing talent for today and tomorrow.* Singapore: Adecco. Retrieved from www.insead.edu/sites/default/files/assets/dept/globalindices/docs/GTCI-2014-report.pdf.

Lanvin, B., & Evans, P. (2016). *The global talent competitiveness index, 2015–2016: Talent attraction and international mobility; Growing talent for today and tomorrow.* Retrieved from www.insead.edu/sites/default/files/assets/dept/globalindices/docs/GTCI-2015-2016-report.pdf.

Lanvin, B., & Evans, P. (2017). *The global talent competitiveness index, 2017: Talent and technology.* Retrieved from www.insead.edu/sites/default/files/assets/dept/globalindices/docs/GTCI-2017-report.pdf.

Ministry of Education, Cultural Affairs and Science. (2011). *Kwaliteit in verscheidenheid. strategische agende hoger onderwijs, onderzoek en wetenschap.* The Hague: Ministry of Education, Cultural Affairs and Science.

OECD (2017). *Gross domestic product (GDP).* Retrieved on September 30, 2017 from data.oecd.org/gdp/gross-domestic-product-gdp.htm.

Onderwijsinspectie. (2017). *Onderwijsverslag. De staat van het onderwijs.* Den Haag: Ministerie van Onderwijs, Cultuur en Wetenschap.

Ooijevaar, J., & Verkooijen, L. (2015). *Expat, wanneer ben je het? Een afbakening van in het buitenland geboren werknemers op basis van loon.* Den Haag: Centraal Bureau voor de Statistiek.

Paauwe, J. (2004). *HRM and performance: Achieving long-term viability.* Oxford: Oxford University Press on Demand.

Portegijs, W., & Van den Brakel, M. (2016). *Emancipatiemonitor (2016).* Den Haag: Sociaal en Cultureel Planbureau/Centraal Bureau voor de Statistiek.

Rathenau Instituut. (2017). *Factsheet Wetenschappelijke output.* Retrieved from www.rathenau.nl/nl/page/wetenschappelijke-output.

Scullion, H., Collings, D. G., & Caligiuri, P. (2010). Global talent management. *Journal of World Business, 45*(2), 105–108.

Shi, Y., & Handfield, R. (2012). Talent management issues for multinational logistics companies in China: Observations from the field. *International Journal of Logistics Research and Applications, 15*(3), 163–179.

Sociaal en Economische Raad (SER). (2017). *Regionaal samenwerken. Leren van praktijken.* Retrieved from www.ser.nl/nl/publicaties/adviezen/2010-2019/2017/regionaal-samenwerken.aspx.

Thunnissen, M., Boselie, P., & Fruytier, G. (2013). A review of talent management: 'Infancy or adolescence?' *The International Journal of Human Resource Management, 24*(9), 1744–1761.

Thunnissen, M., & Gallardo-Gallardo, E. (2017). *Talent management in practice: An integrated and dynamic approach.* Bingley: Emerald Publishing.

Times Higher Education. (2017). *World university rankings 2018.* Retrieved from www.timeshighereducation.com/world-university-rankings/2018/world-ranking#!/page/0/length/25/locations/NL/sort_by/rank/sort_order/asc/cols/stats.

UNICEF Office of Research. (2013). *Child well-being in rich countries: A comparative overview.* Innocenti Report Card 11, UNICEF Office of Research, Florence.

Van Dalen, H., Henkens, K., Henderikse, W., & Schippers, J. (2006). *Dealing with an ageing labour force: What do European employers expect and do?* Report 73. The Hague: NIDI.

Van Dalen, H., Henkens, K., & Schippers, J. (2010). Productivity of older workers: Perceptions of employers and employees. *Population and Development Review, 36*(2), 309–330.

Van Echtelt, P., Croezen, S., Vlasblom, J. D., & De Voogd-Hamelink, M. (2016). *Aanbod van Arbeid 2016.* Den Haag: Sociaal en Cultureel Planbureau.

Van Echtelt, P., Schellingerhout, R., & De Voogd-Hamelink, M. (2015). *Vraag naar arbeid 2015.* Den Haag: Sociaal en Cultureel Planbureau.

Van Grinsven, V., Van der Woud, L., & Elphick, E. (2016). *Kansengelijkheid in het onderwijs. Meningen en ideeën vanuit het onderwijs zelf.* Utrecht: DUO Onderzoek.

Verkenningscommissie wetenschap en technologie primair onderwijs. (2013). *Advies Verkenningscommissie wetenschap en technologie primair onderwijs.* Retrieved from www.poraad.nl/files/legacy_files/advies_verkenningscommissie_wetenschap_en_technologie_po.pdf.

VSNU. (2017). Aantal ingeschreven studenten. Retrieved September 30, 2017 from www.vsnu.nl/f_c_ingeschreven_studenten.html.

World Economic Forum. (2013). *Human capital report 2013.* Retrieved from www3.weforum.org/docs/WEF_HumanCapitalReport_2013.pdf.

World Economic Forum. (2016). *Human capital report 2016.* Retrieved from www3.weforum.org/docs/HCR2016_Main_Report.pdf.

9

Macro Talent Management in Australia

Balancing Industrial Relations, Isolation and Global Competitiveness

Sharna Wiblen and Anthony McDonnell

Introduction

Australia is a country of striking landscapes, a rich ancient culture and one of the world's strongest economies. It is the sixth-largest country in land area and is the only nation to govern an entire continent.

(Australian Government Department of Foreign Affairs and Trade, 2016, p. 6)

Although the country we know today as "Australia" arose from the arrival of the First Fleet at Botany Bay in New South Wales in 1788, the country is home to one of the world's oldest cultures, with Australia's Aboriginal people arriving on the vast land mass at least 60,000 years ago. The country today, and the talent management context is firmly rooted in Australia's historical evolution and the convict heritage whereby the first penal colonies were established by convicts, marines and their families, from the British Empire. In 1901, the previously formed penal colonies united to form the Federal Commonwealth of Australia. To this day, the country remains a colony of the British Empire and part of the Commonwealth.[1] No matter one's perspective of Australia's history, it is evident that migration has been pivotal in shaping modern-day Australia with the penal history leading to the development of a strong labour and employment relations context whereby conciliation and arbitration are central and key influencers on issues of attracting and managing talent.

Talent management continues to be a pressing concern for Australian industry (ManpowerGroup, 2017). Gaining insights into the current and future challenges of the HR profession, a survey of more than 5,500 executives from 109 countries found that most industries and countries will experience a widening talent gap, notably for high skilled positions and for the next generation of middle and senior leaders (Strack et al., 2010). Moreover, it is clear that for each country, managing talent is a critical factor of importance for organisational success (Strack et al., 2010). Despite the prevalence of such discourses, national responses to recent economic events have differed across countries, as has the war for talent. In contrast to other parts of the world which sought to downsize their investments in human resources in response to the Global Financial Crisis (GFC), the salience of the war for talent in Australia shows limited sign of abating (Wiblen, Dery, & Grant, 2012). Australia is an interesting case in that employment appeared to be largely protected vis-à-vis many other western economies through and directly post-GFC (Boyle & McDonnell, 2013). Reports examining Australia's national talent context (see Hays, 2011; P. Wilson, 2010) predict that skills shortages, at all organisational levels, will continue to challenge management such that 'the ability to overcome skills shortages and secure top talent will be critical to business success' (Hays, 2011, p. 2). Overall, the ability for Australian organisations to attract and identify the 'best people' or 'talent' continues to be a significant challenge and the processes and tools deployed fervently debated.

In this chapter, we draw from pivotal components of Khilji and Schuler's (2016) framework in offering applicable data and information about historical and contemporary factors associated with macro talent management within Australia. To garner an understanding of the opportunities and challenges associated with how organisations enact talent management strategies, we first expand on the macro factors arising from Australia's national culture and the prevailing influence of employment relations, while also highlighting the pivotal role of unions and employer associations. Next, we highlight Australia's demographics, including its small internal talent pool and ageing population. After recognising the country's divergent opinions about the need for, and benefits of, immigration and mobility, we then discuss attitudes towards, and the support for, formalised education. To provide a coherent picture of Australia's position worldwide, we also discuss the country's competitiveness. Our chapter concludes with an overview of these factors and poses numerous questions about the sustainability of current practices, as well as potential opportunities and challenges.

The Macro Talent Management (MTM) Factors

We commence with an overview of the macro environmental factors that significantly influence talent management within the context of Australia.

National Culture

Labour, Employment and Industrial Relations

Labour and employment relations influenced the evolution of Australia with industrial relations, more specifically, underpinning Australia's national culture. The influence of industrial relations on present-day talent management activities is rooted in the country's early history as a penal colony. Most convicts arriving in Australia from 1788 onwards did so from various British colonies including India and Canada, as well as Maoris from New Zealand, Chinese from Hong Kong and slaves from the Caribbean (Lawrence & Davies, 2011). Individuals convicted of crimes such as larceny, robbery or rural crimes, on numerous occasions were "transported" as "punishment" by boat to Australia. Working convicts who, upon being allocated tasks according to previous occupations and skills, underpinned a system of labour that included carpenters, brick makers, nurses, servants, cattlemen, shepherds and farmers. Female convicts upon arrival fulfilled the role of wives and mothers. Females could escape their criminal and convict status through marriage. Convicts were seen as sources of labour from 1810, with their labour and skills employed to advance the British colony's presence in Australia and establish many foundational attributes of society. This centred on public facilities such as roads, causeways, bridges, courthouses and hospitals (Australian Government, 2016).[2]

The Constitution of the Commonwealth of Australia, introduced at federation in 1901, afforded the newly established federal government the power to make industrial laws. These industrial laws could, however, only be made in respect to "conciliation and arbitration for the prevention and settlement of industrial disputes extending beyond the limits of any one State" (section 51, para xxxv). Adopted by the federal jurisdiction in 1904, the Australian system of conciliation and arbitration sought to address political and economic challenges that had arisen from periods of economic development and the inherent trade relationship between some colonies in Australia and the mother country, Britain. A booming domestic manufacturing industry, combined with declining prices for commodities exports in the late 19th Century, had resulted in conflict as labour and capital groups fervently debated who would bear the costs of changes in international trade relationships. This period of political and economic unrest gave rise to tensions between business and trade unions resulting in a series of strikes.

The Australian system of conciliation and arbitration was further formalised through the *Commonwealth Court of Conciliation and Arbitration Act 1904*. This Act legitimated and empowered unions to represent workers and make claims to the Court on behalf of all employees in an industry. Unions were also able to force employers to compulsory conciliation and arbitration, even if unwilling. Furthermore, once a decision about pay or other terms of employment was arbitrated, those conditions were from thereon legally enforceable and referred to as an "award" (Lansbury & Wailes, 2004). This was the first body of its kind in the world, and therefore clearly making Australia a unique employment context. In 1908, based on the *Harvester Case*, the first minimum wage was set by this Court. This landmark event stated that the basic living wage for a (male) worker was an amount that allowed him to support a family of five (5).

The introduction of the 1904 Act and Court set the foundations for Australia's industrial relations system. This system, whereby there is an iterative negotiation between employers and employees, requires all organisations to provide all employees with a set of minimum standards. This includes, but is not limited to: a 38-hour working week; 10 days sick leave; 4 weeks annual leave; equal pay for equal work; 12 months unpaid maternity leave; and 18 weeks paid maternity leave at the minimum wage. Australia's lowest paid workers (from July 1, 2017) receive AU$18.29 per hour or AU$694.00 per 38-hour week (before tax).

The International Labour Organisation's (ILO) latest *Global Wage Report* demonstrates 'that the extent of wage inequality within enterprises—and its contribution to total wage inequality—has perhaps been underestimated in the past . . . [but] evidence shows that broad collective bargaining coverage contributes to a narrower distribution of income and more stable growth' (International Labour Organization, 2016, p. iv). The perceived relationship between wages and collective bargaining, a dominant feature of Australia's national culture and labour relations, may help explain why Australia's wage growth is above that of other countries. Australia ranks 2nd of G20 countries behind the Republic of Korea for real wages growth since 2006 (10 per cent). Australia is positioned above Canada (9 per cent), Germany (7 per cent), and the United States (5 per cent), and significantly above Japan, Italy and the United Kingdom where real wages declined (by 2, 6 and 7 per cent, respectively) (2016, p. 11).

Australia's minimum wage is the most generous in the world. Internationally, Australia is proud of this achievement and the ability to protect the most vulnerable individuals in the workforce. Domestically however, there are various debates and sentiments arguing that a high minimum wage negatively impacts jobs and employment growth, with the potential for businesses to avoid expanding into or competing in Australia because the country has one of the most, if not the most expensive, labour markets in the world (for an example see Oliver & Buchanan, 2014).

Non-Governmental Organisations

Non-governmental organisations, and specifically the embedded antagonist relationship between unions and employer associations, are two important factors that influence the legal, economic and political context of Australia.

- *Unions*

Establishment of the conciliation and arbitration system, as noted previously, facilitated the rapid growth of unions and employer associations. This, coupled with a long history of tensions between employers and employees, has afforded both unions and employer associations with an ability to influence HRM and workplace relations. Although union density and membership numbers dwarf the levels of 1921 when close to half of Australia's labour force was unionised, about 17.4% of full or part-time employees are union members. Unions, therefore, currently represent 1.9 million individuals (Roy Morgan, 2017). Comparatively, the influence of unions in Australia is relatively powerful. While in the US, 14.6 million workers are union members, this represents only 10.7% of wage and salary workers (United States Department of Labor, 2017). Academics and policymakers have widely viewed unions as critical to improving the conditions and entitlements of workers and mitigating the perceived power of organisations and capital structures. Moreover, they are often presented as an essential party to workplace negotiations with unions playing a key, and at times, antagonist role, in organisational practices. Many unions are privy to workplace discussions at the state, industry, and organisational level.

The Australian Council of Trade Unions (ACTU) is the peak body for Australian unions, and in a similar vein to the United States and the UK, this confederation comprises of ". . . 38 affiliated unions who together represent about 1.8 million workers and their families" (ACTU, 2017). Since 1927, the ACTU has publically campaigned for the right for workers to organise and bargain collectively. For foreign enterprises, Australia may seem like a challenge to managerial prerogative vis-à-vis other liberal market economies.

- *Employer Associations*

Employer associations are actively involved in shaping the legislative and competitive landscape impacting talent in Australia. Employer associations arose from the previously noted evolution of unions. They feature prominently and are committed to representing the commercial interests of the Australian business community, both domestically and internationally with a core operational and strategic priority to curtail union power and influence.

It, however, appears that employer associations are less organised than their union counterparts. This may be the result of the inherent need for employer associations to compete for the same pool of members (Australian businesses). Tensions between employer associations also play out publicly. While larger associations control much of the coverage and debates, smaller industry-based associations largely focus on issues pertaining specifically to their members (Barry & You, 2017).

Building on a shared antagonism with unions, all employer associations in 2015 sought legitimacy for a business-centric approach to industrial laws and instruments. Employer associations while campaigning for a Productivity Commission Inquiry into Australia's workplace relations framework collectively argued that arrangements must change to suit new workplace realities (Barry, 2016). Issues about the need for workplace laws and bargaining instruments to become less rigid and more flexible, the curtailing of penalty rates and union power were to the fore of submissions and discussions. Barry (2016) notes that employers widely hold concerns about union bargaining rights within Australia. This is of significance for organisations operating in sectors such as manufacturing, construction and resources where industry-wide pattern bargaining occurs. Continued endeavours to enhance the competitiveness of Australia's organisations has encouraged employer associations to remain committed to representing the interests of small and medium-sized firms who are subjected to the same degree of award provisions as larger organisations and limiting the power and influence of unions in the processes of bargaining and the right to take industrial action.

At the time of writing, employer associations were set to achieve large concessions with impending changes to public holiday, evening and after midnight work penalty rates. Employers and employer associations have been pushing for cuts to higher Sunday penalty rates (Barry & You, 2017), and although Sunday concessions will be introduced over 3 or 4 years depending on the award and employment type (Fair Work Ombudson, 2017), key employer associations infer that such changes are essential to enhance Australia's productivity. Thus, it could be argued that Australia is increasingly becoming more supportive of the business lobby.

The Relationship Between Government and Employment Relations: Policies, Programs and Activities

There is a long history of industrial relations and governance in Australia. Industrial relations underpin aspects of government policies, programs and activities for numerous reasons. Specifically, the Australian Labor Party (ALP), Australia's oldest political party, is intertwined with the evolution of the labour movement of the country (outlined in *Labour, Employment and Industrial Relations*). Formally appearing in the 1890s, the Australian Labor Party was the product of the evolutionary process of unionism with the foundation framework explicitly underpinned by the trade union movement. As in these early times, the ALP represents the interests of the working class and is considered a fundamental political step forward for Australian workers. This relationship influences voting patterns with a significantly greater proportion of individuals that vote for the ALP belonging to a union, than those individuals that support the policies of the Liberal National, Greens and other minor parties. The ALP remains one of a ". . . small number in the world where unions affiliate directly with the political party. This gives the unions significant representation in the party's internal structures and forums, and influence in choice of parliamentary candidates" (Markey, 2016). The historical relationship between unions and the ALP has resulted in a situation where union representatives can transition into a political career. While the proportion of former union officials who are ALP members of parliament has declined from 79% in 1901 to 45% in 2016, there remains a de-facto relationship between trade union membership, politics and governance in Australia (Markey, 2016). For example, the current Opposition Leader and Leader of the ALP William 'Bill' Shorten, before entering parliament, worked as a union organiser, lawyer, union secretary and a member of the Australian Council of Trade Unions (peak trade union body) (Australian Labor Party, 2017).

Federal election changes the associated mechanism for managing talent. As Chris F. Wright (2017, p. 2) notes, 'federal election years in the recent past have heralded significant changes in Australian industrial relations'. This includes, but is not limited to, the Howard (Liberal) Government's ability to introduce *WorkChoices* (2004), the trade union movement's Your Rights At Work Campaign influenced the 2007 election result (Ellem, 2013; Wilson & Spies-Butcher, 2011), which gave the Labor Party a mandate to repeal WorkChoices and with it the Howard government's most individualistic and anti-union policy measures (Cooper, 2009). Further evidence of the entwined relationship between industrial relations, unions, government and legislation in Australia, was the recent 2016 Federal election. Prime Minister Malcolm Turnbull, because of an inability to pass two pieces of his government's industrial relations legislation *Fair Work (Registered Organisations) Amendment Bill* and the *Building and Construction Industry (Improving Productivity) Bill*, requested both houses of parliament be dissolved and a double-dissolution election be held. Campaigns and electoral debates focused on raising Australia's economic performance through improving business confidence and improving labour flexibility, deregulating the labour market and limiting union involvement (Barry & You, 2017). While the Turnbull Liberal government returned to power, they did so with a smaller majority. Despite passing both pieces of industrial relations legislation in November 2016, the Liberal government and employer associations continue to face staunch resistance to the continued deregulation of Australian markets and workplace relations.

Demographics: The Australian Talent Pool

The sheer quantity of a country's talent pool has important implications for talent management in a global context (Chand & Tung, 2014; Khilji, 2012). This section outlines how and why population, demographics, immigration and mobility factors are particularly pertinent to Australia.

- *Population*

Australia has a population of 24.4 million people which is small in comparative terms. According to *The World Factbook*, published by the Central Intelligence Agency (United States), Australia is ranked 56th regarding total country-based population and talent pool. This is well behind significant players in globalised markets. China tops the population pool with 1.37 billion, followed by India 1.25 billion, and the United States with approximately 324 million. Other countries that dwarf Australia's population include Brazil (205 million), Indonesia (258 million), Japan (126 million), Philippines (102 million), and Malaysia (31 million).

Despite the small population pool, Australia has a vast area of 7,692,024km^2. Australia is the 6th largest country after Russia, Canada, China, the United States, and Brazil and accounts for five per cent of the world's total land area. The vast array of land mass when compared to the small population size ensures that Australia has one of the lowest population density ratios in the world—at June 2015 this was 3.1 people per square kilometre or 7 per square mile (Australian Bureau of Statistics, 2016a). The majority of residents reside along the outer parameters and coastlines meaning that some parts of Australia are even less densely populated. While population density is projected to increase to 4 by 2030 and 6 by 2100 (Department of Economic and Social Affairs Population Division, 2015a, p. 79), Australia will remain one of the least densely populated countries worldwide.

The projected population growth until 2050 in the Oceania region, which Australia is part of, is placed behind Asia, Northern America, Latin America and the Caribbean (Department of Economic and Social Affairs Population Division, 2015a). Notably, Europe is projected to have a smaller population in 2050 than today (2015a, p. xxv). Much of this population growth will derive from enhanced fertility rates. The exponential growth of developing countries presents an interesting set of challenges for smaller countries, including Australia, with questions about the ability of businesses operating in these locations to capitalise on the commercial opportunities associated with emerging markets due to resource and location constraints. The talent challenges that have been raised with internationalisation are therefore only likely to be magnified if such projections materialise.

Although not located in one of most urbanised regions of the world, Australia is following the trend towards urbanisation (2015c, p. xxi). In 2014, approximately 89 per cent of Australia's population was living in urban regions (2015c, p. 201). More specifically, 15.9 million individuals, around two-thirds of the population, live in a Greater Capital City (Sydney, Melbourne, Brisbane, Perth, Adelaide, Darwin and Canberra). The largest pools of potential talent, therefore, are in these capital cities. While issues relating to the rise of "megacities" (cities with more than 10 million inhabitants) do not feature in domestic discourse, they highlight the talent and population pool challenges that Australia and Australian businesses inherently face in this interconnected world, largely due to its small population and (perceived) geographical isolation.

Sustainability issues are associated with the move towards urbanisation with countries needing to facilitate economic and social development actively, while also seeking to mitigate the adverse impact of greater levels of consumption and production on the environment (Department of Economic and Social Affairs Population Division, 2015c). This requires collaborations between industry and governments to ensure the viability of commercial markets for today, and into the future. The changes required of countries, and the organisations within, will inherently impact on the skills and capabilities required of employees and potentially lead to a greater emphasis on ethical, responsible and sustainable leadership and talent.

Australia's Demographic Picture

Like many other countries, Australia's population is ageing. This results from sustained low fertility and increasing life expectancy. The median age of an Australian has increased by 3 years over the last two decades to 37.4 years old (Australian Bureau of Statistics, 2016b). Notably, individuals aged 65 years and over comprised 14 per cent of the population in 2012. This figure is projected to grow rapidly to 25 per cent in 2101. Similarly, the 85-year-olds and over will also experience significant growth, with the projection that this cohort of individuals will make up 6 per cent of Australia's population by 2101 (Australian Bureau of Statistics, 2013).

There is evidence that all advanced industrialised countries are confronted with challenges associated with managing an ageing population. The *Australian Bureau of Statistics* discussed how Australia's ageing population fairs internationally. For the vast majority of analysed countries, the increase in the older population is accompanied by a decrease in the youngest citizens, children aged between 0 and 14 years old. Changing demographic patterns means that overall the workforce is shrinking and more people are retiring than are entering the workforce (Axelrod, Handfield-Jones, & Welsh, 2001; Blass, 2007; Calo, 2008). An ageing population further compounds the aforementioned macro talent management challenges, as it has an array of implications for the health industry and its resources, the size of the working-age population, housing and the demand for skilled labour.

Retirement patterns have various implications for talent management, and in particular knowledge management, as valuable knowledge skills and capabilities, as well as talented employees, depart an organisation. Despite many debates arguing the need for organisations to deal with an ageing workforce and their retirement, it is also important to recognise that those still involved in the workforce also have talent management implications. Organisations will need to consider the best way to utilise the talents of older employees in a manner that still adds value to the organisation (Calo, 2008) and how to transition their knowledge and experience to a younger workforce.

Recognising the value of older workers in this latter capacity, the labour-force participation of mature-age workers is attracting attention. There are differences in the approaches being adopted in different countries, although in general, these focus on restructuring tax arrangements and retirement income policies, development of policies that provide more intensive assistance to support active labour participation and legislation that deters age discrimination (Encel, 2003). Age discrimination is prohibited under the *Age Discrimination Act (2004)*. This legislation and the facilitation of older workers is supported via the *Restart* program in Australia. In 2011, Australia introduced its first Age Discrimination Commissioner which morphed into Age and Disability in 2014. Also in 2014, Australia's Department of Employment provided a financial incentive of up to AU$10,000 (approximately US$7500 or 5800 British pounds) "to encourage businesses to hire and retain mature age employees who are 50 years of age and over" (2017). Additional Government rhetoric asserts

> Employees are an investment for any business. Hiring a mature aged worker can be a great investment, bringing many years of experience and knowledge. Mature aged workers have often built up knowledge and skills during their time in the workforce . . . If your business welcomes mature aged workers, you'll be seen as a more attractive employer to a growing proportion of the workforce.
> (Australian Government Business, 2017)

Immigration and Mobility

Immigration

> The impact of economic immigration on Australia's population, economy and labour market is virtually unmatched among advanced economies.
> (Wright, Clibborn, Piper, & Cini, 2016, p. 2)

Australia is experiencing substantial growth in Net Overseas Migration (NOM). NOM accounted for 55% of Australia's total population growth in 2016 (Australian Bureau of Statistics, 2017). Between 2015 and 2050, the top net receivers of international migrants (more than 100,000 annually) are projected to be the US, Canada, UK, Australia, Germany, Russia and Italy (Department of Economic and Social Affairs Population Division, 2015a, p. xxviii).

Although internal and international migration can be positive forces for economic and social development as they offer a mechanism to rebalance labour markets in areas of origin and destination, and to accelerate the diffusion of ideas and technologies (Department of Economic and Social Affairs Population Division, 2015b, p. xxviii), immigration is not consistently framed as in Australia's national interest. This has over the past decade become more apparent in terms of public commentary and government action. At the time of writing, the Australian (Liberal National) Government had announced significant changes to talent-related immigration. Australia's Prime Minister Malcolm Turnbull, when announcing the changes, stated that "We are putting jobs first. We are putting Australians first . . . Australian workers must have priority for Australian jobs." Thus, there appears to be an increasingly nationalist type narrative developing. The Howard Government's "457 visa" program (introduced in 1996) which permitted a four-year working visa and the potential to migrate to Australia, will be replaced by two new visa programs which aim to better target "genuine" skill shortages. Tighter restrictions are to be placed on requirements for previous work experience and English language proficiency. Employers will be required to advertise positions before foreign workers can fill them. The list of occupations eligible for temporary visa status will decrease to 435 from 651. This includes Human Resource Advisors, Web Developers, Training and Development Professionals, and ICT Support Technicians (Hanrahan, 2017). The consequences of these policy changes on the operation of domestic and multinational enterprises have both direct and indirect implications for talent management and the size of the talent pool.

In spite of recent changes, Australia is still considered one of the most multicultural countries in the OECD with the country's overseas-born population 28.5 per cent of the total population in 2014 (OECD, 2016b). The multicultural population has great importance for Australian industry as it means that business has access to a diverse workforce with different cultural understanding and language capabilities. This is evidenced by some 30% of the Australian labour force being born outside of Australia (Australian Bureau of Statistics, 2016d).

The recent policy changes can, on the face of things, appear somewhat surprising given it is regarded that Australia has been relatively successful in managing the strong levels of economic migration with minimal impacts in terms of major social and political upheaval (Wright et al., 2016).

Migrants bring new ideas and perspectives from their home country leading to improvements in productivity and innovation. This can take the form of talent developing new technology, altering existing business models to provide opportunities in new markets, propose and implement better processes and practices within organisations and establishing new business (Jensen, 2014). Given the centrality being placed on business innovation to drive Australia's future economic competitiveness and prosperity, any alteration in policy that could negatively impact on innovative capabilities must be a concern.

Diaspora and Mobility

Concerning mobility and diaspora, Australians are commonly viewed as possessing a strong willingness to move and work abroad. Hugo (2006) pointed to more than 1 million Australians living overseas on a long-term or permanent basis. By 2030 it is predicted that the Australian diasporic community in Asia will be a minimum of 450,000 people (PWC, 2016). Interestingly, Australia appears to be quite distinct to other developed, liberal market economies on this with the population of the US, UK and Ireland considerably less likely to be willing to work abroad (Boston Consulting Group, 2014). Showing a global average of almost 64% amongst 200,000 survey participants who are already living abroad or are willing to do so, the Boston Consulting Group (2014) report depicts Ireland, UK, US, Germany and Denmark in the less than 50% category but Australia as being in the second highest category (80%–90% range). This study indicates a sector effect to exist whereby those in engineering and technical jobs represent the most willingly mobile workers. The medical and social work domains are amongst the lowest in terms of people willing to move abroad.

Turning to the attractiveness of Australia as a destination for people to work in we find that it typically ranks highly in comparative terms and thus is viewed as a very appealing location. Data from the Boston Consulting Group (2014) places Australia in 7th position as a potential work destination behind the US, UK, Canada, Germany, Switzerland and France. Moving to the more specific attractiveness question Sydney and Melbourne are traditionally ranked in the world's top cities to work in (Boston Consulting Group, 2014). Australia's Asian diaspora appears to have grown exponentially and given the linguistic skills and global and cultural networks that this provides Australia can be well placed to strengthen further and expand economic links with Asia. The Chinese diaspora in Australia is estimated to be 1.2 million, along with 610,000 Indians (Liu, 2016). While potential exists, there has been criticism that this rich Asian diaspora is underutilised (Rivzi, Louie, & Evans, 2016) an argument also made with respect to the Australian diaspora in Asia.

> PwC's view is that Australia does have the talent to succeed in Asia, but we are not doing enough to foster, prepare and deploy this talent in the region.
> (PwC, 2016, p. 4)

Education

Education and the ability to develop skills and create knowledge will become more salient as many economies, including Australia, transition to a knowledge-based economy. Knowledge-intensive economies, and knowledge-intensive organisations, where the skills and capabilities of talent are critical for competitive advantage and success (McDonnell, Lamare, Gunnigle, & Lavelle, 2010; Wiblen et al., 2012) will increase in importance. Synthesis of these factors, with technological innovations and a rapidly changing global economy, succeed in embedding the salience of formalized education.

The OECD argues that equipping citizens with the knowledge and skills necessary to achieve their full potential, contribute to an increasingly connected world, and converting better skills into better lives is the central aim of governments and policy makers worldwide OECD (2016c). Therefore, education is particularly pertinent to macro talent management as the next generation of employees, leaders and talent are educated for the world of work within a country's primary, secondary and tertiary education system.

Although education is framed as of critical importance to economic growth, as well as organisational and country competitiveness, Australian students lag behind top-performing countries. This is despite Australia having a highly educated workforce as judged by the quality of its strong secondary and tertiary education participation rates, student mobility and overall education system. We describe the processes and performance of Australia's education system in this section.

- *Schools and Universities*

Australia ranks 1st in the OECD for the length of instruction time for compulsory education. Primary (Kindergarten to Year 6) and Secondary (Year 7 to 12) school lasts 11 years, with students required to attend school until the conclusion of Year 10 or they are 17 years old (OECD, 2016a).

Many bodies, both domestically and internationally, report on Australia's school system performance. For example, results from the OECD's Program for International Student Assessment (PISA) shows that while Australia performs better than the OECD average in

Science, Mathematics and Reading, this has been in decline since 2006. Notably, the performance gap between immigrant and non-immigrant students is better than the OECD average and has remained stable. In the latest PISA 2015 evaluation, Australia was significantly outperformed (overall) by nine countries. They ranked below New Zealand, but above the UK and Germany. Singapore outperforms all countries in science. Singapore, Hong Kong (China), Canada and Finland top the world rankings in reading. Singapore again tops the rankings in mathematics. Only in Canada, Estonia, Finland, Hong Kong (China), Japan, Macao (China) and Singapore do at least four out of five 15 year olds master the baseline level of proficiency in science, reading and mathematics (OECD, 2016b, p. 4). Despite these specific results, primary and secondary schooling plays a significant role in consolidating knowledge and aims to prepare all students, regardless of their country, for admission into the labour market.

The OECD reports that educational and schooling results are no longer directly influenced by the wealth of a country. The OECD (2016b) remarks that while all countries have excellent students, few countries have successfully enabled all students to excel. This is interesting to note as Australia's total (public and private) expenditure on primary to tertiary education is slightly higher than the OECD average of 5.2 per cent totalling 5.6 per cent of gross domestic profit (GDP). Australia is also spending more money per student than the average. There was an increase in expenditure per student of 11 per cent between 2008 and 2013. The vast majority of expenditure is attained from private, rather than public sources, although public spending increased by 27 per cent between 2008 and 2013 (OECD, 2016a).

Based on the positive influence of tertiary education on the quality of the labour market and the skills and capabilities of the talent pool, Australia is positioned to compete in this globalised and interconnected world. Australia has one of the highest shares of tertiary-educated adults (43 per cent) among OECD countries (behind Canada, Japan, Israel, United States and the United Kingdom). The vast majority of these possess a bachelor's degree. Australia's university completion rates are the 3rd highest in the OECD, placing ahead of the United States and the United Kingdom (Universities Australia, 2017).

The University and Other Higher Education in Australia market generated AU$31 billion dollars of revenue in 2016. The sector added an estimated AU$140 billion to the Australian Economy in 2014 (Universities Australia, 2017). Australian domestic students face some of the highest tuition fees in the world (above US$4000 per year and behind the UK and the US, but above New Zealand). While viewed as generous, these are significantly less than the arrangements in many Nordic countries (such as Denmark, Finland, Iceland, Norway and Sweden) where students pay no tuition fees (OECD, 2017).

At least 85 per cent of (domestic) students receive some level of support from public loans or scholarships and grants. Domestic students, under a government-supported scheme, can accumulate a debt for their university education and can delay compulsory loan repayments until they earn AU$54,869. No interest is payable. However, the final amount is indexed in accordance with inflation. This contributes to the facilitation of an inclusive approach to education, whereby attending university and extending the period of formalised and tertiary education is possible for many low-income students.

This sector has experienced significant change over the past five years, with the Australian Government transitioning away from a capped arrangement, towards a demand-driven funding model. This has removed numerous barriers to entry faced by students with universities now able to gain additional government supported places for domestic students. While people from major cities are twice as likely to hold a degree than those from regional and remote areas (Universities Australia, 2017), there is limited competition between universities. This may be because there is limited student mobility between universities with students typically attending universities within their home states or territories (IBISWorld, 2017).

Vocational education also plays a pivotal role in preparing individuals for workforce participation and skill development. This industry helps participants to acquire practical knowledge and work-based learning, while also supporting apprentices and trainees. It also contributes significantly to the country's economic competitiveness. Graduation rates from vocational programs have increased by more than 40 per cent since 2005. This is significant as the average of OECD countries was 4 per cent (OECD, 2017).

Education of international students is big business in Australia with the export of education a core part of their socio-economic development strategy. Valued at AU$21. 8 billion a year (Universities Australia, 2017), recent figures show that education is Australia's third-largest export after coal and iron ore. International education is Australia's largest service export. Changes to student visa requirements were part of the university and education review. This enabled significant growth in the number of international student enrolments in Australia's universities. Of the 1.4 million students studying at Australian Universities in 2015, over 363,000 were international students (approx. 38 per cent) (Universities Australia, 2017). Over half of all masters and doctoral students in 2014 were from China (35 per cent), India (15 per cent) and Malaysia (6 per cent) (OECD, 2016a). The average tuition fees for these students is significantly higher than domestic students. In situations where government support is absent, the fees can be over three times higher (OECD, 2016a). Although there is the potential for these higher fees to discourage future students, the contribution of international students to Australia's economy is significant. There is, however, concern that changes in immigration policy can negatively impact the availability of international student graduates from taking up employment in Australia post study.

Country Competitiveness

> . . . countries that offer enticing economic, political and social incentives send a strong signal to the global labour market that they are open for business and to a variety of types of talented workers.
>
> (Harvey & Groutsis, 2014, p. 35)

So how does Australia fare concerning country competitiveness on key macro conditions? Australia ranks 22nd out of 138 countries on the Global Competitiveness Index which is based on 12 pillars that make up the three sub-indexes of basic requirements, efficiency enhancers and innovation and sophistication factors. Australia ranks no lower than 28th in any of the 12 pillars although it performs poorest with regard to labour market efficiency (although this has been significantly improving) and business sophistication. It is ranked in the top 10 for financial market development, higher education and training and health and primary education. The strengths of access to and quality of education are noteworthy in the context of this chapter. Of concern may be the result that two of the five most problematic factors for doing business were restrictive labour regulations and poor work ethic in the national labour force (World Economic Forum, 2016).

Regarding productivity, Australia has been enjoying a relatively strong period whereby labour productivity growth has exceeded increases in real wages (Australian Bureau of Statistics, 2016c). Specifically, Australia experienced an increase of just over 8% in average labour productivity in the 2010–2016 period, while real labour costs only rose by 1.5%.

While the impact on productivity involves more than talent, it is recognised that human capital acts as a significant driver (Banks, 2010).

Notwithstanding, the comparatively small population and size of its internal talent pool, The Global Human Capital Index ranks Australia 20th (out of 130 countries) in terms of how well the country develops its human capital. The report notes that Australia and its regional counterpart New Zealand (ranked 7th), have "solid track records" in maximizing their internal labour pool's contribution to the wider East Asia and Pacific region. According to this report's theoretical ideal Australia adequately utilises the skills and capabilities of 71 per cent of its total population (World Economic Forum, 2017) in pursuit of its national productivity and competitiveness goals, although the country's ranking could rise if there was a significant improvement in the employment rates of younger citizens (15–24 years). This signals the presence of numerous opportunities for Australia to further enhance its international standing and the country's competitiveness.

Conclusion

Australia, like much of the developed world, has talent challenges which in some sectors and occupations are quite acute. Global workforce shortages have placed a level of importance greater than ever before witnessed on the ability of countries to attract and retain their most highly valued. Central to this is ensuring cities are attractive locations to both live and work in, having a strong education system, the provision of an efficient and an effective public health system. Australia has a well-recognized and ranked educational system, availability of skilled labour and strong scientific research institutions. Australia can be viewed as a multicultural society in that almost 30 per cent were born overseas, 1.3 million speak a European language, and 2.1 million speak an Asian language (Austrade, 2017). The role that immigration has played in Australia is apparent in these language statistics; however in more recent times there appears to be a more restrictive approach taken to migration policy which may prove detrimental to Australian industry in the years ahead. Overall, there is a range of supply and demand factors impacting the need for talent. This raises a range of issues for organisations and governments.

For organisations, there is a need to understand better what their potential talents want. Operating in a manner that worked in the past may not necessarily be the best approach into the future. It will be important for organisations to understand the workforce challenges they face now and into the future including the ageing workforce conundrum and greater levels of diversity now evident. Ensuring their approaches to recruitment, rewards, development, retention and motivating are fit for purpose will be crucial to whether they can operate sustainably and successfully. In sum, a central question that exists at the organisational level is, are organisational responses effective in addressing the talent shortages and challenges?

There are more fundamental concerns regarding the labour market hollowing out to too great a degree in a relatively short period. There has been a significant loss of low skilled jobs as traditional manufacturing has seen many organisations close and move elsewhere. When one factors in the potential for automation and digital technology advancements in the coming years there must be a major concern over disruption to labour markets and the skills that will be required. According to Durrant-White, McCalman, O'Callaghan, Reid and Steinberg (2015) up to 40% of current jobs are at risk of being lost over the next 15 years as a result of technological advancement and disruption. There is a need to better understand the impact of technological and automation disruption in the years ahead and grasp the types of skills that may be required into the future. Seeking to then develop greater coordination between educational institutions, training bodies, employers, and public policy makers will be vital to ensure Australia is adequately prepared for the challenges of tomorrow. A logical question that follows is whether current approaches to education and workplace learning are fit for purpose. Also, what impact will the continued lack of willingness vis-à-vis past decades for employers to make long-term investments in employee skill development (Oliver & Wright, 2016)? An overarching question exists regarding what are the strategies, policies and processes that government and business need to operationalize to address the ongoing talent challenges and the potential for major disruption to labour markets caused by technological advancements? This should naturally see governments look at their education system and the extent to which it will be fit for purpose in the new economy.

The changes in immigration policy are also something that needs greater consideration as there is a danger that this move will serve to undermine the Australian economy as opposed to protecting it. Given political developments such as the Brexit vote and the tough approach on migration by the Trump administration, there may, in fact, be a great opportunity to attract high skilled talent to Australia. The talent challenges of changing global demographics are very evident with governments needing to plan appropriately. For example, the rapidly ageing populations will require an expansion of health-care and retirement services. There is however also a need for greater consideration as to retain ageing workers in organisational roles for longer. In sum, the talent challenges that exist are great, and government and organisational decision making in the near term will have a significant say over how well placed they are to deal with these as they become more acute in the future.

Notes

1. Consult "Australia in Brief" publications, attainable from Australian Government Department of Foreign Affairs and Trade www.dfat.gov.au for current information about Australia and its history.
2. Consult Australia's official pages via Australia.gov.au, the primary reference for this section, for official information about the history and composition of Australia.

References

ACTU. (2017). *About the ACTU*. Retrieved from www.actu.org.au/about-the-actu.
Austrade. (2017). Why Australia: Benchmark Report 2017. Retrieved from file:///C:/Users/swiblen/Downloads/Australia-Benchmark-Report.pdf.
Australian Bureau of Statistics. (2013). *3222.0—Population projections, Australia, 2012 (base) to 2101. 2013_11_26*. Retrieved from www.abs.gov.au/ausstats/abs@.nsf/Lookup/3222.0main+features32012%20(base)%20to%202101.
Australian Bureau of Statistics. (2016a). *3218.0—Regional population growth, Australia, 2014–15* [Press release]. Retrieved from www.abs.gov.au/ausstats/abs@.nsf/Previousproducts/3218.0Main%20Features152014-15?opendocument&tabname=Summary&prodno=3218 0&issue=2014-15&num=&view.
Australian Bureau of Statistics. (2016b). *3235.0—Population by age and sex, regions of Australia, 2015*. Retrieved from www.abs.gov.au/AUSSTATS/abs@.nsf/Latestproducts/3235.0Main%20Features102015?opendocument&tabname=Summary&prodno=3235.0&issue=2015&num=&view=.
Australian Bureau of Statistics. (2016c). *5206.0—Australian national accounts: National income, expenditure, and product time series workbook*. Retrieved from www.ausstats.abs.gov.au/ausstats/meisubs.nsf/0/9355EEA037741EDFCA258248000BC099/$File/52060_dec%202017.pdf.
Australian Bureau of Statistics. (2016d). *6291.055.001—Labour force, Australia*. Retrieved from www.abs.gov.au/AUSSTATS/abs@.nsf/DetailsPage/6202.0Dec%202016?OpenDocument.
Australian Bureau of Statistics. (2017). *Stronger growth in net overseas migration* [Press release]. Retrieved from www.abs.gov.au/ausstats/abs@.nsf/Latestproducts/3101.0Media%20Release1Sep%202016?opendocument&tabname=Summary&prodno=3101.0&issue=Sep%202016&num=&view.

Australian Government. (2016). *Convicts and the British colonies in Australia: A penal colony*. Retrieved from www.australia.gov.au/about-australia/australian-story/convicts-and-the-british-colonies.

Australian Government Business. (2017). *Mature aged people*. March 9, 2017. Retrieved from www.business.gov.au/info/run/employ-people/equal-opportunity-and-diversity/mature-aged-people.

Australian Government Department of Employment. (2017). *Restart—help to employ mature workers*.

Australian Government Department of Foreign Affairs and Trade. (2016). *Australia in brief*. Retrieved from dfat.gov.au/about-us/publications/Documents/australia-in-brief.pdf.

Australian Labor Party. (2017). *We'll put people first—Bill Shorten*. www.billshorten.com.au/people_first/.

Axelrod, E. L., Handfield-Jones, H., & Welsh, T. A. (2001). War for talent, part two. *McKinsey Quarterly, 2*, 9–12.

Banks, G. (2010). *Advancing Australia's 'human capital agenda'*. The fourth Ian Little Lecture. Retrieved from www.pc.gov.au/news-media/speeches/advancing-human-capital Melbourne.

Barry, M. (2016). Employer and employer association matters in Australia in 2015. *Journal of Industrial Relations, 58*(3), 340–355. doi:10.1177/0022185616634092.

Barry, M., & You, K. (2017). Employer and employer association matters in Australia in 2016. *Journal of Industrial Relations*.59 (3), 288-304. doi:10.1177/0022185617693873.

Blass, E. (2007, November). *Talent management: Maximising talent for business performance*. Executive Summary, London. Retrieved from www.ashridge.org.uk/Website/IC.nsf/wFARPUB/Talent+Management:+Maximising+talent+for+business+performance?opendocument.

Boston Consulting Group. (2014). *Decoding global talent: 200,000 survey responses on global mobility and employment preferences*. Retrieved from www.bcg.com/publications/2014/people-organization-human-resources-decoding-global-talent.aspx.

Boyle, B., & McDonnell, A. (2013). Exploring the impact of institutional and organizational factors on the reaction of MNCs to the global financial crisis. *Asia Pacific Business Review, 19*, 247–265.

Calo, T. J. (2008). Talent management in the era of the aging workforce: The critical role of knowledge transfer. *Public Personnel Management, 37*(4), 403–416.

Chand, M., & Tung, R. L. (2014). The aging of the world's population and its effects on global business. *Academy of Management Perspectives, 28*(4), 409–429. doi:10.5465/amp.2012.0070.

Cooper, R. (2009). Forward with Fairness? Industrial relations under labor in 2008. *Journal of Industrial Relations, 51*(3), 285–296. doi:10.1177/0022185609104298.

Department of Economic and Social Affairs Population Division. (2015a). *World population prospects the 2015 revision volume II: Demographic profiles*. Retrieved from esa.un.org/unpd/wpp/publications/Files/WPP2015_Volume-II-Demographic-Profiles.pdf.

Department of Economic and Social Affairs Population Division. (2015b). *World population prospects the 2015 revision: Key findings and advance tables*. New York, United States. Retrieved from esa.un.org/unpd/wpp/publications/files/key_findings_wpp_2015.pdf.

Department of Economic and Social Affairs Population Division. (2015c). *World urbanization prospects the 2014 revision*. Retrieved from esa.un.org/unpd/wup/Publications/Files/WUP2014-Report.pdf.

Durrant-White, H., McCalman, L., O'Callaghan, S., Reid, A., & Steinberg, D. (2015). The impact of computerisation and automation on future employment. In Australia's future workforce? June 2015 (pp 56-64). CEDA Retrieved from www.ceda.com.au/CEDA/media/ResearchCatalogueDocuments/Research%20and%20Policy/PDF/26792-Futureworkforce_June2015.pdf S.

Ellem, B. (2013). Peak union campaigning: Fighting for rights at work in Australia. *British Journal of Industrial Relations, 51*(2), 264–287. doi:10.1111/j.1467-8543.2011.00878.x.

Encel, S. (2003). *Age can work: The case for older Australians staying in the workforce*. Retrieved from www.actu.org.au/media/308820/agedoc.rtf.

Fair Work Ombudson. (2017). *Penalty rates & allowances*. Retrieved from www.fairwork.gov.au/pay/penalty-rates-and-allowances.

Hanrahan, C. (2017, April 20). HR, coders and manufacturing: The occupations most affected by the 457 visa changes. *ABC News*.

Harvey, W., & Groutsis, D. (2014). Reputation and talent mobility in the Asia Pacific. *Asia Pacific Journal of Human Resources, 53*, 22–40.

Hays. (2011). *Bridging the skills gap: Research and insights that can impact on your world of work 2011*. Retrieved from www.hays.com.au/news/ausworkplace/bridgingskillsgap.pdf.

Hugo, G. (2006). An Australian Diaspora. International Migration, 44(1), 105-133. doi.org/10.1111/j.1468-2435.2006.00357.x.

IBISWorld. (2017). *University and other higher education in Australia*. Retrieved from www.ibisworld.com.au/industry-trends/market-research-reports/education-training/university-other-higher-education.html.

International Labour Organization. (2016). *Global wage report 2016/17: Wage inequality in the workplace.* Geneva, Switzerland. Retrieved from www.ilo.org/wcmsp5/groups/public/-dgreports/-dcomm/-publ/documents/publication/wcms_537846.pdf.

Jensen, P. (2014). Understanding the impact of migration on innovation. *Australian Economic Review, 47*(2), 240–250.

Khilji, S. E. (2012). Editor's perspective: Does South Asia matter? Rethinking South Asia as relevant in international business research. *South Asian Journal of Global Business Research, 1*(1), 8–21. doi:10.1108/20454451211205914.

Khilji, S.E. & Schuler, R. (2016). Talent management in the global context. In D. Collings, K. Mellahi, and W. Cascio (Eds.), *Oxford handbook of talent management* (pp. 399–419). Oxford: Oxford Press.

Lansbury, R. D., & Wailes, N. (2004). Employment relations in Australia. In G. J. Bamber, R. D. Lansbury, & N. Wailes (Eds.), *International and comparative employment relations: Globalisation and the developed market economies* (pp. 119–145). Crows Nest, Australia: Allen & Unwin.

Lawrence, S. & Davies, P. (2011). An Archaeology of Australia since 1788. New York: Springer.

Liu, X. (2016). Australia's Chinese and Indian Business Diasporas: Demographic Characteristics and Engagement in Business, Trade and Investment. Report for the Australian Council of Learned Academies, Melbourne, Australia. Retrieved from acola.org.au/wp/PDF/SAF11/Liu%20Xuchun.pdf.

ManpowerGroup. (2017). *ManpowerGroup employment outlook survey Australia: Q4 2017.* Retrieved from www.manpowergroup.com.au/documents/MEOS/2017/MEOS-AU_Q4-2017.pdf.

Markey, R. (2016, April 27). How the influence of trade unions on the Labor Party is overestimated. *The Conversation.*

McDonnell, A., Lamare, R., Gunnigle, P., & Lavelle, J. (2010). Developing tomorrow's Leaders: Evidence of global talent management in multinational companies. *Journal of World Business, 45*(2), 150–160.

OECD. (2016a). Australia. In OECD (Ed.), *Education at a glance 2016: OECD indicators.* Paris: OECD Publishing. Retrieved from www.keepeek.com/Digital-Asset-Management/oecd/education/education-at-a-glance-2016/australia_eag-2016-41-en#.WTitSmh96Uk#page5.

OECD. (2016b). *International migration outlook 2016.* Retrieved from www.oecd-ilibrary.org/social-issues-migration-health/international-migration-outlook-2016_migr_outlook-2016-en.

OECD. (2016c). *PISA 2015 results* (Vol. I). Paris: OECD Publishing.

OECD. (2017). *Education at a glance 2016.* Paris. Retrieved from www.keepeek.com/Digital-Asset-Management/oecd/education/education-at-a-glance-2016_eag-2016-en#.WTjBsmh96Uk#page49.

Oliver, D., & Buchanan, J. (2014). *Australian business gets a good deal from the minimum wage.* Retrieved from theconversation.com/australian-business-gets-a-good-deal-from-the-minimum-wage-27698.

Oliver, D., & Wright, C. F. (2016). Australia's shifting skills ecosystem: Contemporary challenges in education, training and immigration. In K. Hancock & R. D. Lansbury (Eds.), *Industrial relations reform: Looking to the future* (pp. 163–186). Sydney: Federation Press.

PwC. (2016). 19th Annual Global CEO Survey: Redefining Business Success in a Changing World. PwC. Retrieved from www.pwc.com/gx/en/ceo-survey/2016/landing-page/pwc-19th-annual-global-ceo-survey.pdf.

Rizvi, F, Louie, K, and Evans, J (2016). Australia's Diaspora Advantage: Realising the potential for building transnational business networks with Asia. Report for the Australian Council of Learned Academies, www.acola.org.au.

Roy Morgan. (2017). *Who are Australia's union members? You may be surprised* [Press release]. Retrieved from www.roymorgan.com/findings/7104-who-are-australias-union-members-you-might-be-surprised-201701101609.

Strack, R., Caye, J.-M., Lassen, S., Bhalla, V., Puckett, J., Espinosa, E., . . . Haen, P. (2010, September). *Creating people advantage 2010: How companies can adapt their HR practices for volatile times.* Boston Consulting Group and World Federation of People Management Associations (WFPMA).

United States Department of Labor. (2017). *Union members summary: Economic news release.* Bureau of Labor Statistics. Retrieved from www.bls.gov/news.release/union2.nr0.htm.

Universities Australia. (2017). *Universities Australia data snapshot 2017.* Deakin, ACT. file:///C:/Users/swiblen/Downloads/Data%20snapshotv6%20webres%20(1).pdf.

Wiblen, S., Dery, K., & Grant, D. (2012). Do you see what I see? The role of technology in talent identification. *Asia Pacific Journal of Human Resources, 50*(4), 421–438.

Wilson, P. (2010). *people@work/2020: The future of work and the changing workplace: Challenges and issues for Australian HR practitioners.* Melbourne.

Wilson, S., & Spies-Butcher, B. (2011). When labour makes a difference: Union mobilization and the 2007 Federal Election in Australia. *British Journal of Industrial Relations, 49,* s306–s331. doi:10.1111/j.1467-8543.2010.00788.x.

World Economic Forum. (2016). Country/ Economic Profiles: Australia. Retrieved from www3.weforum.org/docs/gcr/2015-2016/AUS.pdf.

World Economic Forum. (2017). *The global human capital report 2017: Preparing people for the future of work.* Retrieved from www3.weforum.org/docs/WEF_Global_Human_Capital_Report_2017.pdf.

Wright, C. F. (2017). Australian industrial relations in 2016. *Journal of Industrial Relations.* 59 (3), 237–253 doi:10.1177/0022185617701513.

Wright, C. F., Clibborn, S., Piper, N., & Cini, N. (2016). *Economic migration and Australia in the 21st century.* Retrieved from www.lowyinstitute.org/sites/default/files/wright_et_al_economic_migration_and_australia_in_the_21st_century_0_0.pdf.

Appendix
Useful Research Sources, Talent Rankings and Cross-Country Indices

Digest and Summary of Websites Used by Randall Schuler in Macro Talent Management

knowledge.insead.edu/talent-management/global-talent-competitiveness-index-2932

This site is for the Global Talent Competitiveness Index (GTCI) of INSEAD. This has six pillars (enabling, attracting, growing, retaining, vocational knowledge and global knowledge) and approx. indicators per pillar. Covers 103 countries.

www.imd.org/wcc

This site is for the World Talent Report and Rankings from IMD. It has descriptions of three country-level talent factors, namely investment and development, appeal and readiness.

www.weforum.org/reports/the-global-competitiveness-report-2016-2017-1/

This site is for the World Competitiveness Index that ranks 183 countries of the world on various factors for competitiveness on 14 pillars, 4 of which are directly related to country level talent management. The other 10 factors are supportive, macro level factors at the country level.

www.weforum.org/reports/the-human-capital-report-2016/

This site is from the World Economic Forum in conjunction with LinkedIn. The first report was in 2013, and then 2015. It is an excellent source of information about how 130 countries teach, train and develop their human capital. It provides many example of what countries are doing to help improve the extent to which they use and develop their human capital potential for the future.

www.globaltalentindex.com/pdf/Heidrick_Struggles_Global_Talent_Report.pdf

This report provides benchmark information on the capacity of countries for developing, attracting and retaining talent. These aspects of countries overlap with those from the WEF and INSEAD and IMD. But each is unique and warrants inclusion here so that the researcher can delve more deeply in each of them. Also see the reports for 2013 and 2015:

www3.weforum.org/docs/WEF_HumanCapitalReport_2013.pdf
www.mercer.com/content/dam/mercer/attachments/global/Talent/WEF_2013_Human_Capital_Report.pdf

These sites provide a nice description of the development of the Human Capital Talent Report. Over these reports the focus and coverage varies, but remains very complementary and useful. So it is good to review all three of these reports. The examples that are provided vary and thus provide additional insights.

www.bcgperspectives.com/content/articles/leadership_talent_human_resources_global_leadership_talent_index/

This site has the Boston Consulting Group's (BCG) Global Leadership and Talent Index (GLTI). This looks at the relationship between firm financial performance and talent and HR management activities (so one level below the country-level analysis).

www.ilo.org/global/statistics-and-databases/lang—en/index.htm

This site has a great deal of data and statistics on the nature and quality of jobs being created and the talent needed for them across more than 140 countries. Good information on migration across countries as well.

www.ilo.org/global/research/global-reports/weso/2016/WCMS_443480/lang—en/index.htm

Great report on the trends in employment, unemployment and social trends around the world.

www.oecd.org/pisa/keyfindings/

This site has the educational attainment levels of countries on three major categories: math, science and reading.

www.doingbusiness.org/reports/global-reports/~/media/GIAWB/Doing%20Business/Documents/Annual-Reports/English/DB16-Chapters/DB16-Labor-Market-Regulation.pdf

This site provides information related to a country's regulations that impact how companies can utilize its human capital/talent if they wish to operate in their country.

www.mckinsey.com/industries/public-sector/our-insights/measuring-the-state-of-us-states?cid=other-eml-alt-mip-mck-oth-1702

This site has great data on the talent levels on all the states in the United States. It also includes many measures of the environments of all the states as well. Very useful for measuring the talent of states!

www.hays-index.com/the-index/introduction/

This site provides another extensive database for use in evaluating global skills indicators across countries and the many relevant country characteristics that help support those indicators within and across countries. The skills indicators include education flexibility, labour market participation, labour market flexibility, talent mismatch, overall wage pressure, wage pressure in high-skill industries, and wage pressure in high-skill occupations.

www.businessinsider.com/the-best-countries-in-the-world-according-to-us-news-and-world-report-2017-3

This is a very useful place to see the listing of the best countries in the world. Country level talent is certainly an important factor in determining the ranking of each country.

Additional Websites for Further Country-Level Data of Potential Relevance to MTM

- The corruption perception index: www.transparency.org/cpi2015
- The National Career Readiness Certificate (NCRC): www.act.org/content/act/en/products-and-services/workforce-solutions.html
- The global cities index: www.atkearney.com/research-studies/global-cities-index/2015
- Foreign Direct Investment (FDI) Confidence Index: www.atkearney.com/research-studies/foreign-direct-investment-confidence-index/2015
- The commitment to Development Index: www.cgdev.org/cdi-2015
- Global Connectedness Index 2014: www.dhl.com/en/about_us/logistics_insights/studies_research/global_connectedness_index/global_connectedness_index.html#.VvgijfkrJ1N
- Best Countries for Business: www.forbes.com/best-countries-for-business/list/
- Country Brand Index: www.futurebrand.com/foresight/cbi
- Happy Planet Index: www.happyplanetindex.org/data/
- OECD Indicators of Employment Protection: www.oecd.org/employment/emp/oecdindicatorsofemploymentprotection.htm
- Web Index: thewebindex.org/
- Human Development Reports and the Human Development Index (HDI) from the United Nations: www.humandevelopmentreports.org

Comparative Indices of Interest to IB Scholars and Students

Prepared by Betty Jane Punnett in November 2017 (with input from AIB Colleagues) and listed here with her permission. These sources can be found via web search engines.

- DHL: Global **Connectedness** Index
- Transparency International: **Corruption** Index
- Index of **Economic Freedom**
- GINI Index (**Income Inequality**)
- Global **Gender Gap** Index
- **Happy Planet** Index
- United Nations **Human Development** Index, Global Index of **Talent Competitiveness**
- Global EDGE: **Emerging Market** Potential index, **Business Climate** Ranking
- World Bank: **Ease of Doing Business** Index, Worldwide **Governance** Index
- World Economic Forum: **Global Competitiveness** Rankings, **Networked Readiness** Index, **global risks**
- Foreign Policy Journal: **Failed States** Index
- Property Rights Alliance: International **Property Rights** Index
- World Justice Project: **Rule of Law** Index
- Heritage Foundation: **Trade Freedom** Index
- Information Network (Columbia University): **Environmental Performance** Index
- KOF **Globalization** Index: globalization.kof.ethz.ch/
- **Global Peace** Index: visionofhumanity.org/

- Grant Thornton **Global Dynamism** Index: www.globaldynamismindex.com/gdi.html
- ATKearney: **Global cities** index, **Emerging cities** index, **Global Services** Location Index, **FDI Confidence** Index, **Globalization** index (may not be updated)
- Schotter & Beamish: **Hassle** Factor (updated later this year): www.hasslefactor.info
- **Market Potential** Index: globaledge.msu.edu/mpi
- UN **World Risk** Index
- Economist: Big Mac Index, Starbucks Index—**Purchasing Power Parity/ Exchange Rates**
- Global **Social Tolerance** Index (Zanakis S., W. Newburry & V. Taras—2016—Journal of International Business Studies, 47.4: 480–497): link.springer.com/article/10.1057/jibs.2016.5
- World's Values Survey has a number of useful indices such as those on "propensity to **trust**" and "**opportunism score**"
- Cato Institute has a "**Human Freedom** Index"
- Marsh Group, the Coface Index (**Political risk**)
- Reporters Without Borders: **Press Freedom** Index
- Coastlight Capital reports a **Global Financial Stress** Index that measures solvency and liquidity risk in national financial systems
- Bank of America also has a competing **GFSI** with the same goals.
- Global **Access to Health Care** Index (Economist Intelligence Unit)
- OECD **Wellbeing**
- Ibrahim Index of **African Governance**

Other Relevant Sources

- World Bank: National Economic Data, Enterprise Surveys
- OECD: National data, International Investment Agreements
- The Economist: Economist Intelligence Unit data
- Eurasia Group (consultancy): Top Global Risks
- Mercer Group (consultancy): Cost of Living Survey, Quality of Living Survey
- US Department of State: Investment Climate Statements
- Market Access Database: Trade Barriers Database
- Cost of living surveys (e.g. Mercer, ECA International, EIU)
- Passport GMID (Euromonitor): National and industry level data (e.g. business environment, income and expenditure)
- Yale Center for Environmental Law and Policy and the Center for International Earth Science
- World Economic Forum Global Agenda
- CIA Country Reports

Index

Page numbers in *italics* indicate figures and in **bold** indicate tables on the corresponding pages.

Aalto University 173–174, 180
absorptive capacity 78
academics 83, 113, 198
Accenture 35
ACT 35
Adecco 6, 20
African countries, country image 136–137
agency effects 92–97, *93–94*
aging populations 25–26; Australia 212–213; Finland 177; Germany 11, 104, *105*; Netherlands 198–199; Spain 130, *131*; United Kingdom 89
Air Berlin 101
Alberta Education 54
American men job loss among 27–28, 35–36
Amsterdam, Netherlands 13
anti-corruption laws 49
apprenticeship levy 83
apprenticeship programs 51, 53, 83, 103, 180, 183
artificial intelligence (AI) 52, 55, *55*, 64, 79–80
Asian countries country image 136–137
Asia Pacific countries, aging populations 26
Assembly of First Nations 46
A.T. Kearney 60
Australasia, developed markets 8
Australia 14–15, 206–222; Aboriginal people 206; competitiveness 217–218; demographics 211–213; developed markets 8; educational system 215–217; employer associations 209–210; government-employment relations 210–211; immigration policy 14, 213–214, 218; income distribution 14; industrial relations 208–209; labor market 207–209; labor unions 14, 208, 209, 210; minimum wage 14; national culture 207–209; NGOs 209–210; as penal colony 206, 207; population growth 14; urbanization 212; "war for talent" 14; workforce skills levels 86

automation, implication for talent management 181–182
auto mechanic training programs 35

baby boomer generation 28
baby buster (generation X) generation 28
Bangladesh 25–26
Bank of England 46, 75, 78
basketball 60
BCG *see* Boston Consulting Group (BCG)
Belgium 85, 86, 88–89
Bertelsmann Foundation, European Lifelong Learning Index 115
best employer awards 48, 51–52
bilingual education 127
Blackberry smartphone 60
BMW 35
Boston Consulting Group (BCG) 6, 20, 215
brain circulation, definition 106
brain drain *see also* diaspora 9, 12, 46, 52, 106, 130
Brazil 85
Brexit 75, 76–77, 79, 83–85, 87, 133
Brooking Global Cities Initiative 90
Bush, George W. 33

Canada 9, 40–69; competitiveness 40, 60–61; corporate strategy and leadership 54–55; demographics 46; developed markets 8; diaspora of labor from 9, 46, 58–59; ease of doing business in 61, 62–63; economic development 60–61; educational attainment 9, 56, 57–58, 216; educational system 44–45, 47, **49**, 54, 56; employment-supportive institutions 53; financial environment 44; foreign investment in 44; G7 membership 40–41, 43, 47–48; gender wage inequality 63; global connectedness 40–41; globally-oriented governmental policies 43–44; immigrant population 40; immigration policies 9, 25, 40, 45–46, 49, *50*; Indigenous People 45, 46, 48, 53, 54, 62; infrastructure investments 79; innovation in 60, 62–63; institutional environment 44; internationalization of economy 9; labor force growth 62; labor laws 45; labor market 45; linguistic diversity 47; national culture 40, 47; national health care system 53–54; NGOs 44; population 43–44, 58–59; productivity 60; regulatory environment 44; talent attraction to 51–52; talent development in 51; talent mobility in 58; talent planning in 50–51; talent retention in 51–52; trade agreements 35, 43, 44; workforce skills levels 86; working-age population 88–89

capitalism varieties of 6–7
Carney, Mark 46
Central Ohio Technical College 34
Chartered Institute of Personnel and Development (CIPD) surveys 6, 73–74, 83–84
Chile 88–89
China 25–26, 27, **33**, 75, 85, 88–89
CIPD *see* Chartered Institute of Personnel and Development surveys
cities *see also specific cities*: economic importance ranking 60; global 90–91, 95
City Talent Competitiveness Index 178
cluster initiatives 135
CMEs *see* coordinated market economies
co-determination 102
collective agreements/bargaining 102, 132, 158–160, 162, 192, 208, 209, 210
Commonwealth 44
competitiveness *see also* Global Competitiveness Index (GCI) rankings; Global Competitiveness Report rankings; Global Talent Competitiveness Index (GTCI) rankings: Australia 217–218; Canada 40, 60–61; definition 28; Denmark 154; Finland 170–17, **171**; France **138**, **140**; Germany 116, 137, **138**, **140**; Italy 137, **138**, **140**; macroeconomic outcomes 92; Spain 8, 123, 139, **140**; states (U.S.) 34; United Kingdom 74–75, *93*; United States 8, 21, **22**, 28–30, **29**, 32, 34, 116, 137, 139, **140**
Comprehensive Economic and Trade Agreement (CETA) 9, 44
computer programs 35
construction sector 132
consulting firms, talent management involvement 6, 18, 20
continuing education *see* lifelong education
contracts 45, 200, 201
coordinated market economies (CMEs) 6–7, 12–13, 156

Copenhagen Capacity 165, **165**
core processes, of MTM, definition 31
corruption, in the public sector 49, 60–61, 62
cross-national research, in MTM 7
cultural factors: in HRM styles 72–73; in MTM 91–92
cybersecurity 51, *61*, 64
Czech Republic 85, 86

Danish talent paradox 154–155
deep learning 55, *55*, 64
DeepMind 55
demographics *see also* aging populations; population; population decline; population growth: agency effects of 95; Australia 211–213; Canada 46; Germany 101, 104, *105*; Spain 129–131, *131*; United Kingdom 88–89
Denison University 34
Denmark 12–13, 154–169; competitiveness 154; as coordinated market economy 12–13, 156; educational system 158, 159, 161–163; flexicurity policy 12, 158, 177; Global Talent Index rankings *24*; immigration policies 156–157, 164; labor market 157, *157*, 158–161; labor relations 12; MTM-related policies 163–166; national culture 156; talent growth and development 154, 161–163; talent readiness for technology 182; workforce 156; workforce skills 85, 86
Deutsche Bahn 101
developed countries, aging population 26
developed markets, categorization 8
diaspora: Asia 215; Australia 14, 214; Canada 9, 46, 52, 58–59, 63; China 14, 215; Germany 11, 106–107; governmental policies regarding 17; India 14, 215; Spain 11, 12, 130; talent development and 30; talent retention and 30; United States 27
digitalization 11, 79–80, 112–113
digital native (Generation Z) generation 28
disabled persons, employment 110, 132–133
disadvantaged groups, employment gap 132–133
diversity 26, 46, 47–48, 65
Dow Jones 8
Dutch language 195–196

East Asian countries, educational attainment 81–82
Economist, Global Talent Index *see* Global Talent Index (GTI)
ecosystem partnerships 182–183
educational attainment: Australia 215–216; Canada 9, 56, 57–58, 216; China **33**; East Asian countries 81–82; Estonia 216; Finland 216; as foreign investment incentive 34; funding for 35; Germany 103, 111, 112, 115, **141**, 216; Hong Kong 216; Italy **141**;

Japan 216; Korea 82; MTM outcomes and **32**, 32–33, **33**; National Career Readiness Certificate (NCRC) 35; Netherlands 194–196; New Zealand 216; OECD countries 33, **33**, 140, **141**; overeducation 86; recommendations for 36; of the self-employed 134; Singapore 82, 216; Spain 11, 128, 130, 140, **141**, 142; undereducation 86; United Kingdom 78–79, 81–83, 88, 216; United States 33, **33**, 140, **141**; of women 194, 198
educational institutions, role in MTM 24
educational systems: for 21st century workforce 181–182; Australia 215–217; Canada 44–45, 47, **49**, 54, 56; Denmark 158, 159, 161–163; Finland 13, 172, 178, 179–181; gender equality of 47; Germany 11, 102–104, 111–113; for gifted children 161, 162; inequality in 195–196; international collaborations 9; Netherlands 13–14, 193, 194–197, 199, 202; Spain 126–128, 141, 142–143, **144–145**; Switzerland 179, 180; as talent development factor 175; United States 21, 22, **22**, 24, 35, 36
egalitarianism 28, 172, 178, 183, 194–195, 196–197
Eindhoven, Netherlands 13, 193–194
emergent markets, categorization of 8
emerging economies, population growth in 25–26
emigrants, returning to native country *see* returnees
emigration, reversal of *see* returnees employer branding 133
employment, government subsidization of 36
employment rate 49, 57, 75, 86, 91, 109, 123 *see also* unemployment rate
employment services/systems 53, 182
English language 47, 154, 214
entrepreneurship 133–135, 173–174, 180, 183–184, 193–194
environmental factors, in MTM, *5*; Australia 207–218; Canada 42–50, **43**; Germany 102–108; Spain 126–137; United Kingdom 72–77, *93*; United States *19*, 21–30
equality 47, 178, 179
equal opportunity 178, 179, 183
Estonia 86
euro 125
European Economic Community 125
European Lifelong Learning Index, 115
European Monetary Union 125
European Union (EU): Blue Card 110–111; Cohesion Policy 143; Comprehensive Economic and Trade Agreement (CETA) 9; hourly wages 79; socio-economic arrangements 11; trade agreements 44; unemployment rate 84; United Kingdom's departure from (Brexit) 75, 76–77, 79, 83–85, 87, 133; vocational education investments 84–85; workforce undereducation 86

European Union-28 zone 107
European Union A8 countries 87
Europe *see also specific countries*: aging population 26; national business system diversity 10
Eurozone 83, 84

family-owned businesses 134
Ferguson, Kroitor, and Kerr 60
FiatChrysler 35
financial crisis (2008) 14, 91, 123, 129, 130, 132, 134, 174, 199, 206–207
Finland 13, 170–189; competitiveness 170–171, **171**, 175–176; economy 171–174; educational system 172, 178, 179–181; entrepreneurship 173–174, 183–184; foreign direct investment in 177; Global Talent Index rankings *24*; industrial structure policies 76; labor laws 176–177; labor market 176; national culture 172, 178; overeducation in 86; regulatory landscape 176; talent readiness for technology 182; talent retention 181; technology-driven economy 171–174; technology sector 170, 173–174, 182, 183–184
Finnish language 177, 178
Fintech Campaign 165
First Nations 46
flexicurity policy 12, 158, 177
Forbes Best Countries for Business rankings 61, 62
foreign direct investment 34, 44, 75, 92, *93*, 177
Foresight Company 80
Fortune 500 companies 34
France: aging population 26; competitiveness 139, **140**; G7 membership 40–41; gender pay gap 107; HRM culture 72; industrial structure 76; infrastructure investments 79; Mediterranean mixed market economy 7; overeducation in 86; productivity 79; workforce skills 85, 86
Franco, Francisco 125, 132
freedom of speech 170
freedom of the press 60–61
French language 47
FTSE 8
functions and processes, in MTM, *5*; in Canada 48–56, **49**, *50*; cultural context 7; in Germany 109–114; in United States *19*, 30–32

gender equality 47, 107–108, 109–110, 178–179
gender inequality 79, 112, 197–198
gender wage inequality 57–58, 63, 107–108, 133, 179
generational divide, global 27

Germany 10–11, 101–122; aging population 26; competitiveness 116, 137, **138**, **140**; demographics 104, *105*; developed markets 8; economy 7, 11, 101, 102; educational attainment 115; educational system 102–104, 111–113; gender equality initiatives 107–108, 109–110; HRM culture 72; immigration policies 25, 105–106, 110–111; industrial structure 76; infrastructure investments 79; labor market 107–108; national culture 108; overeducation in 86; talent attraction to 109–111; talent development in 111–112; talent mobility in 106–107; talent retention in 113–114; workforce skills levels 86; working-age population 104, *105*

Girls Who Work 35

"glass ceiling" 198

Global Affairs Canada 58, 59

Global Competitiveness Index (GCI) rankings, 6, 20; economic focus of 30; Finland, 170; France **138**; Germany 137, **139**; Italy 137, **138**; Spain 137–139, **138**; twelve pillars of 28–29, **29**, 31; United Kingdom 75; United States 21, **22**, 137, **138**

Global Competitiveness Report rankings 59; Canada 61; Germany 116; Spain 123

Global Connectedness Index 40–41, 60

Global IT Readiness Index 182

globalization, governmental policies for 163

global knowledge skills 175

global labor markets, new worker entries into 27

Global Skills Index 6, 18, 20, 24, 36, 85

Global Talent Competitiveness Index (GTCI) rankings 6, 20, 21; Australia **171**; Canada 59, 61; Denmark 154, **171**; description 174, 190–191; educational attainment rankings 32, **32**; Finland 170–171, **171**, 175–176, *176*, **184–185**; France **140**; Germany 114, *115*, **140**; input pillars 174–175; Italy **140**; Luxembourg **171**; neo-liberal perspective 14; Netherlands 191; Norway **171**; output pillars 175; reliability 174; Singapore **171**; Spain 139, **140**; Sweden **171**; Switzerland **171**; twelve pillars **32**; United Kingdom 75, **171**; United States **32**, 139, **140**, **171**

Global Talent Index (GTI) rankings 6, 20, 59; Canada 48; Denmark *24*; dimensions of 34; Finland *24*; Norway *24*; overlap with Human Capital Reports 34; Singapore *24*; United States 23, *24*

global talent management model 92

GLOBE studies 47, 108, 136

Google 55

governmental organizations, talent management involvement 18

government policies, for talent management 2–3

Greece 86

"green cards" 25

gross added value (GAV) 10

gross domestic product (GDP): Canada 49, 60; Finland 172, 173; Germany 101, 102, 103; Group of 7 countries 40–41; immigration and 95, *96*; Netherlands 192; Spain 123, 124, *124*

Group of 7 (G7) countries 40–41, 43, 47–48, 58, 79

Group of 20 (G-20) countries 53

Hays: Global Skills Index 6, 18, 20, 24, 36, 85; talent management capability descriptions 18, 20

HCI *see* Human Capital Index

health, job loss and 27–28, 35–36

health care expenditures, of OECD countries 54

health care sector 89–90, 162

health care systems: Canada 53–54; Netherlands 193; Spain **138**, 139; United Kingdom 53, 89–90; United States **29**, 30

Heidrick & Struggles 6, 20

Heineken 192

Helsinki, Finland 178

hockey 60

Hong Kong 88–89

human capital: Australia 218; definition 29–30, 126, 142; Germany 115; measurement of 74–75; Spain 123; United Kingdom 74–75, 85, *93*

Human Capital Analytics Group 163

Human Capital Index/Report rankings 6; description 190, 191; Finland 75; focus of 30; France **142**; Germany 75, 115, **142**; Italy **142**; Japan 75; MTM core processes and **29**, 32; Netherlands 191; overlap with Global Talent Index 34; Spain 123, 141, **142**; United Kingdom 75; United States 20, 26, **29**, 29–30, 36, 75, **142**

Hungary 85

Iceland 86

IMAX movie system 60

IMD *see* International Institute for Management Development (IMD)

immigrants: illegal 26; as percentage of U.K. workforce 87; as percentage of U.S. population 25; quotas on 25; return policies for 130; unemployment rate of 87–88

immigration, gross domestic product and 95, 96

Immigration Act of 1965 26

immigration policies 2; Australia 14, 213–214, 218; Canada 9, 25, 40, 45–46, 49, *50*; Denmark 156–157, 164; Germany 25, 105–106, 110–111; immigrant-friendly 17; skills-based 40, 45–46;

Spain 130–131; talent attraction and 31; United Kingdom 83, 87–88; United States 25, 27
inclusion 47–48, 65, 202
income distribution 14
income inequality 13–14, 116, 126, 193, 200 *see also* gender wage inequality
income levels 63, 132
income tax 58, 63
India 25–26, 27, 54, 85, 88–89
indigenous people: of Australia 206; of Canada 45, 46, 48, 53, 54, 62
individualism 28, 108
Indonesia 88–89
industrial-relations systems 11, 158
Industrial Revolution, fourth (Industry 4.0) 181–182
industrial structure 76–77, 92, *93*, 102, 126, 192
industry-education partnerships 44
information and communications technology 60, 80, *81*
infrastructure investments 79
innovation: in Canada 60, 62–63; in Finland 180; in France **138**; in Germany 103, **138**; global talent mobility and 31; in Italy **138**; in manufacturing 35; in the Netherlands 192, 193–194; in Spain 139; in United States 21, **22**, **29**, 30, **138**
innovation-driven development 41
INSEAD *see also* Global Talent Competitiveness Index (GTCI) rankings: talent management capability descriptions 18, 20
institutional theory 97
intellectual property protection 48
International Association for the Evaluation of Educational Achievement (IEA) 82
international education initiatives 54 *see also* international students
International Experience Canada (IEC) program 51, 58
International Institute for Management Development (IMD): talent management capability descriptions 18, 20; World Competitiveness Center 2, 17; World Talent Report 6, 20, 22, **22**, 48, 59, 139, **139**
International Labor Organization (ILO) 18, 20, 191, 208
International Monetary Fund 8, 125
International Passenger Survey 83
international students: in Australia 217; in China 82; in Egypt 82; exchange programs 127; from Germany 104; in Germany 114; in Malaysia 82; in Saudi Arabia 82; in Spain 127; talent mobility of 82–83; in United Arab Emirates 82; in United Kingdom 82; in United States 24–25

internet usership 60
Ireland 85, 86, 88–89
Italy 7, 11, 40–41, 79, 85, 137, **138**, **140**

Japan: aging population 26; country image 136–137; developed markets 8; G7 membership 40–41; HRM culture 72; infrastructure investments 79; production systems 7; workforce skills levels 86; workforce skills shortage 85
Jensen, Kristian 154
job loss, health-related 27–28, 35–36

Khan, Naqeeb 166
knowledge-based economy 171–174
knowledge-based services 102
knowledge flow 31
knowledge-intensive industries 76, 156
knowledge management 213
knowledge sharing 52–53
knowledge transfer 78
Kone 171
Korea 82, 86, 88–89

labor laws 23, **23**, 45, 48, 176–177, 192, 208, 210
labor market: active policies 177, 182; Australia 207–209; Canada 45; Denmark 157, *157*, 158–161; Finland 176–177; Germany 107–108; global 89–90, 95, 107; Netherlands 192; older model of 192; Spain 131–133; women in 197–198
labor market efficiency 11, 21, **22**, **29**, 30, **49**, 58, 74, 138, **138**
labor market flexibility 24, 114, 177, 192, 201–202
labor market forecasting 9
labor unions 14, 158, 160, 161, 176–177, 208, 209, 210, 211
Latin American countries, country image 136–137
Latin European countries, HRM culture 72
leadership 47, 54–55, 109–110
learning 52–53, 175, 181
Leitch Report 77–78
liberal market economies (LMEs) 6–7
Licking County Ohio 34, 36
life expectancy 104, 126–127, 142, 198
lifelong education 115, 139, 159, 160–161, 175, 181–182, 200–201
life satisfaction 58, 63
line managers 51
LinkedIn, Human Capital Report *see* Human Capital Index/Report rankings
literacy rates 44–45

local governments, MTM initiatives 21
London, England 10, 90–91

Macro Talent Management: A Global Perspective on Managing Talent in Developed Markets 1–2
Macro Talent Management in Emerging and Emergent Markets: A Global Perspective 1, 3
macro talent management (MTM) *see also* environmental factors, in MTM; functions and processes, in MTM; outcomes, in MTM: complexity of 36–37; core functions 5; definition 1, 18, 41, 190; development of 1–2, 17; framework 4–7; implications/applications 34–36
Malaysia 88–89
Management 64, 178
management capability 51, 56
manufacturing, innovation in 35
mathematics, educational attainment in 82
mathematics research 44
McKinsey 2, 6, 17, 18, 20
Mediterranean mixed market economies 7
men, labor force participation rates 27–28
Mercer Consulting 29
Merkel, Angela 106
meso talent management 3
Metsa Group 171
Mexico 35, 43, 86, 88–89
Microsoft Corporation 29
micro talent management 3
migrants: educational levels 11; supply and demand situation 107
migration managed 87
millennials 27, 28, 133
minimum wage 14, 45, 208–209
MITACS 44
mixed market economies 7, 11–12, 125
mobile gaming industry 174
mobile telephone market 173–174
MSCI 8
MTM *see* macro talent management (MTM)
multiculturalism 45, 214
multinational enterprises (MNEs) 177; competition with global cities 90–91; in Denmark 156; HRM globalization processes 75; human capital availability for 12; macro-level issues affecting 4; in the Netherlands 192; Nordic 12; skills and productivity relationship in 77; in Spain 134, 136; talent management in 167–168; workforce skills shortage and 84

Naismith, James 60
National Carrer Readiness Certificate (NCRC) 35
national champion organizations 13
national culture: Australia 207–209; Canada 9, 40, 47; Denmark 156; Finland 172, 178; Germany 108; Netherlands 193; Spain, 135–137; United States 28
National Health Service (U.K.) 53, 89–90
neo-liberalism 193
nested systems, 167
Netherlands 13–14, 190–205; competitiveness 116; economy 192; educational system 193, 194–197; health care system 193; immigrant population 191–192, 195–196; immigrant workforce 199–200; labor market flexibility 201–202; national culture 193; talent attraction to 197–200; talent growth and development 194–197; talent retention 197–201; Triple Helix collaboration 193; workforce skills levels 86; workforce skills shortage 85
New European Economy 34
New Zealand 8
Nigeria 25–26
No Child Left Behind campaign 33
Nokia 13, 171, 172–174, 183
nongovernmental organizations (NGOs) 2–3, 18, 20, 44, 209–210
Nordic countries, values of 178
Nordic Passport System 162, **164**
North America, developed markets 8
North American Free Trade Agreement (NAFTA) 9, 43, 52
Northern Ireland 86
Norway *24*, 86

Obama, Barack 33
Ohio, foreign investments in 34
Ohio State University 34
oil, gas, and energy industries 54–55
older workers: in Australia 212–213, 218; employment gap 132–133; in Germany 113, 114; of multinational enterprises 26; in the Netherlands 198–199; in Spain 141
Organization for Economic Cooperation and Development (OECD) 2, 17; Canadian membership 53; economic survey of United Kingdom 77; educational spending 45; founding members 41; Gender Equality in Education Report 47; health care expenditures 54; human capital measurement method 74–75; International Skills Model 78; Online Education Database 86; Program for International Student Assessment (PISA) 20, **33**, 81–82, 103, 140, **141**, 142; Spain's membership 125; tertiary education in 45; unemployment rate 132; Well-Being Index 116, *116*, 123

outcomes, in MTM *5*; in Canada 56–61, **57**, *61*; educational attainment and **32**, 32–33, **33**; in Germany 114–116; levels 32–34; in Spain 137–142; in United States *19*
overeducation 86, 95, *96*
overtime work 45

Pakistan 25–26, 27
parental leave policies 48, 110, 159
patterns of agency 10, 70–71, 80, 92–97
performance appraisal 73
plurality nation, United States as 26
Poland 85, 86
polder-model, of national business systems 14
political asylum seekers/refugees 11, 106, 111, 165–166
political economies 6–7, 11
population: Australia 211–212; Canada 43–44, 58–59; Finland 177; Germany 104; Netherlands 191–192
population decline 25–26, 88, 101, 104, 212
population growth 25–26; Australia 14, 212, 213; Belgium 88; developing countries 212; Germany *129*; Italy 88, *129*; Netherlands 88; Oceania region 212; Portugal *129*; Spain 129, *129*, 132; Sweden 88; United Kingdom 88; United States *129*
Portugal 11, 86
preschool education 172
primary education: Australia 215; Canada 45, 47, **49**; Denmark 156, 161; Finland 172; France **138**; Germany 103, **138**; Italy 138; Netherlands 194, 195, 196; Spain 127, 128, **138**, 139, 141; United States 21, **22**, **29**, 30, 35, 36, **138**; as workforce capability indicator 30–31
private sector employment, government subsidization for 36
productivity: Australia 217–218; Canada 60; effect of global financial crisis on 79; industrial structure and 92; Netherlands 13–14, 192; of older workers 199; United Kingdom 77, 79–81; workforce expansion and 84; workforce skills relationship 77–78, 79–81, *81*, *94*, 95
professional organizations, as MTM information source 6, 20
Program for International Student Assessment (PISA) scores **33**, 81–82, 103, 115, 140, **141**, 142, 172, 179
property rights 74
prosperity, relation to productivity 28
Prosperity Cup 34–35

QS World University Rankings 104
quality of life 58, 193

Race to the Top 33
recession (2008) 14, 91, 123, 129, 130, 132, 134, 174, 199, 206–207
recruitment, of talent *see* talent attraction
refugees *see* political asylum seekers/refugees
research and development (R&D) *138*, **138**, 139, 192 *see also* innovation
Research in Motion Technologies 60
retirement age 141, 198, 199
returnees: to Canada 46–47, 52; to Germany 106–107, 110; to Spain 130
Revitalize American Manufacturing and Innovation Act 35
Rotterdam 13
Routledge Global Human Resource Management Series (Werner) 4, 8, 11
Rovio 174
Royal Bank of Canada 55
Royal Dutch Shell 192
Russia 85

Scandinavia *see also specific countries*: coordinated market economies 7
Schwab, Klaus 36
science, educational attainment in 81–82
science, technology, engineering, and mathematics (STEM) 34, 112, 127, 161, 196
scientific research 44
Scotland, workforce skills shortage 86
secondary education: Australia 215; Canada **49**; Denmark 162; Germany 103, 112; Netherlands 194, 195; Spain 127, 128, 141; United States 35, 36; as workforce capability indicator 30–31
self-employment 133–134, 181
Shorten, William 'Bill' 210
SHRI 6
Silicon Valley 27
Singapore **24**, 82, 85, 116
Singer Audrey 26
Sino-Danish Center for Education and Research 156
skilled worker shortages 84–86, 107, 108, 109, 160, 163–165
Slovak Republic 86
small- and medium-sized enterprises (SMEs): Denmark 156; Finland 173; Germany 102; Netherlands 192; Spain 126, 133, 134, 136; United Kingdom 77
social democracy 7
social market economy 11, 102
social mobility 178
Social Progress Index 154
Society for Human Resource Management 6, 20
socio-economic forces, effect on human resource management 11

"soft power" 9, 49
S&P 8
Spain 11–12, 123–153; aging population 26; competitiveness 123, 137–139, **138**, **140**; country image 136–137; demographics 129–131, *131*; economy 7, 11–12, 124–126; educational system 126–128, 141, 142–143, **144–145**; entrepreneurship 133–135; immigration policies 130–131; labor market 131–133; labor market reforms **145–146**; national culture 135–137; overeducation in 86; talent growth and development 139, **140**; talent retention 139, **140**; workforce skills shortage 85
Spanish language 127, 137
STEM (science, technology, engineering, and mathematics) 34, 112, 127, 161, 196
Stora Enso 171
Supercell 174
Sweden 85, 86
Swedish language 177
Switzerland 85, 116
systems theory 56

talent attraction: Australia 215; Canada 46–47, 48, **49**, 51–52, 57; Denmark 154–155, *155*, 164–165, 166; external openness aspect 175; Finland 178; France **140**; Germany 109–111, 114, *115*, **140**; internal openness aspect 174–175; Italy **140**; Netherlands 193, 197–200; Spain 123, 139, **140**, 143; United Kingdom 83–89, 95, *96*; United States **140**
talent growth and development: Canada **49**, 51; Denmark 154, 161–163, 166; educational attainment and 81–83; factors affecting 175; France **140**; Germany 111–112, 114, *115*, **140**; Italy **140**; Netherlands 194–197; Spain 139, **140**; states' programs for 34–35; United Kingdom 77–83; United States 34–35, **140**; vocational education and training (VET) strategy 78–81, *94*, 95
talent hubs 90–91, 95
talent magnets 191, 192, 193
talent management: country level *see* macro talent management (MTM); cultural factors in 73–74; definition 73–74, 142, 157; individual (micro) level 2, 3, 17; organizational (meso) level 2, 3, 17; in United Kingdom 72–74; in United States 17
talent mismatch 24
talent mobility 31, 58, 78, 82–83, 106–107
talent planning 50–51
talent retention: Canada **49**, 51–52; components of 175; Denmark 154–155; Finland 181; France *139*, **140**; Germany 113–114, *115*, **139**; Italy 139, *139*; Spain 139, *139*, **140**, 143, 193, 197–201; United Kingdom 83–89, 95, *96*
taxation 58, 63, 181

teachers, professionalism of 179
technology, talent readiness for 181–182
tertiary education *see also* universities: Australia 216–217; Canada 45, **49**, 52; Finland 180; Germany 104, 112–113; Netherlands 196–197; Spain 127, 141; United Kingdom 79, 82; as workforce capability indicator 30–31
Times Higher Education World University Rankings 45, 104, 127–128, 196
Toronto, Ontario, Canada 60, 62
Trade Adjustment Assistance program 35
trade agreements 9, 35, 43, 52
training programs *see also* vocational education and training: for job re-entry 28; of states 34–35
Transparency International 49, 170
Triple Helix collaboration 193
Trudeau, Justin 47
Turkey 88–89
Turnbull, Malcolm 214

Uncertainty 28, 108, 136
UNCTAD 75
Undereducation 86
Underemployment 141, 197–198, 199–200
unemployed workers, training program access 35
unemployment insurance 48, 53, 107, 158, 177
unemployment rates: declines in 84; Finland 172; Germany 101, 107, *143*; global 107; of immigrants 87–88, 111; Italy *143*; Netherlands 197; OECD countries 132; of older workers 199; Portugal *143*; Spain 131–132, 141, *143*; United Kingdom 84; United States *143*
UNESCO 82, 191
Unilever 192
United Kingdom 70–100; as advanced economy 10; Commission for Employment and Skills (UKCES) 80; competitiveness 74–75; demographics 88–89; departure from European Union (Brexit) 75, 76–77, 79, 83–85, 87, 133; developed markets 8; educational attainment 78–79, 81–83, 88, 216; foreign direct investments 75; G7 membership 40–41; gender pay gap 107; healthcare sector employment 89–90; human capital 74–75, 85; immigrant workforce 87–88; immigration policies 83, 87–88, *96*; industrial structure 76–77; infrastructure investments 79; MTM analysis 92–97; overeducation in 86; patterns of agency 10, 70–71; productivity 77, 78, 79–81, 92, 95; talent attraction 83–89, 95, *96*; talent growth and development 77–83; talent management style 72–74; talent retention 83–89; unemployment rate 84; vocational education and training 78–81; webs of action 10; workforce skills levels 78–81, *81*, 86; workforce skills-productivity relationship 77–78, 79–81, *81*, *94*, 95; workforce skills shortages 84–86; working-age population 88–89

United Kingdom Employer Skills Survey (UKCES) 85–86
United Nations 43, 125
United Nations Council Committees 53
United States 8–9, 17–39; competitiveness 8, 21, **22**, 28–30, **29**, **32**, 116, 139, **140**; country image 136–137; developed markets 8; educational attainment 33, **33**, **140**, **141**; educational system 21, 22, **22**, 24, 35, 36; foreign investment in 34; G7 membership 40–41; immigration policies 25; industrial structure 76; investments in United Kingdom 75; labor market efficiency 21, **22**; labor market regulations 23, **23**; liberal market economy 7; national culture 28; population growth 25–26; primary education in 35, 36; research and development innovation in 21, **22**; trade agreements 35, 43; workforce skills levels 86; workforce skills shortage 85; working-age population 26, 88–89
U. S. Department of Education, "Final Teacher Preparation Regulations" 35
U. S. Labor Department, Trade Adjustment Assistance program 35
universities *see also specific universities:* Australia 216–217; Canada 52; Denmark 162–163; Finland 178, 180; Germany 104, 112–113; Netherlands 196–197, 198; open 112–113; Spain 127–128, 142; Times Higher Education World University Rankings 45, 104, 127–128, 196; United Kingdom 82, 83
Universities UK 82, 83
University of Alberta *55*
University of Toronto 45
UPM 171

visa/work permit programs 25, 58, 106, 110–111, 114, 162, **164**, 166
Vistage 77
vocational education and training: Australia 217; Denmark 159, 160–162; employer spending on 84–85; Finland 172, 175, 179–180; Germany 103, 107, 113, 114, *115*; as MTM outcome 32, **32**; Netherlands 195, 196; Spain 128, 141, 142; Switzerland 179, 183; United Kingdom 78–81, *94*, 95; United States **32**, **33**

vocational skill levels 139, **140**
volunteer jobs, subsidization of 36

wage equality 48
wage inequality 208; gender-based 57–58, 63, 107–108, 133, 179
wage pressure 24
wage regulation 45
wages: of European Union member countries 79; in Germany 102–103; of immigrants 88
Wales 86
war for talent 2, 14, 17, 101, 206–207
webs of action 10
Well-Being Index 116, *116*, *123*
Western Europe, developed markets in 8
women: business opportunities 114; educational attainment 194, 196, 198; STEM education 112, 127; underemployment 197–198; unemployment 197–198; wage inequality 57–58, 63, 107–108, 133, 179
workforce: inclusion in 48, 53, 65; multicultural 14; projected shortage 27
Workforce Development and Training Offices 35
Workforce Innovation and Opportunity Act of 2014 35
workforce skills levels: effect on productivity 77–78, 79–81, *81*, *94*, 95; in global cities 91; vocational 139, **140**
working poverty rates 107
workplace inclusion 47–48
World Bank: Doing Business Index rankings 5, 20, 22, **23**, 34, 59, 61, 75, 134, *135*; Employing Workers indicator 5, 20; talent management capability descriptions 18, 20
World Economic Forum (WEF) 2, 17; Executive Opinion survey 62–63; founder and executive chairman 36; Global Competitiveness Index (GCI) *see* Global Competitiveness Index (GCI) rankings; talent management capability descriptions 18, 19, 20; talent management reports 6
World Federation of People Management (WFPMA) 6, 20
World University Rankings 127–128

Youth Summit 43

Zalando 101